Long-term Treatment of Depression

This series has been supported by an educational grant from
SmithKline Beecham Pharmaceuticals

PERSPECTIVES IN PSYCHIATRY VOLUME 3

Long-term Treatment of Depression

Edited by

S.A. Montgomery
St Mary's Hospital Medical School, London, UK

and

F. Rouillon
Hôpital Louis-Mourier, Paris, France

JOHN WILEY & SONS

Chichester · New York · Brisbane · Toronto · Singapore

Other Wiley Editorial Offices

John Wiley & Sons, Inc., 605 Third Avenue,
New York, NY 10158-0012, USA

Jacaranda Wiley Ltd. G.P.O. Box 859, Brisbane,
Queensland 4001, Australia

John Wiley & Sons (Canada) Ltd, 22 Worcester Road,
Rexdale, Ontario M9W 1L1, Canada

John Wiley & Sons (SEA) Pte Ltd, 37 Jalan Pemimpin # 05-04,
Block B, Union Industrial Building, Singapore 2057

Library of Congress Cataloging-in-Publication Data

Long-term treatment of depression / edited by S.A. Montgomery and F.
Rouillon.
        p.   cm. — (Perspectives in psychiatry : v.3)
    Includes bibliographical references and index.
    ISBN 0 471 92892 5
        1. Depression, Mental—Treatment.   I. Montgomery, S.A.
II. Rouillon, F.   III. Series: Perspectives in psychiatry
(Chichester, England) : v. 3
        [DNLM: 1. Depressive Disorder—therapy.   2. Long Term Care.   WM
171 L857]
RC537.L65   1992
616.85'2706—dc20
DNLM/DLC
for Library of Congress   91-40088
                                                                                CIP

British Library Cataloguing in Publication Data

A catalogue record for this book is
available from the British Library

ISBN 0 471 92892 5

Typeset by Inforum Typesetting, Portsmouth
Printed in Great Britain by Biddles Ltd, Guildford

Contents

Contributors

M.T. Abou-Saleh   *University Department of Psychiatry, Royal Liverpool Hospital, PO Box 147, Liverpool L69 3BX, UK*

H.S. Akiskal   *University of Tennessee, College of Medicine, Department of Psychiatry, 66N. Pauline, Suite 633, Memphis, TN 38105, USA*

J. Angst   *Psychiatric University Hospital of Zurich, Research Department, PO Box 68, 8029 Zurich, Switzerland*

G.B. Cassano   *II Chair of Clinical Psychiatry, University of Pisa, 56100 Pisa, Italy*

M.J. Filteau   *Hôpital de L'Enfant Jesus, 1401–12eme Rue, G1J 124, Quebec, Canada*

E. Frank   *Department of Psychiatry, University of Pittsburgh School of Medicine, 3811 O'Hara Street, Pittsburgh, PA 15213, USA*

P. Freeling   *St George's Hospital Medical School, Jenner Wing, Cranmer Terrace, London SW17 0RE, UK*

S. Johnson   *Department of Psychiatry, University of Pittsburgh School of Medicine, 3811 O'Hara Street, Pittsburgh, PA 15213, USA*

D.J. Kupfer   *Department of Psychiatry, University of Pittsburgh School of Medicine, 3811 O'Hara Street, Pittsburgh, PA 15213, USA*

M. Lejoyeux   *Service de Psychiatry, Hôpital Louis Mourier, 178 Rue des Renoulliers, 92701 Colombes, France*

S.A. Montgomery   *Department of Psychiatry, St Mary's Hospital, Praed Street, London W2 1NY, UK*

D.B. Montgomery *Department of Psychiatry, St Mary's Hospital, Praed Street, London W2 1NY, UK*

G. Perugi *Institute of Clinical Psychiatry, University of Pisa, 56100 Pisa, Italy*

R.M. Post *Biological Psychiatry Branch, NIMH, Building 10, Room 3N212, 9000 Rockville Pike, Bethesda, MD 20892, USA*

F. Rouillon *Assistance Publique, Hôpital Louis Mourier, 178 Rue des Renouilliers, 92701 Colombes, France*

M. Savino *Institute of Clinical Psychiatry, University of Pisa, 56100 Pisa, Italy*

A. Tylee *St George's Hospital Medical School, Jenner Wing, Cranmer Terrace, London, SW17 0RE, UK*

Preface

The recent shift of emphasis towards long-term treatment parallels the recognition that, as well as being a commonly occurring disorder, most of depressive illness is recurrent. The epidemiological studies have revealed that a higher proportion is recurrent than we previously thought and have helped to show that the different patterns of recurrence are important clinical indicators of the type of depression. It is important to establish that the efficacy of treatment is maintained in the long term and that treatments are able to reduce both relapses and the risk of new episodes of depression.

The regulatory authorities in the European Community have made it clear that long-term efficacy must not be assumed for an antidepressant simply because short-term efficacy has been demonstrated. They require the demonstration of long-term efficacy in separate properly conducted studies. These studies have important implications for the use of antidepressants and should examine the evidence for relapse prevention as well as prophylaxis.

It is now clear from the relapse prevention studies that antidepressants used in the short term do not provide adequate treatment but have to be continued for a period of at least four to six months following apparent resolution of symptoms in order to consolidate the response. This means that any episode of depression, whether in first time or recurrent illness, should be continued for approximately six months. Premature discontinuation would lead to a return of the inadequately treated episode in half the cases.

An increasing number of studies have documented the ability of various treatments to reduce the chances of developing a new episode of depression. These prophylactic studies have only just begun to separate out effective from ineffective treatments and to discover whether particular treatments reduce the risk of new episodes or merely delay them.

Treatments are required to be safe both in short-term and in longer-term usage. Long-term studies are a powerful scientific tool to investigate aspects of safety inaccessible in short-term studies. In these studies unexpected side effects are sometimes uncovered, such as the potential for suicide provocation seen in the study of maprotiline.

The long-term studies of depression have been fruitful in generating hypotheses on the nature of depressive illness. The differential response to long-term treatment has demonstrated a separate pharmacology for bipolar and unipolar depressive illness and this is an important criterion for regarding these two forms of depression as separate. Likewise the ability of the tricyclic antidepressants to provoke rapid cycling in certain individuals suggests the existence of a further subgroup of depression having a different pharmacology. Investigation into possible mechanisms which alter onset, cycle length, and switch processes are only just beginning but are likely to produce important insights into different forms of depressive illness.

Long-term studies provide a more comprehensive method of testing the efficacy of treatments and remain the best available means to examine aspects of course modification for the different kinds of depressive illness.

Stuart Montgomery
Frederic Rouillon

1

How recurrent and predictable is depressive illness?

Jules Angst

Introduction

This chapter will briefly review some clinical and mainly epidemiological data from community studies in order to obtain a representative view of the prevalence and the course of depressive illness.

An extensive overview of *patient studies* on the course of affective disorders was given by Angst (1988a). The results do not agree with the textbook view that schizophrenia has a poor and affective disorder a good prognosis: it is common clinical experience that depressives treated as out-patients or in-patients recover to a great extent from a single episode, but suffer from high recurrence and have to be treated or readmitted again and again. According to our own data, about 15–20% of clinical patients develop chronicity and 10–20% commit suicide. According to a follow-up of 20 years, after the onset of the illness about 20% of lifetime is spent in episodes. Between episodes patients frequently suffer from residual symptoms which lower quality of life. Relapse rates do not decrease with age; most bipolar and about half of unipolar depression remain recurrent until age 80. It is still an open question how many patients experience a single episode or a recurrent type of depression. A single-episode unipolar depression was for instance observed in 20% (Angst and Frey, 1976) of first hospitalized early-onset cases. Single-episode bipolar cases are extremely rare in clinical samples.

Long-term Treatment of Depression. Edited by S.A. Montgomery and F. Rouillon
© 1992 John Wiley & Sons Ltd

Until now the course of psychiatric disorders has not found the interest of *epidemiologists*. Hoping to provide useful data for the planning of health services, they focused more on prevalence and incidence rates. Therefore, although being provided with strong data on point and one-year prevalence rates of depression, we know very little about the course of depression observed in the general population.

Diagnostic classification

Modern diagnostic classification of depression is operational, i.e. based on syndromes, which include severity (minor versus major depression) and course (defined by length and frequency of manifestations). This approach has the advantage of being descriptive and avoiding aetiological assumptions, e.g. 're-active, neurotic, endogenous, exogenous, organic'. At present, both American diagnostic systems (DSM-III and DSM-III-R) and the WHO system (ICD-10) distinguish between single-episode and recurrent depressive disorder.

The following review is mainly based on the DSM-III categories of depression: major depressive disorders, dysthymia and other depression. In addition it will also give data on recurrent brief depression which was first observed in general practice (Paskind, 1929) and recently defined in a study of the normal population (Angst *et al.*, 1988, 1990).

Prevalence of depression

Prevalence rates are mainly given as point or period prevalence rates. They are much more reliable than lifetime prevalence rates. Some investigations based on diagnostic criteria of normal population samples are listed in Table I.

The point prevalence rate of *major depressive disorder* is around 4%. The six-month and one-year prevalence rates generally vary between 3% and 6%. As mentioned before, lifetime prevalence rates are not reliable. Common estimates of 4–8% may be much too low, the best estimation being probably around 18%. The largest study (ECA) has suspiciously low lifetime prevalence rates (4.4%), which compared to the point prevalance rates of 1.5% appear questionable.

Dysthymia as defined by DSM-III includes a two-year course with at least 50% time spent in depression. The point and one-year prevalence rates are around 3%. Lifetime prevalence rates are again unreliable, the wide range between 3% (USA) and 20% (Finland) being very suspect (Table II). Dysthymia almost completely overlaps with major depression and may not be useful as a separate diagnostic category (Angst and Wicki, submitted for publication). For this reason we will not consider it further.

Table I.   Prevalence rates of major depressive disorder (DSM-III/RDC)

		Prevalence rates		
		Point	6 months* or 1 year	Lifetime
Weissman and Myers (1978)	New Haven (USA)	3.7[a,f]		18.0
Blazer and Williams (1980)	North Carolina (USA)	3.7[b]		
Murphy (1980)	Stirling County (Can.)	4.1		16.0
Uhlenhuth *et al.* (1983)	National Survey (USA)		5.1	
Haellstroem (1984)	Gothenburg (S)	6.9[d]		
Elliott *et al.* (1985)	National Survey (USA)		5.5*	8.4
Faravelli and Incerpi (1985)	Florence (I)	3.8	5.2	
Oliver and Simmons (1985)	St Louis (USA)	6.0[e]		19.5
Lehtinen (1986)	Turku (SUO)	4.9		
Surtees and Sashidharan (1986)	Edinburgh (GB)	3.1[d,f]		
Kashani *et al.* (1987)	Columbia (USA)	4.7		
Wittchen and v. Zerssen (1987)	Munich (D)	1.7		9.0
Bland *et al.* (1988)	Edmonton (Can.)	2.3	3.2*	8.6
Kivelae *et al.* (1988)	Tampere (SUO)	3.7		
Weissman *et al.* (1988)	ECA (USA)	1.5	2.6	4.4
Angst and Wicki (1990)	Zurich (CH)		4–9	16.7[c]

[a] Males, 12.3, females 15.8.
[b] Age > 65 years.
[c] Ten-year prospective study from age 20 to 30.
[d] Females only.
[e] Sample: 61% females.
[f] RCD.

Table II.   Prevalence rates of dysthymia (DSM-III)

		Prevalence rates		
		Point	6 months* or 1 year	Lifetime
Faravelli and Incerpi (1985)	Florence (I)	1.2	2.3	
Kashani *et al.* (1987)	Columbia (USA)	3.3		
Wittchen and v. Zerssen (1987)	Munich (G)	3.9		3.9
Bland *et al.* (1988)	Edmonton (Can.)	3.7	3.7*	3.7
Kivelae *et al.* (1988)	Tampere (SUO)			20.6
Weissman *et al.* (1988)	ECA (USA)			3.1
Angst and Wicki (1991)	Zurich (CH)		2.6	

Brief depressive episodes, which last less than two weeks and therefore do not meet criteria for major depression, are quite common in the normal population. Usually they are present for one to three days, but are highly recurrent (10–12 or more episodes per year). This class of *recurrent brief depression*

(Angst *et al.*, 1988) has a one-year prevalence rate of 4–6% in the age group of 20–30 years. There are no data available yet for older groups.

There is a marked sex difference in depression, the female prevalence rates being about twice those of males. The reason for the sex difference has been discussed frequently and has been the subject of many articles. A recent review is given by Ernst and Angst (submitted for publication).

Prevalence of bipolar disorder

Bipolar disorder is difficult to investigate in the normal population. The presently available figures probably underestimate its true occurrence. The point prevalence rates reported in the literature (Table III) vary between 0.1% and 0.7%, the one-year prevalence rates between 0.6% and 1.7%. The lifetime prevalence rates, which may again be unreliable, vary between 0.6% and 1.2%. In view of the high recurrence of bipolar illness the small difference between point and lifetime prevalence is suspect. In a recent study Wicki and Angst (1991) developed a new definition for hypomania and found a one-year prevalence rate at age 28–30 years of 3.9%, which is comparable to the prevalence of cyclothymic disorder reported by Oliver and Simmons (1985).

Table III.   Prevalence rates of bipolar disorder

	Prevalence rates		
	Point	6 months* or 1 year	Lifetime
Weissman and Myers (1978)	–		1.2
Murphy (1980)		0.6	
Faravelli and Incerpi (1985)	0.76	1.7	
	0.47[a]	1.4[a]	
Oliver and Simmons[a] (1985)	2.3		3.3
Wittchen and v. Zerssen (1987)	0.0		0.2
Bland *et al.* (1988)	0.1	0.1*	0.6
Weissman *et al.* (1988)	0.7	1.0	1.2
Angst and Wicki (1990)		4.0[b]	

[a] Cyclothymic disorder.
[b] Including hypomania, cyclothymia.

Single and multiple-episode depression

The distinction between single and multiple-episode depression is important from a theoretical and practical point of view. Single-episode major depression

Table IV.   Prospective community studies of depressives (minimal length 5 years)

		Sample	Cases	Length (years)	Single episodes (%)
Murphy *et al.* (1986)	'Stirling County'	123	64	17	44
Wittchen and von Zerssen (1987)	Munich	483	46	7	28.3
Fichter *et al.* (1987)	Upper Bavaria	1386	244	5	60.9
Hagnell (1988)	Lundby	2550	262	25	50–52
Fichter (1990)	Upper Bavaria	1342		5	
Lehtinen *et al.* (1990)	Turku (SUO)	723	215	16	

has a later age of onset, often lacks a family history of depression and may form a separate diagnostic category (Cassano *et al.*, 1989; Angst, 1990a; Merikangas *et al.*, in preparation). Reliable data can only be collected prospectively. But there are only very few prospective community studies which give data on single-episode major depression (Table IV). They suggest that about 50% of all depressives suffer from single episodes, but this rate may be too low, as any loss of information inflates the rate of single-episode cases. The latter depends mainly on the duration of the prospective investigation and on the frequency of assessments. The community study of Wittchen and von Zerssen (1987) in Munich over seven years found only 28% single-episode cases. A rate of 23% was found in an out-patient psychiatric study in Pisa (Cassano *et al.*, 1989). So multiple episodes may befall 70–80% of community depressives. This conclusion is supported by the Zurich study.

Recurrence of depression in the Zurich study

In Zurich (Switzerland) a prospective epidemiological study was carried out over ten years in a cohort first interviewed at age 20/21 and followed up until age 30. Four semi-structured interviews were given (age 21, 23, 28, 30). We used DSM-III criteria to diagnose major depression (MDD) and our own criteria for recurrent brief depression (RBD). By the frequency of episodes we classified major depression into monophasic (single episode), oligophasic (two to three episodes), polyphasic (more than three episodes), and continuously cycling courses (major depression plus highly recurrent recurrent brief depression with weekly, short depressive mood spells). RBD is by definition periodic. By the frequency of episodes we classified RBD into a polyphasic type with 10–12 episodes over a year and a continuous cycling type with weekly depressive spells.

Table V gives the average one-year prevalence rate assessed by four interviews between age 20 and 30 and in addition the ten-year prevalence rates from age 20 to 30. The one-year prevalence rates from age 20 to 30. The one-year prevalence rate for major depressive disorder was on average 7%, and for recurrent brief depression 5%. The ten-year prevalence rate was 17% for MDD and 11% for RBD.

Table V.   One-year prevalence rates of subtypes of depression and association with hypomania

		Age 20–30 average 1-year preval. rate[a]	10-year preval. rate	3-year preval. rate of associated	
				Dysthymia[b]	Hypomania[c]
No depression		87.8	72.2	2.5	2.2
MDD	Monophasic	4.1	7.2	0.1	0.2
	Oligophasic	1.5	2.9	–	0.6
	Polyphasic	0.4	2.0	0.2	1.3
	Cont. cycling	1.1	4.6	2.2	0.6
RBD[d]	Polyphasic	4.1	9.6	0.2	0.6
	Cont. cycling	1.0	1.5	0.3	0.05
MDD	All	7.1	16.7	2.5	2.7
RBD[d]	All	5.1	11.1	0.5	0.7
Dysthymia	All			2.9	
Hypomania	All				5.5

[a] Average of four interviews.
[b] Three-year prevalence rate 2.9%.
[c] Three-year prevalence rate 5.5%; one-year prevalence rate 3.4–4.4%.
[d] RBD and MDD are mutually exclusive; MDD takes preference in cases of overlap.

Table V also shows the prevalence rates for subgroups defined by the course of depression. Monophasic (single) episode major depression has a one-year prevalence rate of 4% and a ten-year prevalence of 7%. Over one year about 30% of all depressives were single-episode cases, over ten years about 25%. But the latter figure may still be an overestimation because ten years were covered by only four interviews.

In Table V prevalence rates of the association between subtypes of MDD and RBD with dysthymia or hypomania are given. As expected, dysthymia strongly overlaps with the continuous cycling subtype of unipolar major depressive disorder. The two disorders may form a continuum.

The one-year prevalence rates for hypomania vary between 3.4% and 4.4% and the three-year prevalence rate (age 28–30 years) amounts to 5.5%; 3.3% were bipolars, while hypomania without a diagnosis of depression was observed in 2.2%. So two-thirds of the cases with hypomania are bipolar cases. Among the 'unipolar hypomanics', however, the majority of cases manifested depressive symptoms without reaching a diagnostic threshold. The number of bipolar depressives may therefore increase over time. Hypomanic syndromes are mainly associated with the recurrent subtypes of depression, which is compatible with the fact that bipolar illness is an almost exclusively recurrent disorder.

Prediction of depression

In this context we will only consider two aspects of course prediction, i.e. prediction of recurrence and prediction of outcome. The prediction of recovery from an actual episode will be left out.

Most of the results of studies on prediction are sample dependent and not cross-validated by another sample. Without cross-validation, however, a result remains a well-founded hypothesis. This problem has been dealt with extensively by Hamilton (1974).

Prediction of recurrence
The prediction of recurrence is extremely difficult and in individual cases usually not possible at all. In a review of patient studies (Angst, 1988b) very few factors were found to correlate with recurrence of depression. Recurrence is predicted by bipolarity of the disorder (Angst, 1966; Angst and Weis, 1967; Angst, 1980; Coryell *et al.*, 1989), which itself is correlated with early age of onset and high number of previous episodes. Early age of onset predicts recurrence (Astrup *et al.*, 1959; Angst and Weis, 1967; Bratfos and Haug, 1968; Kay *et al.*, 1969; Keller and Shapiro, 1981; Keller *et al.*, 1983; Billings and Moos, 1984; Kovacs *et al.*, 1984; Murphy, 1986; Giles *et al.*, 1989) as does the number of previous episodes (Angst and Weis, 1967; Bratfos and Haug, 1968; Weissman *et al.*, 1978b; Keller and Shapiro, 1981; Keller *et al.*, 1982). More recently this finding was also confirmed by a community study (Lewinsohn *et al.*, 1988). Previous hospitalizations also correlate with readmissions in the follow-up period (Kiloh *et al.*, 1988). In a follow-up study over 15 years, endogenous depressives were clearly more often readmitted (63%) than neurotic depressives (48%) (Andrews *et al.*, 1990).

In this context the research on expressed emotion is of interest, as it gives some evidence that the presence of a sick spouse may increase the relapse rate (Vaughn and Leff, 1976; Leff and Vaughn, 1980; Hooley and Hahlweg, 1986).

From the available clinical data it is obvious that recurrent course is best predicted by earlier course (age of onset, number of previous episodes) and bipolarity.

Prediction of outcome
The outcome of affective disorders is highly individual and varies between complete recovery, residual symptoms or severe chronicity. Earlier studies give only rough rates of remissions or rates of chronicity (defined as uninterrupted illness of at least two years length). More recently semi-quantitative measures were applied

to assess residual states, for instance the Global Assessment Schedule of Endicott *et al.* (1976) or measures of subjective suffering or quality of life. A multi-modal assessment of outcome is to be recommended.

It is remarkable that both community and clinical studies show that *many socio-demographic variables do not predict outcome*, for instance, race, social class, school education, professional education, marital status, religion, presence of a broken home in early childhood, intelligence, a positive family history, and probably also sex and age (see review of Angst, 1990b, in press).

In the Stirling County study (Murphy *et al.*, 1986), which comprises follow-up data over 17 years of a normal population sample of 618 subjects, a log-linear analysis showed that neither age nor sex nor severity of the illness had any impact on the prognosis of outcome. It is well known that among psychosocial factors life events can precipitate depression, but it is not clear at all whether acute or chronic stressors have an impact on recovery or chronicity of depression.

The impact of social support on the quality of remission of depression is unclear. The study of George *et al.* (1989) suggests that patients of middle and higher age may have a better recovery rate after 6–30 months in the presence of a good social support. But a recent comprehensive review of the clinical literature (Cooper, 1990) gives a more sceptical and controversial view of the situation. Further research in this area is needed.

Other *psychosocial factors* are of interest: the presence of a sick spouse may impair the quality of remission (Gangil *et al.*, 1982; Merikangas *et al.*, 1983; Billings and Moos, 1984). The presence of a confiding relationship may provide a protective buffer against a symptomatic response to life stress and therefore also protect against recurrence of depressive symptoms (Brown and Harris, 1978; Surtees, 1980). The Upper Bavarian field study (Dilling *et al.*, 1988) suggests that demoralization measured by the PERI is linked on one hand with deficiencies in childhood care and on the other hand with the severity of later psychological syndromes (a mixture of depressive, anxious and psychosomatic syndromes).

In a large questionnaire study carried out in Alameda County, California, by Kaplan *et al.* (1987) with a follow-up of nine years (1965–1974), high levels of depressive symptoms were predicted by social isolation, uncertain situations, baseline physical symptoms, physical disablement and perceived poor health. On the whole *physical health* was one of the strongest predictors. This is compatible with general practice investigations (Kukull *et al.*, 1986; Hankin and Locke, 1982).

In the ECA study, at a follow-up of one year (Sargeant *et al.*, 1990), 20% of the subjects were still depressed, especially women older than 30 years, women with an unstable marital history or with less than a high school education. For men only poor education was significantly associated with persistence of depression. Poorer outcome was also correlated with a history of depression prior to index episode, increased index episode severity, and greater index comorbidity. On the whole, *comorbidity or multimorbidity* indicated poorer outcome. These factors had more impact than the sociological factors mentioned before (Sargeant *et al.*, 1990).

One of the best established clinical and epidemiological findings is the prognostic value of *premorbid personality features*. This was shown for low intelligence (Astrup *et al.*, 1959), hysterical personality traits (Kay *et al.*, 1969; Kerr *et al.*, 1972) and high neuroticism scores (Kerr *et al.*, 1972; Paykel *et al.*, 1974; Weissman *et al.*,1978; Henderson *et al.*, 1981; Duggan *et al.*, 1990), whereas high extraversion scores predicted a more favourable outcome. Both recovery rates and Global Assessment Schedule scores correlate with premorbid social deviation. This finding was shown to be reproducible in unipolar and bipolar affective disorders (Angst, 1990b; in press). Duggan *et al.* (1990) showed that in a follow-up study over 18 years of a consecutive series of admissions to the Maudsley Hospital high scores for obsessional traits were associated with poor long-term outcome.

Conclusions

Single-episode depression is certainly less frequent than the estimate of 50% provided by several community studies would suggest. More recent prospective data indicate that only about one-quarter, or even less, of all depressives are affected once in their lifetime. Today we can assume that 75–80% of depressive cases are recurrent.

Recurrent depression mainly takes on the form of major depression and of recurrent brief depression. Major depression has a lifetime prevalence rate of 17% or more, recurrent brief depression of 11% or more. A prospective clinical study showed that recurrence of both unipolar depression and bipolar disorder does not diminish with age, but this finding needs further confirmation. Recurrence is difficult to predict. It is higher in bipolar disorders and in patients with early age of onset and with recurrent episodes prior to index episode. Future course is best predicted by past course.

Contrary to recurrence, outcome (chronicity versus recovery) is influenced by numerous—probably additive—factors, of which each may contribute a small amount to the variance. Comorbidity, multimorbidity and the presence of physical disorders predict poor outcome, as does an inadequate, premorbid personality or maladjustment. To a probably minor extent other psychosocial factors may contribute, for instance poor childhood care, lack of social support, the absence of a confidant, the presence of a sick partner and strong expressed emotions in personal relationships.

Acknowledgement

This project was supported by grant 3.873.0.88 from the Swiss National Science Foundation.

References

Andrews G, Neilson M, Hunt C *et al.* (1990) Diagnosis, personality, and the long-term outcome of depression. *Br J Psychiatry* **157**, 13–18.

Angst J (1966) Zur Aetiologie und Nosologie endogener depressiver Psychosen. Eine genetische, soziologische und klinische Studie. *Monographien aus dem Gesamtgebiete der Neurologie und Psychiatrie*, Heft 112. Berlin: Springer.

Angst J (1980) Verlauf unipolar depressiver, bipolar manisch-depressiver und schizo-affektiver Erkrankungen und Psychosen. Ergebnisse einer prospektiven Studie. *Fortschr Neurol Psychiat* **48**, 3–30.

Angst J (1988a) Clinical course of affective disorders. In: Helgason T, Daly RJ (eds) *Depressive Illness: Prediction of Course and Outcome*, pp. 1–48. Berlin: Springer.

Angst J (1988b) Risikofaktoren für den Verlauf affektiver Störungen. In: von Zerssen D, Moeller HJ (eds) *Affektive Störungen: Diagnostische, epidemiologische, biologische und therapeutische Apekte*, pp. 99–110. Berlin: Springer.

Angst J (1990a) Course as classifier for depression. Paper presented at the *International Symposium on Recurrent Mood Disorders*, Monte-Carlo (Monaco) (in press).

Angst J (1990b) Prädiktoren des Spontanverlaufs affektiver Psychosen. Paper presented at the *9. Düsseldorfer Psychiatrie-Symposion, Prädiktoren des Therapieverlaufs bei endogenen Psychosen*, Düsseldorf 1990 (in press).

Angst J, Frey R (1976) Die Prognose endogener Depressionen jenseits des 40. Lebensjahrs. *Zentralbl Gesamte Neurol Psychiatr* **215**, 235.

Angst J, Weis P (1967) Periodicity of depresive psychoses. In: Brill H, Cole JO, Deniker P *et al.* (eds) *Neuro-Psychopharmacology: Proceedings of the Fifth International Congress of the Collegium Internationale Neuro-Psychopharmacologicum*, Washington, DC, 1966, pp. 703–710. Amsterdam: Excerpta Medica.

Angst J, Wicki W (1991) The Zurich Study. XI. Is dysthymia a separate form of depression? Results of the Zurich Cohort Study. *Eur Arch Psychiatry Clin Neurosci* **240**, 349–354.

Angst J, Vollrath M, Koch R (1988) New aspects on epidemiology of depression. In: Angst J, Woggon B (eds) *Lofepramine in the Treatment of Depressive Disorders: Review of the Past 10 years and Future Prospects*, pp. 1–14. International Symposium organized by the Psychiatric University Hospital Zurich, Lugano, 1987. Braunschweig: Vieweg-Verlag.

Angst J, Merikangas K, Scheidegger P, Wicki W (1990) Recurrent brief depression: a new subtype of affective disorder. *J Affective Disord* **19**, 87–98.

Astrup C, Fossum A, Holmboe R (1950) A follow-up study of 270 patients with acute affective psychoses. *Acta Psychiatr Scand* (Suppl) 135.

Billings A G, Moos R H (1984) Chronic and nonchronic unipolar depression: the differential role of environmental stressors and resources. *J Nerv Ment Dis* **172**, 65–75.

Bland RC, Newman SC, Orn H (eds) (1988) Epidemiology of psychiatric disorders in Edmonton. *Acta Psychiatr Scand* (Suppl) 338.

Blazer D, Williams CD (1980) Epidemiology of dysphoria and depression in an elderly population. *Am J Psychiatry* **137**, 439–444.

Bratfos O, Haug JO (1968) Course of manic-depressive psychosis: a follow-up investigation of 215 patients. *Acta Psychiatr Scand* **44**, 89–112.

Brown GW, Harris T (1978) *Social Origins of Depression: A Study of Psychiatric Disorder in Women*. London: Tavistock.

Cassano GB, Akiskal HS, Musetti L *et al.* (1989) Psychopathology, temperament, and past course in primary major depression. II. Towards a re-definition of bipolarity with a new semi-structured interview for depression (SID). *Psychopathology* **22**, 278–288.

Cooper Z (1990) Psychosocial factors in the onset and course of depression: some issues of method. Paper presented at the *Meeting of Duphar Medical Relations: Predictions and Treatment of Recurrent Depression*, London, 1990.

Coryell W, Keller M, Endicott J *et al.* (1989) Bipolar II illness: course and outcome over a five-year period. *Psychol Med* **19**, 129–141.

Dilling H, Katschnig J, Weyerer S, Fichter MM (1988) Zur Prävalenz affektiver Störungen: Ergebnisse der oberbayrischen Feldstudie. In: von Zerssen D, Möller HJ (eds) *Affektive Störungen*, pp. 71–83. Berlin: Springer.

Duggan CF, Lee AS, Murray RM (1990) Does personality predict long-term outcome in depression? *Br J Psychiatry* **157**, 19–24.

Elliot D, Huizinger D, Morse BJ (1985) *The Dynamics of Deviant Behavior. A National Survey: Progress Report*. Boulder, CO: Behavioral Research Institute.

Endicott J, Spitzer RL, Fleiss JL, Cohen J (1976) The Global Assessment Scale: a procedure for measuring overall severity of psychiatric disturbance. *Arch Gen Psychiatry* **33**, 766–771.

Ernst C, Angst J (1992) The Zurich Study. XII. Sex differences in depression. Evidence from longitudinal epidemiological data. *Eur Arch Psychiatry Clin Neurosci* (in press).

Faravelli C, Incerpi G (1985) Epidemiology of affective disorders in Florence: preliminary results. *Acta Psychiatr Scand* **72**, 331–333.

Fichter MM (1988) *The Upper Bavarian Study: Course of Mental Illness in the Community* (in cooperation with Meller J, Witzke W, Weyerer S, Koloska R, Rehm J). Final report to the 'Deutsche Forschungsgesellschaft' (DFG), Munich.

Fichter MM (Collaborators: Meller I, Witzke W, Weyerer S, Rehm J, Dilling H, Elton M) (1990) *Verlauf psychischer Erkrankungen in der Bevölkerung*. Berlin: Springer.

Fichter MM, Rehm J, Witzke W *et al.* (1987) Der Verlauf affektiver und psychosomatischer Störungen am Beispiel der oberbayerischen Feldstudie: ein lineares Kausalmodel verlaufsbeeinflussender Faktoren. In: von Zerssen D, Müller HJ (eds) Affektive Störungen, S84–98. Berlin, Heidelberg, New York: Springer.

Gangil OP, Kumar A, Yadav BS, Jain RK (1982) Family history of mental illness as factor in relapse and nonrelapse of discharged functional psychotics. *Indian J Psychiatry* **24**, 84–87.

George LK, Blazer DG, Hughes DC, Fowler N (1989) Social support and the outcome of major depression. *Br J Psychiatry* **154**, 478–487.

Giles DE, Jarrett RB, Biggs MM *et al.* (1989) Clinical predictors of recurrence in depression. *Am J Psychiatry* **146**, 764–767.

Haellstroem T (1984) Point prevalence of major depressive disorder in a Swedish urban female population. *Acta Psychiatr Scand* **69**, 52–59.

Hagnell O (1988) *Affective Diseases: Their Course in a Longitudinal Perspective; the Lundby Study*. Strasbourg: Vortrag AEP (in press).

Hamilton M (1974) Prediction of response to E.C.T. in depressive illness. In: Angst J (Chairman) *Classification and Prediction of Outcome of Depression*, pp. 273–279. Stuttgart: Schattauer.

Hankin JR, Locke BZ (1982) The persistence of depressive symptomatology among prepaid group practice enrollees: an exploratory study. *Am J Publ Health* **72**, 1000–1007.

Henderson AS, Byrne DG, Duncan-Jones P (1981) Neurosis and the Social Environment. London: Academic Press.

Hooley JM, Hahlweg K (1986) The marriages and interaction patterns of depressive patients and their spouses. In: Goldstein MJ, Hand I, Hahlweg K (eds) Treatment of Schizophrenia: Family Assessment and Intervention, pp. 85–96. Berlin: Springer.

Kaplan GA, Roberts RE, Camacho TC, Coyne JC (1987) Psychosocial predictors of depression: prospective evidence from the human population laboratory studies. Am J Epidemiol 125, 206–220.

Kashani J, Carlson GA, Beck NC et al. (1987) Depression, depressive symptoms, and depressed mood among a community sample of adolescents. Am J Psychiatry 144, 931–934.

Kay DWK, Garside RF, Roy JR, Beamish P (1969) 'Endogenous' and 'neurotic' syndromes of depression: a 5- to 7-year follow-up of 104 cases. Br J Psychiatry 115, 389–399.

Keller MB, Shapiro RW (1981) Major depressive disorder: initial results from a one-year prospective naturalistic follow-up study. J Nerv Ment Dis 169, 761–768.

Keller MB, Shapiro RW, Lavori PW, Wolfe N (1982) Relapse in major depressive disorder: analysis with the life table. Arch Gen Psychiatry 39, 911–915.

Keller MB, Lavori PW, Lewis CW, Klerman GL (1983) Predictors of relapse in major depressive disorder. JAMA 250, 3299–3304.

Kerr TA, Roth M, Schapire K, Gurney C (1972) The assessment and prediction of outcome in affective disorders. Br J Psychiatry 121, 167–174.

Kiloh LG, Andrews G, Neilson M (1988) The long-term outcome of depressive illness. Br J Psychiatry 153, 752–757.

Kivelae SL, Pahkala K, Laippala P (1988) Prevalence of depression in an elderly population in Finland. Acta Psychiatr Scand 78, 401–413.

Kovacs M, Feinberg TL, Crouse-Novak M et al. (1984) Depressive disorders in childhood: II. A longitudinal study of the risk for a subsequent major depression. Acta Gen Psychiatry 41, 643–649.

Kukull WA, Koepsell TD, Inui TS et al. (1986) Depression and physical illness among elderly general medical clinic patients. J Affective Disord 10, 153–162.

Leff J, Vaughn C (1980) The interaction of life events and relatives' Expressed Emotion in schizophrenia and depressive neurosis. Br J Psychiatry 136, 145–153.

Lehtinen V (1986) The prevalence of depression. Vox 8, 69–75.

Merikangas KR, Bromet EJ, Spiker DG (1983) Assortative mating, social adjustment, and course of illness in primary affective disorder. Arch Gen Psychiatry 40, 795–800.

Merikangas KR, Wicki W, Angst J (1990) Heterogeneity of depression: classification of depressive subtypes by longitudinal course (submitted).

Murphy JM (1980) Continuities in community-based psychiatric epidemiology. Arch Gen Psychiatry 37, 1215–1223.

Murphy JM, Olivier DC, Sobol AM et al. (1986) Diagnosis and outcome: depression and anxiety in a general population. Psychol Med 16, 117–126.

Oliver JM, Simmons ME (1985) Affective disorders and depression as measured by the Diagnostic Interview Schedule and the Beck Depression Inventory in an unselected adult population. J Clin Psychol 41, 486–576.

Paskind HA (1929) Brief attacks of manic-depressive depressions. Arch Neurol (Chicago) 22, 123–134.

Paykel ES, Klerman GL, Prusoff BA (1974) Prognosis of depression and the endogenous–neurotic distinction. Psychol Med 4, 57–64.

Sargeant JK, Bruce ML, Florio L, Weissman MM (1990) Factors associated with one year outcome of major depression in the community. Arch Gen Psychiatry 47, 519–526.

Surtees PG (1980) Social support, residual adversity, and depressive outcome. *Soc Psychiatry* **15**, 71–80.

Surtees PG, Sashidharan SP (1986) Psychiatric morbidity in two matched community samples: a comparison of rates and risks in Edinburgh and St. Louis. *J Affective Disord* **10**, 101–113.

Uhlenhuth EH, Balter MB, Mellinger GD *et al.* (1983) Symptom checklist syndromes in the general population: correlations with psychotherapeutic drug use. *Arch Gen Psychiatry* **40**, 1167–1173.

Vaughn CE, Leff JP (1976) The influence of family and social factors on the course of psychiatric illness: a comparison of schizophrenic and depressed neurotic patients. *Br J Psychiatry* **129**, 125–137.

Weissman MM, Myers JK (1978) Affective disorders in a US urban community: the use of research diagnostic criteria in an epidemiological survey. *Arch Gen Psychiatry* **35**, 1304–1311.

Weissman MM, Myers JK, Harding PS (1978a) Psychiatric disorders in a US urban community. *Am J Psychiatry* **135**, 459–462.

Weissman MM, Prusoff BA, Klerman GL (1978b) Personality and the prediction of long term outcome of depression. *Am J Psychiatry* **135**, 797–800.

Weissman MM, Leaf PJ, Tischler GL *et al.* (1988) Affective disorders in five United States communities. *Psychol Med* **18**, 141–153.

Wicki W, Angst J (1991) The Zurich Study X: Hypomania in a 28–30 year old cohort *Eur Arch Psychiatry Clin Neurosci* **240**, 339–348.

Wittchen HU, Zerssen D von (1987) *Verläufe behandelter und unbehandelter Depressionen und Angststörungen: Eine klinisch-psychiatrische und epidemiologische Verlaufsuntersuchung.* Berlin: Springer.

2

Depression missed or mismanaged in primary care

Paul Freeling and Andre Tylee

Review of the evidence of incidence and prevalence of depression in primary care

The problem of caseness

It has always been difficult to determine the frequency with which GPs are consulted by depressed patients because of the problem of 'caseness' (Bebbington *et al.*, 1981). What one GP calls a 'case' of depression is not always the same as the usage adopted by another. Self-evidently the variation may arise either because a GP diagnoses as suffering from depressive illness a patient who would not be so labelled by a 'gold-standard' method, or through a failure to identify as depressed a patient who would be given the label by the 'gold standard'. It is only relatively recently that two-stage approaches have been adopted using first a screen and then a structured interview technique. These techniques, which draw on instruments developed by research psychiatrists, have provided more reliable figures for the number of cases of depression seen in primary care. Earlier descriptions are illuminating but probably said as much about the doctors concerned as about their patients.

An early indication that depressive illness accounted for a high proportion of the workload of primary care was provided by the prospective recording of data by Dr Arthur Watts, a British GP working in a rural area (Watts, 1947). He described a lifetime risk in his practice over 20 years for clinically significant

Long-term Treatment of Depression. Edited by S.A. Montgomery and F. Rouillon
© 1992 John Wiley & Sons Ltd

depression of approximately 10 cases per thousand (Watts, 1966). He described the tiny proportion who died by suicide in a single year, the low frequency of admission to mental hospital and the relatively low rates of people who saw psychiatrists as out-patients, at home or in the courts. He contrasted these with the 12–15 per 1000 patients who were depressed and consulted only GPs.

The practice of another eminent British GP was described retrospectively (Dunn and Skuse, 1981) over the 20 years up to 1976. One in every six women and one in every 20 men registered received a diagnosis of depression. An American GP from Indiana reviewing 15 years of care found that 23.5% of patients seen 'continuously' had been suffering from depression (Justin, 1976).

Porter (1970) conducted a treatment study of depression in 1970 in his single-handed English practice and using his own somewhat idiosyncratic diagnostic criteria obtained a rate of 1.7% in men and 7.8% in women consulting him; he calculated an annual incidence of 6.5 per 1000 for men and 29.3 per 1000 for women.

These four practitioners may each have been studying a different population rather than using different criteria for their diagnoses of depression. However, it is clear that different GPs have used the term to describe pathological change in mood with or without a variety of other symptoms in varying severity or quantity. A first step towards uniformity of case labelling in studies of depression in general practice was taken with the application of psychiatric rating scales.

The use of rating scales for recognition

Salkind (1969) applied the Beck Depression Inventory (BDI) (Beck *et al.*, 1961) to 80 consecutive attenders at his London practice using a cut-off score of 11 to define 'depressed' and surprisingly identified 48% of his sample as being in a 'depressed state'. Two later studies in the USA utilized the same instrument to produce markedly different results. Nielsen and Williams (1980) found that only 19.8% of 562 primary care medical attenders scored over 10, whilst Williamson (1987) found only 15.3% of 131 males and 15.7% of 223 females at or over this threshold. It is unusual for an equal proportion of males and females to be reported as depressed and Parker and colleagues (1986), also from the USA, reported 25% of females as opposed to 17% of males as having a BDI score of greater than 9.

The logistics of primary care screening favour the use of instruments purpose designed for self-completion: a widely applied one has been the Zung Self Rating Depression Scale (SDS) (Zung, 1965). Application of the SDS in primary care in the USA identified as 'symptomatically depressed', using a cut-off of 55, 13.2% of 1086 attenders (Zung *et al.*, 1983) and 12% of 499 attenders (Zung and King, 1983). In contrast, a third study (Rosenthal *et al.*, 1987) identified 21% of 123 whilst a fourth Bradshaw and Parker (1983) also identified 21% of 251 attenders in Sydney, Australia, using a lower cut-off point of only 40.

Other cut-off points have been used by other workers and a score of 50 identified 45% of 212 attenders in North Carolina (Moore *et al.*, 1978), 51% out of 95 in Los Angeles (Linn and Yager, 1984) and 41% out of 377 in Louisiana (Davis *et al.*, 1987). Such a variation in cut-off points is irritating to the reviewer but must reflect something about variations in clinical judgement and belief systems.

An instrument which has been used with a consistent cut-off is the Depression Scale of the Centre for Epidemiological Studies (CES-D) (Radloff, 1977). In studies reported from North America consistency of cut-off has not led to consistency in rates of depression reported. These have ranged from 12% of 1554 (Schulberg *et al.*, 1985) through 21% of 1921 attenders (Hankin and Locke, 1983) and 27% of 262 (Duer *et al.*, 1988) in different parts of the USA to 33.2% of 1250 attenders in Canada (Barnes and Prosen, 1984).

The Hospital Anxiety Depression Scale (HADS) (Zigmond and Snaith, 1983) was developed to avoid the problem of concurrent physical illness artificially elevating the psychiatric score. When assessed against the more commonly used 30-item General Health Questionnaire (Goldberg, 1978), HADS was found to be more sensitive when used with general practice attenders who found it simpler to complete (Wilkinson and Barczak, 1988).

Even when rating scales produce consistent findings it may be dangerous to assume that diagnoses are standardized. The problems caused by relying on non-standardized diagnoses are well illustrated by the fact that the second National Morbidity Study (RCGP/OPCS/DHSS, 1979), which had an annual case rate for neurotic depression of 31 per 1000, reflected a 20-fold increase over a similar study in the 1950s (Crombie, 1974). A significant difficulty in relying on reporting of depression by GPs is that they tend to identify for studies only those patients to whom they have prescribed a drug (Watson and Barber, 1981; Burton and Freeling, 1982) although they manage by non-drug methods the depressive illness of at least as many other patients (Sireling *et al.*, 1985a). In the third National Morbidity Study (RCGP/OPCS/DHSS, 1986) GPs from England and Wales in 1981–1982 reported a persistent rate of depression of 28 patients per year per thousand at risk.

GPs also report a substantial rate of false positives if compared with a diagnostic gold standard. Only half of the patients given antidepressants by their GP received diagnoses of major depression (Sireling *et al.*, 1985a) although 96% were categorized as having some kind of psychiatric diagnosis by a formal standardized psychiatric interview external to the GP consultation.

Two-stage designs

The difficulties associated with the use of the scales mentioned so far have been superseded by the addition of a second-stage standardized psychiatric interview. Instruments with well-defined thresholds for disorder developed in the UK (Wing *et al.*, 1974) and in the USA (American Psychiatric Association,

1980) are applied after screening consecutive attenders to identify likely cases.

There have been a number of studies of this nature in the USA. Hoeper and colleagues (1984) used the Schedule for Affective Disorders and Schizophrenia (SADS) (Endicott and Spitzer, 1978) as their second stage with 1327 patients over three months in one primary care setting and found point prevalence rates of 5.8% for major depressive disorder, 5% for intermittent depression and 3.4% for minor depressive disorder. Wright and colleagues (1980) found that such a two-stage design obtained poor compliance but estimated that 17% of their sample of 199 consulting patients in a Kentucky family practice had depressive disorder as defined by the Research Diagnostic Criteria (RDC) (Spitzer *et al.*, 1978). In Baltimore, just over half of the 41 patients who reached the second stage were depressed as judged by the Feighner criteria (Feighner *et al.*, 1972) (Nielsen and Williams, 1980). Coulehan and colleagues (1988) used the third version of the Diagnostic Interview Schedule (DIS) (Robins *et al.*, 1981) and found that 7.1% of 294 primary care attenders to three practices in Pittsburgh had DSM-III major depressive disorder. Block and colleagues (1988), also in Pittsburgh, found that 9.2% of 294 new attenders at three primary care clinics met DSM-III criteria for depressive disorder. Von Korf and colleagues (1987) found a 5% prevalence for DSM-III major depression in a Baltimore group practice using the DIS as second stage with 809 patients. When the usual second stage was turned into a self-rated instrument (based on the DSM-III) attenders to a practice in Nebraska showed much higher rates for depression: 18.5% of 54 males and 19.2% of 146 females (Yates *et al.*, 1985).

In the UK, Bridges and Goldberg (1987), using the third version of the *Diagnostic and Statistical Manual of Mental Disorders* (DSM-III) (American Psychiatric Association, 1980) as the second interview stage, found that nearly 13% of 590 consecutive attenders aged 15 and over who consulted a GP for a new episode of illness had major depressive disorder. A rigorous depression study in an Inner London practice (Blacker and Clare, 1988) reports a prevalence of 4.3% for RDC major depressive disorder among 2308 consecutive attenders who included an excess of young adults. If 70–90% of people with depressive disorder consult their GP for help (Wing *et al.*, 1974; Brown and Harris, 1978; Weissman and Myers, 1978) this would produce a prevalence rate for depression similar to the common estimate of 5% in the community (Paykel, 1989a).

In the Sydney practices of 12 GPs (Parker *et al.*, 1986), only 29% of screen-positive potential depressives accepted further study: 83% were considered cases on subsequent interview using the Present State Examination (PSE) (Wing *et al.*, 1974): the effect was that 29 out of 564 attenders (64% female) who were screened were found to be depressed.

Despite this vogue for psychiatric scales and schedules, Williams and Skuse (1988) found that depressive thoughts were so commonly reported by a sample of attenders to one practice in south London that they concluded that attention should be paid to content rather than simply expressing depression as a total score or as being above a threshold score.

Recognition of depression (grade 1) by primary care practitioners

It has been estimated that only half the cases of psychiatric disorder are recognized as such by the GP (Goldberg and Huxley, 1980). When patients aged 16–60 are screened in GP waiting rooms, just over half of those found to have major depression are not recognized as depressed by their doctor during the interviews which follow. This occurs whether patients are consulting for a new episode (Bridges and Goldberg, 1987) or for any reason (Skuse and Williams, 1984; Freeling *et al.*, 1985). Recognition of depression appears more accurate in the elderly although acknowledgement of the depression by the GP remains a major problem (MacDonald, 1986). It seems that GPs may recognize depression in the elderly yet decide not to acknowledge it because of a reluctance to prescribe a tricyclic or because it may be felt that depression is characteristic of declining years and reactive to life events.

American family physicians also fail to recognize depressive illness whether they be established practitioners (Nielsen and Williams, 1980; Hoeper *et al.*, 1980; Hankin and Locke, 1983; Zung *et al.*, 1983; Zung and King, 1983; Zung *et al.*, 1985) or trainees (Moore *et al.*, 1978; Goldberg *et al.*, 1980a; Goldberg *et al.*, 1980b).

Which depressions are unrecognized?
Two USA studies describe patient outcome after the non-recognition of their depression: Weissman and colleagues (1981) reported that there are some patients who once missed stay that way for a long time; Widmer and Cadoret (1978), on the other hand, described how depressives are eventually recognized. However, in the UK, unrecognized depressives were more likely than recognized depressives to have had their illness for more than a year (Freeling *et al.*, 1985).

The depressives in these studies who went unrecognized were somewhat less dedressed than those whose depression was recognized although there was considerable overlap between the two groups in terms of symptoms experienced, such as pessimism, guilt, impaired activity, loss of energy, and insomnia, and also in the global severity. Not only were unrecognized depressives as a group less markedly ill, they were harder to recognize because they were less likely to admit to or complain of the symptom depression, and they looked less miserable and behaved in a less depressed fashion. They were, however, more likely to show a 'distinct quality of mood' (Paykel, 1985), a category of symptom representing a change in internal feelings including descriptions such as 'coldness', 'deadness' or 'emptiness' inside.

We have studied video-taped interviews between depressed people and their GPs to determine any differences in content or interviewing style between consultations which result in major depression being correctly acknowledged, those in which major depression remains unacknowledged, and consultations with patients who have normal affect. Acknowledgement was defined at the minimum level as a GP stating to a researcher at the end of a consulting session that a particular patient might have been depressed and that the patient was returning within 14 days. The two groups of depressed patients had an external psychiatric interview (Sireling, 1985b) and the video-tapes were analysed using the Consultation Analysis by Triggers and Symptoms (CATS) (Tylee and Freeling, 1987) and the Consultation Analysis by Behaviour and Style (CABS). CATS codes content and GP micro-behaviours.

CABS covers doctor-interviewing behaviours globally including interviewing skills; problem definition; the selection, naming, solving or management of key problems; the emotional tone of the consultation; the degree of empathy manifested; and the appropriate use of authority. Preliminary findings using CATS have been reported (Tylee and Freeling, 1989) from comparisons of the first twenty-odd trios of consultations. It was found that in the group in which major depression was correctly acknowledged, a depression cue was presented as the opening utterance in more than a third of the consultations. Three-quarters of these consultations contained the first depression cue within the first four patient utterances. Opening cues included items such as 'depressed', 'so nervous', 'nerves gone', 'can't cope', 'problems sleeping'. Very occasionally, a patient was newly acknowledged by their GP as depressed without a verbal depression cue, suggesting that the communication of emotional disorder occurred at a non-verbal level.

In the group whose major depression went unacknowledged by the GP, a third of the opening patient utterances were not about depression although a fifth of the consultations opened with a possible depression cue including 'feeling at point zero' and 'not eating'. Only a third of these consultations during which depression went unacknowledged actually contained a stated depression cue among the first four patient utterances. Thus it is not too surprising that the GP went down another track in the consultation.

It is important to recognize the contribution made to correct acknowledgement by the interviewing styles and behaviours of the doctor, for example listening skills and empathy. A patient who knows that their GP has an open style may feel able to commence the consultation with a psychological symptom. Equally, there are patients who somatize their complaints and such individuals are reported to form the majority of the patients whose major depression goes unrecognized when they present to GPs with a new episode of illness (Bridges and Goldberg, 1987).

With the debate over definition and caseness and the variations in the studies so far outlined, it is hardly surprising that there are difficulties encountered in recognizing depressive disorder in primary care. However, other difficulties can arise from the internal structure and arrangements of the practice itself. British general practice is a good example: having changed by evolution over the past 20 years (Freeling and Fitton, 1983), it is now in a period of much more rapid change as it attempts to adapt to the 'New GP Contract, 1990'.

The number of group practices has increased, and it is commonplace for several partners to share their 'lists' of patients with each other and with vocational trainees so that Balint's (1957) 'collusion of anonymity' can occur with the patient simply moving around within the arrangements of a group practice. The somewhat impersonal structure described seems to appeal to some patients who can play on the lack of intimacy. The emphasis on proactive care with practice nurses providing preventive care for defined conditions may affect their ability to recognize underlying depression unless suitably trained.

Improving recognition of depression

Most GPs in Western Europe have a similar job description that includes making early diagnoses in physical, psychological and social terms. This requires the ability to look and listen for any cues to such disorder within the undifferentiated collection of symptoms presented by patients. Although GPs conduct short interviews these can be repeated frequently, within the structural confines described, so that contact can in effect be continuous (RCGP, 1972). This provides an opportunity for the patient to effect change between consultations (Freeling and Barry, 1982). It also allows the GP to organize the undifferentiated symptoms presented by the patient in a way that reduces unnecessary intervention (Freeling and Harris, 1984; Grol, 1989). Many of the symptoms offered by patients are acute and self-limiting but some represent the beginning of inevitable deterioration towards handicap and disability (Freeling, 1985).

Blacker and Clare (1988) in a London practice found that six symptoms were highly significantly associated with depressive disorder and distinguished between other forms of psychiatric disorder taken collectively and those with physical illnesses. In order of statistical importance the symptoms were: insomnia; fatigue; loss of interest; morbid self-opinion; and finally, with equal importance, impairment of concentration, and hopelessness with or without recurrent suicidal thoughts. Symptoms which distinguished depression from anxiety included: loss of interest; insomnia; and morbid self-opinion, with or without morbid guilt.

These phenomenological descriptions of symptom complexes derived directly from general practice may be of importance in helping to account for apparent discrepancies between GPs and psychiatrists in recognizing depressive disorder. Such discrepancies might arise if the two types of practitioner require different numbers or types of symptoms to be present in order to reach a diagnosis. Such differences in criteria would produce both false-positive and false-negative diagnoses when GPs are assessed against a research psychiatrist's 'gold standards'. GPs also may give different weight to particular symptoms and it appears that others will weight a symptom by the number of times a patient repeats it rather than eliciting the functional disturbance which it causes.

We suggest that GPs need a pragmatic aid to the recognition of depressive disorder that is particularly linked to patient outcome. Now that we know that benefits from drug intervention are predicted for depression that is of a level of severity of at least Research Diagnostic Criteria (RDC) probable major depression (Hollyman *et al.*, 1988) we have adopted the RDC criteria in everyday practice. We have found the definitions used in the RDC described by Spitzer and colleagues (1978) (see Table I) easy to memorize and apply in everyday British general practice. The use of such an instrument tackles the problem of 'caseness' and can easily be used by the GP in response to any depression 'cue' in the same manner as the cue word 'pain' triggers a standard response set in most physicians. The RDC will suffice until general practice can generate its own response set of criteria that take account of the use of somatic symptoms in the RDC that may reflect physical disorder.

GPs adopt a pragmatic, problem-solving approach based often on probabilities (Crombie, 1963; RCGP, 1972) and linked to notions of the risk associated with a condition together with the effectiveness of available interventions. GPs often make management decisions first and then formulate a diagnosis to justify those decisions (Howie, 1972). Where psychiatric conditions are concerned, studies of decision making by GPs (Jenkins *et al.*, 1985) and by GP trainees compared with psychiatric trainees (Wilkinson, 1988) have shown low agreement within and between groups. This could be related to the ability or the willingness of individual doctors to elicit the symptoms of conditions such as depressive illness. Certainly, when studying associations between scores on a psychiatric screening questionnaire and the number of cues to psychological

---

Table I.   Probable major depression (RDC)

Two weeks with:

A.   Dysphoric mood or pervasive loss of interest

AND

B.   At least four of the following:
     appetite or weight change
     change in sleep pattern
     anergia, fatigue, or tiredness
     psychomotor agitation or retardation
     loss of interest or pleasure in usual activities
     feelings of self-reproach or excessive guilt
     diminished thinking or concentration
     recurrent thoughts of suicide or death

disturbance given in the consultation, Davenport and his colleagues (1987) concluded that some doctors are better able than others to detect psychiatric illness because they are more likely to allow patients to express verbal cues about lowered mood as well as somehow permitting 'vocal' (paraverbal) cues such as sighing. This giving of permission is probably related to, and may account in part for, the wide variation among GPs in their ability to detect psychiatric disorders (Shepherd *et al.*, 1966) which has been attributed to the personal bias of individual doctors towards or away from such problems (Marks *et al.*, 1979).

This has led to a series of efforts to improve GPs' performance with patients who have emotional disorder. From the 1950s these efforts lay largely in Balint training, which consists of small group discussion of case reports with the emphasis on understanding the patient by considering the nature of the relationship and transaction between doctor and patient. Successful training, which may involve weekly sessions for many years, was reported to produce a small but significant change in the doctor's personality (Balint *et al.*, 1965). The continuing responsibility of the doctor for the patient was seen originally as very important although more recently vocational trainees have experienced benefit from a more time-limited process.

It is probable that doctors can best polish their social and interpersonal skills of interviewing and extend self-knowledge and understanding in an interactive small group with a skilled leader. Another component or alternative method to improve professionally is to devote long consultations to some patients, and this learning process may be similar to that of psychotherapy training where time spent with the patient seems as good a predictor of benefit as the school of origin of the therapist.

An audit of GP management of depression was carried out by two groups of GPs (Burton and Freeling, 1982; Freeling and Burton, 1982). These GPs described how they were first 'cued' to consider depressive illness and then applied a checklist of symptoms. If depressive illness seemed likely, they assessed recent life events, and 'depressive tendencies' which include past or family history of depressive illness, or an adverse upbringing. Management decisions are based on this information. The GPs' most commonly used cue proved to be a volunteering by the patient of a single symptom of depression (82%); second was the patient saying 'I feel depressed' (52%); third was the ill-defined cue that the doctor 'felt' the patient was depressed (53%); and fourth was the recurrent presentation of symptoms without identifiable organic cause (44%). Only rarely did a single cue trigger the process of seeking supporting evidence.

The doctors had said during their discussions that if a depressed patient had few recent life events and no obvious depressive tendency they would not prescribe but reconsider the diagnosis, and if a patient had a low depressive tendency but many life events they would rely on counselling instead of drugs.

When they recorded their audit, every depressed patient had been prescribed an antidepressant drug, although 36% of them were in one of these 'won't prescribe' groups.

Providing American family doctors with scores from the 28-item GHQ (Goldberg and Hillier, 1979) produced no increase in the recognition of mental disorder (Hoeper *et al.*, 1984) although one British GP with a known interest in psychiatry found the results of the 60-item GHQ helpful (Johnstone and Goldberg, 1976). It has been suggested that rather than replacing the emotional antennae of the GP with a screening test result it would be sensible to replace the GP with a specially trained worker for some groups known to be at high risk, such as women with postnatal depression. Health visitors trained in Rogerian counselling seeing such women for eight weekly visits obtained significant improvements in psychiatric morbidity at three months when compared with a control group receiving routine help (Holden *et al.*, 1989).

Interviewing behaviours taught to American family practice trainees have been known to increase their accuracy in recognizing psychiatric disorders, although those who performed poorly at onset seemed also to need teaching about approaches to management (Goldberg *et al.*, 1980a, 1980b). The technique of problem-based interviewing developed at McMaster University (Lesser, 1985) has been taught successfully to GP trainees (Gask *et al.*, 1988) and to a self-selected group of established GPs (Gask *et al.*, 1987). The latter improved their skills in psychiatry, which were already good (Gask *et al.*, 1987). We suspect that such improvement in performance is partly an effect of the group work and not completely dependent on the technique learnt. However, it has been demonstrated that communication skills training of GPs has increased patient satisfaction (Evans *et al.*, 1987) and also that interviewing skills taught to undergraduates persist into professional life (Maguire *et al.*, 1986), so that the acquisition of appropriate techniques is in itself likely to be of lasting value. It remains important to identify skills which are associated with accurate identification of depression by GPs.

How might GP diagnosis and management of depression be improved?

Management of depressive disorder aimed at relieving lost cognitive function, emotional drive and social performance requires firstly acknowledgement of the condition by the GP followed by an explanation of depression as a syndrome rather than a single symptom or normal mood which might be treated easily by the sufferer. Next, management should be jointly decided upon, with the patient considering benefits and risks of the different methods available. Not surprisingly GPs sometimes decide to use a sequence of consultations rather than a single one in order to achieve all these goals.

We have touched already upon the possibility that the act of recognition itself may improve outcome, and patients with unrecognized major depressive disorder did fare slightly worse when followed up after three months (Freeling *et al.*, 1985) than the recognized patients who were prescribed inadequate dosages of antidepressant drugs and rarely had a return appointment within the study follow-up period, a finding which is in accord with previous studies (Johnson, 1973). As well as affecting drug compliance, such poor follow-up precludes even the use of simple support let alone specific psychotherapeutic techniques.

Whatever the attitude of GPs may be to following up patients with major depression, drugs specific for the condition are frequently dispensed. In 1985 alone more than 6.7 million prescriptions for antidepressants were dispensed by the NHS pharmaceutical services in England and Wales. Sireling and colleagues (1985b) found that patients prescribed antidepressants were more likely to have 'caseness' on the Index of Definition (Wing, 1976), higher scores on the Hamilton Rating Scale for Depression (HRSD) (Hamilton, 1967), and higher Raskin ratings (Raskin *et al.*, 1970) than those whose depression was acknowledged but treated in some other way.

That very few patients complete a minimal therapeutic course of antidepressant drugs in general practice (Johnson, 1973; Parish, 1971; Tyrer, 1973) may still be true despite the proven value of amitriptyline in major depression treated in general practice (Paykel *et al.*, 1988; Hollyman *et al.*, 1988). In this study general practice depressives were treated for six weeks with amitriptyline (reaching mean doses of 119 mg) or placebo. Drug effect was markedly superior to placebo and response was independent or demographic characteristics, history of illness, endogenous symptomatology, and precipitating stress. Drug effect was related only to the severity of the depression. In particular the drug was found to be superior to placebo in patients with initial score on the HRSD of 13 or more but not in those with scores below that level, and similarly it was superior to placebo in subjects whose state at entry at least conformed to probable major depression (RDC) on entry.

People recruited into a drug trial are different from those patients in general practice who do not want drug treatment or who subsequently drop out of it. Suitable management for these patients remains to be determined. We also cannot assume that the unacknowledged patients will benefit from the same treatments as acknowledged ones. On the other hand, since severity was the only predictor for outcome for patients within the trial the indications are good. Not only have we yet to prove the outcome of treating previously unacknowledged depression with drugs, we have yet to determine what benefits these patients may receive simply from being acknowledged. Depressed patients about whose outcome their doctors were optimistic and who were therefore not prescribed antidepressants fared significantly worse than those who were treated (Zung *et al.*, 1985).

Whether or not GPs will be more willing both to acknowledge depressive illness and to treat it with antidepressant drugs remains to be determined. Many GPs are discouraged by the unpleasant, unwanted, effects of anticholinergic activity of the tricyclics. Other factors are the two-week delay in producing benefit and that they can be lethal in overdose. Newer potentially less toxic antidepressants affecting serotonin uptake must have their efficacy and safety tested in general practice depressives.

Montgomery (1989) has pointed out that until recently studies of antidepressant drugs whether new or old have simply assessed the efficacy and adverse events in the acute phase of depressive illness. More information is needed about the efficacy of antidepressants in the continuation phase of treatment (i.e. between six weeks and six months after commencement of treatment) as well as the efficacy in prophylaxis of recurrence.

It is important to elicit stresses and life events from patients even if their presence does not predict the effectiveness of drugs. A depressed patient often needs a certain degree of improvement in function to be able to make decisions and achieve changes that are needed in their life. Drug treatment is often helpful in giving the patient the impetus to achieve necessary change and respond to counselling. Benefit is likely from simple, sympathetic, social support supplied while the effect of the drug is being monitored.

There is a wide range of specific psychotherapies available but they are all expensive of time and commitment and are perhaps best reserved for second-phase deployment in primary care. Cognitive therapy (Beck, 1976) has, however, been used increasingly in primary care, mainly by clinical psychologists (see Chapter 8). Some positive results are reported (Blackburn *et al.*, 1981, 1986; Teasdale *et al.*, 1984) though Paykel (1989b) called it the 'Yuppie of the anti-depressant therapies: a child of the 1970's, verbal, exciting, a little pushy, perhaps riding for a fall'.

Virtually all psychiatric disorder presents initially to GPs and only one in 20 patients with mental illness is referred to a psychiatrist (Fahy, 1974; Grad de Alarcon *et al.*, 1975).

The majority of depressed patients will continue to make their first contact with their general practitioner and the primary care team in numbers that make it impractical to refer many to specialist services. Most sufferers can be helped relatively simply and inexpensively once acknowledged.

Training at all levels of undergraduate and postgraduate activity needs to address the many factors that affect the recognition of depression and to develop and disseminate appropriate management protocols to follow for the different degrees of severity and different patient types. Depressive illness will continue to be a challenge to the clinical acumen of the GP and to the treatment skills of the whole primary care team.

References

American Psychiatric Association (1980) *Diagnostic and statistical manual of mental Disorders* (3rd ed). Washington, DC.

Balint M (1957) *The Doctor, the Patient, and the Illness*. London; Pitman Medical.

Balint M, Balint E, Gosling R, Hildebrand PA (1965) *A Study of Doctors*. London: Pitman Medical.

Barnes GE, Prosen H (1984) Depression in CaJadian general practice attenders. *Can J Psychiatry* **29**, 2–10.

Bebbington PE, Tennant C, Hurry J (1981) Adversity and the nature of psychiatric disorder in the community. *J Affective Disord* **3**, 345–366.

Beck AT (1976) *Cognitive Therapy and the Emotional Disorders*. New York: International Universities Press.

Beck AT, Ward CH, Mendelson M *et al.* (1961) An inventory for measuring depression. *Arch Gen Psychiatry* **4**, 561–571.

Blackburn IM, Bishop S, Glen IM *et al.* (1981) The efficacy of cognitive therapy in depression: a treatment trial using cognitive therapy and pharmacotherapy, each alone and in combination. *Br J Psychiatry* **139**, 181–189.

Blackburn IM, Eunson KM, Bishop S (1986) A two year naturalistic follow-up of depressed patients treated with cognitive therapy, pharmacotherapy and a combination of both. *J Affective Disord* **10**, 67–75.

Blacker CVR, Clare AW (1988) The prevalence and treatment of depression in general practice *Psychopharmacology* **95**, S14–S17.

Block M, Schulberg HC, Coulehan JC *et al.* (1988) *J Am Board Family Practice* **1**, 91–97.

Bradshaw G, Parker G (1983) Depression in general practice attenders. *Aust NZ J Psychiatry* **17**, 361–365.

Bridges K, Goldberg D (1987) Somatic presentation of depressive illness in primary care. In Freeling P, Downey LJ, Malkin JC (eds) *The Presentation of Depression: Current Approaches*. London: Royal College of General Practitioners.

Brown G, Harris T (1978) *Social Origins of Depression*. London: Tavistock.

Burton RH, Freeling P (1982) How general practitioners manage depressive illness: developing a method of audit. *J R Coll Gen Pract* **32**, 558–561.

Coulehan JL, Schulberg HC, Block MR, Zettler-Segal M (1988) Symptom patterns of depression in ambulatory medical and psychiatric patients. *J Nerv Ment Dis* **176**, 284–288.

Crombie DL (1963) Diagnostic methods. *J R Coll Gen Pract* **6**, 579–589.

Crombie E (1974) Changes in patterns of recorded morbidity. In Taylor D (ed) *Benefits and Risks in Medical Care*. London: Office of Health Economics.

Davenport S, Goldberg D, Millar T (1987) How psychiatric disorders are missed during medical consultations. *Lancet* **ii**, 439–440.

Davis TC, Nathan RG, Crouch MA, Bairnsfather LE (1987) Screening depression in primary care: back to the basics with a new tool. *Fam Med* **19**, 200–202.

Duer S, Schwenk TL, Coyne JC (1988) Medical and psycho-social correlates of self-reported depressive symptoms in family practice. *J Fam Pract* **27**, 609–614.

Dunn G, Skuse D (1981) The natural history of depression in general practice: stochastic models. *Psychol Med* **11**, 755–764.

Endicott J, Spitzer RL (1978) A diagnostic interview: the Schedule for affective Disorders and Schizophrenia. *Arch Gen Psychiatry* **35**, 837–844.

Evans J, Kiellerup FD, Stanley RO *et al.* (1987) A communication skills programme for increasing patients' satisfaction with general practice consultations. *Br J Med Psychol* **60**, 373–378.

Fahy TJ (1974) Pathways of specialist referral of depressed patients from general practice. *Br J Psychiatry* **124**, 231–239.

Feighner JP, Robins E, Guze SB (1972) Diagnostic Criteria for use in psychiatric research. *Arch Gen Psychiatry* **26**, 57–63.

Freeling P (1985) Health outcomes in Primary Care: an approach to the problem. *Fam Practice* **2**, 177–181.

Freeling P, Barry S (1982) *In-Service Training: A Study of the Nuffield Courses of the Royal College of General Practitioners*. Windsor: NFER/Nelson.

Freeling P, Burton RH (1982) General practitioners and learning by audit. *J R Coll Gen Pract* **32**, 231–237.

Freeling P, Fitton P (1983) Teaching practices revisited. *Br Med J* **287**, 535–537.

Freeling P, Harris CM (1984) *The Doctor–Patient Relationship*. Edinburgh: Churchill Livingstone.

Freeling P, Rao BM, Paykel ES (1985) Unrecognized depression in general practice. *Br Med J* **290**, 1880–1883.

Gask L, McGrath G, Goldberg DP, Millar T (1987) Improving the psychiatric skills of established general practitioners: evaluation of group teaching. *Med Educ* **21**, 362–368.

Gask L, Goldberg D, Lesser AL, Millar T (1988) Improving the psychiatric skills of the general practice trainee: an evaluation of a group training course. *Med Educ* **22**, 362–368.

Goldberg DP (1978) *Manual of the General Health Questionnaire*. Slough: NFER/Nelson.

Goldberg DP, Hillier VF (1979) A scaled version of the General Health Questionnaire. *Psychol Med* **9**, 139–145.

Goldberg D, Huxley P (1980) *Mental Illness in the Community*. London: Tavistock.

Goldberg DP, Steele JJ, Smith C (1980a) Teaching psychiatric interviewing skills to family doctors. *Acta Psychiatr Scand* **62**, 41–47.

Goldberg DP, Steele JJ, Smith C, Spivey L (1980b) Training family doctors to recognise psychiatric illness with increased accuracy. *Lancet* **ii**, 521–523.

Grad de Alarcon J, Sainsbury P, Costain WR (1975) Incidence of referred mental illness in Chichester and Salisbury. *Psychol Med* **5**, 32–54.

Grol R (1989) *To Heal or to Harm: The Prevention of Somatic Fixation in General Practice* (3rd edn). London: Royal College of General Practitioners.

Hamilton M (1967) Development of a rating scale for primary depressive illness. *Br J Soc Clin Psychol* **6**, 278–296.

Hankin JR, Locke BZ (1983) Extent of depressive symptomatology among patients seeking care in a prepaid group practice. *Psychol Med* **13**, 121–129.

Hoeper EW, Nycz GR, Regier DA *et al.* (1980) *Am J Psychiatry* **137**, 207–210.

Hoeper EW, Kessler LG, Burke JD, Pierce W (1984) The usefulness of screening for mental illness. *Lancet* **i**, 33–35.

Holden JM, Sagovsky R, Cox JL (1989) Counselling in a general practice setting: a controlled study of health visitor intervention in treatment of post-natal depression. *Br Med J* **298**, 223–226.

Hollyman JA, Freeling P, Paykel ES *et al.* (1988) Double-blind placebo-controlled trial of amitriptyline among depressed patients in general practice. *J R Coll Gen Pract* **38**, 393–397.

Howie JGR (1972) Diagnosis: the Achilles heel. *J R Coll Gen Pract* **22**, 310–315.

Jenkins R, Smeeton N, Marinker M, Shepherd M (1985) A study of the classification of mental ill health in general practice. *Psychol Med* **15**, 403–409.

Johnson DAW (1973) Treatment of depression in general practice. *Br Med J* **2**, 1061–1064.

Johnstone A, Goldberg D (1976) Psychiatric screening in general practice: a controlled trial. *Lancet* **i**, 605–606.

Justin RG (1976) Incidence of depression in one family physician's practice. *J Fam Practice* **3**, 438–439.

Lesser AL (1985) Problem-based interviewing in general practice: a model. *Med Educ* **19**, 209–304.

Linn LS, Yager J (1984) Recognition of depression and anxiety by primary physicians. *Psychosomatics* **25**, 593–600.

MacDonald AJD (1986) Do general practitioners 'miss' depression in elderly patients? *Br Med J* **292**, 1365–1376.

Maguire G, Fairbairn S, Fletcher C (1986) Benefit of feedback training in interviewing as students persist. *Br Med J* **i**, 268–270.

Marks JN, Goldberg D, Hillier VF (1979) Determinants of the ability of general practitioners to detect psychiatric illness. *Psychol Med* **9**, 337–353.

Montgomery SA (1989) Developments in antidepressants In Herbst K, Paykel ES (eds) *Depression: An Integrative Approach.* Oxford: Heinemann.

Moore JT, Silimperi DR, Bobula JA (1978) Recognition of depression by family medicine residents: the impact of screening. *J Fam Practice* **7**, 509–513.

Nielsen AC, Williams TA (1980) Depression in ambulatory medical patients, prevalence by self-report questionnaire and recognition by non-psychiatric physicians. *Arch Gen Psychiatry* **37**, 999–1004.

Parish PA (1971) The prescription of psychotropic drugs in general practice. *J R Coll Gen Pract* **21** (suppl 4), 1–77.

Parker G, Homes S, Manicavasagar V (1986) Depression in general practice attenders. *J Affect Dis* **10**, 27–35.

Paykel ES (1985) The clinical interview for depression: development and validity. *J Affect Dis* **9**, 85–96.

Paykel ES (1989a) The background: extent and nature of the disorder. In Herbst K, Paykel ES (eds) *Depression: An Integrative Approach.* Oxford: Heinemann.

Paykel ES (1989b) Treatment of depression: the relevance of research for clinical practice. *Br J Psychiatry* **155**, 754–763.

Paykel ES, Hollyman JA, Freeling P, Sedgwick P (1988) Predictors of therapeutic benefit from amitriptyline in mild depression: a general practice placebo controlled trial. *J Affect Dis* **14**, 83–95.

Porter AMW (1970) Depressive illness in a general practice: a demographic study and a controlled trial of imipramine. *Br Med J* **1**, 770–778.

Radloff LS (1977) The CES-D scale: a self-report depression scale for research in the general population. *Appl Psychol Measurements* **1**, 385–401.

Raskin A, Schulterbrandt J, Reatig N, McKeon JJ (1970) Differential response to chlorpromazine, imipramine and placebo: a study of sub-groups of hospitalised depressed patients. *Arch Gen Psychiatry* **23**, 164–173.

Robins L, Helzer J, Croughan J *et al.* (1981) National Institute of Mental Health Diagnostic Interview Schedule: its history, characteristics and validity. *Arch Gen Psychiatry* **38**, 381–389.

Rosenthal MP, Goldfarb NI, Carlson BL *et al.* (1987) Assessment of depression in a family practice center. *J Fam Practice* **25**, 143-149.

Royal College of General Practitioners (1972) *The Future General Practitioner: Learning and Teaching.* London: British Medical Journal.

Royal College of General Practitioners, Office of Population Censuses and Surveys, Department of Health and Social Security (1979) *Morbidity Statistics from General Practice: Second National Study 1971–2.* London: HMSO.

Royal College of General Practitioners, Office of Population Censuses and Surveys, Department of Health and Social Security (1986) *Morbidity Statistics from General Practice: Third National Study 1981–1982.* London: HMSO.

Salkind MR (1969) Beck Depression Inventory in general practice. *J R Coll Gen Pract* **18**, 267–271.

Schulberg HC, Saul M, McClelland M *et al.* (1985) *Arch Gen Psychiatry* **42**, 1164–1170.

Shepherd M, Cooper M, Brown AC, Kalton G (1966) *Psychiatric Illness in General Practice.* Oxford: Oxford University Press.

Sireling LI, Paykel ES, Freeling P (1985a) Depression in general practice: case thresholds and diagnosis. *Br J Psychiatry* **147**, 113–119.

Sireling LI, Freeling P, Paykel ES, Rao BM (1985b) Depression in general practice: clinical features and comparison with out-patients. *Br J Psychiatry* **147**, 119–125.

Skuse D, Williams P (1984) Screening for psychiatric disorder in general practice. *Psychol Med* **14**, 365–377.

Spitzer RL, Endicott J, Robins E (1978) Research Diagnostic Criteria: rationale and reliability. *Arch Gen Psychiatry* **35**, 773–782.

Teasdale JD, Fennell MJV, Hibbert GA, Amies PL (1984) Cognitive therapy for major depressive disorders in primary care. *Br J Psychiatry* **144**, 400–406.

Tylee AT, Freeling P (1988) The recognition, diagnosis and acknowledgement of depressive disorder by general practitioners. In Herbst K, Paykel E (eds) *Depression: An Integrative Approach.* Oxford: Heinemann.

Tylee AT, Freeling P (1989) The Consultation Analysis by Triggers and Symptoms (CATS): a new objective technique for studying consultations. *Fam Practice* **4**, 260–265.

Tyrer P (1973) Drug treatments of depression in general practice. *Br Med J* **ii**, 18–20.

Von Korf N, Shapiro S, Burke JD *et al.* (1987) Anxiety and depression in a primary care clinic: comparison of diagnostic Interview Schedule, General Health Questionnaire and practitioner assessments. *Arch Gen Psychiatry* **44**, 152–165.

Watson JM, Barber JH (1981) Depressive illness in general practice: a pilot study. *Health Bull* **39**, 112–116.

Watts CAH (1966) *Depressive Disorders in the Community.* Bristol: John Wright.

Watts CAH (1947) Endogenous depression in general practice. *Br Med J* **1**, 11.

Weissman M, Myers JK (1978) Rates and risks of depressive symptoms in a US urban community. *Acta Psychiatr Scand* **57**, 219–231.

Weissman MM, Myers JK, Thompson WD (1981) Depression and its treatment in a US urban community 1975–76. *Arch Gen Psychiatry* **38**, 417–421.

Widmer RB, Cadoret RJ (1978) Depression in primary care: changes in pattern of patient visits and complaints during a developing depression. *J Fam Practice* **7**, 293–302.

Wilkinson G (1988) A comparison of psychiatric decision-making by trainee general practitioners and trainee psychiatrists using a simulated consultation model. *Psychol Med* **18**, 167–177.

Wilkinson MJB, Barczak P (1988) Psychiatric screening in general practice: comparison of the general health questionnaire and the hospital anxiety depression scale. *J R Coll Gen Pract* **38**, 311–313.

Williams P, Skuse D (1988) Depressive thoughts in general practice attenders. *Psychol Med* **18**, 469–475.

Williamson MT (1987) Sex differences in depression symptoms among adult family medicine patients. *J Fam Practice* **25**, 591–594.

Wing JK (1976) A technique for studying psychiatric morbidity in inpatient and out-patient series and in general population samples. *Psychol Med* **6**, 665–671.

Wing JK, Cooper JE, Sartorius N (1974) *The Measurement and Classification of Psychiatric Symptoms.* Cambridge: Cambridge University Press.

Wright JH, Bell RA, Kuhn CC (1980) Depression in family practice patients. *South Med J* **73**, 1031–1034.

Yates WR, Hill JW, Petty F, Filipi M (1985) Presenting problem and depression in a rural family practice. *Nebraska Med J* October, 367–369.

Zigmond AS, Snaith RP (1983) The hospital anxiety and depression scale. *Acta Psychiatr Scand* **67**, 361–370.

Zung WWK (1965) A self-rating depression scale. *Arch Gen Psychiatry* **12**, 63–70.

Zung WWK, King RE (1983) Identification and treatment of masked depression in a general medical practice. *J Clin Psychiatry* **44**, 365–368.

Zung WWK, Magill M, Moore JT, George DT (1983) Recognition and treatment of depression in a family medicine practice. *J Clin Psychiatry* **44**, 3–6.

Zung WWK, Zung EM, Moore J, Scott J (1985) Decision making in the treatment of depression by family medicine physicians. *Compr Ther* **11**, 19–23.

3

The minimum length of treatment for recovery

David J. Kupfer and Ellen Frank

Introduction

In this chapter we propose to explore the key issues surrounding the minimum length of treatment for recovery from an episode of major depression. Although this monograph is concerned with the long-term treatment of depression, it is our contention that successful long-term treatment of depression rests on a precise understanding of the various phases of treatment including the acute phase, the continuation phase and the maintenance or prophylactic phase.

We will first introduce a conceptual framework for an episode in order to best pose the questions necessary in articulating the definitions that are appropriate to demarcate the various change points in an episode of depression. We will particularly emphasize the definition of relapse. In doing so, it is important to separate out relapse from recurrence. To accomplish this task, we will turn to two different efforts to resolve this issue. The first of these relates to a work group established by the John D. and Catherine T. MacArthur Foundation Network on Depression and Related Disorders to develop a consensus on definitions of those terms that are used routinely in describing an episode of depression (Frank *et al.*, 1991). The second effort is illustrated by summarizing a recent approach developed by Hollon and colleagues to separate out relapse and recurrence.

The second major area examined in this chapter is concerned with the factors

Long-term Treatment of Depression. Edited by S.A. Montgomery and F. Rouillon
© 1992 John Wiley & Sons Ltd

that are important in determining how long treatment should occur during an episode of depression (i.e., the continuation phase). In assessing this particular issue, we will refer to a short review article published by Prien and Kupfer in 1986, the Pittsburgh study on long-term treatment of depression in mid-life, preliminary data from a study of late-life depression using a similar design for maintenance treatment, a review article by Loonen and Zwanikken, and finally another review article by Belsher and Costello.

The third section of this chapter will deal with a number of other issues which are related to the minimum length of treatment. They include predictors of relapse, the transition to maintenance treatment with a specific emphasis on discontinuation, and the relationship of continuation therapy to maintenance treatment.

Finally, we will attempt in the concluding section of this chapter to outline what the current problems are and summarize our conclusions regarding these issues, having attempted to derive a consensus from the results of the naturalistic studies, as well as the controlled treatment trials that have been conducted to date.

Conceptual framework for an episode of depression*

Effective pharmacological and psychotherapeutic treatments for affective disorders have been developed, but despite their extensive testing in clinical trials our understanding of their differential effectiveness is very limited. While more treatment research and novel treatment modalities are needed to improve side-effect profiles, onset to recovery, and give more specialized symptom profiles for drug choice, we also need to pay more attention to the development of consistent operational criteria in examining the episode of depression.

Early in the planning process of a programme on the Psychobiology of Depression and Related Disorders sponsored by the John D. and Catherine T. MacArthur Foundation it was concluded that while treatment research *per se* is sufficiently well funded by government agencies and the pharmaceutical industry, none of the many sponsors has found room to support work on the vital and basic problem of the lack of generalizability of reports on treatment outcome and the efficacy of various treatment modalities which is impeding research. The enormous variability in the use of labels to identify change points in the course of illness (such as 'response', 'recovery', 'recurrence' and 'relapse') has created 'Tower of Babel' conditions in the field and rendered comparison of results across treatment studies virtually impossible.

Prien and colleagues (1991) reviewed research articles published in nine journals over a two-year period, focusing on studies of unipolar depression that utilized a

---

* Adapted from Frank *et al.*, 1991, with permission.

criterion-based diagnostic system and involved some form of therapeutic manoeuvre in order to determine how critical changes in the clinical course of depressive disorder are defined in the research literature. These change points, labelled by terms such as response, recovery and relapse, are critical for evaluation and communication of study results. The review found marked inconsistency in the labelling and definition of change points and indicated the need for more precise conceptual definitions and operational criteria to enhance comparison, generalization, and application of results from clinical studies of depression.

Even one example will suffice to make the point of their review article: if one study defines 'recovery' from depression as a 50% symptom reduction at the eight-week point (irrespective of whether or not the patient still meets syndromal criteria for the disorder), while another study considers 'recovery' as being symptom free for a period of eight months (the presumptive end of the 'episode' of depression), and yet a third study considers the former a 'response' and the latter a 'remission', defining 'recovery' as something in between, it is clear that one cannot compare these 'recoveries' and easily evaluate which of the treatment procedures described in these three studies was most 'effective'. Moreover, many study reports fail to specify how exactly they defined the terms employed to label change points in course. In summary, while treatment studies are well supported and there is a large body of literature, its findings are less definitive than is generally assumed. This conclusion has major public health implications in that it not only affects research progress, but constitute a major impediment to optimizing clinical care.

A task force from the Network on Depressions was formed with three related goals: (1) arriving at consensus definitions of the relevant terms; (2) proposing tentative operational criteria for each of the definitions; and (3) testing these operational criteria for validity. In developing preliminary consensus definitions of terms relating to course of affective illness, attention was given to base the definitions exclusively on observable symptomatology rather than on any theoretical model of the disease. Theoretical models tend to be based on assumptions about the nature of the underlying, but inherently unobservable, course of the illness and tend to differ between treatment researchers of different backgrounds and theoretical persuasions. In an iterative process, preliminary consensus definitions were developed and methods for testing these definitions in existing data sets were devised.

Three principles were used to construct the definitional scheme: (1) the definitional scheme is based on observable, measurable phenomena; (2) the initiation or withdrawal of any form of treatment may change the *meaning* of the terms remission, recovery, relapse and recurrence, but not their phenomenologic expression (i.e., observable events); and (3) the temporal focus of the definitional scheme is life long rather than episode specific. Authors of the consensus document (Frank *et al.*, 1991) concluded that only six terms were required to designate the relevant change points in the course of unipolar

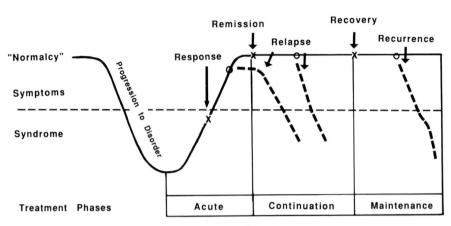

Figure 1.   Response, remission, recovery, relapse, recurrence. (Reprinted from *The Journal of Clinical Psychiatry*, 1991, 52 (2, suppl.), 12–16. Copyright 1991, Physicians Postgraduate Press.)

depressive illness. They also realized that a coherent definitional scheme for these terms leads to a definition of what constitutes an 'episode' of illness (and vice versa). As shown in Figure 1, a prototype of an episode of major depression can be portrayed. Two types of variation were fundamental to their definitions: (a) *severity* (number and/or intensity of symptoms); and (b) *duration* (of symptomatic deterioration or improvement). By this simplification they hoped to isolate the part of the problem of definition that depends on the description of the number and intensity of symptoms from the part that is tied to the timing of changes in symptoms.

The six terms are episode, response, remission, recovery, relapse and recurrence, and are described by Frank *et al.* (1991).

Episode
Conceptualization of episode   An 'episode' is a period of time, lasting longer than D days, during which the patient is consistently within the fully symptomatic range on a sufficient number of symptoms to meet syndromal criteria for the disorder. Syndromal criteria are defined by any of several criterion-based assessment systems, such as the Research Diagnostic Criteria or the Diagnostic and Statistical Manual of Mental Disorders. It should be noted that some of these assessment systems specify a pattern as well as number, severity and duration of symptoms.

Any time period prior to the patient's first episode, during which the patient is in the asymptomatic range except for short periods ($<D$ days), is said to be *disorder free*. A short ($<D$ days) time period during which the patient is outside the asymptomatic range is called a 'flurry'. A flurry can occur either prior to

onset or after the resolution of an episode. An episode does not end until a patient reaches recovery (see below).

Rationale for the conceptualization of episode Both clinicians and researchers must decide when a patient is clearly ill. For the clinician, this typically triggers a decision to treat; for the researcher, this designation signals the appropriateness of including the patient in a group of individuals with the same illness.

Response and partial remission

Conceptualization of partial remission A 'partial remission' is a period of time during which an improvement of sufficient magnitude is observed such that the individual is no longer fully symptomatic (i.e., no longer meets syndromal criteria for the disorder), but continues to evidence more than minimal symptoms. Treatment is not a requirement of the definition; partial remission can be spontaneous.

A 'response' can be thought of as the point at which a partial remission begins. Theoretically a response, unlike a partial remission, *does* require treatment and, thus, implies that the cause of the change in the patient's condition is known, which may or may not be a valid assumption.

Rationale for the conceptualization of partial remission In deciding when and how to intervene, the clinician usually chooses to intervene when the patient suffers from the disorder. If the disorder is in partial remission (either by natural course or in association with treatment), the clinician may choose to observe rather than alter the patient's regimen. If a partial remission fails to become a full remission after a reasonable period of time, the clinician will typically alter treatment, either by increasing the intensity (through a higher dose of medication or more frequent therapy sessions) of the current treatment, adding additional treatments to the one associated with the partial remission, or by switching to a new treatment. If the disorder is not being treated and partial remission fails to become a full remission after a reasonable period of time, the clinician will typically initiate treatment. For the researcher, the failure to proceed from partial to full remission in a naturalistic study may imply the need for placing the subject in a separate category of patients. In a treatment study with a specified treatment protocol, it may imply the need to drop the subject from the study.

Full remission

Conceptualization of full remission A 'full remission' is a relatively brief ($>E$ days, but $<F$ days) period of time during which an improvement of sufficient magnitude is observed such that the individual is asymptomatic (i.e., no longer meets syndromal criteria for the disorder and has no more than minimal symptoms). Again, treatment is not a requirement; full remission can be spontaneous.

Rationale for the conceptualization of full remission   A declaration of remission implies that no increase in the intensity of the treatment regimen is required. Depending upon the treatment and assumptions about its mechanisms of action, a full remission might imply that a decrease in the intensity of treatment could be attempted.

Recovery

Conceptualization of recovery   A remission which lasts $\geq F$ days is a 'recovery'. Recovery can be spontaneous and can last for an indefinite period. The term is used to designate recovery from the episodes, not from the illness *per se.*

Rationale for the conceptualization of recovery   In a clinical setting, a declaration of recovery raises the possibility that: (a) treatment can be discontinued; or (b) if continued, the aim is prevention of a subsequent episode. In a research setting, it might mean that treatment efforts can now be focused on maintenance of the well state or that the subject moves on into a no-treatment follow-up phase in which the focus is the extent to which treatment-associated improvement is maintained.

Relapse

Conceptualization of relapse   'Relapse' is a return of symptoms satisfying the full syndrome criteria for an episode which occurs during the period of remission, but prior to recovery as defined above. Relapse can represent a change from either partial or full remission to full syndrome criteria for the disorder.

Rationale for the conceptualization of relapse   A relapse signals a need for treatment intervention or modification of ongoing treatment since the disorder has returned. In a study of acute or continuation treatment it may represent one outcome of interest.

In the distinction between a relapse and a recurrence (see below) relapse represents the return of the symptoms of a still ongoing, but symptomatically suppressed episode, while a recurrence represents an entirely new episode; however, in a definitional scheme based exclusively on observable events, this distinction must be made in probabilistic terms.

Recurrence

Conceptualization of recurrence   A recurrence implies: (a) need for treatment; and (b) a revision in the history of the course of illness (i.e., a new episode has occurred). The latter may have prognostic and treatment implications. In studies of maintenance therapy, recurrence is typically the outcome of primary interest.

Distinction between relapse and recurrence   Implicit in this approach is the distinction between relapse and recurrence. Although an arbitrary distinction was suggested by Klerman *et al.* (1974) as well as other investigators several years ago to separate relapse from recurrence, it is extremely important to clarify this distinction through the use of empirical techniques. Hollon and colleagues (1990) have commented on this issue extensively and have suggested that the expected length of an episode averages about six to nine months in out-patients and 9–12 months in in-patients. Using survival analytic techniques in naturalistic studies, Lavori and colleagues (1984) have established estimated risks for 'renewed symptoms'. They conclude that when new symptoms occur within the time period normally required for spontaneous remission (six to nine months) one should consider it a relapse irrespective of whether the new symptoms occur following medication withdrawal. In support of a distinction between relapse and recurrence, the earlier literature of Zis and Goodwin (1979) also suggests that the period between completely new episodes of depression, so-called recurrences, in fully remitted patients might very well be on the average of three years.

Hollon and colleagues (1990) have attempted to demonstrate the value of this distinction using a 'two-process risk model' to suggest that renewed symptomatology during the first several months following treatment-induced remission is likely to be a clinical relapse or a return of the syndrome associated with the index episode. While some of these renewed symptomatic presentations may represent wholly new episodes, the majority of them are likely to represent relapses. In support of their hypothesis, they reviewed the data from three studies: Evans *et al.* (submitted), Glen *et al.* (1984) and Prien *et al.* (1984).

Hollon *et al.* (1990) suggest that interventions of depression can be divided into three different kinds: (1) suppressive interventions; (2) curative interventions; and (3) prophylactic interventions. Suppressive interventions are those which block the expression of manifest symptoms, but do little to alter the underlying episode. They argue that it would appear that tricyclic antidepressants administered during an acute episode are largely symptom suppressive when used with non-bipolar populations. Curative interventions are those which actually alter the course of the underlying episode, reducing risk for relapse during the time-limited period that the untreated episode would have been expected to have run. The third category of intervention is the prophylactic intervention and includes medications (e.g., lithium carbonate and 'possibly' tricyclic antidepressants) which may actually prevent new episodes from emerging. In conclusion, they argued for the change in treatment designs to try to capitalize on the chance of differentiating relapse from recurrence (Ingram and Hollon, 1986).

In this section we have reviewed several current efforts to define in operational terms change points in the course of a depressive episode. The most interesting strategies are those developed by Frank *et al.* (1991) and Hollon *et al.* (1990).

Nevertheless, confusion still remains and we will use relapse/recurrence if the specific study is unclear on the operational criteria for those terms.

How long should we treat?

This section focuses on the issue of how long to treat, or what is the best way to prevent relapse? In 1986 Prien and Kupfer reviewed the existing literature on how long continuation drug treatment of depressive episodes should be maintained to ensure that the episode is over. A systematic review of the six extant placebo-controlled investigations of continuation drug therapy in depression led to the conclusion that the relapse rate over a two to eight-month period of observation on placebo was 50%, and that the relapse rate on active drug which consisted in most cases of a tricyclic antidepressant was 22% (Table I).

Table I. Results of placebo-controlled studies of continuation drug therapy of depression

| Study | Treatment | | Patients | |
| | | | Relapsed | |
		N	N	%
Seager and Bird (1962)	Imipramine	12	2	17
	Placebo	16	11	69[a]
Mindham *et al.* (1973)	Amitriptyline or imipramine	50	11	22
	Placebo	42	21	50[a]
Prien *et al.* (1973)	Lithium	45	12	27
	Imipramine	38	14	37[a]
	Placebo	39	26	67
Klerman *et al.* (1974)	Amitriptyline	50	6	12
	Placebo/no pill	49	14	29[a]
Coppen *et al.* (1978)	Amitriptyline	13	0	0
	Placebo	16	5	31[a]
Stein *et al.* (1980)	Amitriptyline	29	8	28
	Placebo	26	18	69[a]
Total	Active drug	237	52	22
	Placebo/no pill	188	94	50[a]

[a] $p < 0.05$, Fisher's exact probability test.

This table originally appeared in: Prien RF, Kupfer DJ: Continuation drug therapy for major depressive episodes: how long should it be maintained? *Am J Psychiatry,* **143**, 18–23, 1986. Copyright 1986, the American Psychiatric Association. Reprinted by permission.

The authors utilized the NIMH–PRB collaborative study on long-term psycho-pharmacological treatment to evaluate the length of symptom-free periods among depressed patients before treatment and examined the rate of relapse during the eight weeks after assignment to double-blind maintenance treatment with either placebo, imipramine, or imipramine and lithium. They concluded that the patient should be free of significant symptoms for 16–20 weeks before treatment is discontinued and that before one concluded that a 'syndromal declaration' represented a new episode and, therefore, evidence of a pro-phylactic failure rather than a continuation of a previous episode, it should be preceded by an interval of 16–20 weeks without significant psychopathology. It was also concluded from this empirical analysis that the first eight weeks fol-lowing discontinuation of active medication constituted the period of highest risk for symptomatic changes leading to the declaration of a depressive syn-drome. Finally, the authors stressed the need to focus on mild, as well as moderate and severe symptoms, since even mild symptoms in patients who usually do not function at that level, might represent an indication that the episode had not run its course. Later when we discuss issues of factors contrib-uting to relapse, we will return to this issue of mild symptomatology or so-called residual symptomatology in face of an apparent clinical remission.

The recently completed Pittsburgh study by Frank, Kupfer and colleagues (Frank *et al.*, 1990b) represented another opportunity to examine issues relating to continuation treatment and the rate of relapse during continuation treatment. In this study on combination maintenance treatment (imipramine and interper-sonal psychotherapy (IPT)) an open treatment phase was conducted during acute and continuation prior to the double-blind randomized maintenance trial. In the acute and continuation phases all patients received combination treat-ment. Of the 157 patients who entered the continuation phase, 128 completed the 17 weeks of this treatment phase. Only 12 patients (7.6%) experienced a relapse during continuation treatment. Among the remaining 17 patients who failed to complete the continuation treatment phase, 3 were discontinued from the study because of intolerable side effects, one developed a secondary psy-chiatric illness, 5 dropped out or were terminated for non-compliance, and 8 left the study for other reasons.

In the context of this protocol, the continuation of acute or 'full'-dose imi-pramine (mean = 215 mg per day) was associated with few adverse effects, excellent compliance and a markedly lower rate of relapse and other difficulties during continuation treatment than had been observed in previous investiga-tions (Kupfer and Frank, 1987). The data on the group of 157 who entered the continuation phase demonstrates that the combined treatment approach (tri-cyclic antidepressants and IPT) is highly efficacious in achieving a sustained remission of symptoms. Furthermore, side effects were a relatively minor con-sideration after four months of treatment and seem to have played a very small role in the period between the beginning of continuation and assignment to the maintenance phase (Frank *et al.*, 1990a). When the data on drop-out and non-adherence rates in this study were compared to those of the NIMH–PRB collaborative study, it appeared that the design of the present study had affected treatment adherence in a positive way (Frank *et al.*, 1985). Two features of the design which may be responsible for this difference are the addition of psychotherapy to the treatment regimen and a strong emphasis on educating both patients and their family members regarding the nature of the illnesses and the nature of the treatments being used.

A review of 'naturalistic' treatment follow-up of depression suggests that the cumulative rate of relapse/recurrence after recovery for individuals with primary depression is approximately 15% at six months and 22% at one year (Keller *et al.*, 1982a). While the patients on whom these data are based met criteria for primary depression, most of them had had fewer than three episodes. A further refinement in the analyses of these data indicates that 11% of the patients who had fewer than three episodes relapsed within 12–15 weeks, but 43% of the patients who had had three or more episodes suffered a relapse by the 12th week (Keller *et al.*, 1982b). Thus, these patients with recurrent unipolar depression, who were not entered into a controlled drug trial, experienced a >40% relapse rate within three months after recovery. These data from the Collaborative Study on the Psychobiology of Depression are consistent with the review of continuation treatment by Prien and Kupfer (1986) which, as we indicated, demonstrated that the relapse rate was at least 22% for patients in active drug conditions versus 50% for those in placebo conditions.

Data from the Pittsburgh studies indicated that the addition of psychotherapy, as well as a family educational workshop, may reduce the rate of relapse to below 10%. The overall relapse rate of 7.6% observed in the Pittsburgh sample during continuation treatment is remarkably low for this patient population and certainly merits replication (Kupfer and Frank, 1987; Frank *et al.*, 1990a). It also appears that combined continuation treatment has an advantage in terms of keeping patients engaged in treatment. Only 7% of the subjects dropped out or needed to be terminated for non-compliance (Frank *et al.*, 1990a). A randomized trial in which combined psychotherapy and pharmacotherapy is compared with pharmacotherapy alone during the continuation phase of treatment would present the opportunity for the most definitive confirmation of the benefits of combined treatment and family education in prevention of relapse and maintenance of a strong treatment alliance.

A protocol which is derived from the 'mid-life' maintenance study just described is the late-life maintenance treatment trial currently being conducted by Reynolds and colleagues (personal communication). In this study, the treatment strategy for recurrent depression in the elderly is to compare alone and in combination nortriptyline and a late-life version of maintenance IPT. Two hundred patients aged 60–80 meeting RDC criteria for recurrent, non-bipolar, non-psychotic major depression (minimum of two lifetime episodes) are being enrolled in the study. The index episode is treated with a combination of nortriptyline (NT) and IPT. After acute treatment and a 16-week period of continuation, treatment responders are randomized to one of four maintenance therapy conditions: (1) medication clinic with NT; (2) medication clinic with placebo; (3) IPT with placebo; (4) combined therapy with NT and IPT. Maintenance therapy lasts for two years or until recurrence of a major depressive episode.

While this study is currently in progress, a number of preliminary results concerning the open phase of this investigation (acute and continuation) are relevant. At the present time during the first 20 months of the study, 64 individuals have entered the acute phase, and 41 patients have entered the continuation phase. During the continuation phase 8 patients have suffered a relapse using the criteria for full syndromal depression that was used in the mid-life depression investigation. While this 19.5% rate of relapse is somewhat higher than the combined treatment trial in the mid-life cohort, there are clear indications that issues concerning compliance, as well as long-term treatment strategies, may be somewhat different in this investigation. However, it should be pointed out that this relapse rate is consistent with the relapse figures from the Prien and Kupfer review (1986).

At the other end of the age spectrum, there have been no controlled treatment trials that truly deal with continuation and issues of relapse/recurrence in either pre-pubertal or adolescent depression. An obvious need exists for such investigations, and it would be hoped were we to review this field several years from now that studies in this age category could be included.

Recently, several new published reviews of the literature on continuation treatment and relapse have appeared. Two reports are of particular relevance for their level of comprehensiveness and integration. A review by Loonen and Zwanikken (1990) analysed the literature to ascertain the clinical benefits of long-term drug treatment in recurrent major depression. They specifically evaluated and commented on the design and quality of over 25 identified studies, which included 18 studies of continuation therapy and seven on maintenance treatment. Loonen and Zwanikken (1990) noted the great difficulty in finding a consistent definition of relapse or recurrence. In many reports, no clear-cut definition was given and in others relapse was defined in terms of the development of affective symptoms which either required specific treatment (drugs, ECT and/or hospital admission) or, while less often, exceeded a specific severity rating or met specific diagnostic criteria for an affective episode. This inconsistency made it very difficult to perform a metanalysis of the extant studies.

On the basis of their review of the literature, Loonen and Zwanikken concluded that after continuation treatment of four months a clinician should evaluate each patient's needs individually, deciding whether patients' medications should be continued, discontinued, or replaced, in some cases, by preventive use of lithium carbonate. They also recommended that when antidepressant treatment is to be discontinued, the clinician should proceed very gradually (i.e., over a period of several months by 25–33% monthly decrements). These guidelines were based on their review of numerous studies even though they concluded that there were only six placebo-controlled trials of continuation therapy which were of reasonable quality and had sufficiently homogeneous study results.

The report of Belsher and Costello (1988) is particularly interesting since it examines the rates of relapse/recurrence from reports on controlled drug treatment trials and naturalistic studies, as well as studies involving primarily psychotherapy interventions in unipolar depression. What is noteworthy is their attempt to compare these studies using survival analysis. At two months postremission, they reported a relapse rate of 20–24%, at four months postremission, they reported a relapse range of 28–44%, and at six months postrecovery the relapse range was 27–50%. At the 12-month point they showed a range of 37–54%. Their analysis clearly suggested a 'flattening of the risk over time' (Figure 2).

Belsher and Costello also pointed out a number of major methodological points that had not received sufficient attention. Since patient-related factors,

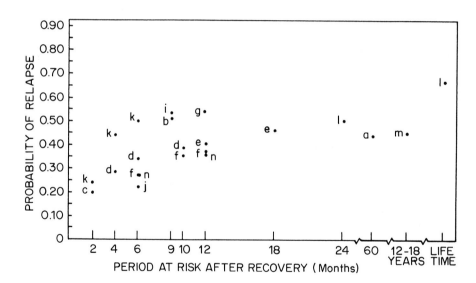

Figure 2.   Rates of relapse after recovery (a = Copeland, 1983; b, Hooley *et al.*, 1986; c = Keller and Shapiro, 1981; d = Keller *et al.*, 1982b; e = Keller *et al.*, 1983a; f = Keller *et al.*, 1983b; g = Gonzales *et al.*, 1985; h = Paykel and Tanner, 1976; i = Vaughn and Leff, 1976; j = Targum, 1984; k = Kirkegaard, 1981; l = NIMH/NIH Consensus Statement, 1985; m = Bland and Orn, 1982; n = Simons *et al.*, 1986). (From Belsher G, Costello CG: Relapse after recovery from unipolar depression: a critical review. *Psychol Bull* **104**, 84–96, 1988. Copyright 1988 by the American Psychological Association. Reprinted by permission).

such as the number of previous episodes, have been found to relate to the probability of relapse, they suggest that any investigation should control for differences between groups on such variables. Second, it would be important to control the duration of 'well' time preceding the onset of the clinical trial. Third, the definition of remission is extremely important. Fourth, it would be important to understand that there may be differential responsiveness to types of intervention. Finally, relapse itself should be determined on the basis of regular follow-up interviews rather than according to medical records or subsequent hospital admissions. They conclude that relapse/recurrence is frequent even after unipolar depression has been successfully treated.

In this section we have sought to review the most pertinent literature that relates to the question: how long do we treat to prevent or minimize the likelihood of a relapse during a depressive episode? It should be apparent from both controlled and naturalistic treatment data that a continuation treatment period of four to five months should reduce relapse rates to approximately 20%, perhaps even lower with combined treatment.

'Predictors' of relapse

Belsher and Costello (1988) suggested that within two years of remission approximately 50% of patients had experienced a new episode. It was also suggested the longer patients stay well the less likely they are to relapse or recur. As shown in Table II, recent environmental stress or 'life events' (Faravelli *et al.*, 1986; Brown *et al.*, 1986), the absence of social support from family members (Vaughn and Leff, 1976; Hooley and Teasdale, 1989), a history of prior depressive episodes (Keller *et al.*, 1982b) and persistent neuroendocrine dysregulation after recovery from depression (Arana *et al.*, 1985; Braddock, 1986) all increase the probability of relapse or recurrence. Maintenance dosages of a tricyclic antidepressant or lithium carbonate decrease the probability of relapse (Prien *et al.*, 1973, 1984). At the present time, researchers have failed to demonstrate

Table II. Factors contributing to relapse/recurrence

Environmental stress	
Expressed emotion	+
Life events	+
Number of prior episodes	+
Neuroendocrine dysregulation	++
Residual symptoms	++
Poorer social adaptation	?
More pathological personality profile	?
Lower TCA plasma levels on equivalent dose	?

significant associations between relapse and gender, marital status or socio-economic status.

These conclusions are in relative harmony with most of the other investigations that have examined predictors of relapse. Faravelli and colleagues (1986) demonstrated that in individuals who were followed through remission after an index episode, relapses showed higher levels of residual symptoms and less social adaptation, a more pathological mean personality profile and lower tricyclic plasma levels despite similar dosage (Table II). They concluded that their findings were supportive of a hypothesis of an incomplete recovery from the index episode as the key factor for relapse within one year. Furthermore, their findings were consistent with the reports of Keller and colleagues (1982b) which found that three or more previous episodes predicted an increased rate of relapse. Of those who are suffering from their first episode of depression, on the other hand, those who are older are more likely than those who are younger to relapse, as are patients whose depression is secondary to a non-affective psychiatric disorder.

Discontinuation or transition to maintenance

In reviewing the available literature on discontinuation treatment, several things become clear. One point is that with respect to psychopharmacological intervention, a reasonably good consensus has emerged that the minimum length of treatment even after symptomatic remission is between four and six months of continuous treatment. The recommendation for a gradual rather than an abrupt discontinuation is also consistent with the guidelines that can be derived from the literature. The Prien *et al.* investigation (1984) from which the four to six-month criteria were derived is also instructive with respect to discontinuation. A recent reanalysis (Greenhouse *et al.*, 1991) clearly points out the risk of late relapse or early recurrence as a result of the abrupt discontinuation in this study. It suggests that the conclusion reported by Prien *et al.* (1984) that imipramine and the combination treatment were more effective than lithium and placebo in preventing the recurrence of depression in unipolar patients may be incorrect. The Greenhouse *et al.* analysis shows a dramatic increase in the risk of early recurrence associated with being abruptly withdrawn from imipramine. Thus, patients assigned to the lithium and placebo groups who had a 'recurrence' within the first eight weeks of maintenance therapy may, in fact, be experiencing a drug withdrawal reaction that creates symptomatology that mimics a depressive episode or that precipitates an episode of depression.

The issues of the relative merits of gradual versus abrupt discontinuation is not totally resolved. Our own experience (Frank *et al.*, 1990b) using a two-phase maintenance therapy design with gradual withdrawal showed that only 3 of 75 (4%) patients randomized to imipramine discontinuation had an early recurrence/late relapse within eight weeks of maintenance treatment. It is instructive, however, to review the transition to maintenance carried out in this particular investigation since the general issues concerning drug withdrawal are important in interpreting all studies which deal with relapse and recurrence. At the end of the continuation phase, patients were randomly assigned to one of five maintenance treatment cells: (1) maintenance interpersonal psychotherapy (IPT-M) alone; (2) IPT-M and active imipramine (at the acute treatment dose); (3) IPT-M and placebo; (4) medication clinic visits and the treatment mean being blind to active medication of placebo pills.

The general principle shaping the withdrawal schedule for those patients assigned to a placebo or no-pill condition was a reduction of 33% per week for the first three weeks after random assignment. Thus, the patient receiving 300 mg would be reduced to 200 mg by the end of the first week, 100 mg by the end of the second week, and to all placebo or no pills by the end of the third week.

To deal with the problem of discontinuation it may be necessary to implement a tapering strategy of several months to mirror clinical practice. Certainly, data available from maintenance monoamine oxidase inhibitor (MAOI) trials (Robinson *et al.*, 1991) indicate that abrupt or rapid taper strategies are counterproductive for long-term treatment efficacy trials for the other classes of antidepressants.

This particular study has raised issues concerning the rate at which MAOIs should be tapered both in a controlled trial and also in clinical practice. Since the authors included a defined symptom-free period before maintenance treatment, the issue of whether the syndrome following drug withdrawal is a relapse or a recurrence is not resolved. Indeed, they pointed out that depressive episodes can exist for a length of time greater than a year in many individuals. Robinson *et al.* argued that the usual episode length may be 7–14 months, which is longer than other investigators have suggested. On the other hand, they suggest that relatively abrupt discontinuation may serve as an important 'probe' to test the need for long-term active drug maintenance treatment.

Thus, a related unresolved issue with regard to discontinuation strategies relates to the natural course of the index episode. Currently used discontinuation strategies have probably confounded the definitional schema of 'relapse' versus 'recurrence'. As we have seen, in the study of Prien *et al.* (1984) the early recurrences/relapses in the lithium-treated and placebo-treated groups could be interpreted as providing evidence of the efficacy of the drug combination treatment with which the index episode had been successfully stabilized. However, this impression may be more a reflection of the combination's ability to maintain control over the ongoing episode in treatment responders than its ability to prevent a new episode. The possibility that the poorer results with the lithium and placebo treatments during maintenance may have been the result of exacerbation of the still-ongoing index episode rather than a new episode is also a possible explanation for the number of early recurrences. In summary, discontinuation designs have the potential to confuse the distinctions between a relapse and a 'true' recurrence.

Current problems and opportunities

Based on the current review of the literature, it becomes clear that a number of methodological problems remain. One of the most important issues is establishing the risk of relapse/recurrence and this was addressed by Lavori and colleagues (1984) several years ago in reanalyses of controlled and naturalistic follow-up studies using life table methods. In their reanalysis of nine published reports on relapse after remission they showed a common finding that the hazard of relapse/recurrence declines steadily for the first three years after recovery. The Lavori report also demonstrated the difficulties that investigators have had in clarifying issues relating to relapse, continuation and maintenance treatment.

There are a number of problems with follow-up studies of acute or continuation and maintenance treatment. First, they are often non-representative as they are confounded by an overabundance of responders and a failure to follow up the entire sample. Second, there needs to be a clearer separation between relapse and recurrence, and in order to accomplish this task specified lengths of treatment which are consistent across studies need to be established. In this regard, Hollon *et al.* (1990) have made a valiant attempt to try to hypothesize different models for the separation of relapse from recurrence. Clearly, further work needs to be performed in this area.

The third problem is that in many studies insufficient attention is paid to ensure the quality of treatment delivery both in terms of adequate dosage schedules and the maintenance of consistent dosage schedules whether they be in psychopharmacological intervention studies or, in those studies with combined treatment, in terms of delivery of psychotherapy. The fourth issue relates to a lack of standard or reference treatment. As discussed by Montgomery *et al.* (1988), at present we need to give more weight to placebo-controlled studies since we lack a well-validated active reference compound for use in comparison. This would be an important advance in the technology of the conduct of these studies as well as their interpretation. The fifth issue relates to the application of contemporary analytic strategies, rather than the earlier reliance on box scores. These earlier analyses did not take into account the element of 'time', as well as the inability to use all data on subjects entered into a clinical trial. The introduction of survival analytic strategies as a standard tool has facilitated better interpretation of the more recently completed clinical trials. Finally, the sixth issue deals directly with the need to pay more attention to discontinuation strategies and a parallel problem, which is the issue of compliance. In this regard, we have not developed analytic tools to dissect out what role combined treatment plays in reducing non-compliance and establishing an alliance between clinical staff and patients/families.

In a randomized clinical trial to evaluate the relative efficacy of treatments in the prevention of a recurrent disorder, we believe that it is essential to admit patients to the study during an acute episode of the illness so that patients are comparable with respect to the timing of the 'natural' cycle of their illness. However, in any prospective study patients will withdraw or drop out for various reasons, often for reasons related to the treatment they are receiving. How, then, can a maintenance therapy trial be conducted which minimizes potential sources of bias? A possible solution suggested by Greenhouse *et al.* (1991) is to design a study for all patients in an acute, continuation and maintenance treatment strategy. Patients who satisfy admission requirements would enter the study in an acute episode and would be randomized simultaneously to a treatment for the preliminary phase, to control the index episode, and to a treatment for the maintenance phase, to prevent recurrence.

In summary, we have dealt in this chapter mostly with issues of continuation treatment and questions of relapse. It is important to note, however, that our understanding of relapse and continuation is preparatory to any attempt to understand issues of maintenance therapy. There are several important issues relating to maintenance treatment which are dependent on our understanding of relapse and continuation. One example is whether continuation itself has any relationship to predicting the type of maintenance required or the probability of recurrence. Does the course of continuation treatment predict recurrence of illness? We examined the experience of three groups of patients in the maintenance phase of the Pittsburgh study defined on the basis of whether they had experienced a 'blip' (i.e., an HRSD score of >9 during the 20-week period of continuation). Whereas 81 (63%) of the 128 patients never experienced an HRSD score higher than 9 during the 20-week continuation period, 26 patients (20%) experienced at least one symptomatic 'blip' (HRSD >10) and 21 patients (16%) experienced two or more blips. Because we know that, at least for the first 18 months of the maintenance phase, the different maintenance treatments have significantly different survival rates associated with them (Frank *et al.*, 1989), we examined the three blip groupings' experience in maintenance treatment, controlling for their maintenance treatment assignment; we found absolutely no difference with respect to survival time in maintenance. In other words, those patients who experienced no symptomatic exacerbations during continuation treatment had neither longer nor shorter survival time than those who experienced such exacerbations during the continuation treatment phase. The course of combined continuation treatment thus does not appear to have predictive value with respect to new episodes of major depression.

Finally, it is noteworthy that even though we have only begun to separate out continuation and maintenance treatment conceptually, studies such as the Frank *et al.* (1990a) and Montgomery *et al.* (1988) investigations do point to the impact of maintenance pharmacology on the likelihood of recurrence. When we consider what the appropriate designs are for such maintenance treatment investigations, it becomes clear on the basis of our literature review that a six-month continuation period before maintenance is vital to increasing our understanding of prophylaxis in recurrent depression. In fact, as we learn more about the minimum length of treatment for recovery in depression, our overall knowledge base concerning the treatment of depression for all phases of the disorder will be enhanced considerably.

Acknowledgements

This work was supported in part by National Institute of Mental Health grants MH–30915, MH–29618 and a grant from the John D. and Catherine T. MacArthur Foundation Research Network on the Psychobiology of Depression.

References

Arana GW, Baldessarini RJ, Ornsteen M (1985) The dexamethasone suppression test for diagnosis and prognosis in psychiatry. *Arch Gen Psychiatry* **42**, 1193–1204.

Belsher G, Costello CG (1988) Relapse after recovery from unipolar depression: a critical review. *Psychol Bull* **104**, 84–96.

Björk K (1983) The efficacy of zimilidine in preventing depressive episodes in recurrent major depressive disorders: a double-blind placebo-controlled study. *Acta Psychiatr Scand* **68** (Suppl 308), 182–189.

Bland RC, Orn H (1982) Course and outcome in affective disorders. *Can J Psychiatry* **27**, 573–578.

Braddock L (1986) The dexamethasone suppression test: fact and artifact. *Br J Psychiatry* **148**, 363–374.

Brown GW, Bifulco A, Harris T, Bridge L (1986) Life stress, chronic subclinical symptoms and vulnerability to clinical depression. *J Affective Disord* **11**, 1–19.

Copeland JRM (1983) Psychotic and neurotic depression: discriminant function analysis and five-year outcome. *Psychol Med* **13**, 373–383.

Coppen A, Ghose K, Montgomery S *et al.* (1978) Continuation therapy with amitriptyline in depression. *Br J Psychiatry* **133**, 28–33.

Evans MD, Hollon SD, DeRubeis RJ *et al.* (submitted) Differential relapse following cognitive therapy, pharmacotherapy, and combined cognitive-pharmacotherapy for depression: IV. A two year follow-up of the CPT Project.

Faravelli C, Ambonetti A, Pallanti S, Pazzagli A (1986) Depressive relapses and incomplete recovery from index episode. *Am J Psychiatry* **143**, 888–891.

Frank E, Prien R, Kupfer DJ, Alberts L (1985) Implications of non-compliance on research in affective disorders. *Psychopharmacol Bull* **21**, 37–42.

Frank E, Kupfer DJ, Perel JM (1989) Early recurrence in unipolar depression. *Arch Gen Psychiatry* **46**, 397–400.

Frank E, Kupfer DJ, Levenson J (1990a) Continuation therapy for unipolar depression: the case for combined treatment. In Manning DW, Frances AJ (eds) *Combined Phar-*

macotherapy and Psychotherapy for Depression, Ch. 5, pp. 135–149. Washington, DC: American Psychiatric Press.

Frank E, Kupfer DJ, Perel JM *et al.* (1990b) Three-year outcomes for maintenance therapies in recurrent depression. *Arch Gen Psychiatry* **47**, 1093–1099.

Frank E, Prien RF, Jarrett RB *et al.* (1991) Conceptualization and rationale for consensus definitions of terms in major depressive disorder: remission, recovery, relapse, and recurrence. *Arch Gen Psychiatry* **48**, 851–855.

Glen AIM, Johnson AL, Shepherd M (1984) Continuation therapy with lithium and amitriptyline in unipolar depressive illness: a randomized, double-blind controlled trial. *Psychol Med* **14**, 37–50.

Gonzales LR, Lewinsohn PM, Clarke GN (1985) Longitudinal follow-up of unipolar depressives: an investigation of predictors of relapse. *J Consult Clin Psychol* **53**, 461–469.

Greenhouse JB, Stangl D, Kupfer DJ, Prien RF (1991) Methodologic issues in maintenance therapy clinical trials. *Arch Gen Psychiatry* **48**, 313–318.

Hollon SD, Evans MD, DeRubeis RJ (1990) Cognitive mediation of relapse prevention following treatment for depression: implications of differential risk. In Ingram RE (ed.) *Psychological Aspects of Depression*, pp. 117–136. New York: Plenum Press.

Hooley JM, Orley J, Teasdale JD (1986) Levels of expressed emotion and relapse in depressed patients. *Br J Psychiatry* **148**, 642–647.

Hooley JM, Teasdale JD (1989) Predictors of relapse in unipolar depressives: expressed emotion, marital distress, and perceived criticism. *J Abnorm Psychol* **98**, 229–235.

Ingram RE, Hollon SD (1986) Cognitive therapy for depression from an information processing perspective. In Ingram RE (ed.) *Information Processing Approaches to Clinical Psychology*, pp. 259–281. New York: Academic Press.

Janicak PG, O'Connor E (1990) Major affective disorders: issues involving recovery and recurrence. *Curr Opinion Psychiatry* **3**, 48–53.

Kane JM, Quitkin FM, Rifkin A *et al.* (1982) Lithium carbonate and imipramine in the prophylaxis of unipolar and bipolar II illness: a prospective, placebo-controlled comparison. *Arch Gen Psychiatry* **39**, 1065–1069.

Keller MB, Shapiro RW (1981) Major depressive disorder: initial results from a one-year prospective naturalistic follow-up study. *J Nerv Ment Dis* **169**, 761–768.

Keller MB, Shapiro RW, Lavori PW, Wolfe N (1982a) Recovery in major depressive disorder: analysis with the life table and regression models. *Arch Gen Psychiatry* **39**, 905–910.

Keller MB, Shapiro RW, Lavori PW, Wolfe N (1982b) Relapse in major depressive disorder: analysis with the life table. *Arch Gen Psychiatry* **39**, 911–915.

Keller MB, Lavori PW, Endicott J *et al.* (1983a) 'Double depression': two-year follow-up. *Am J Psychiatry* **140**, 689–694.

Keller MB, Lavori PW, Lewis CE, Klerman GL (1983b) Predictors of relapse in major depressive disorder. *JAMA* **250**, 3299–3304.

Kirkegaard C (1981) The thyrotropin response to thyrotropin-releasing hormone in endogenous depression. *Psychoneuroendocrinology* **6**, 189–212.

Klerman GL, DiMascio A, Weissman M *et al.* (1974) Treatment of depression by drugs and psychotherapy. *Am J Psychiatry* **131**, 186–191.

Kupfer DJ, Frank E (1987) Relapse in recurrent unipolar depression. *Am J Psychiatry* **144**, 86–88.

Lavori PW, Keller MB, Klerman GL (1984) Relapse in affective disorders: a reanalysis of the literature using life table methods. *J Psychiatr Res* **18**, 13–21.

Loonen AJM, Zwanikken GJ (1990) Continuation and maintenance therapy with antidepressive agents: an overview of research. *Pharm Weekbl (Sci)* **12**, 128–141.

Mindham RH, Howland C, Shepherd M (1973) An evaluation of continuation therapy with tricyclic antidepressants in depressive illness. *Psychol Med* **3**, 5–17.

Montgomery SA, Dufour H, Brion S *et al.* (1988) The prophylactic efficacy of fluoxetine in unipolar depression. *Br J Psychiatry* **153**, 69–76.

NIMH/NIH Consensus Development Conference Statement (1985) Mood disorders: pharmacologic prevention of recurrences. *Am J Psychiatry* **142**, 469–476.

Paykel ES, Tanner J (1976) Life events, depressive relapse and maintenance treatment. *Psychol Med* **6**, 481–485.

Prien RF, Kupfer DJ (1986) Continuation drug therapy for major depressive episodes: how long should it be maintained? *Am J Psychiatry* **143**, 18–23.

Prien RF, Klett CH, Caffey EM (1973) Lithium carbonate and imipramine in prevention of affective episodes. *Arch Gen Psychiatry* **29**, 420–425.

Prien RF, Kupfer DJ, Mansky PA *et al.* (1984) Drug therapy in the prevention of recurrences in unipolar and bipolar affective disorders. *Arch Gen Psychiatry* **41**, 1096–1104.

Prien RF, Carpenter LL, Kupfer DJ (1991) The definition and operational criteria for treatment outcome of major depressive disorder: a review of the current research literature. *Arch Gen Psychiatry* **48**, 796–800.

Robinson DS, Lerfald SC, Bennett B *et al.* (1991) Continuation and maintenance treatment of major depression with the monoamine oxidase inhibitor phenelzine: a double-blind placebo-controlled discontinuation study. *Psychopharmacol Bull* **27**, 31–39.

Seager CP, Bird RL (1962) Imipramine with electrical treatment in depression: a controlled trial. *J Ment Sci* **108**, 704–707.

Simons AD, Murphy GE, Levine JL, Wetzel RD (1986) Cognitive therapy and pharmacotherapy for depression. *Arch Gen Psychiatry* **43**, 43–48.

Stein MK, Rickels K, Weise CC (1980) Maintenance therapy with amitriptyline: a controlled trial. *Am J Psychiatry* **137**, 370–371.

Targum SD (1984) Persistent neuroendocrine dysregulation in major depressive disorder: a marker for early relapse. *Biol Psychiatry* **19**, 305–318.

Vaughn CE, Leff JP (1976) The influence of family and social factors on the course of psychiatric illness. *Br J Psychiatry* **129**, 125–137.

Zis AP, Goodwin FK (1979) Major affective disorder as a recurrent illness: a critical review. *Arch Gen Psychiatry* **36**, 835–839.

4

Prophylactic treatment in recurrent unipolar depression

Stuart A. Montgomery and Deirdre B. Montgomery

Introduction

The investigation of the efficacy of psychotropic drugs in the treatment of depression has focused overwhelmingly on symptomatic response during the acute episode. The majority of clinical efficacy studies are consequently short in duration, usually from four to six weeks, when a difference between an active drug and placebo has been most reliably demonstrated in acute studies. It is, however, recognized that the treatment of the depressive episode to the point where symptoms apparently resolve is insufficient and a much longer treatment period is needed. Placebo-controlled studies of the efficacy of antidepressants have provided a convincing demonstration of the need for antidpressant treatment to continue for some months after response of the acute episode is seen.

The basis of prophylactic treatment is conceptually different from the treatment of acute episodes of illness. Prophylaxis is aimed at keeping people well, at intervention to prevent the return of an illness, rather than the non-interventionist approach of waiting for the next acute episode to occur before instituting treatment. The principle of preventative treatment is well established in medicine and is widely discussed in psychiatry. In schizophrenia and in bipolar illness, for example, the need for continuing pharmacotherapy for secondary prevention is accepted, yet in practice relatively little prophylaxis is undertaken in recurrent unipolar depression.

Long-term Treatment of Depression. Edited by S.A. Montgomery and F. Rouillon
© 1992 John Wiley & Sons Ltd

It is possible that this aspect of treatment may have been neglected in the past partly because the size of the population at risk was underestimated. Estimates of the proportion of depressions that occur as single episodes have varied, depending to some extent on the length of the follow-up undertaken (Angst, 1973; Coryell and Winokur, 1982). From recent epidemiological studies it has, however, become increasingly evident that the original estimates of 60% of depression being recurrent were too low. With careful and prolonged follow-up many more depressions are seen to be recurrent (see Chapter 1) and the potential need for prophylactic treatment is substantial. The cost of depressive illness, both in human and economic terms, the associated excess morbidity and mortality from suicide and from physical illness serve as reminders of the importance of reducing the risk of repeated depressive episodes.

Given the high incidence of recurrent depression it is perhaps surprising that so few well-conducted studies of prophylactic treatment or secondary prevention have been undertaken. This type of study, which investigates patients over long periods of a year or longer, are, however, some of the most difficult to carry out. Prophylactic studies require a far greater investment of resources than short-term efficacy studies, both in financial terms and in commitment from researchers and their patients, and these factors may help to explain why there are relatively few studies. More studies are now being initiated to investigate the prophylactic efficacy of antidepressants and this change is encouraged by the Committee on Proprietary Medicinal Products (CPMP) guidelines for the investigation of new antidepressants now accepted by regulatory authorities in the European Community. The need to assess efficacy in both medium and long-term treatment separately from efficacy in acute treatment is recognized and underlined in these guidelines.

This is a welcome development, particularly because, in the absence of a large body of controlled studies, there has been a tendency on the part of clinicians to assume that an antidepressant that is effective for acute treatment is also effective in long-term treatment. This assumption of efficacy has not been tested for many of the older, widely used antidepressants and may not be justified in some cases. An example of the risk inherent in this assumption is seen in the study of Georgotas *et al.* (1989), which found that nortriptyline was not effective in reducing new episodes of depression although a monoamine oxidase inhibitor (MAOI) was.

While there is general acceptance on the part of clinicians that antidepressant treatment needs to continue for some months following apparent response of an episode in order to consolidate response, the value of prophylactic treatment in patients who suffer from recurrent unipolar depression has been viewed with less unanimity. There has to be good evidence of the value of undertaking long-term medication before clinicians will feel justified in making a recommendation to patients. The treating physician would like answers to a series of practical questions to help make decisions concerning long-term treatment. Which antidepressants have been shown to be effective in reducing the occurrence of episodes of depression? How sound is the evidence, to what extent are they effective, and over what periods of time? Which antidepressants are to be preferred, in which patients, and at what dosage? The studies in whose results the answers to these questions must be sought have been set up in different decades and have often taken many years to complete and, as might be expected, the approach and the methodology adopted vary considerably. Clear, definitive answers have not been found for some of the questions though there can be no doubt that there is now a solid body of evidence of the value of prophylactic treatment for recurrent unipolar depression.

Assessing prophylactic efficacy

Prophylaxis is a specific aspect of the possible efficacy of an antidepressant and reflects its ability to reduce the likelihood of the occurrence of a new episode of depression. The particular requirements of prophylactic studies have not always been well understood and it may be helpful to review the errors of trial design that are commonly made and to discuss the minimum criteria which need to be adopted for a study to be able to test the effectiveness of an antidepressant in reducing the risk of a new episode of depression.

Response to acute treatment
Since the aim of prophylactic studies is to test the ability of an antidepressant to prevent recurrence it is sensible that the patients included in this type of study should have responded to continuation treatment with an antidepressant in the acute episode. It is, however, possibe that the three phases of treatment—acute, continuation and prophylaxis—operate by separate mechanisms.

The definition of response should be in terms of an absolute score, e.g. <12 on the Montgomery and Asberg Depressioa Rating Scale (MADRS) (Montgomery and Asberg, 1979), or a score of 8 or 10 on the Hamilton Rating Scale (HRS) (Hamilton, 1967), at the end of six or eight weeks treatment rather than the 50% reduction criterion which is sometimes used in acute studies. The reason for taking an absolute rather than a relative score is that a 50% reduction may still leave an individual with significant symptomatology and mild or moderate severity of depression which should continue to improve with further antidepressant treatment. There is evidence that residual depressive symptomatology increases the risk of relapse whether this is measured by a self rating (Mindham *et al.*, 1973) or by the HRS (Montgomery *et al.*, 1991).

The patient group studied should of course satisfy the same diagnostic criteria as are used in acute efficacy studies: patients should have suffered from moderate to severe depressive illness of more than two weeks duration, meeting the criteria defined in recognized diagnostic scales. There are insufficient data to establish whether prophylaxis is more or less important in severe or moderate depression and it is therefore important to record information on the initial severity and timing of response during acute treatment.

Need for a symptom-free period
To test the prophylactic efficacy of an agent it is clear that patients included in studies should not only be responders to antidepressants but should also have fully recovered from the previous episode of depression. The distinction between relapse, i.e. the resurgence of symptoms of the acute episode following apparent response, and recurrence, i.e. the appearance of a new episode of depression, is of critical importance in assessing prophylactic efficacy.

For prophylactic studies it is necessary to ensure that the depression has been adequately treated but, as the studies of continuation treatment of depressive illness have shown, response of the acute episode cannot be relied upon as an indicator that the episode is fully recovered. Patients need to have remained well during a period of continuation treatment beyond the period when relapse of symptoms of the episode would be expected on discontinuation of medication. Unfortunately it is not possible to be sure of the likely length of a particular episode in an individual patient in spite of the extensive epidemiological data that have been gathered on the duration of depression. Some depressions may run a chronic course, the duration of episodes may lengthen slightly with recurrence, and the natural length of an episode in individual patients is difficult to estimate because of the effect of intervention with antidepressants on earlier episodes.

The likely length of necessary treatment is indicated in the studies of continuation treatment. Three placebo-controlled studies of amitriptyline in patients who had responded to treatment of their acute episode have shown the significant benefit of continuing therapy with amitriptyline compared with placebo (Mindham *et al.*, 1973; Klerman *et al.*, 1974; Stein *et al.*, 1980) and a similar advantage is seen with imipramine though the results are less consistent (Seager and Bird, 1962; Mindham *et al.*, 1973; Prien *et al.*, 1973). Analysis of the data of Mindham *et al.* (1973) suggests that there was a relapse rate of approximately 20% in the first four weeks after early discontinuation of antidepressant treatment, which by the end of 16 weeks had risen to 40%. In other words the most likely period of relapse was in the first four weeks but there was still a risk of relapse up to four months. These results are generally consistent with the analysis of Prien and Kupfer (1986) who retrospectively analysed the relapse rates on placebo following early discontinuation of antidepressant treatment in an earlier study (Prien *et al.*, 1984). A relatively high relapse rate was seen in the first 16 weeks (44%), the highest rate occurring in the first eight weeks (38%).

Unless patients have been free of symptoms for a sufficient period before entering a prophylactic study, it is not possible to say whether a relapse represents the reappearance of symptoms of the inadequately treated original episode or the occurrence of a new episode. The length of continuation or consolidation treatment is likely to vary between patients and this may well represent the length of the underlying depressive episode which the acute antidepressant treatment has suppressed but not abolished. The symptom-free period of four to six months following apparent response of the acute episode, which is supported by most investigators, therefore represents the continuation period of treatment which appears sufficient to ensure full response in the generality of patients. Those prophylactic studies that have used a minimum four-month symptom-free period appear to have been able to identify a population where the recurrence rate is reduced by prophylactic treatment and where the occasional mislabelling of a late relapse as an early recurrence is not critical. In the study of fluoxetine (Montgomery *et al.*, 1988), for example, the first three months of placebo treatment following a four and a half month symptom-free period contained an estimated possible two late relapses judged by comparison with the subsequent recurrence rate from three months to 12 months.

Withdrawal problems and relapse assessment
One of the problems in discontinuation trial designs is that the abrupt discontinuation of treatment is sometimes accompanied by symptoms which may be mistaken for relapse. Discontinuation of tricyclic antidepressants, for example, has been reported to be associated with a short-lived adjustment reaction with increased nervousness, anxiety and sleep disturbance in some patients. These phenomena are generally reported to occur over a one to two-week period and are thought to be related to the withdrawal of the sedative antihistamine action. Withdrawal reactions have also been reported with MAOIs. Withdrawal from both tricyclic antidepressants and MAOIs seems to be more of a problem when the drugs are discontinued abruptly and reactions seem to be more common if the dose was high immediately prior to discontinuation.

In relapse prevention studies it may therefore be appropriate to analyse the apparent relapses occurring in the first two weeks or so separately from those occurring later in order to avoid contamination from the possible effects of withdrawal. The assessment of withdrawal phenomena is sometimes difficult in relapse prevention studies since a high proportion of relapses are expected in the first two months. A more reliable method of assessment is provided in prophylactic studies which investigate individuals who have remained symptom free for four months. In these studies an early recurrence would be relatively less common and a high proportion of 'recurrences' in the first month might indicate the presence of withdrawal phenomena or late relapses.

The possible confounding effects of discontinuation phenomena need to be examined for each drug separately. For example, in the abrupt discontinuation of 40 mg of fluoxetine in the prophylactic study of Montgomery *et al.* (1988) there was very little to indicate any withdrawal phenomena. To avoid the possible contamination one method, which was adopted in the study of Bjork (1983), is to discontinue treatment for all patients for one month before the start of the double-blind prophylactic trial. This device is probably more important in studies of drugs known to be associated with withdrawal effects, for example high-dose tricyclics. An alternative would be a tapered reduction in dosage prior to the study.

Previous history of recurrence

An important consideration in studies designed to test prophylactic efficacy is the need for sufficient morbidity within the study period to be able to test the hypothesis. The entry criteria for a prophylactic study should therefore include a measure of recurrence in the previous history in order to ensure that sufficient new episodes will be seen during a study for meaningful analysis. Different recurrence criteria have been adopted, for example, three previous episodes with two occurring in the past three years, three episodes in four years, and two episodes in the previous five years.

A previous history of frequent recurrence has been suggested as a predictor of poor prognosis, and at first sight the higher recurrence rate on placebo seen in the prophylactic studies that used a high recurrence history entry criterion (Prien *et al.*, 1973; Bjork, 1983; Frank *et al.*, 1990) might appear to support this hypothesis. However, in the studies patients with a less frequent history, but who nevertheless satisfy the criterion of two episodes in five years, seem very likely to have a new episode. For example, in the study of fluoxetine (Montgomery *et al.*, 1988) using the less stringent criteria 57% of patients had a recurrence on placebo in a one-year study.

It is apparent, if the recurrence rates on placebo treatment are compared in the different studies, that the longer the study period the higher the recurrence rate reported on placebo (Table I). There are still insufficient data to analyse late and early recurrences to determine with confidence whether the risk of recurrence reduces or increases with time. However, the ratio of recurrence to those still at risk and remaining on placebo in the studies suggests a steady and continuing risk. This suggests that once patients satisfy the criterion of two episodes in five years or three previous episodes the risk of new episodes is then constant.

The other side of this picture is that antidepressants seem to exercise a prophylactic effect in patients whether they have a history of more frequent or less frequent recurrence. Greater frequency of illness as measured by the number of previous episodes does not appear to reduce the level of efficacy of the active antidepressant seen in the studies. The levels of recurrence reported during active treatment are very similar. The data have not been adequately analysed to be sure but it would appear that effective prophylactic

Table I. Percentage of patients suffering a recurrence of depression on placebo in controlled studies

Study	Duration	Recurrence on placebo (%)
Prien *et al.* (1973)	20 months	85
Prien *et al.* (1984)	1 year	65
Frank *et al.* (1990)	3 years	78
Coppen *et al.* (1978)	1 year	31
Glen *et al.* (1984)	3 years	89
Georgotas *et al.* (1989)	1 year	65
Bjork (1983)	18 months	84
Mongomery *et al.* (1988)	1 year	57

treatments work in both those with frequent and less frequent recurrence histories. It seems in general that patients with recurrent depression who have had at least one episode in the five years prior to the index episode may halve the risk of a further recurrence of depression by prophylactic treatment with antidepressants.

Placebo-controlled comparisons
The likelihood of a new episode in any individual patient is not easy to predict and it may be difficult to assess whether a patient remains free of new episodes because of the beneficial effect of a treatment or because they would not have experienced a new episode within a given study period. We cannot be sure that an antidepressant is effective unless it has been tested in a study of adequate size in a double-blind comparison with placebo. The CPMP guidelines have recommended using a placebo as a control for testing prophylactic effect be-cause of the lack of an established reference compound. The reference tricyclic antidepressants which are used in comparisons of acute efficacy have not been sufficiently well studied to serve as a standard for prophylactic efficacy. Com-parisons with a reference antidepressant would in any case present great practi-cal difficulties since the statistical constraints of demonstrating equivalent efficacy would require very large numbers of patients to be treated in long-term studies—considerably larger than most of the prophylactic studies that have been carried out. Prophylactic studies are very demanding and time consuming and are much more susceptible than acute studies to the effects of increased numbers of patient withdrawals during the study.

Response measures
The principal criterion of efficacy is the number of new episodes recorded in each treatment group. The ability of an antidepressant to delay the appearance of a new episode may be an important extra response criterion. A secondary analysis of time to recurrence, using survival analysis to examine the probability

of remaining well during the study, takes this into account. These two analyses measure different but related phenomena. The raw recurrence rate on drug compared with placebo provides the best evidence of efficacy. However, in small studies the number of recurrences may be too small to adequately test efficacy and here the more sensitive survival analysis is useful. It is possible that a treatment may delay the recurrence to a slight but significant degree and yet not affect the overall recurrence rate in the long term. This treatment should be regarded as inferior to a treatment which both delayed new episodes and reduced their number.

It is also possible that an effective prophylactic treatment will reduce the severity of the subsequent depressive episode. This may be taken into account by examining the severity of depression at recurrence, but rather few studies have been set up to examine this phenomenon. A measure that takes the severity of recurrence into account is the affective morbidity index, which has been widely used in studies of lithium (Coppen *et al.*, 1971).

This measure is, however, not appropriate in studies of new antidepressants in unipolar depression as it measures a more complex, possibly synergistic, interreaction between the prophylactic agent and the antidepressant treatment used for the newly arising episode. Analysis is further complicated by the lack of distinction between the continuation phase and prophylactic phase of treatment following the occurrence of a new episode arising during the study. Measurement of the severity of the subsequent recurrence using standard severity scores should be used more widely.

The definitions of a new episode in the studies of prophylactic treatment have varied, which accounts for some of the variation in recurrence rates reported. The most widely used has been the clinician's global impression but a more satisfactory definition would be if symptoms return to the level that would qualify for entry to an acute depression study, e.g. MADRS score greater than 22 or HRS score greater than 18. The requirement used in some studies that the new episode should fulfil the full formal diagnostic criteria of, for example, DSM-III-R major depression may be unnecessarily stringent in patients who have been carefully diagnosed at the start of treatment and might delay the institution of necessary treatment.

The evidence for prophylactic efficacy

The relatively low level of prophylactic treatment undertaken in the community may reflect the need for clinicians to be convinced of the sound basis of the evidence of efficacy, and for this reason a review of the studies that have been carried out may be timely. The studies which compared two antidepressants without including a placebo control are difficult to interpret because of the small numbers and the lack of an accepted reference agent. The comparisons with lithium in particular are largely flawed because of a failure to take account of the withdrawal effects which may arise when patients previously stabilized on lithium are switched to the antidepressant. Unequivocal evidence of efficacy can only be obtained from studies comparing the recurrence rate on the drug with the recurrence rate on placebo in properly conducted studies. This review therefore concentrates entirely on the evidence of efficacy from placebo-controlled studies (Tables II and III).

Amitriptyline

Amitriptyline, one of the most thoroughly investigated antidepressants in the treatment of the acute episode due to its wide use as a standard reference, has received very little attention in prophylactic studies. The early study of Coppen *et al.* (1978), which found a significant advantage for amitriptyline compared with placebo in reducing recurrences during the one-year study period, had a number of design flaws and the results should be assessed with appropriate caution. There were only 32 patients in the study and three of these were

Table II. Placebo-controlled studies of prophylactic efficacy of antidepressants in unipolar depression

Study	Symptom-free period	Study length	Drug	*n*	Outcome
Coppen *et al.* (1978)	6 weeks	1 year	Amitriptyline Placebo	13 16	AMI > P
Kane *et al.* (1982)	6 months	2 years	Imipramine Lithium Placebo	6 7 5	IMI = P LI > IMI or P
Bjork (1983)	4 months	1 year	Zimelidine Placebo	19 19	ZIM > P
Prien *et al.* (1984)	2 months	2 years	Imipramine Lithium Placebo	39 37 34	IMI > P LI = P
Montgomery *et al.* (1988)	4½ months	1 year	Fluoxetine Placebo	88 94	FLX > P
Georgotas *et al.* (1989)	4 months	1 year	Phenelzine Nortriptyline Placebo	15 13 23	Ph > P Ph > Nor
Frank *et al.* (1990)	20 weeks	3 years	Imipramine Placebo IPT	Total 75	IMI > P IMI > IPT
Robinson *et al.* (1991)	16 weeks	2 years	Phenelzine 60 mg Phenelzine 45 mg Placebo	16 12 19	Ph > P

Table III.   Long-term efficacy in placebo-controlled studies without a symptom-free period

Study	Duration	Drug	n	Outcome
Prien et al. (1973)	2 years	Imipramine	21	IMI = Li
		Lithium	22	IMI > P
		Placebo	13	
Glen et al. (1984)	3 years	Amitriptyline	7	Am = P
		Lithium	12	Li = P
		Placebo	9	Am + Li > P
Doogan and Caillard (1988)	44 weeks	Sertraline	184	SER > P
		Placebo	110	
Rouillon et al. (1989)	1 year	Maprotiline 75 mg	385	MAP > P
		Maprotiline 37.5 mg	382	MAP75 > MAP37.5
		Placebo	374	
Eric et al. (1991)	1 year	Paroxetine	68	Parox > P
		Placebo	67	

excluded from the analysis when measurement of their drug plasma concentrations revealed them to be non-compliers with medication. The design did not allow similar non-compliers on placebo to be eliminated. The definitions of recovery and recurrence are clearly given but some of the recurrences reported are likely to have been relapses of the index depressive episode since the symptom-free period following response before randomization to treatment with amitriptyline or placebo was short at six weeks, and nearly all of the episodes occurred in the first six months of the study. The number of patients with new episodes was low in this study, with a strikingly low rate during amitriptyline treatment. This low rate may reflect the recurrence history of the patient sample, some of whom had only one episode of depression, although it would not account for the drug–placebo difference. Another more disturbing possiblity is that the treatment of a first episode with amitriptyline produces a faster recurrence than would have been expected when the treatment is stopped. This concept is allied to the observation that tricyclic antidepressants may induce rapid cycling (see Chapter 7).

The second study of amitriptyline (Glen et al., 1984) began at much the same time as the study of Coppen et al. (1978) and also suffers from design flaws which make it difficult to base a claim for the prophylactic efficacy of amitriptyline on the findings. Patients with a history of one episode in the previous five years prior to the index episode were randomized to treatment with amitriptyline, lithium or placebo following response of the acute episode, with no defined intervening period of symptom-free continuation treatment. The failure to include a symptom-free period in the design makes it difficult to separate out possible efficacy in relapse prevention from prophylactic efficacy in reducing new episodes. This was a three-year study and, had sufficiet numbers of patients been included, this problem might have been addressed by separate analysis of early and late appearances of depressive symptoms. It might have been possible, for example, to examine the outcome in the group of patients who had remained well for the first six months separately from the rest. As far as one can tell only four patients in the placebo treatment group and six patients in the amitriptyline-treated group remained in the study after six months. With the inclusion of such small numbers the study is too small to provide any valid evidence of the prophylactic efficacy of amitriptyline.

Imipramine

The best evidence that a tricyclic antidepressant (TCA) has efficacy compared with placebo in reducing the risk of further episodes of depression is provided by studies of imipramine. The distinction between efficacy in preventing relapse of an episode and efficacy in preventing new episodes is a difficult one, but three studies of imipramine fulfilled the criteria for prophylactic studies by investigating long-term efficacy in patients who had recovered from their acute episode of depression and had remained well for a defined period before randomization to placebo or active treatment.

The most recent study of imipramine's efficacy in long-term treatment is discussed in Chapters 3 and 8 (see also Kupfer *et al.*, 1989; Frank *et al.*, 1990). This was an ambitious study with a longer period of investigation—three years—than many studies have attempted. The rather low minimum severity criterion for the index episode may have influenced the recurrence rate recorded in the study; however, the methodological requirements for prophylactic investigations are well addressed. The depressive illness was defined on Research Diagnostic Criteria and patients had a recurrence history of at least three episodes. Possible contamination from the inclusion of chronic depressives or partially recovered depressives was reduced by the requirement of a minimum ten-week interval between the previous and the index episode and patients had to complete a symptom-free period of 20 weeks following response of the acute episode. Recurrence was defined both as a score on the HRS and by meeting the diagnostic criteria for a major depressive episode. The study was conducted in a single centre, which is likely to enhance the reliability and validity of the ratings and would help counteract the disadvantage of the relatively low numbers of patients (23–28) included in each of the five treatment cells. In this study there was a clear, significant advantage in reducing recurrences for imipramine (22% of patients with recurrence), compared with placebo (78%) and also compared with interpersonal psychotherapy (62%).

The earlier three-way study of Prien *et al.* (1984) comparing imipramine with lithium and placebo used the same criterion of recurrence in the history as the study of Frank *et al.* (1990). When the acute depressive episode, which was treated with imipramine and lithium, had responded, and following a rather short symptom-free period of two months, patients were randomly assigned to treatment with imipramine, lithium, lithium plus imipramine, or placebo. Bipolar patients were also included in this study but the two diagnostic groups were analysed separately. The number of patients with unipolar depression was relatively small (imipramine 39, imipramine plus lithium 38, placebo 37)—lower than would be accepted as safe for demonstrating the efficacy of an antidepressant in acute treatment. Nonetheless imipramine was found to be effective compared with placebo and there was no significant difference between imipramine and the combination treatment. No analysis of the results excluding the first two months was presented to offset the rather short symptom-free period and some of the 'recurrences' are likely to have been relapses of the inadequately treated index episode. Nevertheless the finding that imipramine showed prophylactic efficacy is generally accepted.

The early study of Prien *et al.* (1973) investigated treatment in the longer term following treatment of an acute episode. It is included in the discussion here since, because of its length, an analysis of the morbidity in the later part of the study provides evidence of the prophylactic efficacy of imipramine. The study was rather small and compared the outcome of 25 patients treated with imipramine with that of 26 patients treated with placebo and 27 treated with lithium in recently responding unipolar depression treated with antidepressants or ECT. No criterion of response is given, nor of subsequent relapse or recurrence other than the need for drugs or hospitalization. The overall efficacy of imipramine and lithium separately compared with placebo comprises relapse prevention in the first part of the two-year study, and recurrence prevention in the later part of the study. A subsidiary retrospective analysis published in the original paper excluding relapses occurring in the first four months gives some idea of the prophylactic efficacy of imipramine in 21 patients, compared with lithium (22 patients) and placebo (13 patients). Both imipramine and lithium were associated with significantly less recurrences on this analysis than placebo, and the prophylactic efficacy of imipramine and lithium appeared rather similar.

The study of Kane *et al.* (1982) that produced a negative result with imipramine was flawed by the very small number of patients included. This is a pity since the study was otherwise well designed, with a long, six-month symptom-free period before randomization to active drug or placebo, and a reasonable definition of recurrence. A comparison of six patients treated with imipramine and six treated with placebo is altogether too small to provide valid or meaningful data, and the finding that imipramine was ineffective is likely to have been a chance finding due to small numbers.

Nortriptyline

The only study of the potential prophylactic efficacy of nortriptyline was carried out in a small sample of elderly patients with recurrent major depression that compared nortriptyline, phenelzine and placebo (Georgotas *et al.*, 1989). In spite of its small size the study demonstrated a significant advantage for phenelzine compared with placebo but found no difference between nortriptyline and placebo. The effect was marked and phenelzine was seen to be significantly better than nortriptyline.

Apart from its restricted patient sample and small numbers this was a sound study. The patients had remained well for four months following response to treatment of the index episode and the criterion of response was based on the HRS score. A type II error is possible in this study because of the small numbers (placebo 23, nortriptyline 13, phenelzine 15) though the similarity of the recurrence rate in the nortriptyline and placebo groups argues against this possibility. Nortriptyline is known to be a difficult antidepressant to use properly; however, plasma concentrations were monitored to maintain the patients within the optimum therapeutic range.

It could be argued that nortriptyline's lack of efficacy may only apply to this group of elderly depressives and further studies in the elderly are called for. Nevertheless the finding that phenelzine was effective indicates that the group was drug responsive. On the basis of this study it is difficult to avoid the conclusion that nortriptyline is not an effective prophylactic agent.

Maprotiline

More than 1100 patients, diagnosed as suffering from either major depression or dysthymia, presumably double depression (DSM-III-R), whose depressive episode responded to treatment with maprotiline, were investigated in a one-year study of the long-term efficacy of two doses of maprotiline, 75 mg and 37.5 mg daily, compared with separate placebo groups (Rouillon *et al.*, 1989). Twice as many patients were treated with maprotiline as with placebo. The size of the study makes the finding of a significant advantage for maprotiline compared with placebo in long-term treatment a robust one.

Unfortunately it is not possible to say to what extent this is a true prophylactic effect as patients entered the study following treatment of the acute episode. The study did not include a defined symptom-free continuation treatment period but it has sufficient power to discriminate between relapse prevention in the early part of the study, and recurrence prevention later. The full analysis has not, however, been published yet, and the raw relapse or recurrence scores at the different time points have not been presented in a way which makes it possible to separate the two phases.

Both doses of maprotiline showed long-term efficacy compared with placebo, though there was significantly better efficacy for the 75 mg half-standard dose compared with the lower quarter-standard dose. The relapse/

recurrence rates seen in the two placebo groups is very similar. There is a dose–response relationship with greater long-term efficacy seen in the half-dose maprotiline group compared with the quarter-dose group. This provides important information about the differential efficacy of low doses of maprotiline. However, since this study did not use a full dose of maprotiline it is not possible to know if an even lower rate of recurrence would have been obtained with the full recommended dose.

Phenelzine

Phenelzine is the only MAOI that has been investigated in placebo-controlled studies of prophylactic efficacy. Phenelzine was used as one treatment arm in the study of Georgotas *et al.* (1989) in the elderly and phenelzine was examined in two different doses compared with placebo by Robinson *et al.* (1990).

In the small study in the elderly (Georgotas *et al.*, 1989) a significant advantage was seen for phenelzine compared with placebo, with only 13.3% of patients treated with the MAOI having a recurrence during the one-year study compared with 65.2% treated with placebo and compared with nortriptyline-treated patients, 53.8% of whom had a recurrence.

The difference between phenelzine and placebo is striking though there was a history of a higher rate of recurrence in the placebo-treated group which might have affected the result. A further confounding factor may have been possible adverse effects due to withdrawal from phenelzine. Nine of the placebo-treated patients had received phenelzine prior to randomization and it is possible that effects of withdrawal from the MAOI mimicked recurrence of depression. The possibility that such an effect may have contributed to the striking difference between phenelzine and placebo cannot be ruled out.

This possibility was discussed by Robinson *et al.* (1991) in the report of their study of phenelzine. The acute episode of depression of the patients in this study was treated with phenelzine, which was also the treatment during the subsequent continuation phase. Some of the high recurrence rate in the placebo-treated group may represent the effects of a reaction to the withdrawal of phenelzine, though the withdrawal was gradual in this study. This study was a small one of 47 patients randomly assigned to treatment for two years with phenelzine 60 mg, phenelzine 45 mg or placebo following successful treatment of an acute episode and completion of a continuation treatment period. Both the high and the low doses of phenelzine were reported to be effective in reducing the number of new episodes of depression compared with placebo. This is interesting particularly as the lower dose is below that normally thought to be the therapeutic dose.

Lithium

Lithium was the first medication to be used successfully in the prophylactic treatment of affective disorders and has been established for many years as a reference treatment in bipolar illness (see Chapters 6 and 7). Though the evidence for its efficacy in bipolar illness is indisputable, the evidence in favour of its use in unipolar depression is less robust. The use of lithium was encouraged by the metanalysis made by Schou (1979) of the early studies, which usually included a mixel sample of bipolar and unipolar patients. Schou combined the results on the unipolar patients included in the different studies to examine response in this category of patient and on the basis of this analysis he reported a positive effect for lithium in reducing relapse in unipolar depression. Lithium has been found to be effective in reducing new episodes of depression compared with placebo in one study in which imipramine was also found to be effective (Prien *et al.*, 1973). In this study lithium in combination with imipramine was also effective although the combination did not appear to offer significant additional benefit over imipramine alone. However, the later pivotal placebo-controlled study of Prien *et al.* (1984) did not find a significant difference between lithium and placebo.

Assessing the relative prophylactic efficacy of lithium and antidepressants is made difficult because lithium is frequently associated with marked discontinuation effects. It is a methodological problem to allow for these possible withdrawal phenomena. Patients entering studies of the prophylactic efficacy of lithium have often been stabilized on lithium before randomization to another treatment, and what appears as a recurrence in the double-blind phase of the study may instead represent symptoms caused by the withdrawal from lithium. This might well account for the favourable reports of lithium's efficacy compared with, for example, maprotiline (Coppen *et al.*, 1976).

Lithium is not a simple drug to use in long-term management because of its associated toxicity and teratogenicity, as well as the complication of monitoring of plasma levels. If there were no effective alternatives lithium might gain greater acceptance for unipolar depression in spite of the evidence considered by many to be somewhat equivocal. However, there is clear evidence of prophylactic efficacy for a number of antidepressants which are not beset by problems in management and in unipolar depression the focus has moved to these treatments for prophylaxis.

Serotonin reuptake inhibitors (Table IV)
Zimelidine The importance of the finding of prophylactic efficacy for the serotonin (5-hydroxytryptamine, 5-HT) uptake inhibitor zimelidine was eclipsed by the withdrawal of this drug from the market. The study which found that zimelidine was associated with fewer recurrences than placebo was a relatively small one—38 patients. It was, however, well designed and conducted. Patients were only admitted to the study if they had a history of recurrence of three episodes in four years, and if they had remained symptom free following response of the acute episode for a period of four months. The design also had one useful extra feature, that all patients were withdrawn from active

Table IV.   5-HT reuptake inhibitors in long-term treatment placebo-controlled studies

One-year efficacy continuation and prophylaxis combined

| | Relapse/recurrence rate | | |
	Drug	Placebo	$p <$
Sertraline	39%	62%	0.01
Paroxetine	15%	39%	0.01

Continuation treatment, first four months

		Relapse rate		
Sertraline		18.5%	44.5%	0.05

Prophylaxis (minimum four months symptom free)

		Recurrence rate		
Zimelidine	18 months	32%	84%	0.001
Fluoxetine	1 year	26%	57%	0.01

Prophylaxis (post hoc analysis excluding first four months)

Sertraline		9.3%	22.4%

therapy for one month before they entered the blinded placebo-controlled prophylactic study. The inclusion of this period helped avoid possible confusion between appearances of new episodes and the effects of a withdrawal reaction when an antidepressant was discontinued. A proportion of patients had been treated with lithium before the study and even the one-month period may not have been enough to avoid the known withdrawal effects of lithium. The very high recurrence rate of 84% on placebo over the 18 months study may in part reflect this problem, though it might also have been due to the highly recurrent group chosen (Figure 1). The finding of a significant advantage for zimelidine in reducing the risk of subsequent episodes of depression stimulated the investigation of prophylactic efficacy in the 5-HT uptake inhibitors that followed zimelidine's withdrawal.

Fluoxetine   The study of the 5-HT uptake inhibitor fluoxetine compared with placebo (Montgomery *et al.*, 1988) in the prophylactic treatment of unipolar depression was the first to address adequately the problem of the very large numbers needed to give confidence in the results. Many of the studies of prophylactic studies have reported on rather small group sizes and the problem of achieving even these small numbers is not always acknowledged. Prophylactic studies need to ensure that the patients included are documented responders in order to ensure a valid study. A large number of patients therefore has to be treated to establish response and then followed up to establish continued response. There is an inevitable attrition both for therapeutic and administrative reasons. In the fluoxetine study, out of the 456 patients who were treated openly with fluoxetine 220 responded and remained well for an 18-week

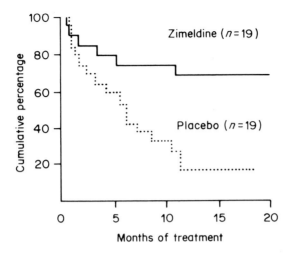

Figure 1.   Time to recurrence, zimilidine placebo-controlled study. Redrawn from Bjork K (1983) *Acta Psychiatr Scand* **68** (Suppl. 308), 182–189, with permission.

symptom-free period and entered the double-blind phase of the prophylactic study. All patients had a history of at least two episodes of major depression in five years. Rigorous criteria of response to acute treatment and to continuation treatment were used, which adds to the validity of the study. The double-blind treatment period with fluoxetine or placebo was one year. There was a highly significant advantage for fluoxetine compared with placebo in reducing the risk of new episodes, 26% of patients having a recurrence during the one-year study in the fluoxetine-treated group compared with 57% in the placebo-treated group. This clear result, based on a large study, showing that the recurrence rate was halved by the antidepressant, has increased general confidence in the prophylactic ability of antidepressants.

Paroxetine   The evidence for the efficacy of paroxetine in long-term treatment comes from one relatively large study which showed the efficacy of paroxetine compared with placebo in long-term treatment over a one-year period (Eric, 1991; Dunbar and Mewett, 1991). Some aspects of the study were well designed. There was an adequate definition of the patients, who had to satisfy the DSM-III-R criteria for recurrent major depression. They had to be moderately depressed, HRS 18 or more, and had to have responded in eight weeks to open treatment with paroxetine 20–40 mg, achieving a final score on the HRS of 8 or less.

The patients had a more highly recurrent pattern than is usual for such studies, with an entry criterion of at least three episodes in four years. The study did not incorporate a symptom-free period so that the assessment of relapse prevention and recurrence prevention is obtained by examining the early and later phases of the study. It is possible that recognition of a relapse was delayed as physicians were permitted to raise the dose during the study instead of using a fixed dose.

The relapse of recurrence criteria used in this study were unusually rigorous and required that an individual fulfilled five separate criteria before being counted as a treatment failure. This has the effect of reducing the relapse rate both on paroxetine and on placebo. In spite of this the study demonstrated a significant advantage for paroxetine over the one-year treatment period.

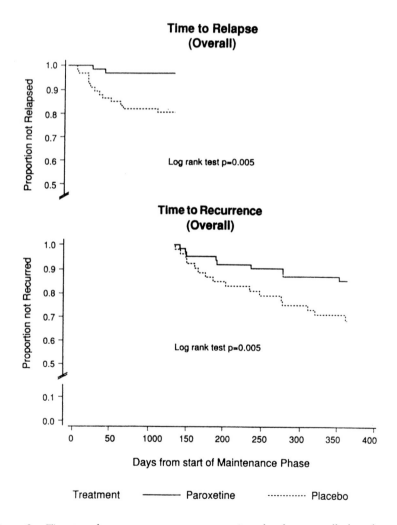

Figure 2.   Time to relapse or recurrence, paroxetine placebo-controlled study.

Out of 135 patients who entered the placebo-controlled trial 39% of patients treated with placebo relapsed, using the full criteria, compared with 15% treated with paroxetine, a difference which was highly significant.

When less rigorous criteria of relapse or recurrence, widely used in other studies, are applied, the relapse/recurrence rates approximated more closely to those reported in other investigations. With these more usual criteria it is possible to examine the data to assess both relapse prevention over the first four-month period and recurrence in the latter part of the one-year study. In this analysis paroxetine is significantly more effective than placebo both in relapse prevention and in prophylaxis or recurrence prevention (Montgomery and Dunbar, in preparation) (Figure 2).

Sertraline   A large study of sertraline provides good evidence of efficacy in continuation treatment, and to a lesser extent in prophylactic treatment (Doogan and Caillard, 1988). The study was large enough to allow subanalyses of groups, though the study design and the methodology employed makes such analyses difficult. The previous recurrence rate of the patients is ill defined and approximately one-third of patients were reported as first-time depressions; twice as many patients were treated with sertraline as with placebo and the study did not apparently define in advance the response criteria, nor did it include a symptom-free period following response of the acute episode. Nevertheless, the post hoc analysis on these data provides evidence that patients who responded to sertraline treatment in the acute phase, response being defined by scores on the HRS or on the clinical global impression, showed significantly fewer relapses during treatment with sertraline than with placebo at four months.

The analysis of the number of late depressive episodes occurring after four months gives some indication of prophylactic efficacy in the subsequent six-month period. Measured by the appearance of significant symptomatology on both the CGI and the HRS, sertraline was associated with significantly fewer recurrences than placebo.

Choice of antidepressant for prophylaxis

There are certain practical problems associated with treatments which are to continue over very long periods. Patients need to be made aware of the advantages of prophylactic treatment and the risks of discontinuing treatment. The problem of compliance with long-term treatment and the natural concerns about possible harmful effects have to be addressed.

Compliance and tolerability
Compliance with medication or lack of it is one of the main practical problems in long-term treatment. There would seem to be an advantage for the

antidepressants with proven long-term efficacy which are also associated with fewer side effects and better tolerability. The new antidepressants appear to have a clear advantage over the older tricyclic antidepressants, which are associated with a higher drop-out rate because of side effects in a number of studies.

Of the newer, better tolerated antidepressants the 5-HT uptake inhibitors have very good evidence of efficacy in prophylaxis and a favourable side-effect profile. The consistent finding of prophylactic efficacy with the 5-HT uptake inhibitors should encourage their use in long-term treatment.

There is rather little information on which to base an assessment of the relative prophylactic efficacy of different antidepressants. The direct comparisons of one antidepressant with another are limited by their small size. If two agents presumed to be active are compared the studies must be of considerably greater size than most of the prophylactic studies in order to have the power to demonstrate equivalence or significant differences. In the absence of an accepted standard reference drug placebo has been the sole comparator in the majority of the studies. The small study of nortriptyline and phenelzine (Georgotas et al., 1989) is therefore of considerable interest as it shows that the assumption of prophylactic efficacy for drugs found effective in the acute treatment of depression is not soundly based. This was, of course, a small study and needs replication but since nortriptyline is associated with the additional disadvantage of a narrow therapeutic range and a high level of unwanted side effects the choice of another, better tolerated antidepressant with clearly demonstrated prophylactic efficacy would seem the better option. Sound data on the efficacy of a number of antidepressants compared with placebo are available and the side-effect problems are well known; it is therefore possible to make a rational choice on the basis of both efficacy and tolerability.

Suicide and suicide attempts

An incidental finding in the study of maprotiline in long-term treatment was that in spite of maprotiline being effective in reducing episodes of depression a significantly increased number of suicide attempts was seen in the maprotiline-treated patients compared with placebo. There were 14 suicide attempts on maprotiline, 5 of which were fatal compared with one suicide attempt which was fatal on placebo. Unfortunately a survival analysis of the suicides and suicide attempts has not been published. Since none of the deaths were from overdose with maprotiline the difference cannot be attributed to maprotiline's direct toxicity.

The total suicide attempt rate is independent of the possible toxicity leading to death and is in any case a better index of whether the drug provokes suicide attempts. This study provides good evidence that maprotiline does provoke suicide attempts. This provocation of suicide attempts appears to be independent of dose, with seven attempts each on both the very low 37.5-mg dose and the 75-mg half-standard dose. This is interesting since it suggests that the

Table V. Suicides and suicide attempts recorded in long-term treatment study of maprotiline

	Maprotiline 75 mg	Maprotiline 37 mg	Placebo
Suicide completed	3	2	1
Suicide attempted	4	5	0
Total suicide attempts	7	7	1

From Rouillon *et al.* (1989).

practice of using a low dose of a potentially toxic drug is unhelpful in that it might compromise efficacy without reducing the risk (Table V).

The ability of maprotiline to provoke suicide attempts appears independent of its long-term antidepressant efficacy. The high suicide attempt rate was seen in the maprotiline group with the least subsequent depressive episodes, and the least attempts were seen on placebo with the highest number of subsequent depressive episodes. Furthermore, the higher, more effective dose in long-term treatment was associated with the same number of attempts as the lower, less effective dose. The inference is that maprotiline provokes suicide attempts in spite of its beneficial effect in reducing the risk of episodes of depression. This suggests that the efficacy in depression and the provoking of suicide attempts are disconnected in some way. It would be helpful to know when the suicide attempts occurred during the study, whether there is a differential effect of time on the drug, and whether the suicides and suicide attempts cluster in the dysthymia patients included in the study or in the patients with pure major depression. The number of suicide attempts was similar in the groups treated with the low and the higher dose of maprotiline, which also suggests that the mechanism of provoking attempts is unrelated to the antidepressant effects, which were seen to be dose related. The low suicide attempt rate in the placebo-treated group, with only one, albeit successful, attempt, is in line with the number of attempts seen in other large studies that included a placebo treatment group.

Dosage of antidepressants in prophylactic treatment

Conventional wisdom proposes that when a patient has recovered from depression a lower dose may be used to prevent the recurrence of a new episode than was needed to treat the acute episode. There is little evidence one way or the other from the controlled studies, most of the prophylactic studies having only tested full doses against placebo.

The suggestion that the use of a high mean dose of imipramine was the reason for the low recurrence rate in the study of Frank *et al.* (1990) goes beyond the data. It may be true but unfortunately the hypothesis has not been directly tested. The majority of studies have opted to use what was considered to be a full standard dose of the antidepressant under investigation. The study of fluoxetine (Montgomery *et al.*, 1988), which, on the basis of data available at the time the study was initiated, was designed to use a lower rather than the expected standard dose, turned out to have used a dose twice that at which the drug was eventually recommended.

Only two studies have directly compared different dosages of the same drug (Rouillon *et al.*, 1989; Robinson *et al.*, 1991). From these studies it appears that low doses of antidepressants are effective in reducing the risk of new episodes. However, a better prophylactic effect is seen with higher doses in the study of maprotiline, which found a significant difference between a half-dose of maprotiline 75 mg and a quarter-dose of maprotiline 37.5 mg. This leads naturally to the question whether further improvement would have been seen with the use of the usual standard dose of maprotiline 150 mg (Rouillon *et al.*, 1989). The study of phenelzine of Robinson *et al.* (1991) also favoured higher doses. Although both the standard dose and the lower dose of phenelzine were effective there was an advantage for the higher dose. Moreover the possibility that subsequent episodes were prolonged following the lower dose needs investigation. Evidence that a low dose might lead to a more chronic illness would be worrying if confirmed.

The balance of evidence for the moment is that full standard doses have been shown to be effective and this is therefore what should be recommended.

Length of prophylactic treatment

The discussion of how long prophylactic treatment should continue needs to be based on data. Do antidepressants continue to exert their prophylactic effect in the long term? This is not an easy question to address in controlled studies. Studies that continue for periods of longer than a year or 18 months are difficult to carry out and suffer from attrition due to loss of motivation on the part of investigators and patients as well as unavoidable administrative factors such as geographical moves. The analysis of patient survival times in the relatively short studies and an examination of when the new episodes occur have to provide the basis for an assessment of whether antidepressants continue to be effective over many years and whether the risk of new episodes reduces with time. There are a small number of studies with lengthy treatment observation periods, but because of the loss of patients from recurrences and from withdrawals a separate analysis of efficacy in the later stages of the study is not possible.

The three-year study of Frank *et al.* (1990), for example, could not answer the question of the persistence of a prophylactic effect in spite of the long study period because the numbers of patients remaining in the study in the placebo and non-drug treatment arms were too small for meaningful comparisons to be made. The problem of attrition in long-term studies is clearly seen. Similarly in the study of Prien *et al.* (1984). The highest recurrence rate was seen in the first year, and the number of patients remaining in the study in the placebo group after the first year is too small to permit the testing of efficacy in the second year separately from the first year. There are in any case difficulties in making direct comparisons of the outcome in the later stages of studies because the comparison groups are no longer similar if substantial numbers have failed on placebo.

Some help in analysing this problem is provided by the analysis of risk during the different phases of the studies. An increase in the number of recurrences in proportion to those at risk during the study might suggest that there is loss of efficacy of the treatment. In the fluoxetine study the proportion of recurrences to those at risk was constant in each quarter of the study in the placebo group, which suggests that the risk of recurrence is time dependent, as one would expect. In the fluoxetine group the recurrences tended to reduce with time, which suggests that there is no loss of efficacy, but rather the opposite, namely that in those who do respond to the 5-HT uptake inhibitor in the first six months there is an increased chance of remaining well in the subsequent six months.

The numbers in this study are large but not sufficiently large to be sure on this point. There are, however, supporting data from the study of Frank *et al.* (1990), namely that there were very few recurrences in the imipramine-treated group in the last two years of the study. The implication of these suggestive findings is that, if an individual remains well on the prophylactic treatment, there is good reason for that treatment to continue.

The longest study period has been three years and it seems reasonable to claim persistent efficacy for this period. However, we cannot be sure because the numbers surviving in the placebo group after one year are too small to permit proper efficacy testing in the separate years. Nevertheless, the evidence that efficacy does not appear to be lost in the group who received antidepressants suggests that the treatment should be continued for years, if not indefinitely. The high risk of recurrence in patients treated with placebo appears to be constant and very few patients remain well after one to two years in the studies, and this contrasts with the apparent sustained efficacy of the antidepressants.

It is sometimes suggested that antidepressants could be discontinued after successful prophylactic treatment for several years. The reluctance to continue a therapy which may not be necessary is understandable, but the rationale for stopping medication is not compelling. There seems to be little reason to consider stopping the effective agent after several years since this could be seen as reintroducing the previously established high risk of recurrence. This aspect of long-term treatment efficacy has not been properly studied, largely because of the formidable obstacles in carrying out appropriate studies, so that exact guidelines are hard to formulate. However, the evidence accumulated to date suggests that in the highly recurrent depressive the successful treatment should be continued for life. If someone wishes to discontinue a long-term medication which has been successfully maintained they should be made aware of the return of the risks of recurrence of depression. The physician would need to substitute more frequent follow-up aor the missing medication in order to institute early treatment of the expected recurrence of depression.

Delaying recurrence but not reducing the rate

One aspect of prophylactic efficacy which the studies have not examined adequately is whether antidepressants, although not eliminating new episodes, may lengthen the interval between episodes. This would require a rather longer study than those carried out so far but the information would be important. The study of Frank *et al.* (1990), which examined the possible effects of non-pharmacological intervention in reducing the risk of new episodes of depression and allowed a direct comparison of the effects of pharmacotherapy and psychotherapy, is interesting in this respect.

Although psychotherapy was clearly less effective than an antidepressant and not apparently different from placebo in reducing recurrences there did appear to be some effect. Psychotherapy could not reduce the number of recurrences but it was apparently associated with a significant delaying effect on their appearance. It is of course not possible to say if this delay represents a delay in recognition, or is due to an increased toleration of early symptoms leading to a delay in reporting, which would fit the behavioural model, or if the onset of the illness is indeed delayed.

These separate findings on outcome do, however, emphasize the need to examine both raw recurrence rates, by which measure psychotherapy is ineffective, and an outcome measure based on life table analysis where psychotherapy showed some small but significant effect.

Which patients need prophylaxis?

The rates of recurrence of new episodes of depression reported during treatment with different antidepressants shown in Table I are a reminder that long-term treatment with antidepressants does not abolish the appearance of new episodes of depression. Prophylactic treatment with an appropriate antidepressant does, however, offer a very significant reduction in the risk of a new episode. The size of the reduction varies from one study to another but a safe estimate is that the risk of a new episode, at least in the following year or so after successful treatment, is halved.

It is sometimes suggested that, since some patients treated with placebo in the studies remained well, an attempt should be made to identify these individuals for whom prophylactic treatment might not confer particular benefit. This argument contains a flaw. It assumes that all patients will have a new episode during the study period and that the lack of a recurrence represents the success of placebo. The periods of remission are, however, variable and it is entirely possible that a proportion of people who will suffer a recurrence may not have done so within the short study period. The studies are not particularly helpful in suggesting ways of identifying these patients in advance. The studies were designed for the demonstration of efficacy of an antidepressant compared with placebo and aimed to select patients with sufficient morbidity to determine group differences from placebo. They were not designed specifically to detect which patients might not benefit or for that matter which patients might benefit the most. The best predictor of an early recurrence that we have is the failure to provide adequate prophylactic pharmacotherapy.

Conclusion

The number of studies that demonstrate the prophylactic efficacy of antidepressants has increased in recent years, and there is now good evidence of long-term efficacy for a range of antidepressants. There is good evidence of efficacy for some of the newer antidepressants, in particular the 5-HT uptake inhibitors. These studies are somewhat larger than earlier ones and clinicians can therefore be more confident in the reports of long-term efficacy. These drugs are also associated with better tolerability compared with the older tricyclic antidepressants and this would make them more suitable for long-term treatment. The results with MAOIs are promising although with only two studies on phenelzine further studies are needed. The efficacy of most of the older TCAs has not been properly investigated. Nortriptyline has shown to be no different from placebo in one study and the studies on amitriptyline are too small or poorly designed to provide an adequate answer. Imipramine is the best investigated of the tricyclics and is associated with good evidence of long-term efficacy.

The results from the well-conducted studies provide a good scientific basis for the widely held clinical view that antidepressants, used in the long term, reduce the chances of new episodes of depression. Since depression is a highly recurrent disorder the increased use of antidepressants in prophylaxis should reduce the overall morbidity.

References

Angst J (1973) The course of monopolar depression and bipolar psychoses. *Pscyhiatr Neurol Neurochir* **76**, 489–500.

Bjork K (1983) The efficacy of zimelidine in preventing depressive episodes in recurrent major depressive disorders: a double-blind placebo-controlled study. *Acta Psychiatr Scand* **68**, 182–189.

Coppen A, Noguera R, Bailey J *et al.* (1971) Prophylactic lithium in affective disorders. *Lancet* **ii**, 275–279.

Coppen A, Montgomery SA, Supta RK, Bailey JE (1976) A double blind comparison of lithium and maprotiline in the prophylaxis of the affective disorders. *Br J Psychiatry* **128**, 479–485.

Coppen A, Ghose K, Montgomery S *et al.* (1978) Continuation therapy with amitriptyline in depression. *Br J Psychiatry* **133**, 28–33.

Coryell A, Winokur G (1982) Course and outcome. In Paykel ES (ed.) *Handbook of Affective Disorders*, pp. 93–106. Edinburgh: Churchill Livingstone.

Doogan DP, Caillard V (1988) Sertraline: a new antidepressant. *J Clin Psychiatry* **49**, 271.

Dunbar GC, Mewett S (1991) A double blind comparative multicentre study of paroxetine and placebo in preventing recurrent major depressive episodes. Presented at the *British Association of Psychopharmacology Annual Meeting*, York.

Eric L (1991) A prospective double blind comparative multicentre study of paroxetine and placebo in preventing recurrent major depressive episodes. *Biol Psychaitry* **29**, 11S, 2545.

Frank E, Kupfer DJ, Perel JM *et al.* (1990) Three-year outcomes for maintenance therapies in recurrent depression. *Arch Gen Psychiatry* **47**, 1093–1099.

Georgotas A, McCue RE, Cooper TB (1989) A placebo-controlled comparison of nortriptyline and phenelzine in maintenance therapy of elderly depressed patients. *Arch Gen Psychiatry* **46** (Suppl. 8), 46–51.

Glen AIM, Johnson AL, Shepherd M (1984) Continuation therapy with lithium and amitriptyline in unipolar depressive illness: a randomized, double-blind, controlled trial. *Psychol Med* **14**, 37–50.

Hamilton M (1967) Development of a rating scale for primary depressive illness. *Br J Soc Clin Psychol* **6**, 278.

Kane JM, Quitkin FM, Rifkin A *et al.* (1982) Lithium carbonate and imipramine in the prophylaxis of unipolar and bipolar II illness. *Arch Gen Psychiatry* **39**, 1065–1069.

Klerman GL, Dimascio A, Weissman M *et al.* (1974) Treatment of depression by drugs and psychotherapy. *Am J Psychiatry* **131**, 186–191.

Kupfer DJ, Frank E, Perel JM (1989) The advantage of early treatment intervention in recurrent depression. *Arch Gen Psychiatry* **46**, 771–775.

Mindham RHS, Howland C, Shepherd M (1973) An evaluation of continuation therapy with tricyclic antidepressants in depressive illness. *Psychol Med* **3**, 5–17.

Montgomery SA, Asberg M (1979) A new depression scale designed to be sensitive to change. *Br J Psychiatry* **134**, 382.

Montgomery SA, Doogan DP, Burnside R. The influence of different relapse criteria on the assessment of long term efficacy of sertraline. *Int Clin Psychopharmacol* **6**, Suppl 2, 37–46.

Montgomery SA, Dufour H, Brion S *et al.* (1988) The prophylactic efficacy of fluoxetine in unipolar depression. *Br J Psychiatry* **3**, 69–76.

Prien RF, Kupfer DJ (1986) Continuation drug therapy for major depressive episodes: how long should it be maintained? *Am J Psychiatry* **143**, 18–23.

Prien RF, Klett CJ, Caffey EM (1973) Lithium carbonate and imipramine in the prevention of affective episodes. *Arch Gen Psychiatry* **29**, 420–425.

Prien RF, Kupfer DJ, Mansky PA *et al* (1984) Drug therapy in the prevention of recurrences in unipolar and bipolar affective disorders. *Arch Gen Psychiatry* **41**, 1096–1104.

Robinson DS, Lerfald SC, Bennett B *et al.* (1991) Continuation and maintenance treatment of major depression with the monoamine oxidase inhibitor phenelzine: a double blind placebo controlled discontinuation study. *Psychopharmacol Bull* **27**, 31–39.

Rouillon F, Phillips R, Serrurier D *et al.* (1989) Rechutes de depression unipolaire et efficacite de la maprotiline. *L'Encephale* **XV**, 527–534.

Schou M (1979) Lithium as a prophylactic agent in unipolar affective illness. *Arch Gen Psychiatry* **36**, 849–851.

Seager CP, Bird RL (1962) Imipramine with electrical treatment in depression: a controlled trial. *J Ment Sci* **108**, 704–707.

Stein M, Rickels K, Weise CC (1980) Maintenance therapy with amitriptyline: a controlled trial. *Am J Psychiatry* **137**, 370–371.

5

Unwanted effects of long-term treatment

Frederic Rouillon, Michel Lejoyeux and Marie Josee Filteau

Introduction

The value of long-term therapy in recurrent affective disorders has been investigated in numerous studies that have demonstrated the efficacy of pharmacotherapy in relapse or recurrence prevention. In general, the side effects of antidepressants are not excessive and represent a small price to pay for the benefit of a reduction in depression. Nevertheless if a medication is to be used for prolonged treatment possible toxicity is of considerable importance. Concerns have also been expressed from time to time that antidepressants may have some unwanted effects that are quite unexpected. One example is the occasional anecdotal reports in the literature of an association with self-destructive behaviour in patients receiving treatment for depression:

> . . . improvement in the activity of patients, which is generally beneficial but should be viewed with caution since it is not accompanied by a clear improvement in the mood disorder, and the patient finds himself in a situation favourable to the implementation of suicidal ideas, until then impossible due to psychomotor inhibition . . . (Montassut *et al.*, 1959)
> . . . a risk of suicide manifested by the removal of motor inhibition before any reduction in anxiety in the treatment of depression with antidepressants . . . (Henon, 1962)

Long-term Treatment of Depression. Edited by S.A. Montgomery and F. Rouillon
© 1992 John Wiley & Sons Ltd

A further area of concern is the possibility that long-term antidepressant treatment may have a detrimental effect on the course of the illness. It has been suggested that illness-free intervals may be shortened or disappear (rapid cycling) and that episodes of hypomania or mania may be precipitated. Valid information is needed on the evidence of such unwanted effects in order to get a reliable estimate of the benefit of long-term treatment with antidepressants.

Technique of pharmacovigilance

Information on unwanted effects of antidepressant treatment can be obtained both from controlled clinical trials and from drug surveillance in clinical practice. Both sources have advantages and disadvantages.

Many systems for detecting adverse reactions of drugs are already in operation. The pharmaceutical manufacturers have their own systems though most rely on voluntary prescriber-initiated reporting. The data are then analysed by international (World Health Organization, WHO) or national drug surveillance systems, e.g. the Arzneimittelkommission der deutschen Ärzteschaft (AMK) in Germany, the Committee on Safety of Medicines in the UK, the Commission Nationale de Pharmacovigilance in France, or the Food and Drug Administration in the USA. Significant underreporting limits the ability of the existing postmarketing monitoring systems to detect adverse drug reactions (Rossi et al., 1983).

Other, more structured, monitoring methods have been proposed for collecting data in ambulatory patients, (Fisher et al., 1986) but they are not universally used. In one system, established by Arzneimittelüberwachung in der Psychiatrie in several German hospitals (Schmidt et al., 1986), specially trained psychiatrists make weekly contact with physicians at collaborating hospitals. The information, which is obtained by a structured interview, is used in case conferences to assess adverse drug reactions (ADR).

All open reporting systems are subject to bias from overreporting of ADRs with new drugs and underreporting with old familiar drugs. Comparative studies initiated by drug safety research units to measure the risk of prescribing antidepressants do not overcome the problem of open reporting, but can put it in perspective. For example, in a study using prescription-event monitoring, Inman (1988) has compared the risk of suicide and the risk of blood dyscrasias associated with amitriptyline and mianserin in 68 963 patients. He concluded that both drugs are associated with a low risk of blood disorders, but mianserin is appreciably safer than amitriptyline because of its significantly lower toxicity in overdosage.

A relatively unbiased estimate of drug safety can be obtained from the controlled efficacy studies of antidepressants, though the estimate is limited with respect to rare ADRs because of the small numbers of patients. Some studies present an exhaustive report of all side effects observed while others focus only on side effects that lead to withdrawal from the study. The causal relation between the occurrence of an ADR and the administration of a drug is often unclear. Nor is it always possible to extend the conclusions from short-term to long-term studies. In a post-marketing study on amitriptyline, for example, Bryant *et al.* (1987) showed that short-term patients are much more likely to attribute their adverse clinical experiences to treatment than long-term patients. There have been less than 20 therapeutic trials evaluating the prophylactic efficacy of long-term antidepressant treatment and until recently most of these have included only 20–30 patients, which is clearly insufficient to evaluate rare ADRs. Comparisons are also difficult because of the methodologies used.

It is in any case difficult to determine and quantify those side effects that are induced by antidepressants and most studies suffer some bias due to the method of collection chosen. Side effects are assessed either with exhaustive checklists or with shorter inventories focused on one type of effect, for example cardiac or neurological effects, or the most well-known and the most commonly occurring effects. Both methods have drawbacks: very detailed checklists are time consuming and are not easy to utilize routinely; shorter inventories run the risk of missing somatic symptoms that have not been systematically researched.

Side-effect-like symptoms must of course be recorded before and after treatment in order to distinguish treatment-emergent effects from the somatic symptoms of depression. A number of checklists have been developed for this purpose. Guelfi *et al.* (1983) proposed the CHESS—a more complete checklist of somatic symptoms than the frequently used Target Emergent Symptoms and Side effects (TESS). In constructing this instrument the authors performed a factorial analysis on the somatic manifestations recorded in a population of depressed subjects. A checklist for identifying tardive dyskinesia and parkinsonism often used to quantify neurological symptoms has been produced by Smith *et al.* (1983) and a method for assessing the eating attitudes and preferences has been constructed by Fernstrom (1990).

Some somatic modifications induced by antidepressants cannot be described simply by the absence or the presence of an identified symptom. There may be changes in appetite, sleep, or baseline anxiety, all of which correspond to clinical dimensions. Such changes need to be quantified using checklists of symptoms as well as clinical rating scales.

The situation in which side effects are recorded can induce bias in the assessment. For example, in studies using a naturalistic approach, where patients are receiving one treatment or combinations of different treatments, the results reflect the natural situation in which prescriptions are given but are not easy to interpret and the occurrence of one side effect cannot be related, in a direct manner, to one drug or another. A more experimental situation with standardized treatments produces side-effect results which are easier to interpret but this gives less information about the way antidepressan s are used in daily practice.

Long-term safety of antidepressants

Long-term studies are of particular value for the assessment of the safety of antidepressants since some side effects, for example convulsions, may not appear during short-term treatment. In order to assess the safety of anti-depressants in long-term treatment we have reviewed long-term efficacy studies. We excluded from our review all retrospective and/or open studies and naturalistic observations of long-term antidepressant use. We found rather few controlled studies of long-term antidepressant treatment and these we separated into those which compared two antidepressants (or lithium) under double-blind conditions and studies versus placebo with or without lithium salts. One of the clearest measures of tolerability of an antidepressant is the incidence of side-effect-related withdrawals from treatment which is reported in the studies.

Controlled studies of two antidepressants (Table I)
In the international literature, we have found six long-term controlled studies comparing two antidepressants or an antidepressant and lithium salts.

In the two studies of Coppen *et al.* (1976, 1978b) comparing maprotiline and lithium and mianserin and lithium, lithium was reported to have better pro-phylactic effect though the result may be biased by the inclusion of patients who had previously been stabilized on prophylactic lithium therapy. The authors reported that there were somewhat more withdrawals due to side effects with maprotiline, 6 cases (33%), and 2 (11%) cases of mania or hypo-mania, which compared with 3 withdrawals from side effects (14%) and 1 (5%) case of mania in the lithium-treated group. In the second study there were no cases of mania or hypomania but there were 3 withdrawals (14%) due to side effects in the mianserin-treated group compared with 1 (5%) in the lithium-treated group.

The studies comparing the long-term efficacy of two antidepressants have for the most part found the antidepressants to have equal efficacy, and few dif-ferences in withdrawals due to side effects are reported. There were 2 drop-outs due to side effects (13%) with phenelzine in the study of Georgotas *et al.* (1989), 3 (14%) with imipramine and 2 (12%) with fluvoxamine in the study of Guelfi *et al.* (1986); and 6 with trazodone and 6 (12%) with imipramine in the study of Fabre and Feighner (1983). This last study is the only one to report cases of mania or suicide: 1 case of mania (2%) with imipramine and 3 cases of suicide (3.5%) in association with trazodone.

Controlled studies of antidepressant versus placebo (Table 2)
Controlled, double-blind studies comparing an antidepressant to a placebo conclude in favour of the active product in the prevention of relapses and/or new episodes of depression. However in the 15 studies presented in Table II,

Table I. Controlled studies of two antidepressants in long-term treatment

Reference	Type of treatment	N	Pre-inclusion	Prophylaxis phase (years)	Drop-out due to side effects	Mania, hypomania	Suicide, attempted suicide
Coppen et al. (1976)	Maprotiline	18	–	1	6 (33%)	2 (11%)	–
	Lithium	21	–	1	3 (14%)	1 (5%)	–
Coppen et al. (1978b)	Mianserin	21	–	1	3 (14%)	–	–
	Lithium	20	–	1	1 (5%)	–	–
Fabre and Feighner (1983)	Trazodone	81	–	1	6 (7.5%)	0	3 (3.5%)
	Imipramine	50	–	1	6 (12%)	1 (2%)	0
Othmer et al. (1983)	Bupropion	41	6 m.	1	–	–	–
	Amitriptyline	19	6 m.	1	–	–	–
Guelfi et al. (1986)	Imipramine	22	4 w.	1	3 (14%)	–	–
	Fluvoxamine	17	4 w.	1	2 (12%)	–	–
Georgotas et al. (1989)	Placebo	23	7–9 w.	1	0	–	–
	Nortriptyline	13	7–9 w.	1	0	–	–
	Phenelzine	15	7–9 w.	1	2 (13%)	–	–

(–), no mention of case(s).

Table II. Controlled studies versus placebo of long-term antidepressant treatments

Reference	Type of treatment	N	Pre-inclusion	Duration of prophylaxis	Drop-out due to side effects (prophylaxis phase)	Mania, hypomania	Suicide, attempted suicide
Seager and Bird (1962)	Imipramine	19	ECT	6 m.	–	–	1 (5%)
	Placebo	21			–	–	0
Kay et al. (1970)	Amitriptyline	59	ETC	7 m.	6 (10%)	–	0
	Diazepam[a]	73			1 (1.5%)	–	3 (4%)
Mindham et al. (1972)	Amitriptyline	34	–	6 m.			
	Imipramine	16			–	–	–
	Placebo	42					
Prien et al. (1973)	Imipramine	25 UP / 13 BP			–	1 (5%) / 6 (67%)	0
	Placebo	26 UP / 13 BP	4 m.	20 m.	–	1 (8%) / 3 (33%)	1 (2.5%)
	Lithium	27 UP / 18 BP			–	2 (9%) / 2 (12%)	0
Klerman et al. (1974)	Amitriptyline	50	4–6 w.	8 m.	–	–	–
	Placebo	50			–	–	–
	No pill	50			–	–	–
Coppen et al. (1978a)	Amitriptyline	16	6 w.	1 y.	–	–	–
	Placebo	16			–	–	–
van Praag and de Hann (1980)	(Cross-over) 5-HT	20 (14 UP–6 BP)	3–6 m.	1 y.	–	3 (15%)	–
	Placebo				–	0	–

Study	Treatment	n					
Stein et al. (1980)	Amitriptyline	29	8 w.	6 m.	—	—	—
	Placebo	26			—	—	—
Kane et al. (1982)	Li + plac. I.	7 UP–4 BP II	—	1 y.	—	0	—
	Li + Imip.	8 UP–6 BP II			—	0	—
	Imip. + plac. Li	6 UP–5 BP II			—	2 (18%)	—
	Plac. I + plac. Li	6 UP–7 BP II			—	1 (7.5%)	—
Bialos et al. (1982)	Amitriptyline	7	3.7 y.[b]	6 m.	—	—	—
	Placebo	10			—	—	—
Glen et al. (1984)	Amytriptyline	58	—	36 m.	8 (12%)	2 (3.5%)	1 (2%)
	Placebo	9			2 (22%)	1 (11%)	—
	Lithium	69			14 (20%)	0	—
Lendresse et al. (1984)	Nomifensine	71	2 m.	6 m.	0	1 (1.5%)	0
	Placebo	72			2 (3%)	0	0
	Nom 2 m. Plac. 4 m.	75			1 (1.5%)	0	0
Prien et al. (1984)	Lithium	⎫ 117 BP	2 m.	2 y.	BP 0, UP 0	BP 11 (26%), UP 0	0
	Imipramine	⎬			BP 0, UP 1 (3%)	BP 19 (53%), UP 3 (8%)	0
	Li + Imip.	⎮ 150 UP			BP 1 (3%), UP 1 (3%)	BP 10 (28%), UP 2 (5%)	0
	Placebo (UP)	⎭			BP —, UP 0	BP —, UP 2 (6%)	0
Montgomery et al. (1988)	Fluoxetine	108	6 m.	1 y.	—	1 (1%)	—
	Placebo	112			—	0	—
Rouillon et al. (1989)	Maprotiline 75 mg	385	2 m.	1 y.	7 (2%)	2 (0.5%)	7 (2%)
	Maprotiline ½ tab.	382			3 (1%)	3 (1%)	7 (2%)
	Placebo 1 tab.	188			0	0	0
	Placebo ½ tab.	186			0	1 (0.5%)	1 (0.5%)
					$(p < 0.04)$	(NS)	$(p < 0.05)$

[a] Diazepam-like placebo.
[b] Patients receiving amitriptyline for approximately 3.7 years.

most only included small groups of patients. There is also considerable variability among the studies in the nature of the disorder (unipolar, bipolar I or bipolar II), duration of the prophylactic treatment (from six months to two or three years), and definition of adverse effects, mania and/or hypomania, suicide and/or attempted suicide, etc. Moreover some authors do not mention the drop-outs due to side effects, mania or suicide and it is difficult to know if such ADRs are absent or simply not reported. Only seven of the studies reviewed reported cases of suicide or attempted suicide; eight studies reported cases of mania or hypomania; and five studies described cases of drop-out due to side effects.

The study of Rouillon *et al.* (1989) is the only long-term study to report a statistical difference between treatments in the number of drop-outs due to side effects and this is probably because of the large number of patients included. There were no side-effect-related drop-outs in the placebo-treated group, whereas in the maprotiline-treated group there were 7 cases (2%) in the group treated with 75 mg of maprotiline and 3 (1%) in the group treated with 37.5 mg of maprotiline.

An overview of all patients included in the long-term studies reviewed gives the following comparisons. In all long-term antidepressant-controlled studies (comparing two antidepressants or an antidepressant versus a placebo), for 1192 patients treated with antidepressants there were 52 drop-outs (4.3%) due to side effects compared with 5 out of 551 patients in the placebo groups (0.9%). The proportion of suicide and attempted suicide is 20/1013 in the antidepressant-treated groups (1.9%) and 5 out of 332 (1.5%) in the placebo-treated groups. There were more cases of mania of hypomania with antidepressants—19 out of 1231 patients (1.5%)—than with placebo—5 out of 555 (0.9%).

Provocation of suicide

Suicide is an important complication of depression. Theoretically, antidepressants should reduce the risk of suicide by improving the clinical prognosis. However, these drugs can be associated with self-destructive behaviour in patients receiving treatment for depression, a finding that was reported early after their introduction by several authors (Delay *et al.*, 1961; Guyotat and Lambert, 1963). The risk associated with overdose is now mentioned in the data sheet of the majority of antidepressants. However, a question remains: is the risk associated with an untreated depression smaller or greater than the risk involved in prescribing a long-term antidepressive treatment? No therapy is infallible, and a depressed patient may be at risk of a suicidal attempt even after treatment has begun, particularly in view of the delay in response often seen. The evaluation of this risk is sometimes difficult, since it would require within-subject and prospective studies involving large cohorts of patients. In addition, the effect of the 'treatment' parameter is difficult to assess without controlled studies.

The frequency of fatal poisoning with a drug depends both on its toxicity and its availability. In the UK, Cassidy and Henry (1987) studied differences in the fatal toxicity of antidepressants, using as an index the number of deaths per million prescriptions for the years 1975 to 1984. They found that tricyclic antidepressants were more often associated with fatalities following overdose than newer drugs. Certain tricyclic drugs such as amitriptyline, dibenzepine, desipramine and dothiepin had a significantly higher toxicity than the mean of all antidepressants, whereas clomipramine, imipramine, trimipramine and the little-used iprindole and protriptyline had an index lower than the mean. These results are in accord with the figures reported by King and Moffat (1983) for the years 1976–1978 in England and Wales. Similarly, in England and Wales in the study by Montgomery and Pinder (1987), the following death rates following overdose were found per million patients treated for the period 1977–1984: amitriptyline, 166; dothiepin, 143; imipramine, 196; doxepine, 106; maprotiline, 103; trimipramine, 87; clomipramine, 32; and mianserin, 13. There are clearly differences in toxicity in overdose also seen in the study of Inman (1988); mianserin was reported to be appreciably safer than amitriptyline because of its low toxicity in overdose. In the same way, Litovitz and Troutman (1983) report a 15.2% mortality rate after 33 amoxapine overdoses in contrast to the 0.7% death rate for all other tricyclic antidepressant overdoses reported in these same centres during the study period.

In their well-known review of the literature, Guze and Robins (1970) quoted 17 within-subject studies which evaluated mortality in depressed patients. The variation in follow-up periods (not defined in certain studies) hinders interpretation but in general there is an estimated annual prevalence of suicide in depressed patients of about 1%, one-third of the estimated annual mortality rate of 3% being due to suicide. Concordant rates are reported by Murphy *et al.* (1974), who monitored 37 depressed patients for an average of five years. The majority of the patients were treated by electroconvulsive therapy (ECT) or antidepressants, yet the authors recorded 7 attempted suicides (20%) and 2 deaths by suicide (6%), corresponding to an average prevalence of around 1% for suicide and 4% for attempted suicide.

Suicides are relatively rare events and following up small samples may not therefore yield representative results. During naturalistic follow-up of 72 patients over one year (after a four-month controlled trial), Rounsaville *et al.* (1980) did not observe a single death by suicide although 2 patients (2.7%) attempted suicide. Shapiro and Keller (1981) reported 7 attempted suicides (5.8%) but no death due to suicide over six months in a cohort of 101 depressed patients. After one year, there were still no suicides but the number of attempted suicides rose to 10, i.e. 10%. The most reliable estimates are provided by very large studies like the Lundby prospective study of a cohort of 3563 subjects, monitored for 25 years. In this study Hagnell *et al.* (1982) noted 28 suicides (23 men and 5 women), half of whom were depressed. According to these authors, the suicide risk of depressed patients was 13 times greater than in the general study population.

These within-subject studies give an overall figure for the suicide rate in depressed patients, regardless of treatment, or indeed, in the absence of treatment. Avery and Winokur (1976) attempted to assess the risk of suicide in relation to management. Starting with the observation that the prevalence of suicide became higher following the introduction of antidepressants than with ECT alone, these authors undertook a three-year prospective study comparing outcome in 519 hospitalized depressed patients (1959–1961) receiving ECT, antidepressants, inadequate treatment or no treatment. Mortality was significantly lower over one year in the group which received ECT (0%) than in the group which received inadequate treatment (0.8%, $p < 0.05$) or the group which received neither ECT nor antidepressant (2.8%, $p < 0.025$). The antidepressant-treated group tended to have a lower mortality rate (1.4% over one or three years) than the group with no treatment at all (2.8% over one or three years), but there was no statistical difference between the two groups. According to the authors, the particularly high suicide rate in the group treated with antidepressant + ECT (2.5% over three years) may be attributed to a selection bias (more severely depressed) since the choice of treatment was not randomized. Overall, there were 8 suicides in 519 subjects over three years, i.e. an annual rate of 0.5%. There were marked differences in the attempted suicide rate in the same cohort of patients, with a greater number of attempts in the antidepressant-treated group (5.1%) than those treated with ECT (0.9%). It is, however, difficult to interpret the differences in the suicide attempt rates since the previous history of attempts differed between the groups.

Many depressed patients who commit suicide or make a suicide attempt were not receiving adequate treatment prior to the event. For example, Modestin (1985) noted that in 61 patients who had committed suicide only a minority (21%) were being adequately treated, 26% were receiving inadequate doses of an antidepressant and 11% received no treatment at all.

In their study involving 100 suicides Barraclough *et al.* (1974) found that although 64% were given a post hoc diagnosis of depression only 21% of the patients were receiving an antidepressant at the time of their death. A comparable proportion was found in a study by Roy (1982): 13 out of 90 suicide victims were treated with more than 75 mg per day of tricyclic antidepressants (14%). Similar proportions are seen with individuals making suicide attempts. Prescott and Highley (1985) noted that less than one-third of the depressed patients admitted to a hospital unit for attempted suicide had previously received antidepressants; the majority were being treated with benzodiazepines. The effect of treatment prior to a suicide attempt is not easy to assess. For example, the study by Roy (1984) comparing two groups of 13 manic-depressive patients, who had or had not exhibited suicide acts, did not find any therapeutic difference between the two groups although they differed in a statistically significant fashion for several clinical and socio-environmental variables. Nevertheless, in his review on the toxicity of antidepressants, Beaumont (1989) noted 'on the basis of the evidence currently available, older antidepressants appear to be more toxic than newer agents'.

The best test of a possible effect of antidepressants on the suicide rate is of course a comparison with placebo, though this is rather difficult since large numbers of patients and/or a long study period are required to test for relatively rare events. To compare rates between two active antidepressants would be even more difficult.

In the few long-term placebo-controlled studies in the literature, 20–30 patients have usually been included in the antidepressant-treated groups. This figure is totally inadequate to evaluate the suicide risk and conclusions cannot therefore be drawn from the one case reported by Prien *et al.* (1973) and the 3 cases in the diazepam-treated group (4%) reported by Kay *et al.* (1970).

The only large placebo-controlled study of long-term antidepressant treatment to report in detail on suicide rates is a study of two doses of maprotiline which included 1141 depressed patients (Rouillon *et al.*, 1989). In this study there were more suicides in the maprotiline-treated group than the placebo group though the difference was not significant:

3 suicides out of 385 (0.8%) in the maprotiline 75 mg group
2 suicides out of 382 (0.5%) in the maprotiline 37.5 mg group
1 suicide out of 186 (0.5%) in the placebo ½ tablet group
0 suicide out of 188 in the placebo 1 tablet group

On the other hand, there was a statistically significant difference between the groups for attempted suicide ($p < 0.03$);

4 attempted suicides out of 385 (1%) in the maprotiline 75 mg group
5 attempted suicides out of 382 (1.3%) in the maprotiline 37.5 mg group
0 attempted suicides in the two placebo groups

One explanation for the effect of maprotiline on suicidal behaviour might be attributed to its specific noradrenaline (norepinephrine) reuptake activity.

The anecdotal report of Teicher *et al.* (1990) of six cases of depressed patients who developed intense, violent suicidal thoughts after a few weeks of fluoxetine treatment (a serotonergic agent) is surprising in view of the reports that serotonergic antidepressants may have an advantage in reducing suicidal thoughts in double-blind studies reviewed by Montgomery and Bullock (in press). Teicher *et al.* (1990) report that these patients had not had a similar experience with any other psychotropic treatment and that the intense self-destructive thoughts persisted temporarily after discontinuation of fluoxetine treatment (range 60–106 days). According to the authors, this side effect occurred in 3.5% of patients receiving fluoxetine. They did not offer any clear explanation for this surprising adverse reaction to a selective serotonergic uptake inhibitor. Such anecdotal reports point to the need for placebo controls to establish whether the effect can be attributed to the drug.

In conclusion, it is difficult to make a general evaluation concerning deaths from suicide in long-term controlled trials, since few studies have been conducted with samples large enough to assess this risk. In addition, certain studies make no mention of the presence or absence of deaths due to suicide. In the studies that do so, there are more cases of attempted suicide or suicide (20/1013) in antidepressant groups (1.9%) than in placebo groups (5/332): 1.5% ($p < 0.05$) ($\chi^2 = 5.32$). Nevertheless, the rates are comparable to those observed in prospective studies involving depressed patients followed up in a naturalistic fashion which suggests an incidence of suicide of around 1–2% per year in the years following an episode of depression. In the naturalistic follow-up report (Lehman, 1983) the suicide rate was 6% in five years and the prevalence of attempted suicide over five years approximately 20%. This attempted suicide rate of 4% per year in depressed patients is similar to those reported by other authors, with rates ranging from 2.7% (Rounsaville et al., 1980) through 4% (Murphy et al., 1974) to 6.8% (Avery and Winokur, 1978), though lower than the 10% rate found by Shapiro and Keller (1981).

There is some evidence that the incidence of suicide varies according to the treatment given during the depressive episode and may be lower after ECT than after antidepressants. This may reflect the superiority of ECT in comparison with other antidepressant treatments, but since there has been no randomized comparison of the effect of antidepressants and ECT on the incidence of deaths from suicide this statement should be accepted with caution. It should in any case be stressed that ECT is not indicated for all depressed patients.

In the review of the toxicity versus benefits of antidepressants, Pinder (1988) concluded that risk of leaving depressed patients untreated far outweighed the risks associated with antidepressant treatment. While it is difficult to be sure whether an antidepressant promotes suicide, it is quite clear that some are more toxic than others in overdosage and that safer antidepressants should be preferred, particularly in long-term treatment.

Review of adverse reactions

The effectiveness of antidepressants has now been well established for 30 years. However, many patients receive inadequate treatments because of non-compliance or as a consequence of physician failure to prescribe adequate dosages (Pollack and Rosenbaum, 1987). Keller *et al.* (1982), for example, showed that only 34% of 200 patients with major depressive disorders, as defined by the Research Diagnostic Criteria, received an adequate dosage of antidepressants, defined as 150–300 mg per day of imipramine or its equivalent for at least four weeks. Keller *et al.* (1982) postulated that the 'low intensity of pharmacotherapy' may be accounted for in part by the physician overconcern with the potential side effects of these medications. However, management of antidepressant-induced side effects is critical for patient compliance, which diminishes as the incidence and the severity of side effects increase (Christensen, 1978). The management of side effects is important in order to achieve doses most likely to be effective. Much so-called treatment-resistant depressions may in fact be attributed to too low a dosage of antidepressant (Pollack and Rosenbaum, 1987). Furthermore, physician's concern about adverse effects will enhance the therapeutic alliance and thus minimize the possibility of premature discontinuation of treatment by patients.

We have divided adverse drug reactions into two sections: the side effects, and the modification of clinical features induced by antidepressants.

Side effects and their incidence

We distinguish seven types of side effects: those which could be related to the anticholinergic action of TCAs, cardiological effects, neurological symptoms, endocrine and metabolic effects, adverse cutaneous reactions, effects on liver and gastrointestinal tract, and blood dyscrasia.

1. Anticholinergic effects These well-known effects, associated with the blockage of the muscarinic receptor (Snyder and Yamamura, 1977), are most frequently seen with tricyclic antidepressants (TCAs). They include dry mouth, blurred vision, urinary retention, constipation and central anticholinergic syndrome.

Dry mouth is a particular problem with antidepressant treatment since it can be exacerbated by anxiety, and is therefore frequently associated with depression. In its severe forms it is associated with the development of dental cavities and stomatitis (Pollack and Rosenbaum, 1987). Patients who are troubled by this effect should be encouraged to use sugarless or lemon-flavoured gum to stimulate salivary flow. Sugar-containing foods should be avoided because of the increased risk of dental cavities.

Blurred vision is often associated with mydriasis, sluggish pupillary reaction to light, cyclopegia (paresis of the ciliary muscles acting on the lens) and presbyopia (disturbed near vision). According to Glassmann *et al.* (1984), blurred vision is less often diagnosed in older patients because of the diminished accommodation capacity already present as a result of ageing.

Constipation is more severe in elderly patients, and faecal impaction and paralytic ileus can be observed in elderly patients treated with TCAs.

Urinary retention can lead to urinary slowness, dribbling, decreased flow, atonic bladder with urinary tract infection secondary to urine stasis, complete urinary retention and even renal failure. Patients with enlarged prostates are especially exposed to this risk.

These side effects, which limit the usefulness of TCAs, are less of a problem with the newer antidepressants. For example, in comparing the first and second generation of antidepressants, Schmidt *et al.* (1986) did not find any case of urinary retention with mianserin and nomifensine, whereas the frequency of this ADR is 0.87% with amitriptyline, 0.58% with clomipramine and 0.73% with dibenzepin.

Anticholinergic effects are mostly observed at the beginning of the treatment and progressively decreasing the dose of TCA is usually sufficient to reduce the symptoms. When drug tapering is not effective, the use of an anticholinesterase inhibitor like physostigmine has been proposed (Granacher and Baldessarini, 1975), but a more rational approach is to prescribe a less anticholinergic anti-depressant (Hayes and Kristoff, 1986). Since the likelihood of adverse drug reactions is increased when more than one drug is used consistently the use of polypharmacy should also be avoided.

2. Cardiological effects   Early studies investigating the effects of antidepres-sants at therapeutic doses reported increases of heart rate, T-wave flattening, and more rarely lengthening of the P–R interval and increase of QRS complex (Kristiansen, 1961). The slowing or lowering is observed at or just above thera-peutic plasma levels and is dose dependent.

Moderate increases in either the P–R interval or QRS complex are not dan-gerous by themselves. These changes are not considered to be clinically import-ant at normal therapeutic antidepressant plasma concentrations in patients free of bundle-branch disease (Glassmann *et al.*, 1984), though patients with pre-existing bundle-branch disease are at risk for atrioventricular blocks (Glass-mann, 1984). Some cases of abnormal intraventricular conduction induced by TCAs have been reported (Warrington *et al.*, 1989) which could increase the risk of sudden death. The abnormal conduction associated with TCAs is of particular importance in overdose.

It has been suggested that some of the cardiac effects of TCAs may be positive, e.g. the *antiarrhythmic effects* reviewed (Warrington *et al.*, 1989). Giardina *et al.* (1979) showed that 10 of 11 patients with premature atrial suppression improved during imipramine therapy. The fact that imipramine is a powerful, quinidine-like antiarrythmic at therapeutic concentrations means that TCA can be used safely in depressed patients with ventricular extrasystoles.

Antidepressant-induced *tachycardia* is a well-known phenomenon but has not been very systematically investigated. Glassmann and Bigger (1981), who studied the cardiac effects of imipramine, did not consider the small increase in pulse rate to be of clinical significance. The increase was maximal in the first week of treatment, averaging 7 beats per minute, and had reduced by the fourth week of treatment to an average of less than 3 beats per minute. It appears that if serious tachycardia occurs as a side effect it is a rare event.

There are differences in the reported incidence of cardiac ADR, with some antidepressants being more cardiotoxic than others. With amitriptyline the rate is reported to be from 4.5% to 10.9%, with clomipramine the rate is 5.2%, with dibenzepin 7.1%, doxepin 7.8%, maprotiline from 2.6% to 13%, and nomifensine from 2.7% to 3.1% (Schmidt *et al.*, 1986).

A much more frequent side effect than serious tachycardia is orthostatic hypotension (Christensen *et al.*, 1985) and this is potentially of greater danger particularly in older patients. In the elderly hypotension is especially severe and can be associated with syncopal episodes, fractures and laceration following falls or even myocardial infarction. Orthostatic hypotension can develop at subtherapeutic plasma concentrations. In a prospective trial (Glassmann *et al.*, 1979) postural fall in blood pressure appeared to be independent of age, pre-existing heart disease and plasma drug concentrations of imipramine. The phenomenon, however, is more likely to be serious in the elderly, where there is an increased risk of fractures due to falls. In this respect the newer antidepressants appear to be much safer (Table III).

Table III.   Significant hypotension reported with antidepressants

Amitriptyline	0.8%
Clomipramine	3.4%
Dibenzepin	3.5%
Doxepin	7.8%
Maprotiline	0.9%
Mianserin	5.3%
Nomifensine	0
Zimelidine	0

From Schmidt *et al.* (1986).

Most TCAs have quinidine-like activity and cause impairment of *contractility* when given to animals at very high doses. In humans, evidence that therapeutic doses of antidepressants can cause an important reduction in cardiac contractility is weak, and these drugs are unlikely to be responsible for precipitating heart failure. TCAs could, however, trigger cardiac failure in the rare patients with little cardiac function reserve. Depression of cardiac contractility by antidepressants is not thought to be an important clinical problem (Warrington *et al.*, 1989).

3. Neurological symptoms   Neurological symptoms are the most frequent ADRs with antidepressants (Table IV).

Table IV. Neurological symptoms reported with antidepressants

Amitriptyline	23.6–28.1%
Clomipramine	48.2%
Dibenzepin	35.7%
Doxepin	35.3%
Maprotiline	27.2–40%
Mianserin	21–26.9%
Nomifensine	11.7–16.6%
Zimelidine	20.3–36.4%

From Schmidt *et al.* (1986).

The causal relationship is, however, difficult to assess for some symptoms, e.g. fine high-frequency *tremor*, which is seen commonly in clinical practice, but can be related either to anxiety or to caffeine intake.

One of the most common neurological side effects of antidepressants is sedation (Glassmann *et al.*, 1984), which can be used to advantage in inducing sleep in patients with disturbed sleep patterns. The sedative effect is more pronounced with some TCAs than others, e.g. amitriptyline, maprotiline. These sedative effects are most prominent upon initiation of drug therapy, or when the dose is raised. Some patients may become paradoxically agitated or over-stimulated by the same compounds. The newer antidepressants with selective and potent serotonergic effects lack the sedation seen with most of the TCAs.

The epileptogenic potential of antidepressants is well known. It is an import-ant consideration in the treatment of depression since seizures are generally observed after long-term treatments with high doses of antidepressants, though they may also occur after rapid escalation of the dose. The seizure induction could be related to high brain concentrations of the drug.

Earlier studies, which suggested that 3–4% of the patients treated with TCAs overestimated the incidence (Leyberg and Denmark, 1959). More recent studies (Jabbari *et al.*, 1985) assess the incidence at 2.2%. Some antidepressants may expose patients to higher risk. For example in the review of drug surveillance data of Schmidt *et al.* (1986) convulsions were reported in 12 of 46 central nervous system reactions due to maprotiline, which represented 63% of all convulsions reported for antidepressants. The comparative frequencies of con-vulsions in these data were 2.1% with amitriptyline, 4% with mianserin, 0.6% with nomifensine, 1.6% with zimelidine and 13.5% with maprotiline (Schmidt *et al.*, 1986). In a recent review of convulsions associated with antidepressants taken from controlled studies Montgomery *et al.* (1990) reported that convul-sions were more likely to be seen with tricyclic antidepressants than with newer antidepressants and that this became a significant problem with an incidence greater than 0.5% when high doses of tricyclic were used.

Myoclonus, defined as an involuntary, usually irregular contraction of a muscle or a group of muscles (Garvey and Tollefson, 1987; de Castro, 1985), was reported by Darcourt *et al.* (1970) in patients treated with antidepressants, and a later case report suggested the phenomenon might be dose related (Lippman *et al.*, 1977a, b). Garvey and Tollefson (1987) reported that 40% of their patients treated with imipramine suffered from a myoclonus and in nine cases was so bothersome that medication had to be changed. The complaints included jaw-jerking, with contractions occurring more than 50 times a day, intermittent upper extremity myoclonus causing patients to drop objects, and noctural myoclonus characterized by a relatively continuous sequence of single myoclonic jerks of various muscles lasting most of the night. The myoclonus usually developed within the first several weeks of therapy and stopped after the discontinuation of treatment. Myoclonus has been related to the TCA-induced increase in serotonin (5-hydroxytryptamine, 5-HT) and to a perturbation of the balance between acetylcholine and 5-HT. However, no biological hypothesis is yet clearly established.

There have been occasional reports of abnormal movements associated with TCAs. It is thought that these movements disorders might have been related to a hyperdopaminergic state and to a decrease of central cholinergic activity. *Choreoathetoid movements* as a toxic manifestation of TCA poisoning have been reported (Burks *et al.*, 1974) and also in therapeutic dosage (Fann *et al.*, 1976; Dekret *et al.*, 1977; Koller and Musa, 1985). Yassa *et al.* (1987) in their review of this topic found 24 cases of tardive dyskinesia in the course of antidepressant therapy, which makes these rare events. The authors also stressed that depression itself can constitute a risk factor for the onset of tardive dyskinesia. Three cases of *akathisia* (Ranga *et al.*, 1984) have been reported in patients treated by clomipramine, amitriptyline and doxepin. All patients were women taking conjugated oestrogens in addition to antidepressants. These cases emphasize the importance of the interaction between antidepressants and oestrogens on dopamine-sensitive adenylate cyclase and on modulation of dopamine receptors.

Confusional states can occur in association with antidepressants though it is more frequent in the elderly (Preskorn and Jerkovich, 1990; Livingstone *et al.*, 1983). For example, Davies *et al.* (1971) in the retrospective study of 150 subjects taking antidepressants found confusional states in 13% of all the patients but in 35% of those older than 40. The confusional states, some of which were quite mild, began with evening restlessness and pacing, followed by sleep disturbance (usually middle-of-the-night awakening), progressing to forgetfulness, agitation, illogical thoughts, disorientation, increasing insomnia and sometimes delusional states. The average episode lasted a week. Often, the confusional episode appeared to be self-limited, with recovery occurring in eight cases without specific therapy except increased attention by the nursing staff. The confusional state tended not to recur and often, following the remission of symptoms, the dosage given previously could be gradually readministered. Preskorn and Simpson (1982) showed that 43% of the patients in their study with high amitriptyline plasma levels suffered from delirium and all patients with a plasma level greater than 450 ng/ml suffered from confusion. This finding is in accord with the results of the study by Meador-Woodruff *et al.* (1988) in adults and that of Preskorn *et al.* (1988) in depressed children. A further risk factor for confusional states is the use of concomitant medication, which is of course more likely to occur in the elderly. However, the concomitant use of lithium, which is as likely in younger as in older patients, has been shown to enhance the risk factor (Meador-Woodruff and Grunhaus, 1986). Old age, high plasma levels and concomitant use of other psychotropic medications thus represent the main risk factors for confusion. Confusion is probably the result of the anticholinergic properties of TCAs. Peripheral signs of cholinergic blocking were observed in only 10% of the patients suffering from a TCA-induced confusion (Livingstone *et al.*, 1983). Moreover Schmidt *et al.* (1986) found a lower incidence of confusional states with antidepressants having less anticholinergic properties: 0.59% with mianserin and 0.55% with nomifensine; the frequency was 1.3% with amitriptyline, 0.58% with clomipramine, 2.45% with dibenzepin, 0.70% with maprotiline and 0.26% with doxepin. The proportion of toxic confusion was very similar: 1.53% (amitriptyline), 0.77% (clomipramine), 2.21% (dibenzepin), 0.26% (doxepin), 1.41% (maprotiline), 0.29% (mianserin) and 0.55% (nomifensine). Plasma drug concentration monitoring would therefore be useful for prevention of confusion.

Paraesthesias are quite rare after TCA treatment. They are characterized (Pollack and Rosenbaum, 1987) by a swollen, stiff, 'pins and needles feeling' of the extremities. In the same way 'jitteriness syndrome' (Pohl *et al.*, 1986) corresponds to a feeling of 'shakiness inside' associated with anxiety. It is induced by TCA treatment and disappears after the addition of the phenothiazine neuroleptic perphenazine.

Impaired speech seems to be related to high plasma levels of antidepressants (Glassmann *et al.*, 1984) and is practically never observed with therapeutic levels. Speech problems in the form of difficulty in word finding, stuttering or of increasing verbal pauses almost always respond to a lowering of the dose.

Several antidepressants in recent years have been withdrawn due to a high incidence of serious adverse reactions which were not detected in the clinical trial programme. This was the case for the 5-HT uptake inhibitor zimelidine, which has been associated with an influenza-like drug reaction and Guillain-Barré syndrome. As zimelidine was the first of a series of 5-HT uptake inhibitors in development this serious ADR caused some concern. However, in her review Aberg-Wistedt (1989) noted that this kind of adverse reaction has not been observed during treatment with other 5-HT uptake inhibitors, and studies (Montgomery *et al.*, 1989) that directly challenged patients who had reacted to zimelidine with another 5-HT uptake inhibitor without unwanted effects have shown that the zimelidine problems were specific to that compound.

4. Endocrinal and metabolic effects   Antidepressant drugs may stimulate prolactin secretion; however, a few of them have been reported to cause distressing galactorrhoea and secondary amenorrhoea. Anand (1985) reports a case suggesting a relationship between clomipramine and the induction of inappropriate lactation. Other uncommon cases of endocrine disturbance have been reported, especially hyponatraemia via the syndrome of inappropriate antidiuretic hormone secretion with amitriptyline (Madhusoodanan and Osnos, 1981) or with clomipramine (Garson, 1979; Pledger and Mathew, 1989).

5. Adverse cutaneous reactions   A recent review of the literature on adverse cutaneous reaction attributed to antidepressant medication concluded that skin reactions appear in approximately 2–4% of patients taking antidepressants (Warnock and Knesevitch, 1988). A variety of cutaneous morphological patterns are reported but the majority are exanthematous (46%), followed by urticaria (23%), erythema multiforme (5.4%), exfoliative dermatitis (3.7%) and photosensitivity (2.8%). The prevalence of rashes is higher for some antidepressants, e.g. maprotiline, which was found in the review by Schmidt *et al.* (1986) to have an incidence of skin ADRs of 29.6%, which compared with 5.3% for mianserin and 7.8% for amitriptyline. Adverse cutaneous eruptions due to antidepressants usually occur in the first two weeks of treatment. It is thus rarely seen during long-term treatment.

6. Effects on gastrointestinal tract and liver   The most frequently reported side effects of the selective 5-HT uptake inhibitors are gastrointestinal symptoms such as nausea and vomiting. These effects seem to be characteristic of this class of antidepressants though the extent to which they are troublesome varies from compound to compound and is also probably dose related.

Gastrointestinal tract ADRs occur with other antidepressants as well, however, and in the review of Schmidt *et al.* (1986) the incidence was reported to be 5.4% with amitriptyline, 6.9% with clomipramine, 3.6% with dibenzepin, 1.9% with doxepin, 1.7% with maprotiline and 10.5% with mianserin. In the same review an incidence of 27.3% was seen with the 5-HT reuptake inhibitor zimelidine.

Impaired liver functions have been observed more frequently in patients taking nomifensine (2.2%) than with other antidepressants (amitriptyline 0.6%, clomipramine 0.9%, dibenzepin 1.9%, maprotiline 0.9%, mianserin 0.6%) by Schmidt *et al.* (1986). In the same way there are 17 voluntary physician reports indicating hepatotoxic effects of nomifensine, which comes first (15.3%) with mianserin (21.1%) for this kind of effect, in comparison to amitriptyline (5.4%), clomipramine (6.9%), dibenzepin (10.7%), doxepin (11.8%), maprotiline (1.7%) and zimelidine (9.1%) in the publication of Schmidt *et al.* (1986).

7. Blood dyscrasias   These serious ADRs have caused some antidepressants to be withdrawn, e.g. nomifensine, which was associated with immuno-haemolythic anaemia, and indalpine, which caused associated agranulocytosis. There is clear evidence that mianserin is associated with an increased rate of blood dyscrasias: 10 cases have been detected in the course of 50000 drug exposures in Australia and 34 cases were noted in response to 12000 mianserin prescriptions in Great Britain (Schmidt *et al.*, 1986). The WHO had collected, by October 1983, 60 cases of blood dyscrasias which involved mianserin (leuco-penia, agranulocytosis, aplastic anaemia, idiopathic thrombocytopenia . . .). These syndromes, some of which had a fatal outcome, occurred during the first to second month of treatment, indicating a myelotoxic reaction. It is, however, known that dyscrasias occur with other antidepressants, and establishing rela-tive risk is difficult using open ADR reporting as the basis for assessment. For example, in a study which compared 26781 patients who had been prescribed mianserin and 42082 who had received amitriptyline Inman (1988) found re-spectively 78 (0.3%) and 151 (0.3%) cases of blood disorders. No patients had aplastic anaemia, agranulocytosis or severe leucopenia. Thus, both drugs pres-ent a low risk of blood disorders.

8. Modification of clinical features induced by antidepressants   Clinical di-mensions such as appetite, sexual function, sleep and memory are modified both by depression and by antidepressants and it is difficult to differentiate between the somatic manifestations of depression and drug-induced effects.

(a) Body weight and appetite   Depressed patients frequently lose weight, though some actually gain weight during their depressive episode (Mezzich and Raab, 1980). On the other hand, the use of frequently prescribed antidepres-sants such as amitriptyline and imipramine is often associated with increase in body weight (Fernstrom and Kupfer, 1988). This effect may not be easy to assess at first since increases in appetite and weight are signs of recovery. To disentangle the drug effects from the course of natural recovery Harris *et al.* (1986) studied seven combinations of antidepressants in double-blind trials and found that trimipramine and isocarboxazid combined had a significant effect in increasing appetite, carbohydrate preference and weight.

Medication-induced changes in body weight and appetite may result from a pharmacological action of the drug, independent of its effect on mood (Fern-strom, 1990); the mechanisms by which the alterations in body weight are produced are not yet understood. They could reflect changes in metabolism produced by alteration in caloric intake, or expenditure, or both. In some patients weight gain could be caused by a reduction in resting metabolic rate and increased energy efficiency during treatment with TCAs, without any in-crease in calory intake.

Food preference can be modified by antidepressants, as reports of carbohy-drate craving induced by amitriptyline treatment have shown (Paykel *et al.*, 1973). Fernstrom (1990) showed that a similar increase in preference for sweet foods occurred in 15% of patients during four months treatment with imipramine, though the change in food preference was not correlated with an increase in weight. The increase in weight which is commonly associated with TCAs is a problem since antidepressants have to be continued over months for an adequate treatment course. For this reason the findings that new 5-HT uptake inhibitors are not associated with excess weight gain has been welcomed (Coppen *et al.*, 1979; Montgomery *et al.*, 1988). With fluoxetine the opposite effect of a reduction in weight is seen which is greater in those with greater body mass.

(*b*) *Sexual dysfunction*　The incidence of sexual side effects is generally low but have been reported with a wide range of antidepressants such as phenelzine, amitriptyline, imipramine and desipramine (de Leo and Magni, 1983). Patients are often reluctant to report sexual changes and some physicians do not routinely inquire about them. However, drug-induced sexual dysfunction, including decreased libido, impaired erection, impaired ejaculation and inhibition of orgasm, may be one of the reasons for non-compliance (Pollack and Rosenbaum, 1987). Sexual dysfunction occurs as part of depression, and to distinguish the sexual symptoms associated with a psychiatric state from the side effects of antidepressants Kowalski *et al.* (1985) compared the effects of amitriptyline, mianserin and placebo on their effects on nocturnal sexual arousal (frequency, amplitude and duration of penile tumescence) in a double-blind trial in a non-psychiatric male population. Both active compounds significantly decreased the amplitude and total duration of nocturnal erections. This study confirms the clinical observation of sexual side effects of antidepressants but does not clarify their mechanism. Some authors have proposed a central mechanism which includes the blocking of 5-HT reuptake, while others suggested a peripheral mechanism and, especially, an anticholinergic action (Mitchell and Popkin, 1983). However, mianserin has only a small effect on central 5-HT reuptake and minor peripheral anticholinergic effects, and an explanation for the sexual dysfunction has still to be sought. Priapism has been reported with the use of trazodone and requires immediate cessation of treatment.

(*c*) *Sleep disorders*　Sleep disorders are part of depressive symptomatology, but certain sleep abnormalities can be more closely related to antidepressive treatment than to depression itself. Neurological symptoms such as nocturnal myoclonus and paraesthesias induced by TCAs have already been described.

Nightmares as well as hypnagogic and hypnopompic hallucinations are often induced by heterocyclic antidepressants (Pollock and Rosenbaum, 1987). The frequency of sleep disturbances reported in drug surveillance studies ranges from 0.2% to 1.55% (Schmidt *et al.*, 1986).

Systematic sleep studies in patients taking zimelidine and indalpine revealed reduced sleep time and increased wakefulness (Nicholson and Pascoe, 1986), which appears to be characteristic of 5-HT reuptake inhibitors. This may appear as insomnia, which may also be related to reduced REM sleep.

(d) Increase of anxiety and 'early tricyclic syndrome' This syndrome is more often associated with more selective 'noradrenergic' antidepressants like desipramine (Rosenbaum, 1984). In particular, patients with panic attacks or panic and depression may experience an increase in anxiety in the first days of treatment which is probably due to acute adrenergic increase and sympathetic stimulation. Benzodiazepines are effective to relieve these symptoms.

An increase in anxiety early in treatment has been described with 5-HT uptake inhibitors in some patients. It seems to be only moderately dose related. A study by Cooper (1988) found anxiety in 15% of patients treated with 20 mg of fluoxetine, 16% in patients receiving 40 mg and 21% in those receiving 60 mg, compared with 11% in the placebo group.

(e) Memory disorders Anticholinergic effects can induce memory impairment which is especially troublesome in older patients, in whom it can lead to acute confusional states, and in patients receiving long-term prophylactic treatment with antidepressants. Drug-induced alterations in memory have to be distinguished from the memory impairments that are manifestations of the depression. There may be qualitative differences in the memory impairment produced by different treatments as was reported by Calev *et al.* (1989), who compared electroconvulsive therapy (ECT) and imipramine in patients with major depression. Both bilateral ECT and imipramine 200 mg daily caused memory impairment in depressed patients but ECT-treated patients showed both anterograde and retrograde memory deficit, whereas imipramine-treated patients showed anterograde memory deficit only.

Course of illness, mania and hypomania

There is a general consensus that antidepressants are able to precipitate mania or hypomania not only in bipolar depressive patients but also in unipolar patients. In addition, they can induce rapid cycling in bipolar patients. Nevertheless, a controversy exists as to the extent that tricyclic antidepressants increase the likelihood of mania. Furthermore, a question remains concerning this adverse effect on mood: does it appear primarily in short-term treament or also in long-term treatment?

For example, in their uncontrolled study, van Scheyen and van Kammen (1979) reported a greater frequency of mania (25%) in unipolar patients treated with tricyclics alone than other controlled studies. In establishing the incidence of mania or hypomania episodes that can be attributed to a drug effect it is important to turn to placebo-controlled studies. In their review of 12 placebo-controlled studies Bunney (1978) and Murphy (1977) suggested that the incidence of mania or hypomania is 9% in unipolar or bipolar patients treated with antidepressants for the acute episode of depression. Other studies have reported lower rates, for example in the study of Kupfer *et al.* (1988) only six of the 230 patients (2.6%) developed hypomania and none experienced mania in the acute phase and 2.5% in the continuation treatment. The bipolar II patients had an incidence of hypomania no higher than the group with recurrent unipolar depression.

Quitkin *et al.* (1981) compared relapse in bipolar I patients treated with imipramine and lithium or lithium and placebo and found the rate was higher in the imipramine group: 24% compared to 10.5%. Although the difference was not significant it suggests that imipramine may be associated with the increased risk for future manic relapse, particularly in mania-prone patients. It may not be possible to assess the true level of precipitation of mania by an antidepressant in the testing programme prior to its introduction, as the episodes may only occur in long-term treatment.

In our review of placebo-controlled long-term antidepressive treatment (Table II) we found eight studies which reported cases of mania or hypomania. Kane *et al.* (1982) described a 4% incidence of manic episodes in the population over an average follow-up duration of one year. The numbers were of course very small and are not consistent with other reports. Prien *et al.* (1984) found fewer manic episodes in bipolar patients treated with lithium (26%) than those treated with lithium + imipramine (28%) or imipramine alone (53%). However, in the absence of a placebo-treated bipolar control group we cannot know if the high incidence of mania resulted from imipramine or from failure of imipramine to prevent naturally occurring manic episodes. In unipolar patients there was no statistical difference in the frequency of manic episodes between the treated groups. There are too few cases of mania of hypomania in the other long-term placebo-controlled studies to make direct comparisons: 3 cases during treatment with 5-hydroxytryptophan (5-HTP) (van Praag and de Hann, 1980); 2 cases with amitriptyline (3.5%) and 1 (11%) with placebo (Glen *et al.*, 1984); 1 case (1.5%) with nomifensine (Lendresse *et al.*, 1984); 1 case (1%) with fluoxetine (Montgomery *et al.*,1988). 5 cases (0.5%) with maprotiline compared with 1 case (0.5%) with placebo.

Overall, in our review of controlled studies of long-term antidepressant treatments (Tables I and II) we have found in bipolar patients:

25 out of 49 cases (51%)   imipramine
13 out of 60 cases (21%)   lithium salts
3 out of 13 cases (23%)   placebo
10 out of 36 cases (28%)   imipramine associated with lithium salts

In unipolar patients we found:

19 out of 1231 (1.5%)   with antidepressants
5 out of 555 (0.9%)   with placebo

The switch phenomenon has been described with almost all new antidepressants. For example, Knobler *et al.* (1986) described three cases of trazodone-induced mania. The symptoms appeared shortly after the beginning of treatment in the two bipolar patients and after ten weeks in the unipolar patients. The switch phenomenon is obviously more frequent in bipolar patients and lithium cannot be guaranteed to prevent them from manic episodes (Solomon *et al.*, 1990). It seems clear that antidepressants induce reversible rapid cycling between mania and depression in some patients but there has been only one placebo-controlled study that has been designed in a way that would permit its detection (Wehr *et al.*, 1988). This study found that 73% of the patients were taking antidepressants at the time of the onset of rapid cycling and that the continuation of rapid cycling was associated with antidepressants in 51% of the patients. As Wehr and Goodwin (1987) concluded, antidepressants can cause mania or rapid cycling in some bipolar patients and a few unipolar patients, but it is still unclear to what extent they do so.

Withdrawal manifestations

Withdrawal phenomena usually following abrupt discontinuation of antidepressants have been known for more than 30 years. Most authors agree that the incidence of this syndrome is surprisingly high, from 21% (Andersen and Kristiansen, 1959) to 55% (Kramer *et al.*, 1961). It appears that long-term treatments with high doses of anticholinergic TCA are more often involved in the genesis of withdrawal manifestations. Antidepressant withdrawal symptoms can be grouped (Dilsaver and Greden, 1984; Dilsaver *et al.*, 1987) into four categories or syndromes:

1. General somatic distress with flu-like symptoms, gastrointestinal disturbances (nausea, vomiting, abdominal pain, anorexia and diarrhoea), somatic distress (myalgias, headache, chills, weakness and rhinorrhoeas), anxiety, agitation and near panic, 'jitteriness' or nervous tension.
2. Sleep disturbances including insomnia or, in contrast, a sense of excessive vivid and early-onset dreaming.
3. Movement disorders, e.g. parkinsonism (Dilsaver *et al.*, 1983) or 'akathisia-like syndrome' (Sathananthan and Gershon, 1973).
4. Miscellaneous withdrawal symptoms: panic attacks (Gawin and Markoff, 1981), cardiac arrhythmias (Boisvert and Chouinard, 1981), delirium (Santos and McCurdy, 1980). Paradoxical activation or time-limited manic reactions can follow discontinuation of antidepressants (Nelson *et al.*, 1983).

Despite all the biological and clinical research concerning antidepressant withdrawal syndromes, the information gained has not had a proper impact on clinical practice and TCAs are usually discontinued without any particular precaution. It is not even regarded as sufficiently severe, difficult or important to warrant a rubric in the DSM-III-R classification, which defines many withdrawal syndromes (alcohol, benzodiazepines, amphetamine, nicotine, etc.).

Antidepressant withdrawal manifestations are more rare among hospitalized patients than in out-patients, which may be because antidepressants are usually slowly tapered in psychiatric units or because these phenomena are not systematically researched (Lejoyeux and Ades, 1989). Withdrawal symptoms may be overlooked and digestive symptoms and general distress are often considered by the patient or by the physician to be flu symptoms.

Conclusion

Antidepressants have been shown to be effective long-term preventive treatments for recurrent unipolar disorders but the occurrence of unwanted effects often complicates long-term prescriptions. They cause on average 4.2% (range 0–33%) of the patients in long-term treatment with antidepressants to discontinue their medication. These unwanted long-term effects are not appreciably different from those associated with treatment of the acute episode. The two main psychiatric complications are suicide and antidepressant-induced mania. Some patients make suicide attempts in spite of antidepressant treatment and the possibility that some antidepressants may provoke this behaviour needs further investigation. The risk of inducing mania or hypomania cannot be avoided though it is more evident in bipolar than unipolar patients.

The significance of unwanted somatic effects, the most important of which are cardiovascular (lowering of intracardiac conduction, orthostatic hypotension) and neurological (seizures and delirium), varies between different antidepressants and between patients. Anticholinergic symptoms such as sedation or urinary retention which would not trouble young healthy patients can have severe consequences in the elderly. Further investigation of the risk factors of unwanted effects is clearly needed. Are there clinical or biological predictors of antidepressant-induced suicide or mania? Can the occurrence of somatic complications be related to the clinical characteristics of the patient (age, somatic diseases, personality disorders, impulsivity, etc.)? Such studies would be helpful in selecting treatments in daily clinical practice. They could also provide heuristic models of biological and clinical abnormalities of depression and the mechanisms by which antidepressants achieve their response.

Acknowledgements

The authors wish to acknowledge the assistance of C. Martineau, C. Massy, C. Revaud and B. Shorter.

References

Aberg-Wistedt A (1989) The antidepressant effects of 5-HT uptake inhibitors. *Br J Psychiatry* **155** (Suppl. 8), 32–40.

Anand VS (1985) Clomipramine-induced galactorrhoea and amenorrhoea. *Br J Psychiatry* **147**, 87–88.

Andersen H, Kristiansen ES (1959) Tofranil treatment of endogenous depressions. *Acta Psychiatr Neurol Scand* **34**, 387–397.

Avery D, Winokur G (1976) Mortality in depressed patients treated with electroconvulsive therapy and antidepressants. *Arch Gen Psychiatry* **33**, 1029–1037.

Avery D, Winokur G (1978) Suicide, attempted suicide and relapse rates in depression occurrence after ECT and antidepressants therapy. *Arch Gen Psychiatry* **35**, 749–753.

Barraclough B, Bunch J, Nelson B (1974) A hundred cases of suicide: a clinical aspect. *Br J Psychiatry* **125**, 355–373.

Beaumont G (1989) The toxicity of antidepressants. *Br J Psychiatry* **154**, 454–458.

Bialos D, Giller E, Jatlow P *et al.* (1982) Recurrence of depression after discontinuation of long term amitriptyline treatment. *Am J Psychiatry* **139**, 325–329.

Boisvert D, Chouinard G (1981) Rebound cardiac arrhythmia after withdrawal from imipramine: a case report. *Am J Psychiatry* **138**, 325–329.

Bryant SG, Fischer S, Kluge RM (1987) Long-term versus short-term amitriptyline side-effects as measured by post marketing surveillance system. *J Clin Psychopharmacol* **712**, 78–82.

Bunney WE (1978) Psychopharmacology of the switch process in affective illness. In Lipton MA, Dimascio A, Kellem KL (eds) *Pharmacology: A Generation of Progress.* New York: Raven Press.

Burks JS, Walker JE, Rumach BA (1974) Tricyclic antidepressant poisoning. *JAMA* **203**, 1405–1407.

Calev A, Ben-Tzvi E, Shapiro B *et al.* (1989) Distinct memory impairments following ECT and imipramine. *Psychol Med* **19**, 111–119.

Cassidy S, Henry J (1987) Fatal toxicity of antidepressant drugs in overdose. *Br Med J* **295**, 1021–1024.

Christensen D (1978) Drug taking compliance: a review and synthesis. *Health Serv Res* **13**, 171–187.

Christensen P, Thomsen HY, Pedersen OL *et al.* (1985) Orthostatic side effects of clomipramine and citalopram during treatment for depression. *Psychopharmacology* **86**, 383–385.

Cooper GL (1988) The safety of fluoxetine: an update. *Br J Psychiatry* **131**, 1237–1264.

Coppen A, Montgomery SA, Gupta RK, Bailey JE (1976) Double blind comparison of lithium carbonate and maprotiline in the prophylaxis of the affective disorders. *Br J Psychiatry* **128**, 479–485.

Coppen A, Ghose K, Rama Rao VA, Peet M (1977) Mianserin in the prophylactic treatment of bipolar affective illness. *Int Pharmacopsychiatry* **12**, 95–99.

Coppen A, Ghose K, Montgomery S *et al.* (1978a) Continuation therapy with amitriptyline in depression. *Br J Psychiatry* **133**, 28–33.

Coppen A, Ghose K, Rama Rao VA, *et al.* (1978b) Mianserin and lithium in the prophylaxis of depression. *Br J Psychiatry* **133**, 206–210.

Coppen A, Rama Rao VA, Swade C, Wood K (1979) Zimelidine: a therapeutic and pharmacokinetic study in depression. *Psychopharmacologica* **63**, 199–202.

Darcourt G, Fadeuilhe A, Lavagna J, Cazac A (1970) Trois cas de myoclonies d'action au cours de traitements par l'imipramine et l'amitriptyline. *Rev Neurol* **122**, 141–142.

Davies RK, Tucker GJ, Harrow M, Detre TP (1971) Confusional episodes and antidepressant medication. *Am J Psychiatry* **128**, 95–99.

de Castro RM (1985) Antidepressants and myoclonus: a case report. *J Clin Psychiatry* **46**, 284–287.

Dekret JJ, Maany I, Ramsey TA, Mendels J (1977) A case of oral dyskinesia associated with imipramine treatment. *Am J Psychiatry* **134**, 1297–1298.

Delay J, Deniker P, Lemperiere T, Ginestet D (1961) Deux années d'expérience de l'imipramine. *Ann Méd Psychol* **1**, 235–249.

de Leo D, Magni G (1983) Sexual side effects of antidepressants drugs. *Psychosomatics* **24**, 1076–1081.

Dilsaver SC, Greden JF (1984) Antidepressant withdrawal phenomena. *Biol Psychiatry* **192**, 237–256.

Dilsaver SC, Kronfol Z, Greden JF, Sackellares JC (1983) Antidepressant withdrawal syndromes: evidence supporting the cholinergic overdrive hypothesis. *J Clin Psychopharmacol* **3**, 157–164.

Dilsaver SC, Greden JF, Snider RM (1987) Antidepressant withdrawal syndromes: phenomenology and physiopathology. *Int Clin Psychopharmacol* **2**, 1–19.

Fabre LF, Feighner JP (1983) Long term therapy for depression with trazodone. *J Clin Psychiatry* **44**, 17–21.

Fann WE, Sullivan JL, Richman BW (1976) Dyskinesias associated with tricyclic antidepressants. *Br J Psychiatry* **128**, 490–493.

Fernstrom MH (1990) Depression, antidepressants and body weight change. *Ann NY Acad Sci* 31–39.

Fernstrom MH, Kupfer DJ (1988) Antidepressant-induced weight gain: a comparison study of four medications. *Psychiatry Res* **26**, 265–271.

Fisher S, Bryant SG, Kluge RM (1986) New approaches to post marketing surveillance. *Psychopharmacology* **90**, 347–350.

Garson M (1979) Syndrome of dilutional hyponatremia secondary to tricyclic antidepressant. *Practitioner* **222**, 411–412.

Garvey MJ, Tollefson GD (1987) Occurrence of myoclonus in patients treated with tricyclic antidepressants. *Arch Gen Psychiatry* **44**, 269–272.

Gawin FH, Markoff RA (1981) Panic anxiety after abrupt discontinuation of amitriptyline. *Am J Psychiatry* **138**, 117–118.

Georgotas A, McCue RE, Cooper TB (1989) A placebo-controlled comparison of nortriptyline and phenelzine in maintenance therapy of elderly depressed patients. *Arch Gen Psychiatry* **46**, 783–786.

Giardina EGV, Bigger JT, Glassmann AH et al. (1979) The electrocardiographic and antiarrhythmic effects of imipramine hydrochloride at therapeutic concentrations. *Circulation* **60**, 1045–1952.

Glassmann AH (1984) The newer antidepressant drugs and their cardiovascular effects. *Psychopharmacol Bull* **20**, 272–290.

Glassmann AH, Bigger TJ (1981) Cardiovascular effects of therapeutic doses of tricyclic antidepressants: a review. *Arch Gen Psychiatry* **38**, 815–820.

Glassmann AH, Bigger JT, Giardina EV et al. (1979) Clinical characteristics of imipramine-induced orthostatic hypotension. *Lancet* **i**, 468–472.

Glassmann AH, Carino JS, Roose SP (1984) Adverse effects of tricyclic antidepressants: focus on the elderly. In Usdin E et al. (eds) *Frontiers in Biochemical and Pharmacological Research in Depression*, pp. 391–398. New York: Raven Press.

Glen AIM, Johnson AL, Shepherd M (1984) Continuation therapy with lithium and amitriptyline in unipolar depressive illness: a randomized double blind, controlled trial. *Psychol Med* **14**, 37–50.

Granacher RP, Baldessarini RJ (1975) Physostigmine: its use in acute anticholinergic syndrome with antidepressants or antiparkinson drugs. *Arch Gen Psychiatry* **32**, 375–380.

Guelfi JD, Pull CB, Guelfi L *et al.* (1983) CHESS utilisation dans la pathologie anxieuse et dépressive, structure factorielle. *Ann Méd Psychol* **3**, 257–278.

Guelfi JD, Dreyfus JF, Pichot P, Gepece P (1986) Fluvoxamine et imipramine: résultats d'un essai contrôlé au long cours. *Actualités Internationales en Psychiatrie*, numéro spécial. Paris: Media Press.

Guyotat J, Lambert PA (1963) L'imipramine. In *Actualités Thérapeutiques Psychiatriques*, pp. 261–271, Paris, Masson.

Guze SB, Robins E (1970) Suicide among primary affective disorders. *Br J Psychiatry* **117**, 437–438.

Hagnell O, Lanke J, Rorsman B, Ojesjo L (1982) Are we entering an age of melancholy? Depressive illness in a prospective epidemiological study over 25 years. The Lundby study, Sweden. *Psychol Med* **12**, 279–289.

Harris B, Young J, Hughes B (1985) Comparative effects of seven antidepressant regimes on appetite, weight and carbohydrate preference. *Br J Psychiatry* **148**, 590–592.

Hayes PE, Kristoff CA (1986) Adverse reaction to five new antidepressants. *Clin Pharm* **5**, 471–480.

Henon H (1962) Mélancolie. *Encyclopédie Méd-Chir Psychiatrie* 37210 A10, 6.

Inman WHW (1988) Blood disorders and suicide in patients taking mianserin or amitriptyline. *Lancet* **ii**, 90–92.

Jabbari B, Bryan GE, Marsh EE, Gunderson CH (1985) Incidence of seizures with tricyclic and tetracylic antidepressants. *Arch Neurol* **42**, 480–481.

Kane JM, Quitkin FM, Rifkin A *et al.* (1982) Lithium carbonate and imipramine in the prophylaxis of unipolar and bipolar II illness. *Arch Gen Psychiatry* **39**, 1065–1069.

Kay DWK, Fahy T, Garside RF (1970) A seven month double blind trial of amitriptyline and diazepam in ECT treated depressed patients. *Br J Psychiatry* **117**, 667–671.

Keller MB, Shapiro RW (1981) Major depressive disorder: initial results from a one year prospective naturalistic follow-up study. *J Nerv Ment Dis* **169**, 761–768.

Keller MB, Klerman GL, Lavori PW (1982) Treatment received by depressed patients. *JAMA* **248**, 1848–1855.

King LA, Moffat AC (1983) A possible index of fatal drug toxicity in humans. *Med Sci Law* **23**, 193–198.

Klerman GL, Di Mascio A, Weissman MM *et al.* (1974) Treatment of depression by drugs and psychotherapy. *Am J Psychiatry* **131**, 186–191.

Knobler HY, Itzhaky S, Emanuel D *et al.* (1986) Trazodone-induced mania. *Br J Psychiatry* **149**, 787–789.

Koller WC, Musa MN (1985) Amitriptyline-induced abnormal movements. *Neurology* **35**, 1086.

Kowalski A, Stanley RO, Dennerstein L *et al.* (1985) The sexual side-effects of antidepressant medication: a double blind comparison of two antidepressants in a non-psychiatric population. *Br J Psychiatry* **147**, 413–418.

Kramer JC, Klein DF, Fink M (1961) Withdrawal symptoms following discontinuation of imipramine therapy. *Am J Psychiatry* **118**, 549–550.

Kristiansen ES (1961) Cardiac complications during treatment with imipramine. *Acta Psychiatr Scand* **36**, 427–442.

Kupfer DJ, Carpenter L, Frank E (1988) Possible role of antidepressants in precipitating mania and hypomania in recurrent depression. *Am J Psychiatry* **145**, 804–808.

Lehman HE (1983) Clinical evaluation and natural course of depression. *J Clin Psychiatry* **44**, 5–10.

Lejoyeux M, Ades J (1989) Le syndrome de sevrage des antidépresseurs. *Psychiatrie Psychobiol* **4**, 335–345.

Lendresse P, Cren MC, Lemarie JC (1984) Traitement prolongé par Nomifensine 75 mg dans les états dépressifs névrotiques et réactionnels. *Psychiatrie Française* **16** (suppl.), 156–158.

Leyberg JT, Denmark JC (1959) The treatment of depressive states with imipramine hydrochloride (Tofranil). *J Ment Sci* **105**, 1123–1126.

Lippman S, Moskovitz R, O'Tuama L (1977a) Tricyclic-induced myoclonus. *Am J Psychiatry* **134**, 90–91.

Lippman S, Tucker D, Wagemaker H *et al.* (1977b) A second report of tricyclic-induced myoclonus. *Am J Psychiatry* **134**, 585–586.

Litovitz TL, Troutman WG (1983) Amoxapine overdose: seizures and fatalities. *JAMA* **250**, 1069–1071.

Livingston RL, Zucker DK, Isenberg K, Wetzel RD (1983) Tricyclic antidepressants and delirium. *J Clin Psychiatry* **44**, 173–176.

Madhusoodanan S, Osnos R (1981) Amitriptyline induced hyponatremia: a case report. *Mount Sinai J Med* **48**, 431–433.

Mann AM, MacPherson A (1959) Clinical experience with imipramine (G22355) in the treatment of depression. *Can Psychiatr Assoc J* **4**, 38–47.

Martin AJ, Wakelin J (1986) Fluvoxamine: a baseline study of clinical response, long term tolerance and safety in a general practice population. *Br J Clin Pract*, **3**, 95–99.

Meador-Woodruff JH, Grunhaus L (1986) Profound behavioral toxicity due to tricyclic antidepressants. *J Nerv Ment Dis* **174**, 628–630.

Meador-Woodruff JH, Akil M, Wisner-Carlson R, Grunhaus L (1988) Behavioral and cognitive toxicity related to elevated plasma tricyclic antidepressant levels. *J Clin Psychopharmacol* **8**, 28–32.

Mezzich JE, Raab JS (1980) Depressive symptoms across the Americas. *Arch Gen Psychiatry* **37**, 818–823.

Mindham RHS, Howland DC, Shepherd M (1972) Continuation therapy with tricyclic antidepressants in depressive illness. *Lancet* **ii**, 854–855.

Mitchell JE, Popkin MK (1983) Antidepressant drug therapy and sexual dysfunction in men: a review. *J Clin Psychopharmacol* **3**, 76–79.

Modestin J (1985) Antidepressant therapy in depressed clinical suicides. *Acta Psychiatr Scand* **71**, 111–116.

Montassut M, Chertok L, Gachkel V, Ferran-Jarame M (1959) Essai d'interprétation clinique de l'action de l'imipramine. *Ann Méd Pschol* **212**, 288–299.

Montgomery SA, Bullock T (1991) Do noradrenaline uptake inhibitors provoke suicide? In Meltzer HY, Nerozzi D (eds) *Current Practices and Future Developments in the Pharmacotherapy of Mental Disorders*, Vol. 1, pp. 131–137. Amsterdam: Elsevier.

Montgomery SA, Pinder RM (1987) Do some antidepressants promote suicide? *Psychopharmacology* **92**, 265–266.

Montgomery SA, Roy D, Montgomery DB (1983) The prevention of recurrent suicidal acts. *Br J Clin Pharm* **15**, 1835–1885.

Montgomery SA, Dufour H, Brion S *et al.* (1988) The prophylactic efficacy of fluoxetine in unipolar depression. *Br J Psychiatry* **193** (Suppl. 3), 69–76.

Montgomery SA, Gabriel R, James D *et al.* (1989) The specificity of the zimelidine reaction. *Int Clin Psychopharmacol* **4**, 19–23.

Montgomery SA, Baldwin D, Fineberg N (1990) Relative toxicity of antidepressants using reports independent of observer bias. *Neuropsychopharmacology* 580–584.

Murphy DL (1977) The behavioral toxicity of monoamine oxidase inhibiting antidepressants. *Adv Pharmacol Chemother* **14**, 71–105.

Murphy GE, Woodruff RA, Herjanic N (1974) Variability of the clinical course of primary affective disorder. *Arch Gen Psychiatry* **30**, 757–761.

Nelson JC, Schottenfield RS, Condrad ED (1983) Hypomania after desipramine withdrawal. *Am J Psychiatry* **140**, 624–625.

Nicholson AN, Pascoe PA (1986) 5-Hydroxytryptamine and noradrenaline uptake inhibition: studies on sleep in man. *Neuropharmacology* **25**, 1079–1083.

Othmer E, Othmer S, Stern WC, Van Wyck-Fleet J (1983) Long term safety and efficacy of bupropion. *J Clin Psychiatry* **44**, 153–156.

Paykel, ES, Meuller PS, De La Vergne PM (1973) Amitriptyline, weight gain and carbohydrate craving: a side effect. *Br J Psychiatry,* **123**, 501–507.

Pinder RM (1988) The benefits and risks of antidepressant drugs. *Hum Psychopharmacol* **3**, 73–86.

Pledger DR, Mathew H (1989) Hyponatremia and clomipramine therapy. *Br J Psychiatry* **154**, 263–264.

Pohl R, Yeragani V, Ortiz A *et al.* (1986) Response of tricyclic induced jitteriness to a phenothiazine in two patients. *J Clin Psychiatry* **47**, 427.

Pollack MH, Rosenbaum, JF (1987) Management of antidepressant-induced side effects: a practical guide for the clinician. *J Clin Psychiatry* **48**, 3–8.

Prescott LF, Highley MS (1985) Drug prescribed for self poisoners. *Br Med J* **290**, 1633–1636.

Preskorn S, Jerkovich GS (1990) Central nervous system toxicity of tricyclic antidepressants: phenomenology, course risk factors, and role of therapeutic drug monitoring. *J Clin Psychopharmacol* **10**, 88–95.

Preskorn SH, Simpson S (1982) Tricyclic-induced delirium and plasma drug concentration. *Am J Psychiatry* **139**, 822–823.

Preskorn SH, Weller E, Jerkovich G *et al.* (1988) Depression in children: concentration-dependent CNS toxicity of tricyclic antidepressants. *Psychopharmacol Bull* **24**, 140–142.

Prien RF, Klett CJ, Caffey EM (1973) Lithium carbonate and imipramine in prevention of affective disorders. *Arch Gen Psychiatry* **29**, 420–425.

Prien RF, Kupfer DJ, Mansky PA *et al.* (1984) Drug therapy in the prevention of recurrences in unipolar and bipolar affective disorders. *Arch Gen Psychiatry* **41**, 1096–1104.

Quitkin FM, Kane J, Rifkin A *et al.* (1981) Prophylactic lithium carbonate with and without imipramine for bipolar I patients. *Arch Gen Psychiatry* **38**, 902–207.

Ranga Rama Krishnan K, France RD, Ellinwood EH (1984) Tricyclic-induced akathisia in patients taking conjugated estrogens. *Am J Psychiatry* **141**, 696–697.

Rosenbaum J (1984) Treatment of outpatients with desipramine. *J Clin Psychiatry* **45** 225–226.

Rossi AC, Knapp DE, Anello C *et al.* (1983) Discovery of adverse drug reactions: a comparison of selected phase IV studies with spontaneous reporting methods. *JAMA* **249**, 2226–2228.

Rouillon F, Phillips R, Serrurier D *et al* (1989) Rechutes des dépressions unipolaires et efficacité de la maprotiline. *L'Encéphale* **XV**, 527–534.

Rounsaville BJ, Prussoff BA, Padian N (1980) The course of non bipolar primary major depression: a prospective 16 month study of ambulatory patients. *J Nerv Ment Dis* **168**, 406–411.

Roy A (1982) Risk factors for suicide in psychiatric patients. *Arch Gen Psychiatry* **39**, 1089–1095.

Roy A (1984) Suicide in recurrent affective disorder patients. *Can J Psychiatry* **29**, 319–322.

Santos AB, Jr, McCurdy L (1980) Delirium after abrupt withdrawal from doxepin: case report. *Am J Psychiatry* **137**, 239–240.

Sathananthan GL, Gershon S (1973) Imipramine withdrawal: an akathisia-like syndrome. *Am J Psychiatry* **130**, 1286–1287.

Schmidt LG, Grohmann R, Muller-Oerlinghausen B *et al.* (1986) Adverse drug reactions to first and second generation antidepressants: a critical evaluation of drug. Surveillance data. *Br J Psychiatry* **143**, 38–43.

Seager CP, Bird RL (1962) Imipramine with ECT in depression: a controlled trial. *J Ment Sci* **108**, 704–707.

Shapiro RW, Keller MB (1981) Initial 6 month follow-up of patients with major depressive disorder. *J Affective Disord* **3**, 205–220.

Smith RC, Allen R, Gordon J, Wolff J (1983) A rating scale for tardive dyskinesia and parkinsonian symptoms. *Psychopharmacol Bull* **19**, 266–276.

Snyder SH, Yamamura HI (1977) Antidepressants and the muscarinic acetylcholine receptor. *Arch Gen Psychiatry* **34**, 236–239.

Solomon RL, Rich CL, Darko DF (1990) Antidepressant treatment and the occurrence of mania in bipolar patients admitted for depression. *J Affective Disord* **18**, 253–257.

Stein MK, Rickels K, Weise CC (1980) Maintenance therapy with amitriptyline: a controlled trial. *Am J Psychiatry* **137**, 370–371.

Teicher MH, Glod C, Cole JO (1990) Emergence of intense suicidal preoccupation during fluoxetine treatment. *Am J Psychiatry* **147**, 207–210.

van Praag H., De Hann S (1980) Depression vulnerability and 5-hydroxytryptophan prophylaxis. *Psychiatry Res* **3**, 75–83.

van Scheyen JC, Van Kammen DP (1979) Clomipramine-induced mania in unipolar depression. *Arch Gen Psychiatry* **36**, 560–565.

Warnock JK, Knesevitch JW (1988) Adverse cutaneous reactions to antidepressants. *Am J Psychiatry* **145**, 425–430.

Warrington SJ, Padgham C, Lader M (1989) The cardiovascular effects of antidepressants. *Psychol Med* (suppl.), 3–40.

Wehr TA, Goodwin FK (1987) Can antidepressants cause mania and worsen the course of affective illness? *Am J Psychiatry* **144**, 1403–1411.

Wehr TA, Sack DA, Rosenthal NE, Cowdry RW (1988) Rapid cycling affective disorder: contributing factors and treatment responses in 51 patients. *Am J Psychiatry*, **145**, 179–184.

Yassa R, Camille Y, Belzile L (1987) Tardive dyskinesia in the course of antidepressant therapy: a prevalence study and review of literature. *J Clin Psychopharmacol* **7**, 243–246.

6

Lithium and bipolar illness

Mohammed T. Abou-Saleh

Introduction

It was Hippocrates who first recognized melancholia as a form of madness in the fourth century BC. Its relationship to mania, however, was first observed by Areateus in the second century AD. Manic-depressive illness, as we recognize it nowadays, was first described independently by Baillarger, 'Folie a double forme', and Farlet, 'Folie circulaire', in 1854. Kraepelin perfected the classification of the functional psychoses, dementia praecox and manic-depresive psychosis. Under the rubric of manic-depressive psychosis he included Farlet's 'Folie circulaire' and all melancholic and manic illnesses, be they single or recurrent, and the variety of morbid fluctuations of mood, be they intermittent or enduring disorders.

The distinction between endogenous affective disorders with both depressive and manic phases (bipolar) and those disorders with recurrent episodes (unipolar) was first suggested by Leonhard *et al* (1962). Investigations by Perris (1966) and Angst (1966) carried out indepedently supported this distinction. Unipolar mania is an extreme variety and shows a similar genetic profile to bipolar depression and thus has been regarded as a random form of bipolar illness.

The unipolar–bipolar dichotomy is supported by genetic, physiological, biochemical, clinical pharmacological, personality and natural history differences between these two types (Perris, 1966). Bipolar illness is more homogeneous an entity than unipolar illness, with the latter showing heterogeneity in severity and

Long-term Treatment of Depression. Edited by S.A. Montgomery and F. Rouillon
© 1992 John Wiley & Sons Ltd

typology, including the controversial typology of neurotic/reactive-endogenous/psychotic distinction. Dunner *et al* (1976) suggested the distinction between bipolar I (severe mania requiring admission) and bipolar II (hypomania). This distinction has recently been supported by the findings of an extensive naturalistic study by Coryell and colleagues (1989), who showed that bipolar II disorder breeds true and is diagnostically stable, in distinction from bipolar I disorder. The study also found that bipolar II patients show complicated histories of psychopathology, with more schizotypal features, neurotic traits in the premorbid personality and more commonly suffer from substance misuse. Angst (1978), however, subclassified bipolar illness into three types: predominantly depressed (Dm), manic (Md), and a group suffering from severe mania and depression (MD). The status of cyclothymic personality disorder is controversial, but has been incorporated into the spectrum of affective disorders in DSM-III and considered a forme fruste of bipolar illness.

The treatment of bipolar illness is often successful and rewarding, with the development of specific and highly effective pharmacological treatment of acute episodes of mania and depression and their long-term management. There is no doubt that the introduction of lithium in the management of bipolar disorders has provided one of the most specific psychotropic drugs in psychiatric practice. It has contributed to the refinement of the major diagnostic distinction of schizophrenia vesus mania and unipolar versus bipolar illness and introduced the most important concept of long-term management of these disorders.

The scope of this chapter is to review briefly the natural history and course of bipolar illness and critically evaluate the place of lithium therapy in its management, particularly in the long-term, with emphasis on its efficacy and safety, optimum dosage and dosage regime and important aspects of its routine in psychiatric practice.

Natural history

The natural course of affective disorders has been well documented and comprehensively reviewed (Zis and Goodwin, 1979; Goodwin and Jamison, 1984). More recent studies have been reviewed by Keller (1987, 1988).

A review by Angst (1988) of 29 studies showed recovery rates of 23–93% over periods of 1–40 years. Recovery rates largely depend on the length of follow-up and the definition of recovery. Overall, these studies show similarity in recovery between bipolar and unipolar disorders. The NIMH programme on the psychobiology of depression, however, showed that manic patients recovered faster than those with index episodes which were purely depressive, whereas those with mixed or cyclic disorders recovered much more slowly. In unipolar illness, up to 79% of patients recovered by 24 months, increasing to 90% recovery by five years. In bipolar illness, slow recovery is indicated by increased severity, longer duration of symptoms and the presence of anxiety and alcohol morbidity.

Angst (1988) concluded from his survey of the literature that a single episode of mania is extremely rare, and bipolar patients experience about twice as many episodes as unipolar depressives. The methodological limitations of these studies have been discussed by Zis and Goodwin (1979) and there is evidence that bipolar patients have an increasing risk for recurrences as they grow older.

The first cycle (time from the beginning of one episode to the beginning of the next one) is considerably longer than subsequent ones. The later age of onset correlates with shorter cycle length, and bipolar illness starts with a shorter cycle length than unipolar depression. Cycle length, however, stabilizes after five episodes of illness. In unipolar illness, those with three or more previous episodes of illness show higher rates of recurrence and shorter well intervals. Noteworthy is that many patients show residual symptoms and psychosocial impairment between episodes of illness.

Chronicity of illness (non-remission for two years) occurs in 10–20% of bipolar and unipolar patients. Chronicity is associated with chronic physical illness in elderly patients. In the NIMH programme, bipolar patients showed a chronicity rate of 22% compared to 21% in non-bipolar patients, whereas those with mixed non-cyclic illness showed a risk of 32% remaining ill after one year.

There is a small literature on the clinical course of bipolar II disorder, which shows shorter and less severe episodes of illness than bipolar I, but a considerably higher relapse rate than unipolar patients.

Lithium therapy

The discovery of the prophylactic effects of lithium opened a new era in the management of affective disorders. Lithium in a number of controlled investigations of variable stringency has been shown to substantially reduce the long-term morbidity of recurrent affective disorders. As an antidepressant, lithium enjoys less popularity than conventional and new antidepressants, despite its established efficacy; 10 out of 13 studies showed lithium to be superior to placebo or as effective as tricyclic antidepressants (TCAs) (Fieve and Peselow, 1983). Lithium is more effective in bipolar than in unipolar depression, and in non-bipolar patients those with endogenous symptom profile, family history of mania and post-partum onset respond more favourably. Moreover, patients with bipolar depression who are treated with TCAs are at risk to suffer hypomanic episodes and in the minority it may provoke rapid cycling illness and lithium prophylaxis failure. Carbamazepine is a less effective antidepressant than lithium in bipolar depression. Bipolar depressive patients who fail to respond to lithium should receive adjunct antidepressant medication, preferably an activating antidepressant such as desipramine, for the commonly associated psychomotor retardation, a monoamine oxidase inhibitor (MAOI) or electroconvulsive therapy (ECT) whilst remaining on lithium to prevent them from switching into hypomania. The advantage of ECT is that it is less likely to contribute to the development of rapid cycling disorder.

Lithium in the treatment of acute mania

Lithium has an established place in the treatment of mania. Four placebo-controlled studies using the cross-over design showed lithium to be superior to placebo in mania. Seven out of nine trials compared lithium and chlorpromazine, and in two trials lithium was compared with haloperidol. These studies showed comparable efficacy for lithium and neuroleptics in the majority of manic patients. The largest of these studies was the multi-centre trial involving 255 patients, which showed chlorpromazine to be more effective than lithium in highly active manic patients, with similar efficacy in the less active ones (Prien *et al.*, 1972).

Lithium is the medication of choice in mania, except for the highly active agitated or disturbed patients, with whom neuroleptics are required for the rapid control of their condition, preferably in combination with lithium. Neuroleptics could then be withdrawn within two to three weeks, by which time lithium effects are established. This arrangement allows minimal exposure to neuroleptics and the use of lithium as continuation treatment for up to three months from recovery unless prophylaxis is indicated, when lithium is continued. Patients with affective disorders are highly vulnerable to develop tardive dyskinesia with brief intermittent exposure to neuroleptics (Mukherjee *et al.*, 1986). Neuroleptics or carbamazepine could, however, be solely used in the management of mania in those patients who are intolerant of lithium and if there is any possibility of pregnancy. The elderly tolerate lithium well, but are highly susceptible to neuroleptic parkinsonian side effects. Manic patients tolerate high doses of lithium due to increased influx into the intracellular space, with tolerance dropping with improvement in association with increased plasma lithium levels. This requires frequent monitoring of lithium levels to prevent intoxication during recovery.

Carbamazepine should be preferred to lithium in patients with neurological conditions such as epilepsy, Parkinson's disease, dementia and tardive dyskinesia and those with compromised cardiac and renal function. Carbamazepine, however, should be avoided in patients with liver disorder and haematopoietic diseases.

Predictors of acute response

Lithium is less effective in manic patients with paranoid-destructive features than those with grandiose-euphoric features (Murphy and Beigel, 1974). Among unipolar patients, those with cyclothymic personality traits, low neuroticism and atypical symptoms (increased appetite and hypersomnia) show more favourable responses than those without these features. Among the biological markers of antidepressant response studied, low platelet MAO activity, low baseline urinary MHPG and low cerebrospinal fluid (CSF) 5-hydroxyindole acetic acid (5-HIAA) have been shown to predict a good antidepressant response to lithium. All these variables, however, have been associated with bipolar status and are therefore not independent correlates of response.

Among manic patients, those with mood-incongruent psychotic symptoms respond less well to lithium. The recommendation that manic patients require higher dosages and plasma levels of lithium above 1.3 mmol/l has not been sustained. There is, however, evidence that manic patients retain lithium to a greater extent than other psychiatric patients. Bipolar patients who continue to show low platelet MAO activity following three weeks of lithium therapy have been shown to have a poor response to lithium (Sullivan *et al.*, 1977).

Lithium in schizoaffective disorders

Lithium is particularly effective in the affective component of schizoaffective disorder, particularly manic symptoms, whilst depressive symptoms are less responsive. There is little evidence that lithium has an antischizophrenic effect in patients with schizoaffective disorder, who often require a combination of lithium and antipsychotic medication. Within schizophrenic disorders, lithium has been shown to be effective in schizophreniform, periodic types which aetiologically may be related to affective disorders. Studies showed that patients with lithium-responsive schizophrenia have a higher familial incidence of affective disorders than those with lithium non-responsive schizophrenia (Sautter and Garver, 1984).

Prophylactic treatment

There is overwhelming evidence for the efficacy of lithium in the prophylaxis of bipolar illness: results of placebo-controlled studies showed that 20–40% of lithium-treated patients relapsed, in comparison to 70–85% of placebo-treated patients (Fieve and Peselow, 1983). Moreover, the aforementioned review of six studies demonstrated that significantly lower proportions of bipolar patients treated with lithium suffered depressive recurrences than those who were treated with placebo.

The efficacy of lithium for bipolar II disorder has been less well investigated. A study by Dunner *et al.* (1982) found lithium superior to placebo, whilst Kane *et al.* (1982) found it superior to imipramine, particularly in preventing manic and hypomanic relapses. Peselow *et al.* (1982), in a retrospective study over two years, however, reported limited efficacy for lithium in bipolar II and cyclothymic patients: 51% of bipolar II and 69% of cyclothymic patients relapsed, in comparison to 64% of unipolar patients.

Prien and co-workers (1984) have recently reported the results of the National Insitute of Mental Health's multi-centre collaborative study comparing lithium, imipramine and their combination in the prophylaxis of unipolar and bipolar illnesses. With bipolar patients, lithium and the combination were superior to imipramine in preventing manic recurrences and were as effective as imipramine in preventing depressive episodes. With unipolar patients, imipramine and the combination treatment were more effective than lithium carbonate or placebo in preventing depressive recurrences. Lithium was superior to placebo in the moderately ill unipolar and no more effective than placebo in the severely ill unipolar patients. The patients involved in the investigation, however, were described as atypical, with a few clear-cut episodes in which the patients were well, which may account for the finding that lithium was no better than placebo in the severely ill unipolar patients. There has been only one study in which the usefulness of lithium was compared with that of long-acting neuroleptic medication in patients with bipolar illness. A Scandinavian multi-centre investigation (Ahlfors *et al.*, 1981) evaluated the efficacy of flupenthixol decanoate and lithium in preventing manic and depressive relapses. Flupenthixol was found as effective as lithium in reducing the frequency of manic episodes, but not as effective in preventing depressive episodes. The study suggested that flupenthixol may be useful with patients who have failed to respond to lithium or not have tolerated it.

Predictors of response to prophylactic lithium (Table I)

The evaluation of long-term outcome of treatment, as in lithium prophylaxis, is fraught with difficulties: it is likely to be biased in favour of the treatment due to the non-specific treatment factors and the tendency among affective disorders for spontaneous recovery. This notion must be set against the tendency of these disorders to recur more often with increasing age. Another methodological difficulty is the measurement of long-term treatment outcome. Most studies have determined outcome by the rate of relapses and fewer studies have used global measures of clinical state. The definition of relapse and lithium-modified

Table I.   Predictors of response to lithium in bipolar illness

A.   Good response is associated with:
 1. Grandious euphoric mania
 2. Mania with mood-congruent psychotic features
 3. Family history of mania
 4. Absence of personality neurotic traits
 5. Restoration to normality between episodes of illness
 6. Rapid onset of retarded depression
 7. Preserved family/social network
 8. High red blood cell/plasma lithium ratio
 9. Augmenting average evoked potential
 10. Good initial response over 6–12 months
 11. Non-suppression to dexamethasone

B.   Poor response is associated with:
 1. Rapid-cycling bipolar illness, slow onset and chronic depression
 2. Alcoholism/drug misuse
 3. Secondary depression
 4. Hypothyroidism
 5. Folate deficiency
 6. Mood-incongruent psychotic features
 7. Marked subjective side effects
 8. Mixed manic and depressive symptoms
 9. Family history of schizophrenia or alcoholism
 10. Severe depressive illness

episodes is not standardized to make meaningful comparisons between the results of different studies.

Clinical predictors

Among bipolar patients, those with frequent episodes (rapid cycling patients) show a greater incidence of prophylaxis failure than those with non-rapid cycling illness (Dunner and Fieve, 1974). Dunner, *et al.* (1976) studied clinical predictors of prophylaxis failure in non-rapid cycling bipolar patients. Whilst none of the clinical variables studied predicted outcome, they observed that patients who received lithium had a similar failure rate to those on placebo in the first six months of treatment. A quarter of their patients had early failure of treatment (within three months) and this tended to predict earlier failure during their continued lithium treatment.

Studies by the author of the long-term outcome of recurrent affective disorder on lithium showed that the most powerful predictor of outcome was empirical: outcome over the first six months and the first year predicted long-term outcome over 2–14 years (Abou-Saleh and Coppen, 1986; Abou-Saleh and Coppen, 1990).

Among the clinical features of affective state investigated, marked psychomotor retardation (a common feature in bipolar depression) was found to be associated with better response (Dunner and Fieve, 1974); whilst paranoid symptoms correlated with a poor response (Abou-Saleh 1980). Studies have reported an association between the presence of family history of bipolar illness and favourable response to lithium (Mendlewicz *et al.*, 1973). A family history of non-bipolar affective disorder was not, however, associated with a more favourable response (Dunner *et al.*, 1976; Abou-Saleh, 1980).

Psychological predictors

Psychological factors have been studied mainly in relation to short-term response to lithium. Two studies examined MMPI profiles of lithium responders and non-responders in a prophylactic situation (Ananth *et al.*, 1979; Burdick *et al.*, 1980) and reported conflicting results. Responders had higher scores on scales of psychopathic deviance and paranoia. The other study used the lithium response scales derived by the aforementioned group and failed to predict outcome (Burdick and Holmes, 1980).

On the Eysenck Personality Questionnaire, responders to lithium had significantly lower neuroticism scores than non-responders in bipolar patients (Abou-Saleh, 1983).

On the Crown–Crisp Experiential Index, responders to lithium had significantly higher obsessionality scores than non-responders (Maj *et al.*, 1984), which confirmed a similar finding by an earlier study in relation to short-term response (Kerry and Orme, 1979). This was interpreted in terms of better compliance in those with obsessional tendencies and thus more likelihood of favourable response. Indeed on the MMPI favourable short-term antidepressant response was associated with higher scores on the acquiescence scale, indicating greater conformity with a pill-taking regime (Steinbrook and Chapman, (1970). On the Foulds Personality Deviance Scale responders to prophylactic lithium had significantly higher dominance scores than non-responders (Abou-Saleh, 1983).

It has been claimed that responders show premorbid mood lability whilst non-responders have premorbid traits of chronic anxiety and obsessiveness (Kupfer *et al.*, 1975; Ananth *et al.*, 1979). On the Marke–Nyman Temperament Scale responders had significantly higher validity and significantly lower stability scores than non-responders (Bech *et al.*, 1976).

Studies have indicated few clinical and psychological predictors of response to prophylactic lithium (Abou-Saleh and Coppen, 1986; Abou-Saleh and Coppen, 1990). In these open studies among unipolar patients, those with endogenous and psychotic features have a better response compared with those with non-endogenous illness. Moreover, patients with pure familial depressive disease (with family history of depression) had comparatively better response than those with sporadic depressive (no family history of depression) and depression spectrum disease (family history of alcoholism or sociopathy). In both bipolar and unipolar patients, those with greater disturbance in their personality characteristics, including neuroticism, introversion, less drive and less self-confidence, responded less well than those with less personality disturbance. A recent study (Coppen and Abou-Saleh, 1988) indicated that lithium in lower doses and levels of 0.45–0.6 mmol/l was highly effective: no or slight morbidity was observed in 78% of unipolar and 73% of bipolar and schizoaffective patients studied for the duration of one year. Moreover, lithium was as effective in the elderly with recurrent affective disorders (aged more than 70 years) as in young and middle-aged patients. Unipolar patients rated as endogenous on the Newcastle scale showed significantly less morbidity than the non-endogenous patients.

Pharmacokinetic predictors

The adequacy of a particular lithium dosage for the individual patient is best determined by the serum level achieved by the daily dosage.

Prien and colleagues (1972), in a retrospective study of a high-risk group of 32 patients over two years, found that 55% of patients maintained on levels of 0.7 mmol/l or less had relapsed compared with 14% of patients maintained on higher levels.

Jerram and McDonald (1978) carried out an open prospective study over one year in which they investigated the efficacy (relapse rates) in groups of bipolar and unipolar patients maintained at three different lithium levels. Relapse rates showed a marked increase in the group maintained at levels between 0.25 and 0.39 mmol/l, indicating that a lithium level of 0.4 mmol/l is probably the minimum effective level.

Waters and colleagues (1982), in the first double-blind study, examined relapse rates of bipolar patients who were randomly assigned to lower levels (0.3–0.8 mmol/l) and higher levels (0.8–1.4 mmol/l) of lithium. Patients in each group were followed up for six months before being switched over to the other group for another six months. They found that significantly more of the relapses (83%) occurred during the low-level phase (mean 0.51 mmol/l), with only 17% occurring during the high-level phase (mean 0.99 mmol/l) of the trial.

A recent study from the USA suggested that bipolar patients require higher dosages to achieve plasma levels of 0.7 mmol/l (Gelenberg *et al.*, 1989). These workers have not, however, evaluated the efficacy of the middle range of levels between 0.6 and 0.8 mmol/l.

In our own study (Abou-Saleh and Coppen, 1989) we examined the morbidity and side effects in 72 patients with recurrent affective disorder under double-blind conditions over a period of one year. The patients had been previously maintained on lithium dosages to give 12-h plasma lithium levels of 0.8–1.2 mmol/l. The patients were randomly allocated either to remain on their previous dosage or to receive a 25% or 50% reduction in dose. No patient had a 12-h serum lithium level of less than 0.45 mmol/l. Morbidity was assessed by a composite index which included measures of severity and duration of symptoms. We found that patients who were maintained at lower serum levels below 0.79 mmol/l had significant reduction in their morbidity (34%) whilst those who remained at levels of 0.8 mmol/l and above had a slight increase in morbidity. Similar results were found for both the unipolar and bipolar patients, except that in the former group those with non-endogenous illness had a more substantial reduction in morbidity (58%). These changes in morbidity were not related to changes in unwanted effects or the prescription of extra medication. The study, however, included patients who were not maintained solely on lithium. Patients who were maintained on plasma levels between 0.45 and 0.79 mmol/l following a 25–50% reduction of dosage experienced fewer side effects, most notable in their complaints of tremor. Patients' weight was lower on lower levels of lithium. Measurements were also made of the patients' plasma thyrotropin (TSH) levels and their 24-h urinary volumes before and after starting the trial. It was found that patients who were maintained on lower plasma levels during the trial had significant reductions in both measures during the trial, indicating a reduction in adverse effects on thyroid and renal functions.

The study by Milln and Patch (1988) using a similar design to the study by Coppen and colleagues (1983) failed to confirm these findings: patients who had 50% reduction in dosage (minimum plasmal levels of 0.3 mmol/l) showed a significantly greater rate of relapse (58%) than those who had no reduction in dosage (17%).

Biological predictors

Suboptimal thyroid function and hypothyroidism has been related to prophylaxis failure: thyroid hypofunction was shown to occur in patients who suffered recurrences including those who have developed rapid cycling bipolar disorder (Extein *et al.*, 1982). Moreover, Coppen and Swade (1986) showed that patients with high TSH levels without hypothyroidism suffered greater affective morbidity during prophylaxis.

A study of biological predictions of response (Abou-Saleh and Coppen, 1989) showed no connection between dexamethasone suppression test and response. Serotonin (5-hydroxytryptamine, 5-HT) transport into platelet, however, predicted response; patients who had an increase in V_{max} had lower long-term morbidity than those with decreased V_{max}.

Platelet MAO activity in bipolar patients was not associated with response to prophylactic lithium (Abou-Saleh, 1983). Good response was, however, observed in those with increased calcium binding to red blood cells (Abou-Saleh,

1980). Increased red blood cell/plasma lithium ratio and low frequency of HLA-A3 antigen was shown to predict good response over two years in a study of 100 bipolar and unipolar patients (Maj *et al.*, 1984).

Indications for prophylactic treatment

A crucial decision for the clinician is when to start prophylactic lithium. A detailed and profound discussion of this topic was put forward by Angst (1981), who decided that it would be desirable to start prophylaxis if a patient was likely to suffer two further episodes in addition to the present one in the subsequent five years. Numerous criteria were examined to see which identified those patients at risk, and the conclusions were surprisingly simple: the presence of one episode in the previous five years in unipolars, in the previous four years in bipolars and in the previous three years in schizoaffectives fulfilled this criteriton for starting prophylactic treatment. The World Health Organization has recently provided guidelines based on these findings: prophylactic treatment should be started in unipolar depression after three episodes, particularly if there was one discrete episode within the last five years, apart from the present episode. In bipolar illness, prophylactic treatment should be given after the second episode.

Management of prophylaxis failure

Schou (1985) has argued that complete response to lithium occurs in 30–60% of patients, partial response in 30–50% and lack of response in 10–20% of patients. Response should be evaluated in relation to previous morbidity prior to starting lithium, e.g. a patient who has many relapses during lithium treatment might still be a relatively good responder as he might have had more frequent relapses if lithium had not been started. Schou has suggested that incomplete or unsatisfactory response to lithium may have many causes, including non-compliance, discontinuation against medical advice, gradual onset of the prophylactic action, non-adjustment of dosage, hypothyroidism, and the need for supplementary or alternative treatment. The clinician confronted with a patient with incomplete response should bear all these factors in mind before discontinuing lithium. Goodwin and Roy-Byrne (1987) provided guidelines for the management of breakthrough mania and depression. For breakthrough mania, an increase in lithium dosage to a maximum tolerable dose level should be the first line of treatment. Alternatively, neuroleptics or carbamazepine should be added to lithium. For breakthrough depression, a re-evaluation is required: thyroid function, development of physical illness and change in the patient's life situation. Lithium dose could be increased to achieve levels above 1.0 mmol/l.

The addition of thyroxine could also be considered even with a normal range of plasma thryoxine. Coppen and Swade (1986) showed an association between affective morbidity during lithium therapy and higher plasma thyrotropin levels and suggested that suboptimal thyroid function may contribute to this morbidity. Those with severe episodes could be treated with antidepressants or ECT.

Coppen and colleagues (1986) have recently suggested that folic acid enhances the effects of prophylactic lithium. In a double-blind trial, folic acid given in physiological dosages (0.2 mg per day) was evaluated in comparison with placebo in a group of 75 patients receiving prophylactic lithium. It was found that patients with the highest plasma folate concentrations during the trial showed a significant reduction in their affective morbidity: patients who had their folate levels increased to 13 ng/ml or above had 40% reduction in their morbidity.

Aagaard and Vestergaard (1990), in a two-year prospective study, showed that non-adherence to treatment was mainly predicted by substance abuse and many earlier admissions. Non-response in those who adhered to treatment was mainly predicted by female sex, younger age and a previous chronic course. A third of the population of patients studied, however, had a chronic illness and half showed social deterioration prior to starting lithium. Life events in the 12 months prior to starting lithium had no influence on outcome on lithium, confirming the findings of Hall *et al.* (1977), who also found that those who relapsed had no more life events prior to their relapse than at other times. Priebe *et al.* (1989), however, showed that patients living with high expressed emotion relatives had worse outcome.

Management of compliance

Poor compliance with lithium is the main reason for prophylaxis failure. This occurs in younger, particularly male patients, with fewer episodes of illness. Reasons given by patients who stop lithium include side effects, missing the 'highs', feeling less creative or productive, feeling well with no need to take lithium or being bothered by the idea that their moods are controlled by medication. Less frequently cited side effects as reasons from discontinuing lithium are weight gain, increased thirst, tiredness, tremor, difficulties with memory, poor concentration and loss of enthusiasm (Jamison, 1987a).

Jamison (1987a) provided guidelines for maximizing lithium compliance, which include monitoring of compliance with frequent enquiries, regular measurement of lithium levels and encouragement of patients to express their concerns about their treatment. Patients should be forewarned of side effects, maintained on minimal effective levels and on a once per day dosage regime. Involving the family in therapy and the use of self-help groups may also be indicated. Cognitive psychotherapy was shown to improve compliance in patients. Jamison (1987b) advocated the use of psychotherapy with lithium in view of the serious personal, interpersonal and social consequences of the severe and recurrent affective disorders. Psychotherapy for these patients requires considerable flexibility of style and technique, aiming to enhance the patients' sense of control over his illness, over and above the effects of lithium. Themes which often emerge in therapy include the loss of 'highs', productivity, creativity, decreased sexuality, fears of recurrence, denial of illness, effects of illness on family, the risk for children and the developmental difficulties in those with early-onset illnesses involving their individuation, development of intimate relationships and loss of career opportunities.

Numerous self-help groups and organizations provide advice and support to patients and their families.

Side effects

Commonly reported side effects in the early stage (within six weeks of starting lithium) include nausea, loose stools, fatigue, muscle weakness, polydipsia, polyuria and hand tremor. During maintenance, weight gain, mild memory impairment and hand tremor are common complaints and polydipsia and polyuria may persist. The rate of occurrence of these side effects and their severity are related to plasma lithium concentrations. Similar complaints, however, have been reported in patients who have received placebo, suggesting that these 'side effects' are also symptoms of depression. Abou-Saleh and Coppen (1983) investigated subjective side effects in patients receiving lithium, drug-free depressed patients and normal control subjects. Side effects reported showed a strong association with the presence of depression and personality disturbance in those patients. The reliability of side effects as rated by clinicians and patients is moderate, with the clinicians rating side effects less often and less severe than the patients themselves (Wancata *et al.*, 1988). Bech *et al.* (1976) showed that patients who received TCAs and neuroleptics complained of more side effects than those on lithium alone or patients who discontinued their lithium. Troublesome lithium tremor improves with propranolol whilst the management of weight gain is more difficult due to the increased craving for carbohydrates and consumption of high-calorie drinks.

Thyroid effects

Only a small percentage of patients develop hypothyroidism or clinical goitre. The frequency of hypothyroidism is around 5% and varies between studies in relation to sample size and criteria for diagnosing hypothyroidism. Thyrotropin concentrations are increased in 10–15% of patients. Women are more susceptible to develop hypothyroidism than men. This may be related to increased disposition of women to develop autoimmune thyroid disease in middle age. Indeed pre-existing thyroid disease is the major vulnerability factor for development of hypothyroidism during lithium therapy. Coppen and Abou-Saleh (1988) studied thyroid function in 125 patients receiving low-dose/plasma levels of lithium. Women had significantly higher levels of thyroid-stimulating hormone (TSH) than men, and all four patients with abnormally high TSH levels were unipolar women. Of the 11 patients who received replacement thyroxine, 10 were unipolar patients.

Thyroid dysfunction has been related to increased affective morbidity during prophylactic lithium and implicated in the development of rapid-cycling bipolar disorder.

Lithium and renal function

Renal morphological abnormalities (sclerotic glomeruli, focal nephron atrophy and interstitial fibrosis) occur in a considerable proportion of patients on lithium. The results from five studies involving 124 patients showed a variable percentage of abnormal biopsies (range 16–100%): in studies where patients were selected on the basis of reduced kidney function, all biopsy specimens were abnormal, but a low rate of abnormality (16%) in studies where patients were selected on the basis of time on lithium (Bendz, 1983). Overall, 5–10% of patients on prophylactic lithium develop tubulo-interstitial nephropathy complicated with glomerular pathology. There is no evidence that these changes are conducive to renal insufficiency. The rare incidents of renal failure on lithium were attributed to lithium intoxication or other causes. Glomerular filtration rate, as determined by 24-hour creatinine clearance, was shown to be abnormal (clearance below 70 ml/min) in 23% of cases (range 3–60%) in four studies involving 567 patients. Polyuria (24-hour urine volume greater than 3 litres) occurred in 29% of patients (mean of ten studies involving 78 patients, range 1–57%). Renal concentrating ability was impaired in 33% of patients.

Coppen and his colleagues (1980), however, found little difference in kidney function between lithium-treated patients and patients with affective disorders who were never treated with lithium. The only difference shown was increased urinary volume in lithium-treated patients.

These investigations suggest that there are potential hazards in the use of lithium that call for careful screening for evidence of renal disease before starting therapy. Patients with polyuria appear to be a high-risk group who need more regular monitoring of plasma lithium and kidney function.

Lithium has a long elimination half-life (12–24 hours), indicating that it need not be prescribed in more than one single dose per day, which alone encourages better compliance.

Lithium intoxication

Prodromal symptoms and signs of lithium intoxication include nausea, vomiting, diarrhoea, coarse tremor, sluggishness and dysarthria, which occur if plasma lithium levels exceed 1.5 mmol/l. Plasma lithium levels exceeding 2.0 mmol/l are associated with moderate to severe intoxication with manifestations of clouded consciousness, muscular hypertonia, fasciculation, coarse tremor, hyperreflexia, epileptiform seizures and, finally, a comatose state.

Management of lithium poisoning is primarily determined by the plasma levels: patients with levels of 4.0 mmol/l and above, and levels of 2–4 mmol/l associated with kidney disease or renal failure, require peritoneal dialysis or haemodialysis.

Plasma lithium levels of 2–4 mmol/l in patients with normal renal function can be managed by: (1) close monitoring of plasma lithium and other electrolyte concentrations, particularly sodium, whilst potassium concentration is best monitored on the ECG; (2) infusion of saline if the patient shows hyponatraemia (low plasma sodium causes a decrease in lithium clearance); (3) induction of diuresis using osmotic diuretics such as urea and mannitol with alkalinization of urine; (4) general cardiopulmonary corrective measures and measurement of fluid input/output.

Lithium interactions

Lithium in therapeutic dosages shows several pharmacological interactions. The drug interacts synergistically with antithyroid medication used in the treatment of hyperthyroidism; with potassium chloride it may induce hypothyroidism.

The most alarming interaction is the observed neurotoxicity in patients receiving lithium combined with antipsychotic drugs, particularly haloperidol (Cohen and Cohen, 1974). These patients, however, suffered from other pathology that could account for these findings. Whether this interaction is due to lithium, neuroleptics or their combination remains uncertain. Neurotoxicity reactions casued by lithium toxicity are similar to those reported on combined lithium and neuroleptics in their clinical features and prognosis. Moreover, these two syndromes are similar to neuroleptic malignant syndrome (NMS), except for the very high fever and high concentations of creatinine phosphokinase in patients with NMS. Although these interactions are rare, it would be prudent to monitor patients for the possibility of their occurrence when combined lithium and neuroleptics are used, particularly in higher dosages. Neurotoxicity reactions have also been reported on lithium combined with carbamazepine. Lithium, however, may counteract the effect of carbamazepine to cause leucopenia, whilst carbamazepine may reduce lithium-induced polyurea.

Lithium may interact with beta-blockers, resulting in the slowing of heart rate, and similar interactions have been noted when lithium is combined with digoxin, with reports of increased risk of sudden cardiovascular death on this combination in predisposed patients.

Thiazide diuretics reduce renal lithium clearance and increase plasma lithium levels by reducing plasma volume, causing an increase in lithium and sodium reabsorption. This interaction is not observed with potassium-sparing diuretics and loop diuretics such as furosemide. Amiloride, however, has been used for treating lithium-induced polyuria and diabetes insipidus. Acetazolamide and osmotic diuretics, however, increase renal lithium excretion and have been used to treat lithium toxicity.

Finally, the widely used non-steroidal anti-inflammatory drugs have been reported to reduce lithium clearance and increase plasma levels, except for aspirin and sulindac. Indomethacin, however, has been used to treat lithium-induced polyuria.

Pregnancy

An international register of lithium babies was started in 1970, showing a high rate of congenital malformation (11%), mostly cardiovascular, in babies exposed to lithium during the first trimester of pregnancy.

Nursing mothers receiving lithium secrete it in considerable concentrations in their breast milk (30–100% of the mother's plasma concentrations). Breast feeding should, therefore, be discouraged. It has been suggested, however, that there is little likelihood that a few additional weeks of lithium exposure adds much in the way of developmental risk for an infant already exposed in utero.

Weinstein (1980) provided guidelines for the management of lithium therapy prior to and during pregnancy.

Women with childbearing potential should be informed of the teratogenic effects and therefore encouraged to avoid pregnancy or inform their doctors if they decide to become pregnant; a pregnancy test is an essential screening test prior to starting lithium. Lithium should be stopped before conception and as soon as possible after the unplanned pregnancy is discovered.

The risk of relapse after lithium withdrawal appears lower in the earlier part of pregnancy. If lithium is introduced after the first trimester of pregnancy, then plasma lithium levels should be monitored more frequently, particularly in the last few weeks of pregnancy, in view of its increased clearance and renal elimination. The lithium dose should be reduced to 50% in the last week of pregnancy and stopped at the onset of labour to prevent lithium intoxication. Lithium could then be reintroduced within the first week post-partum to avoid post-partum relapses.

The dosage regimen

Lithium has a long elimination half-life (12–24 hours), indicating that it need not be prescribed in more than one single dose per day.

Single daily and divided daily dosage regimes produce quite different profiles of serum lithium levels over 24 hours. Lauritsen and colleagues (1981) showed that patients who were maintained on a single daily dosage regimen had early sharp peak lithium levels within 2–4 hours of ingestion of the drug, but had lower levels in the second 12 hours of the day. Patients who had received a similar, but divided daily dosage regimen, however, showed smaller peaks and had a relatively constant level throughout the 24 hours. The two groups had identical mean 12-hour and mean average levels over 24 hours.

Studies of the relationship between the dosage regimen and renal function followed. Plenge *et al.* (1982) found that 24-hour urinary volume showed no association with maximum or 12-hour lithium levels, but was associated with minimal plasma levels: patients who had the greatest 24-hour urine volumes had the highest minimum plasma levels. These preliminary findings were confirmed in a study in which they found that the functional and structural changes were most pronounced in the group of patients who received their lithium in divided doses. They concluded that to avoid kidney damage during long-term lithium treatment, it may be more important to have regular periods with low levels than it is to avoid peaks and they have accordingly strongly advocated a single daily dosage regimen.

Schou and colleagues (1982) instigated a similar study in collaboration with the Copenhagen group, to compare patients who had throughout received a slow-release preparation in a divided dosage regimen, with patients treated by the Copenhagen group with a conventional preparation in a single daily dosage regimen. It was noted that the Copenhagen group of patients were on average older, and had been on lithium for longer and had slightly higher mean plasma concentrations. The results indicated that the dosage regimen had no effect on glomerular function (creatinine clearance) but did influence tubular function as indexed by the 24-hour urinary volume, which was lower in the Copenhagen group. None of these studies, however, were carried out within the same clinic with random allocation of treatment regimen in conjunction with the assessment of clinical and unwanted effects.

These findings suggested that a dosage regimen with even longer intervals between doses, i.e. every second or third day, may be as effective as a daily regimen and less harmful on the kidney. Indeed Jensen and colleagues (1990) evaluated the efficacy and side effects of lithium given every other day in an open study of 10 patients with median duration of 13 months. There was no change in morbidity and side effects were significantly reduced. Such a departure from a daily dosage regimen may lead to less compliance, unless, of course, dummy tablets were to be given on the non-dosage days.

Mortality on lithium

Affective disorders are associated with high mortality: studies have shown that 15% of depressed patients die by suicide and there is an additional increased risk for death by cardiovascular disease and secondary alcoholism. Treatment with lithium exerts a protective effect and lowers the rate of suicide and attempted suicide during prophylaxis (Causemann and Muller-Oerlinghausen, 1988). Norton and Whalley (1984) in a naturalistic study of mortality in 791 subjects treated with lithium observed a standardized mortality rate of 2.83 with excess mortality by suicide in the younger age group (36 times) and cardiovascular disease in the older age group (2.15 times), but no death from nephritis, cancer or leukaemia. Worthy of note was that all 8 suicides had made previous suicide attempts and 3 of these 8 suicides occurred within three months of starting lithium. They also compared the 33 deaths with 33 matched patients selected from the 751 survivors and showed that patients who died on lithium had more severe psychiatric illness and showed more signs of physical disease than the controls: 9 out of 14 patients who died of cardiovascular disease had clinical abnormalities attributable to disease of the cardiovascular system, which was present before the introduction of lithium. The authors indicated the value of careful history taking in the examination of the cardiovascular system with measurement of blood pressure, recording of electrocardiogram and chest X-ray, before starting lithium, and the close monitoring of lithium-treated patients with cardiovascular abnormalities. The findings by Norton and Whalley (1984) contrast with the results of a recent study by Coppen and colleagues (1990) of 104 patients attending the lithium clinic who were followed up for ten years, who showed significantly lower mortality than would be expected from age/sex/year-specific rates for England and Wales. No patient died from suicide. These results suggest a protective effect for lithium.

The occurrence of sudden death in patients on lithium has been related to its effects on cardiac conduction mechanisms (Shopsin *et al.*, 1979).

The routine of lithium therapy

The routine of lithium therapy as a long-term, if not a life-time treatment, involves a number of important steps from the decision to refer patients for assessment by the general practitioner, assessment and screening procedures, indication for commencement of prophylactic therapy, monitoring progress, management of compliance, relapse and side effects and finally the decision to terminate treatment.

Assessment

Referrals for assessment for lithium therapy are often secondary and tertiary ones and very few general practitioners undertake such assessment and initiate treatment. Bipolar patients are invariably referred to psychiatric clinics or, where available, the lithium clinic by their general practitioners; patients with unipolar illnesses are often treated by the general practitioner.

Assessment prior to starting treatment should be thorough and based on the history obtained from the patient and relatives and mental state examination. The assessment of patients involves general psychiatric assessment, with particular emphasis on age of onset, symptom pattern, frequency of episodes, the course of illness, family history and physical condition. Patients with bipolar illness almost invariably receive prophylactic lithium, whilst patients with unipolar illness may also be considered for prophylactic antidepressant medication (Table III).

The list of routine investigations done prior to starting lithium and during treatment is shown in Table II.

Table II.   Routine assessments/investigations prior to starting lithium

- Physical examination
- Haematology and clinical chemistry, including urea, creatinine, electrolytes, thyroxin and TSH, urine test
- Weight
- Pregnancy test if necessary
- ECG

Routine investigations, during treatment	Frequency
• Physical examination, ECG, full blood count, 24-hour urine volume	Once a year
• Clinical chemistry, urea, creatinine, thyroxine, TSH and urine test	Six-monthly
• Weight and electrolytes	With each lithium estimation

Monitoring progress

Once initiated, lithium should be estimated on a weekly basis to adjust dosage to achieve therapeutic plasma levels of 0.6–1 mmol/l. This is particularly important if lithium is started during a manic episode, in view of the fluctuations in plasma lithium levels with increased influx into the intracellular space, resulting in higher plasma levels with the resolution of the illness. The occurrence of side effects is monitored closely for the adjustment of dosage and the reassurance of patients. Once a reproducible plasma lithium level is obtained, patients are monitored less frequently at six to eight-weekly intervals. More careful and close monitoring is indicated in patients with thyroid, cardiovascular and renal disease. Patients should be monitored closely during periods of dieting and advised to ensure adequate hydration and intake of salt during excessive exercise. Those undergoing surgery will require the reduction of dosage to withdrawal for 24 hours before surgery. It could be restarted once fluid and electrolyte balance is restored to normal.

Termination of lithium therapy

There are no guidelines for the termination of lithium therapy and once started it could be continued indefinitely. The decision to stop lithium by the treating clinician is often related to the development of serious side effects or adverse effects, such as renal toxicity as well as situations when it is clearly of no benefit to the patient. Occasionally, patients instigate this termination and more often drop out from treatment for a variety of reasons. Patients who are likely to relapse are those who have not been well controlled on lithium, those who discontinued whilst on extra medication and those with a history of many previous episodes of illness. Greil and Schmidt (1988) found that patients who were maintained on antidepressants and neuroleptics in addition to lithium relapsed in 83% of cases, in contrast to 27% of those who were maintained on lithium alone.

The question whether there is a lithium withdrawal syndrome has not been satisfactorily resolved. A few studies have reported the occurrence of anxiety, irritability, headache, insomnia, fatigue, nausea, diarrhoea and blurred vision within days of stopping lithium. Some of these patients progressed to experience a full-blown episode of illness, whilst others did not (Greil et al., 1982). Whether these symptoms are related to anticipatory anxiety is uncertain. Sashidharan and McGuire (1983) argued against the notion of the lithium withdrawal syndrome on the basis of their findings of a discontinuation study: early relapses were part of the pattern of recurrences occurring over time, with no evidence of rebound episodes of illness. All lithium-related side effects start to subside after discontinuing, with renal concentrating ability and thyroid suppression showing a gradual recovery over a few weeks.

The lithium clinic

The complexities of the management of patients with affective disorders demands the expertise of a team that includes psychiatrists, nurses, social workers and laboratory technicians. These complexities are partly inherent in the nature of these illnesses and the nature of lithium therapy as the main long-term treatment.

The concept of the lithium clinic was pioneered by psychiatrists who carried out the earlier studies on its efficacy in the 1960s, and was part of the movement for the establishment of specialist clinics for patients with conditions such as diabetes, epilepsy and schizophrenia. Lithium-treated patients were also commonly treated in general psychiatric clinics. The proportion of lithium-treated patients managed by their general practitioners is unknown, but presumably small. These clinics serve a number of functions. Primarily they provide expert assessment and treatment settings in which patients' treatment is supervised and their plasma lithium levels monitored on a regular basis, with regular monitoring of thyroid and renal functions. A few clinics, however, provide education to patients and their families on the nature of their condition and the benefits/hazards of lithium therapy. They are often tertiary referral centres, receiving referrals from general psychiatrists and are manned by psychiatrists, nurses, social workers and occasionally laboratory technicians. Some of these clinics have also provided the setting for quality research on lithium. It is estimated that there are at least 200 lithium clinics in the USA, with the large majority based in the university centres and commonly manned by specialist nurses under supervision from psychiatrists. In addition to all the aforementioned functions, these clinics provide psychotherapy services and support groups for patients and their relatives. Studies in the USA have reported greater treatment compliance rate, lower rate of recurrence and fewer episodes of toxicity in patients attending these clinics compared to those attending general psychiatric clinics. Studies in the UK reported similar findings. A recent study which compared a lithium clinic with psychiatric out-patients clinics and general practice supervision found that the lithium clinic provided closest supervision and best control of plasma lithium at a lower mean level. Moreover, glomerular impairment occurred more often in general practice patients who were prescribed their lithium once daily (Masterton *et al.*, 1988).

Lithium clinics are often held in the mornings, an ideal arrangement, which allows measurement of plasma lithium levels 12 hours after the last dose. On arrival, patients have their blood taken for on-the-spot lithium estimation in the close-by laboratory. The patient then joins fellow patients in the waiting room, which provides informal contact and a 'therapeutic milieu': patients who are ill are reassured and encouraged by those who are well, with access to the attending nurse and social worker as required. This time is also used for weighing and, if required, the completion of rating scales/side-effects checklist. Once the plasma level is estimated, they are seen by the clinician for an assessment of their physical and psychiatric status, including their experience of side effects, adjustment of dosage, the prescription of extra medication if necessary and arrangement of routine laboratory investigations and supportive psychotherapy.

Table III.   Indications for lithium therapy

1. *Acute mania:* alone or in combination with neuroleptics for overactive, disturbed and paranoid patients, who could be withdrawn from neuroleptics within two to three weeks and continued on lithium for at least three months after full remission

2. *Acute depression:* alone in bipolar depression; in combination with tricyclics in non-bipolar depression with psychotic features and resistant depression

3. *Continuation therapy following ECT:* in patients with delusional depression, tricyclic-resistant depression and in the elderly

4. *Prophylaxis:* in unipolar/bipolar illness with two episodes in the last three years for early-onset (less than 40 years) and within five years in late-onset (over 40 years) illness

5. *Schizoaffective disorder:* alone or in combination with neuroleptics

6. During the *first manic* episode occurring *in old age* (aged more than 60 years)

Conclusion

Lithium is one of the most specific and effective treatments in psychiatric practice. It is particularly useful in the acute and long-term management of bipolar affective disorders: their morbidity and mortality are substantially reduced and the majority of patients will be able to live a life unencumbered by the severe restraints imposed by these illnesses. Used intelligently with careful monitoring of its effects and adverse effects and in lower doses in a once-per-day dosage regime, lithium is a safe treatment which could be given indefinitely.

References

Aagaard J, Vestergaard P (1990) Predictors of outcome in prophylactic lithium treatment: a 2-year prospective study. *J Affective Disord* **18**, 259–266.

Abou-Saleh MT (1980) Prediction of lithium response in manic-depression illness. MPhil thesis, University of Edinburgh.

Abou-Saleh MT (1983) Platelet MAO, personality and response to lithium prophylaxis. *J Affective Disord* **5**, 55–65.

Abou-Saleh MT, Coppen A (1983) Subjective side-effects of amitriptyline and lithium in affective disorders. *Br J Psychiatry* **142**, 391–397.

Abou-Saleh MT, Coppen A (1986) Who responds to prophylactic lithium? *J Affective Disord* **10**, 115–125.

Abou-Saleh MT, Coppen A (1989) The efficacy of low-dose lithium: clinical, psychological and biological correlates. *J Psychiatric Res* **23**, 157–162.

Abou-Saleh MT, Coppen AJ (1990) Predictors of long-term outcome of mood disorder on prophylactic lithium. *Lithium* **1**, 27–35.

Ahlfors UG *et al.* (1981) Flupenthixol decanoate in recurrent manic-depressive illness: a comparison with lithium. *Acta Psychiatr Scand* **64**, 226–237.

Ananth J *et al.* (1979) Prediction of lithium response. *Acta Psychiatr Scand* **60**, 279–286.

Angst J (1966) *Zur Aetiologie und Nosologie endogener depressiver Psychosen. Eine genetische, soziologische und klinishe Studie.* Berlin: Springer. (Monographien aus dem Gesamtgebiete der Neurologie und Psychiatrie, Heft 112.)

Angst J (1978) The course of affective disorder II. Typology of bipolar manic-depressive illness. *Arch Psychiatr Nevenkr* **226**, 65–73.

Angst J (1981) Clinical indications for a prophylactic treatment of depression. *Adv Biol Psychiatry* **7**, 218–229.

Angst J (1988) Clinical course of affective disorders. In Helgason T, Daley RJ (eds) *Depressive Illness: Prediction of Course and Outcome*, pp. 1–44. Berlin: Springer.

Bech P, Vendsborg PB, Rafaelsen OJ (1976) Lithium maintenance treatment of manic-melancholic patients: its role in the daily routine. *Acta Psychiatr Scand* **53**, 70–81.

Bendz H (1983) Kidney function in lithium-treated patients: a literature study. *Acta Psychiatr Scand* **68**, 303–324.

Burdick BM, Holmes CB (1980) Use of the lithium response scale with an out-patient psychiatric sample. *Psychol Rep* **47**, 69–70.

Causemann B, Muller-Oerlinghausen B (1988) Does lithium prevent suicides and suicidal attempts? In *Lithium: Inorganic Pharmacology and Psychiatric Use*, pp. 23–24. Oxford: IRL Press.

Cohen WJ, Cohen NH (1974) Lithium carbonate, haloperidol, and irreversible brain damage. *JAMA* **230**, 1283–1287.

Coppen A, Abou-Saleh MT (1988) Lithium therapy: from clinical trials to practical management. *Acta Psychiatr Scand* **78**, 754–762.

Coppen A, Swade C (1986) Reduced lithium dosage improves prophylaxis: a possible mechanism. In Hippius H, Klerman GL, Matussek N (eds) *Depressive Illness: Prediction of Course and Outcome*, pp. 126–130. Berlin: Springer.

Coppen A, Bishop ME, Bailey JE *et al.* (1980) Renal function in lithium and non-lithium treated patients with affective disorders. *Acta Psychiatr Scand* **62**, 343–355.

Coppen A, Abou-Saleh MT, Milln P *et al.* (1983) Decreasing lithium dosage reduces morbidity and side-effects during prophylaxis. *J Affective Disord* **5**, 353–362.

Coppen A, Chaudhry S, Swade C (1986) Folic acid enhances lithium prophylaxis. *J Affective Disord* **10**, 9–13.

Coppen A, Standish-Barry H, Bailey J *et al.* (1990) Long-term lithium and mortality. *Lancet* **335**, 1347.

Coryell W *et al.* (1989) Bipolar II illness: course and outcome over a five-year period. *Psychol Med* **19**, 129–141.

Dunner DL, Fieve RR (1974) Clinical factors in lithium carbonate prophylaxis failure. *Arch Gen Psychiatry* **30**, 229–233.

Dunner DL, Fleiss JL, Fieve RR (1976) Lithium carbonate prophylaxis failure. *Br J Psychiatry* **129**, 40–44.

Dunner DL, Stallone F, Fieve RR (1982) Prophylaxis with lithium carbonate: an update. *Arch Gen Psychiatry* **39**, 1344–1345.

Extein I, Pottach ALC, Gold MS (1982) Does subclinical hypothyroidism predispose to tricyclic-induced rapid mood cycles? *J Clin Psychiatry* **43**, 290–291.

Fieve RR, Peselow ED (1983) Lithium: clinical applications. In Burrows GD, Norman TR, Davies B (eds) *Antidepressants* (Vol. 1 of Drugs in Psychiatry Series), pp. 277–321. Amsterdam: Elsevier.

Gelenberg AJ, Kane JM, Keller MB (1989) Comparison of standard and low serum levels of lithium for maintenance treatment of bipolar disorders. *N Engl J Med* **321**, 1489–1493.

Goodwin FK, Jamison KR (1984) The natural course of recurrent affective illness. In Post RM, Ballenger JC (eds) *Neurobiology of the Mood Disorders*, pp. 20–37. Baltimore: Williams and Wilkins.

Goodwin FK, Roy-Byrne MD (1987) Treatment of bipolar disorder. In Hales RE, Frances AJ (eds) *American Psychiatric Association Annual Review*, Vol. 9, pp. 81–107. Washington, DC: American Psychiatric Press.

Greil W, Schmidt ST (1988) Lithium withdrawal reactions. In Birch NJ (ed.) *Lithium: Inorganic Pharmacology and Psychiatric Use*, pp. 147–148. Oxford: IRL Press.

Greil W, Broucek B, Klein HE *et al.* (1982) Discontinuation of lithium maintenance therapy: reversibility of clinical, psychological and neuroendocrinological changes. In Emrich HM, Aldenhoff JB, Lux HD (eds) *Basic Mechanisms in the Action of Lithium* (proceedings of a symposium held at Schloss Ringberg, Bavaria, West Germany, October 1981), pp. 235–248. Excerpta Medica.

Hall KS, Dunner DL, Zeller G *et al.* (1977) Bipolar illness: a prospective study of life events. *Compr Psychiatry* **18**, 497–502.

Jamison KR (1987a) Compliance with medication. In *Depression and Mania: Modern Lithium Therapy*, pp. 117–121. Oxford: IRL Press.

Jamison KR (1987b) Psychological aspects of treatment. In *Depression and Mania: Modern Lithium Therapy*, pp. 121–124. Oxford: IRL Press.

Jensen HV, Olafsson K, Bille A *et al.* (1990) Lithium every second day: a new treatment regime? *Lithium* **1**, 55–58.

Jerram TC, McDonald R (1978) Plasma lithium control, with particular reference to minimum effective levels. In Johnson FN, Johnson S (eds) *Lithium in Medical Practice*, pp. 407–413. Lancaster: MTP Press.

Kane JM *et al.* (1982) Lithium carbonate and imipramine in the prophylaxis of unipolar and bipolar II illness: a prospective placebo-controlled comparison. *Arch Gen Psychiatry* **39**, 1065–1069.

Keller MB (1987) Differential diagnosis: natural course and epidemiology of bipolar disorders. In Hales RE, Frances AJ (eds) *Psychiatry Update: American Psychiatric Association Annual Review* Vol. 9, pp. 10–31. Washington DC: American Psychiatric Press.

Keller MB (1988) Diagnostic issues and clinical course of unipolar illness. In Francis AJ, Hales RE (eds) *Review of Psychiatry*, Vol. 7, pp. 188–212. Washington, DC: American Psychiatric Press.

Kerry RJ, Orme JE (1979) Lithium, manic-depressive illness and psychological test performance. *Br Med J* **i**, 230.

Kupfer DJ, Pickar D, Himmelhoch JM (1975) Are there two types of unipolar depression? *Arch Gen Psychiatry* **32**, 866–871.

Lauritpsen BJ, Mellerup ET, Plenge P *et al.* (1981) Serum lithium concentrations around the clock with different treatment regimens and the diurnal variation of the renal lithium clearance. *Acta Psychiatr Scand* **64**, 314–319.

Leonhard K, Korff I, Schulz H (1962) Die temperamente in den familien der monopolaren und bipolaren phasischen psychosen. *Psychiatr Neurol* (Basel) **143**, 416–434.

Maj M *et al.* (1984) Prediction of affective psychoses response to lithium prophylaxis: the role of sociodemographic, clinical, psychological and biological variables. *Acta Psychiatr Scand* **69**, 37–44.

Masterton G, Warner M, Roxburgh B (1988) Supervising lithium: a comparison of a lithium clinic, psychiatric out-patients clinics and general practice. *Br J Psychiatry* **152**, 535–538.

Mendlewicz J, Fieve RR, Stallone F (1973) Relationship between the effectiveness of lithium therapy and family history. *Am J Psychiatry* **130**, 1011–1013.

Milln PTS, Patch C (1988) Lithium dose reduction trial. In Birch NJ (ed.) *Lithium: Inorganic Pharmacology and Psychiatric Use*, pp. 33–34. Oxford: IRL Press.

Mukherjee S, Rosen AM, Caracci G, Shukla S (1986) Persistent tardive dyskinesia in bipolar patients. *Arch Gen Psychiatry* **43**, 342–346.

Murphy DL, Beigel A (1974) Depression, elation and lithium carbonate responses in manic patient sub-groups. *Arch Gen Psychiatry* **31**, 643–654.

Norton B, Whalley LJ (1984) Mortality of a lithium treated population. *Br J Psychiatry* **145**, 277–282.

Perris C (1966) A study of bipolar (manic-depressive) and unipolar recurrent depressive psychoses. *Acta Psychiatr Scand* (Suppl. 194), 1–189.

Peselow ED *et al.* (1982) Lithium prophylaxis of depression in unipolar, bipolar II, and cyclothymic patients. *Am J Psychiatry* **139**, 747–752.

Plenge P, Mellerup ET, Bolwig TG *et al.* (1982) Lithium treatment: does the kidney prefer one daily dose instead of two? *Acta Psychiatr Scand* **66**, 121–128.

Priebe S, Wildgrube C, Muller-Oerlinghausen B (1989) Lithium prophylaxis and expressed emotion. *Br J Psychiatry* **154**, 396–399.

Prien RF, Caffey EM, Klett CJ (1972) Comparison of lithium carbonate and chlorpromazine in the treatment of mania. *Arch Gen Psychiatry* **26**, 146–153.

Prien RF, Kupfer DJ, Mansky PA *et al.* (1984) Drug therapy in the prevention of recurrences in unipolar and bipolar affective disorders. *Arch Gen Psychiatry* **41**, 1096–1104.

Sashidharan SP, McGuire RJ (1983) Recurrence of affective illness after withdrawal of long-term lithium treatment. *Acta Psychiatr Scand* **68**, 126–133.

Sautter FJ, Garver DL (1984) Schizophrenia in depression and mania. In Johnson FN (ed.) *Modern Lithium Therapy*, pp. 41–44. Oxford: IRL Press.

Schou M (1985) Practical problems of lithium maintenance treatment. *Adv Biochem Psychopharmacol* **40**, 131–138.

Schou M, Amdisen A, Vestergaard P, Rafaelsen OJ (1982) Lithium treatment regimen and renal water handling: the significance of dosage pattern and tablet type examined through comparison of results from two clinics with different treatment regimens. *Psychopharmacology* **77**, 387–390.

Shopsin B, Temple H, Ingwer M *et al.* (1979) Sudden death during lithium carbonate maintenance. In Cooper TB, Gershon S, Kline NS, Schou M (eds) *Lithium: Controversies and Unresolved Issues*, pp. 527–551. Amsterdam: Excerpta Medica.

Steinbrook RM, Chapman AB (1970) Lithium responses: an evaluation of psychological test characteristics. *Compr Psychiatry* **11**, 524–530.

Sullivan JL *et al.* (1977) Platelet monoamine oxidase activity predicts response to lithium in manic-depressive illness. *Lancet* **ii**, 1325–1327.

Wancata J, Simhandl CH, Denk E *et al.* (1988) Reliability of lithium related side-effects. In Birch NJ (ed.) *Lithium: Inorganic, Pharmacology and Psychiatric Use*, pp. 159–160. Oxford: IRL Press.

Waters B, Lapierre YD, Gagnon A *et al.* (1982) Determination of the optimal concentration of lithium for the prophylaxis of manic-depressive disorder. *Biol Psychiatry* **17**, 1323–1329.

Weinstein MR (1980) Lithium treatment of women during pregnancy and in the post-delivery period. In Johnson FN (ed.) *Handbook of Lithium Therapy*, pp. 421–429. Lancaster: MTP Press.

Weissman MM (1979) The psychological treatment of depressions. *Arch Gen Psychiatry* **36**, 1261–1269.

Zis P, Goodwin FK (1979) Major affective disorder as a recurrent illness. *Arch Gen Psychiatry* **36**, 835–839.

7

Rapid cycling and depression

Robert M. Post

Course of illness: life-charting the rapidity of cycling

The course of unipolar (Figure 1) and bipolar affective disorder is characterized by variability and, at the same time, a tendency for recurrence and acceleration. Early observations of Kraepelin and others have emphasized a variability both from patient to patient and within patients over the course of illness (Kraepelin, 1921). Within this multiplicity of patterns, however, some consistent trends have emerged.

Bipolar illness is almost invariably recurrent (Angst, 1986; Zis and Goodwin, 1979; Goodwin and Jamison, 1990) and, in many instances, recurrences tend to follow a course of increasing frequency or severity. In more than 4623 patients studied, there is an average tendency for a pattern of long well intervals between episodes early in the course, and, with successive episodes, a decrease in these well intervals (Swift, 1907; Kraepelin,. 1921; Paskind, 1930; Lundqvist, 1945; Angst and Weiss, 1967; Bratfos and Haug, 1968; Grof *et al.*, 1974; Taschev, 1974; Zis *et al.*, 1980; Roy-Byrne *et al.*, 1985; Goodwin and Jamison, 1990). This potential for progression is also characteristic of many patients with unipolar depression (Grof *et al.*, 1974; Baastrup and Schou, 1967; see Figures 1–4), although such a pattern is by no means uniform (Keller, 1990; Angst *et al.*, 1990). Angst has also described patients with recurrent brief depressions; these may be stable or interchange with major depressions and vice versa over the course of longitudinal observation. Nonetheless, in a subgroup of bipolar

Long-term Treatment of Depression. Edited by S.A. Montgomery and F. Rouillon
© 1992 John Wiley & Sons Ltd

patients, there can be a relentless, malignant progression with rapid and ultra-rapid cycling ultimately becoming manifest.

Although we have utilized the Dunner and Fieve (1974) criteria for rapid cycling (i.e., ≥4 episodes per year), it is noteworthy that a continuum of typical cycling frequencies among individual patients appears to exist, with little evidence that the four episodes per year criterion is any more than an arbitrary cut-off. Kraepelin observed:

> There are indeed slight and severe attacks which may be of long or short duration, but they alternate irregularly in the same case. This difference is therefore of no use for the delimitation of different diseases. A grouping according to the frequency of the attacks might much rather be considered, which naturally would be extremely welcome to the physician. It appears, however, that here also we have not to do with fundamental differences, since in spite of certain general rules it has not been possible to separate out definite types from this point of view. (Kraepelin 1921, p. 149)

Not only do some patients show cycling frquencies on the order of weeks to days (and thus might be labelled ultra-rapid cycling) but Kramlinger and Post (1988) have documented a cyclicity of illness where frequencies of *bona fide* mood switches occur at an extraordinarily rapid rate, such that durations of discrete mood phases are less than 24 hours ('ultra-ultra-rapid cycling'). The cases of 48-hour cycling were previously thought to represent the limit of cycle frequency for classical affective disorder. However, in several instances of cycling faster than once every 24 hours, the patients studied on our unit did present with classical bipolar illness without concomitant personality disorder. Thus, these discrete rapid fluctuations did not appear to be a contamination of bipolar disorder with a component of extreme mood lability often associated with borderline personality disorder. In the small number of patients identified with this ultra-ultra-rapid cycling pattern, it is of some interest that in order to break this cycling pattern they required treatment with a combination of lithium and carbamazepine and, in several instances, adjunctive treatment with other agents including thyroid hormones.

Such a malignant, progressive life-course of illness is illustrated in Figure 2. The patient is a 34-year-old male with a series of depressive episodes that gradually increased in frequency of recurrence and in the accumulation of a baseline continuous mild depression (a double depression). Ultimately, the cycles progressed from a pattern of two episodes per year to one of rapid cycling and ultra-rapid cycling of severe depression with hypomania (bipolar II). At the time of his presentation at the NIMH, he demonstrated a further progression to ultra-ultra-rapid cycling with hypomanic episodes lasting, at times, less than 24 hours. The patient, who was an astronomer and computer programmer, was completely incapacitated by his illness in spite of many types of currently available pharmacotherapy. It is noteworthy that at the NIMH he showed a partial response to carbamazepine augmented by bupropion and, following discharge, continued to do well on bupropion alone.

Thus, while a minority of patients will have single episodes of depression without recurrence or stable patterns over time, when one assesses a large series of patients, as illustrated in Figure 3, an overall pattern emerges of longer well intervals between initial episodes, with an acceleration in frequency and

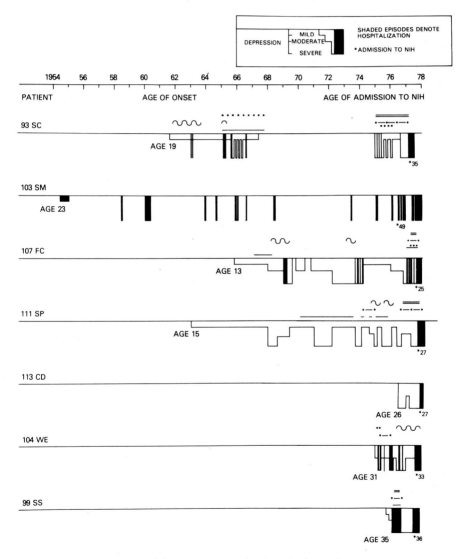

Figure 1(a).   Life courses of depressive episodes in unipolar patients.

142

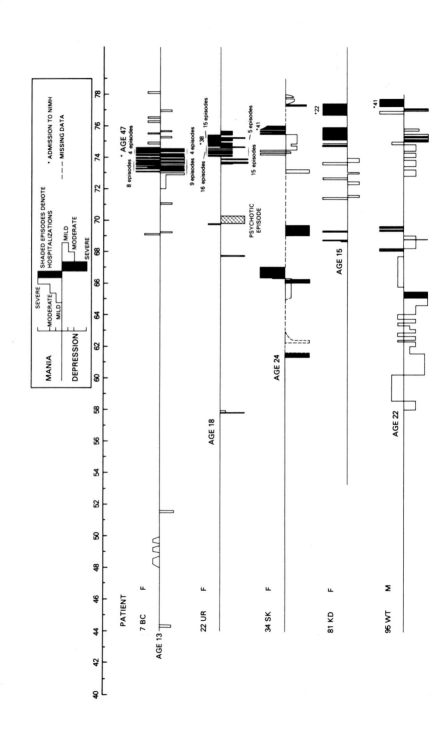

143

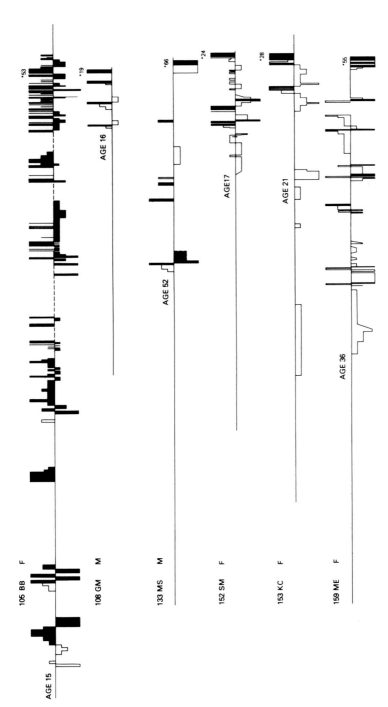

Figure 1(b).   Life course of manic and depressive episodes in bipolar affective illness.

144

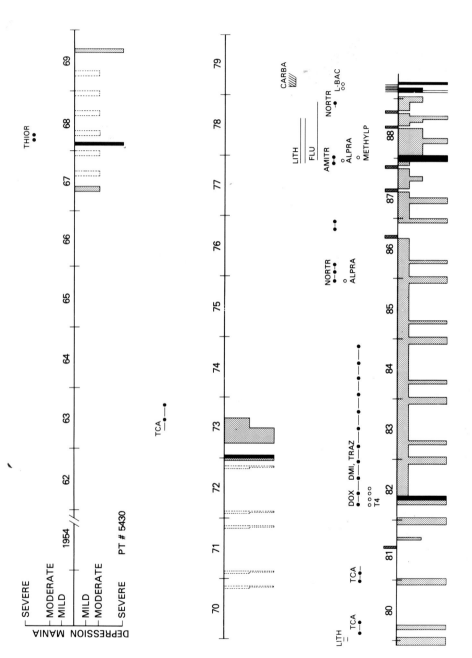

Figure 2. Progressive evolution in cycling frequency in a bipolar II male.

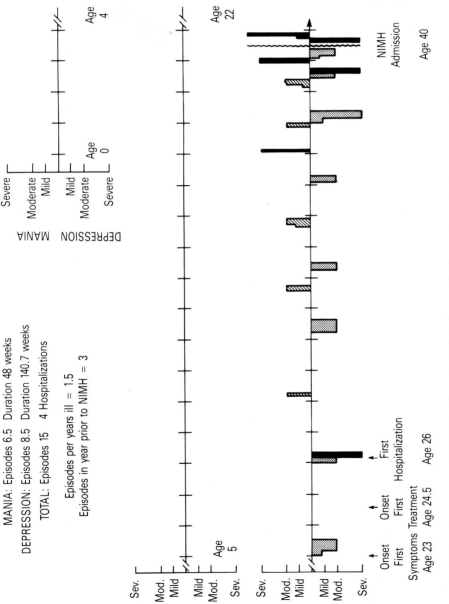

Figure 3. Median course of affective illness in 82 bipolar manic-depressive patients.

severity over time. These data are also summarized in Figure 4, where the well interval is plotted as a function of successive episodes. It seems remarkable that the patients in the pre-psychopharmacological era studied by Kraepelin showed patterns similar to those studied at the NIMH in the post-psychopharmacological era (see Cutler and Post (1982) for a further review of studies). However, when we assessed the number of individual patients showing this pattern of acceleration in cycle frequency in our overall group, we found that it was only about 50%, with the other 50% showing initial rapid cycling with short well intervals from the outset (Roy-Byrne *et al.*, 1985). Thus, while rapid cycling may emerge late in the course of illness, it can also occur at the outset. We surmise that in a more primary care treatment setting with less refractory patients, other subgroups would demonstrate single episodes (extremely rare for bipolar patients but perhaps up to 20–30% of unipolar patients), or a pattern of intermittent recurrences with little evidence of deterioration with successive episodes over the course of illness. Moreover, a small percentage of patients may show an attenuation of the illness frequency over time and eventual 'burning out' of the illness.

Nonetheless, we emphasize the potential for malignant progression of recurrent unipolar and bipolar affective illness because of the critical treatment

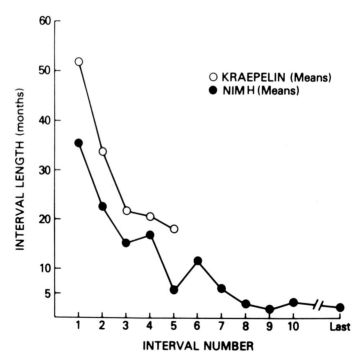

Figure 4.   Decreasing well intervals in recurrent affective illness.

implications for this pattern. We also highly recommend utilization of formal life-charting methodology in order to assess the prior course of manic-depressive illness, both as an indispensable tool for the retrospective and prospective assessment of a given patient, and for documentation of the adequacy of pharmaco-prophylaxis. As described in detail elsewhere (Squillace *et al.*, 1984; Roy-Byrne *et al.*, 1985; Post *et al.*, 1988a), formal life-charting supplies important information and positive feedback for the patient. It assists in uncovering the importance of stressors and other psychosocial events, as well as possible seasonal components to the illness. As the patient helps discretely to map episodes visually, the potentially recurrent nature of an illness becomes harder to deny, which may assist in the institution of and compliance with pharmaco-prophylaxis. The joint endeavour of constructing a life chart will also assist in the medicalization of the illness and in the establishment of the therapeutic alliance, particularly if some of the derivative processes of the life chart methodology are utilized clinically. That is, one may note particularly vulnerable periods for an individual patient and intensify psychotherapeutic or pharmacological interventions at that period of higher risk. One might identify and specify early symptoms typically associated with the onset of severe episodes that would by mutual agreement trigger immediate consultation with a physician should they reappear.

In addition to the relative resistance to pharmacotherapy, several aspects of the symptomatic presentation of rapidly cycling bipolar illness make it unusually difficult to treat. Not only is there tremendous stigma associated with having a psychiatric illness and, in particular, having bipolar affective illness, but the symptom pattern experienced during the different phases leads to unique treatment difficulties. During the depressions, the patient may be so incapacitated and lethargic that he is unable to participate actively in his own help-seeking process. In severe episodes, the patient may be actively help-rejecting and suicidal. There is evidence that severe suicide risk may increase as a function of duration of illness in bipolar patients, with rapid cyclers being particularly vulnerable to a sense of hopelessness caused by relentless recurrence of their depressions (Roy-Byrne *et al.*, 1988). Conversely, during a manic episode (particularly in the bipolar II hypomanic), the patient may have the misguided view that he is not ill at all and may destroy his social and treatment network. Manic behaviour may lead to loss of job, spouse and family fortune, and can severely strain even the most empathic patient–physician relationship. The visualizing of the life course of illness may help curtail these difficulties of symptom recognition and propel action by patients, families and physicians. In addition, it may help to refocus on the distinction between unipolar and bipolar II affective illness, with critical differential implications for acute and prophylactic pharmacotherapy.

Moreover, the effectiveness or ineffectiveness of previous medication may be elucidated in the life-chart process in a way that is not always obvious without

148

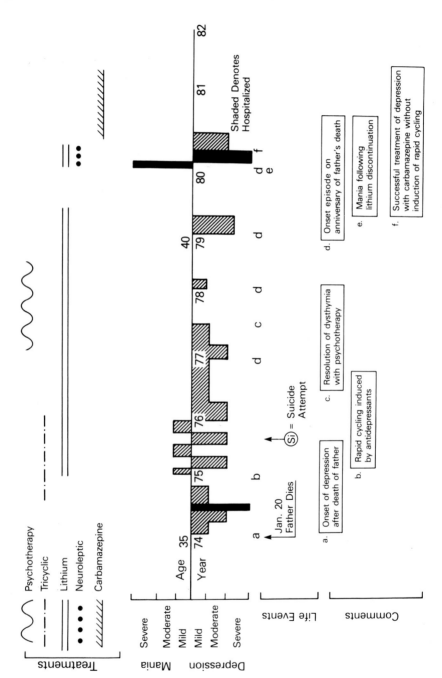

Figure 5(a). Graphing the course of affective illness: prototype of a 'life chart'.

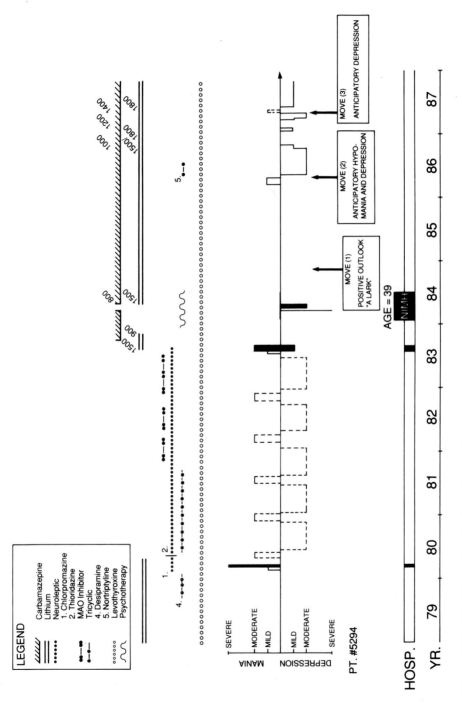

Figure 5(b). Breakthrough episodes with social stressors.

such a formal graphing technique. This is particularly the case in relation to tricyclic-induced cycling or rapid cyling, as discussed below. Many patients who claim to be lithium non-responders are, in fact, partial responders to lithium, and this fact also is important in the reassessment of the need for adjunctive and combination treatment. Examples of how to construct a life chart are indicated in Figures 1 and 2 and more formally outlined in Figures 5(a) and (b).

Although it is clear from early work of Baastrup and Schou (1967), and much subsequent work, that many patients with rapid cycling and even ultra-rapid cycling disorder do respond to single treatment with lithium, there is some consistency in the literature that these patients are relatively more refractory to lithium than their non-rapid-cycling cohort comparison. A less than exhaustive review of the literature reveals that nine studies have indicated that rapid cyclers are relatively less responsive to lithium, whereas four studies indicate no discrimination, and only two studies suggest that rapid cyclers are good responders to lithium. These data are summarized in Table I. In the recent

Table I.   Rapid cycling and response to lithium or carbamazepine

Good response	No prediction	Poor response
Lithium		
Schou (1973)	Svestka and Nahunek	Prien *et al.* (1973)
Page *et al.* (1987)	(1975)	Dunner and Fieve (1974)
3/3	Dostal (1977)	Misra and Burns (1977)
	Itoh and Ishigane (1973)	Kukopulos (1980, 1983)
	Kishimoto *et al.* (1986)	Nolen (1983)
	But 10/42 ↑ cycling	Prien *et al.* (1984)
		Hanus and Zapletalek (1984)
		Abou-Saleh and Coppen
		(1986)
		Goodnick *et al.* (1987)
Carbamazepine[a]		
Okuma *et al.* (1973) (P)		
Post *et al.* (1983b) (P)		
Post *et al.* (1987a) (A)		
Joffe (1991) (A, P)		
Joyce (1988) (P) (7/13		
or 4/12)		
Nolen (1983) (P)		
Stromgren and Boller		
(1985) (P)		
Elphick (1985) (A, P)		
Post *et al.* (1990a) (P)		

[a] Some rapid cyclers have responded to carbamazepine; preferential response is not generally observed.
A, acute.
P, prophylaxis.

Gelenberg *et al.* (1989) study, patients with three or more prior episodes showed poor response to either high- or low-dose lithium regimens.

Kukopulos and colleagues (1980, 1983) have also suggested that patients with rapid cycling and concomitant treatment with tricyclic antidepressants (TCAs) are particularly vulnerable to lithium non-response. Moreover, the continuous form of the illness, where phases rapidly succeed each other (without a definable well interval) is also likely to be less responsive to treatment with lithium.

These latter data raise a number of vexing treatment problems for the rapid-cycling bipolar patient and his physician. For many bipolar I patients and those with bipolar II illness, depressive phases appear to be most refractory to standard and newer treatment modalities with the anticonvulsants. These phases also carry a high morbidity as well as potential for suicide (Roy-Byrne *et al.*, 1988). As such they deserve aggressive treatment, yet preliminary evidence suggests that traditional antidepressant modalities of the heterocyclic and monoamine oxidase inhibitor (MAOI) class may, in some vulnerable patients, either precipitate a manic episode, or induce rapid or continuous cycling. While controversial, these data have recently been reviewed by Wehr and Goodwin (1987) and Wehr *et al.* (1988) and deserve consideration because these patterns of illness may mark a particularly treatment-refractory subgroup (Altshuler and Post, unpublished data), whatever the overall incidence turns out to be (for either drug-induced switches or cycle acceleration) following further systematic study and epidemiological review. Kupfer and associates (1988) found that switches into mania or conversion to rapid cycling were essentially non-existent in unipolar patients treated with TCAs, and were quite rare in bipolar II patients.

Given this divergent literature on the potential impact of the unimodal antidepressants on the occurrence of mania and/or rapid and continuous cycling, we re-examined our own data based on extensive description of the prior course of illness and treatment of refractory patients admitted to our unit, whose illness was carefully retrospectively characterized by systematic life-charting methods. In all bipolar patients exposed to tricyclics, heterocyclics or MAOIs, an assessment was made as to whether these agents were or were not likely to have been involved in a manic switch, or speeding up of the course of illness, or conversion to the continuous form (Altshuler *et al.*, unpublished). Patients' life charts were scored as 'definite' if a switch occurred: (1) rapidly after the introduction of the treatment agent; (2) at a time when a mania was not expected to have occurred on the basis of prior course of illness; or (3) if a manic episode was of greater severity than that previously observed in the medication-free state. The transition to rapid or continuous cycling was also scored 'definite' if the change was temporally closely related to antidepressant treatment and a period of time off medication led to a slowing down or discontinuous pattern. Patients' switches and cycling patterns were scored 'likely' if all of these criteria were non-ambiguously met, or 'unlikely' if their prior course of illness suggested that the switch or pattern change was occurring on the basis of expected natural illness evolution. Patients were also scored as 'no switch' when antidepressant medication was not associated with this phenomenon.

Thirty-five per cent of bipolar I and II patients were reported to have had a 'definite' or 'likely' switch on TCAs. However, not every patient of the 35% demonstrated a 'definite' or 'likely' switch on each occasion of tricyclic exposure. Thirty-four per cent had a 'definite' or 'likely' transition to rapid cycling, while 17% showed conversion to the continuous form of the illness in association with this treatment. In those 35% who did demonstrate an antidepressant-induced switch, there as an increased vulnerability to deterioration in the course of illness; i.e., compared with those scored 'unlikely' or 'no switch', patients who showed 'definite' or 'likely' switch phenomena were significantly more rapid cycling in the year prior to NIMH admission and were hospitalized at NIMH longer, probably reflecting some measure of treatment refractoriness. Whether the switches and cycle progression associated with tricyclic-induced phenomena represent a marker for a more malignant form of illness, or are actually the result of treatment itself, is unclear. Nonetheless, these data do suggest the potential liability of tricyclic and MAOI antidepressant therapy, at least in a subgroup of bipolar patients, further propelling the search for treatment alternatives that are not associated with these triple liabilities (switch, rapid, and continuous cycling), even if these phenomena occur in only a small subgroup or bipolar patients.

In unipolar depressives with several prior recurrences, long-term prophylaxis with either serotonin-active (fluoxetine) or norepinephrine (noradrenaline)-active (malprotiline) unimodal antidepressants is remarkably effective (Montgomery, 1989; Rouillon *et al.*, 1989). What is less clear is whether these agents would be equally effective in rapid cycling unipolar patients, or whether, as in bipolar illness (where rapid cyclers are relatively resistant to standard pharmacotherapy with lithium), this subgroup would also be refractory to standard unimodal antidepressants. It is also possible that with more sustained prophylaxis of unipolar patients, as documented by Montgomery *et al.* (1989) and Rouillon *et al.* (1989), progression to rapid cycling might be prevented. More ominously, it is also possible (as discussed below for lithium) that discontinuation of effective pharmaco-prophylaxis might be associated with episode recurrence and the induction of drug refractoriness even when treatment is reinstituted. This theoretical possibility remains to be directly tested.

In addition to rapid cycling, four investigative groups have also identified a *pattern of episodes* that is differentially associated with response to lithium in bipolar depression. Kulopulos *et al.* (1980), Grof *et al.* (1987), Haag *et al.* (1987) and Maj *et al.* (1989b) have all observed a better response to lithium in patients who show a pattern of manias followed by depressions and then a well interval (M–D–I), as opposed to depressions switching into manias and then followed by a well interval (D–M–I). These patients (who may include the bipolar II subtype) demonstrate the potential difficulties in treating the depressive phases of bipolar illness. The data have interesting mechanistic implications as well and agree with the notion that lithium is a better acute antimanic than antidepres-· sant agent, suggesting that aspects of lithium's antimanic efficacy may be important to its long-term efficacy and prophylaxis. Since carbamazepine, valproate, and the calcium channel blockers also appear to be more effective in acute mania than depression (see below), treatment of depressions in rapid-cycling bipolar patients becomes the most vexing of therapeutic problems.

Thus, a variety of course-of-illness characteristics appear to be associated with a high incidence of non-response to lithium. We may also identify different types of non-response, as illustrated in Figure 6. As schematically illustrated, this might include those patients who show no response to lithium (Figure 6a) from the outset for either manic or depressive episodes. However, there appear to be partial responders to lithium (Figure 6(b) and (c)), where one or both phases of the illness may be partially improved, either in terms of frequency or recurrence or severity of episodes. It is unclear how many patients conform to the pattern of having an initial excellent response, but then experiencing a progressive emergence of episodes through previously adequate lithium prophylaxis (Figure 6(d); e.g., the tolerance pattern), despite adequate blood levels.

Maj *et al.* (1989b) have followed a series of patients who, although they showed an excellent response to lithium for two years, demonstrated very substantial morbidity on long-term follow-up, suggesting that the pattern of loss of efficacy may be more common than previously recognized. Only 44.3% of the complete responders for the first two years of lithium prophylaxis were still complete responders after a subsequent five-year follow-up. The concept of

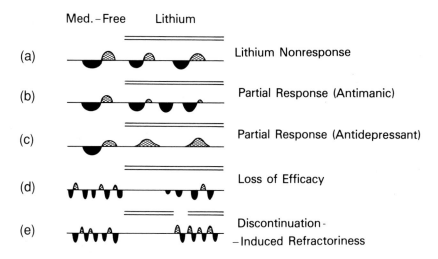

Figure 6.   Patterns of lithium refractoriness.

tolerance to the effects of psychotropic agents has just begun to be recognized as a potential problem and is one to be considered in the evaluation of long-term prophylactic efficacy (Post *et al.*, 1990b). It is also possible that, rather than being explained by the occurrence of tolerance, episodes are emerging in spite of continued adequate lithium treatment and represent a continued progression of the pathophysiological processes involved. Alternatively, pharmacokinetic factors may be of importance, although preclinical models suggest this may not be the case (see below).

We have observed several individuals who appear to follow a novel route to developing lithium refractoriness following discontinuation of otherwise effective pharmacotherapy (Figure 6(e)). These patients (in one instance with physician concurrence) either discontinued or abruptly lowered lithium treatment, leading to the subsequent occurrence of a severe manic or depressive relapse. Upon reinstituting lithium treatment, episodes continued to occur despite multiple attempts at optimizing this regimen and even supplementing lithium with other agents. We have tentatively labelled this phenomenon lithium discontinuation-induced refractoriness, suggesting that episodes occurring upon discontinuation may have an additional liability that goes beyond the occurrence of episodes alone; i.e., the process of having a lithium-induced withdrawal episode may somehow change the patient's responsivity for the longer term.

This process is illustrated schematically in Figure 7. The 57-year-old female patient showed a pattern of occasional manias and recurrent severe depressions in 1972, meeting criteria for rapid cycling. Following renewed occurrence of episodes in 1975, she showed an excellent response to lithium and neuroleptics (1975–1980). Because of the almost complete response for a period of five years, the patient, with physician concurrence, decided to discontinue lithium in 1980. Several months after the discontinuation, she experienced a severe depressive episode (1981). Despite reinstitution of lithium and neuroleptics in combination and, subsequently, the addition of a variety of other psychotropic agents, recurrent depressive episodes interspersed with manias occurred relentlessly.

Jules Angst has also indicated that not only do approximately 80% of his patients, who are well maintained on lithium, relapse, but a subgroup of these patients do not resume their previous degree of lithium responsiveness (personal communication, December 1989). Following lithium discontinuation, deterioration was observed in 21 of 22 recently reported cases, although data on re-response was not reported (Koufen and Consbruch, 1989). The incidence of withdrawal-emergent refractoriness has not been systematically evaluated in the literature and is presented in this case in vignette format simply to warn the clinician and patient of another potential severe consequence of lithium discontinuation.

These observations obviously require further study, as do potential mecha-

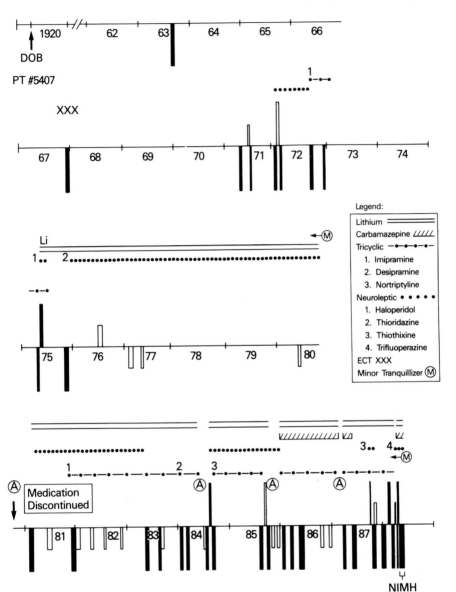

Figure 7.   Lithium discontinuation-induced refractoriness.

nisms underlying this phenomenon. Suitable analogies for this particular phenomenon are difficult to find, although the old saws of 'letting the cat out of the bag' or 'opening Pandora's box' come to mind. Once a process that has been held in check escapes its confines, it may be very difficult to 'recapture.

Analogies from cancer chemotherapy may also be used in considering lithium discontinuation-induced refractoriness in the well-responding patient. One may conceptualize that a primary tumour that is drug responsive when it is localized and encapsulated may no longer respond to the same agents when it has metastasized. New biological processes, including induction of oncogenes and loss of suppressor oncogenes, have been postulated and could explain the change in pharmaco-responsivity. Similarly, removal of the lithium 'brake' and endengering new episodes may, in some individuals, be associated with loss of drug efficacy, consistent with the general formulation that the occurrence of episodes may make one more vulnerable to the occurrence of others (Post *et al.*, 1986b). In this fashion, patients may be inducing lithium refractoriness following repeated bouts of non-compliance and drug holidays (either physician prescribed or not). As noted above, whether this might also be produced in unipolar patients following discontinuation of adequate unimodal antidepressant prophylaxis remains for future investigations.

There are two more well-documented consequences of lithium discontinuation: (1) relapses occurring as expected, based on the prior frequency of occurrence; and (2) relapses occurring immediately upon withdrawal. Mander and London (1988) have emphasized the potential of a lithium withdrawal reaction with patients perhaps being particularly vulnerable in the first two weeks after discontinuation. A variety of investigators (Mander, 1989; Mander and Loudon, 1988; Mander, 1986a, 1986b; Lenz *et al.*, 1988; Tondo *et al.*, 1988; Bouman *et al.*, 1986; Greil and Schmidt, 1988) have also pointed out a series of variables that might be associated with an increased risk for relapse in the period immediately following discontinuation, including an unstable course prior to lithium discontinuation and schizoaffective symptoms. While there may be some debate about the occurrence of the lithium withdrawal syndrome, it is clear from the early controlled lithium discontinuation studies that patients are at a substantially higher risk of relapse when placebo is substituted for active treatment than when patients are continued on lithium maintenance (Schou, 1982; Goodwin and Ebert, 1973).

This author is not aware of systematic studies comparing sudden lithium discontinuation with a more gradual tapering process. Theoretically, to the extent that a true lithium withdrawal syndrome exists, slow tapering should alleviate this process, although it would not be expected to affect the emergence of episodes at the prior expected frequency. Until such data are available, it might be best to engage in a gradual lithium discontinuation tapering process whenever possible. One benefit gained from this procedure might be the avoidance of the putative withdrawal syndrome. In addition, if minor symptoms begin to emerge during the gradual discontinuation process, increases in dose or supplemental medications can be instituted in an attempt to abort the emergence of a full-blown episode, with its dual liabilities of morbidity and potential refractoriness. From the long-term perspective, however, these observations suggest the potential critical importance of maintaining and extending success-ful prophylaxis indefinitely, particularly in patients with a prior history of rapid cycling (which may mark a more malignant pattern of illness). I have observed a patient with a 20-year history of complete lithium response after an extended period of ultra-rapid cycling between profound depressions and secludable manias. Upon lithium discontinuation she showed re-emergence of depression off medication and a subsequent depressive episode even after restarting lithium. Whether or not she eventually shows renewed response or remains refractory, she documents the potential liability of discontinuation of effective prophylactic pharmacotherapy, even after extended periods of complete response.

Tricyclic-induced rapid cycling in bipolar depression

There is an interesting and controversial risk:benefit ratio connected with the use of adjunctive medications for the treatment of breakthrough depressions in the bipolar patient during lithium prophylaxis. The tricyclic or heterocyclic antidepressants (TCAs, HCAs) have long been implicated in the induction of mania and/or rapid cycling. The data on tricyclic and monoamine oxidase inhibitor (MAOI) manic induction appear highly controversial (see above), while the ability of tricyclics to accelerate the cycling in vulnerable individuals, particularly rapid cyclers, appears to be well documented.

Clinically, until further data become available, it would appear wise to mini-mize use of these unimodal agents (TCA and MAOI) in bipolar patients and attempt to use other adjunctive treatments, particularly in the patient who has already demonstrated his/her proclivity for antidepressant-induced switching and/or cycle acceleration. Up to 80% of patients are maintained on these uni-modal antidepressants in some lithium clinics (Page *et al.*, 1987). The utility of bupropion (Wellbutrin), either alone or as an adjunctive treatment to lithium or carbamazepine, deserves further careful consideration in light of the prelimin-ary promising data that this drug, in contrast to other traditional unimodal antidepressants, may not share the proclivity for mania induction (Shopsin, 1983; Haykal and Akiskal, 1990) (and see text regarding outcome in Figure 1).

The ability of a variety of unimodal antidepressants (tricyclic, heterocyclic and MAOI) to increase the frequency of rapid cycling or continuous cycling is less controversial than their ability to induce switches. In the well-controlled studies of Wehr and colleagues (1988), cycle frequency in individual patients was repeatedly demonstrated to shorten during treatment with tricyclics, lengthen during a discontinuation period, and, in some instances, again shorten with reinstitution of this treatment. In our life-chart series, 34% of patients showed 'likely' or 'definite' transition to more rapid cycling and 17% showed conversion from intermittent to continuous cycling while treated with

158

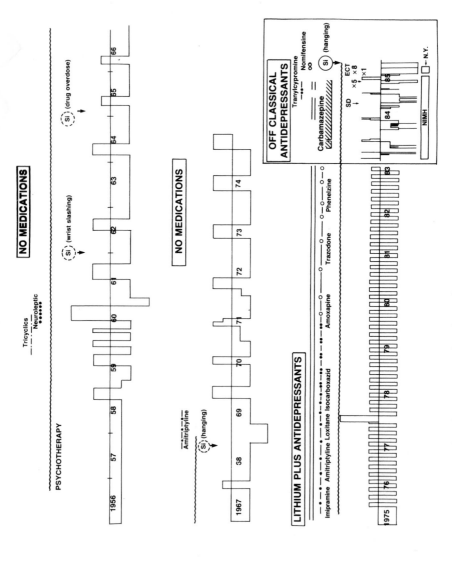

Figure 8.   Rapid cycling associated with antidepressants.

antidepressants. A case is illustrated (Figure 8) of this acceleration of cycling independent of the type of HCA or MAOI employed, even in the face of lithium co-treatment starting in 1975, and cycle slowing off unimodal antidepressant in 1983–1984. Whether this process of cycle induction is largely confined to patients with relatively rapid or continuous cycling disorder, or occurs uniformly in a large group of bipolar patients with slower cycling frequency as well, remains to be further investigated.

This patient (Figure 8) also illustrates the development of refractoriness (tolerance) to two treatment modalities. In 1984 she initially responded dramatically to sleep deprivation (SD), but failed to respond to multiple subsequent SD inductions (not illustrated) (see Roy-Byrne *et al.*, 1984b for illustrations of other patients who became tolerant to the effects of SD). Similarly, she responded rapidly and dramatically to her first course of electroconvulsive therapy (ECT) at NIMH (ECT = ×5), but failed to respond either to ECT prophylaxis or to a second course of ECT (×8) when she was rehospitalized elsewhere. Shortly thereafter, she committed suicide by hanging, using the most lethal method based on her three previous ineffective attempts (wrist, 1962; drug overdose, 1965; hanging, 1968).

Interestingly, there is precedence in other neuropsychiatric illnesses for effective treatment to lose efficacy or lead to cyclic phenomena of increased frequency. The use of L-dopa in the treatment of Parkinson's disease is clearly associated with a honeymoon of therapeutic efficacy that may last for several years, but one that gives way to the induction of severe motor oscillations of the on–off phemonenon, where periods of akinesia oscillate dramatically with periods of uncontrollable dyskinesia. In parkinsonism as well as in bipolar illness, the guidelines for early intervention with agents that incur the risk of cycle induction, as opposed to attempts at withholding these types of treatment until symptom severity reaches a critical threshold, have not been adequately defined.

In the 1970s, the clinician had few choices available for the treatment of breakthrough depressions besides the heterocyclic and MAOI antidepressants for the bipolar patient maintained on lithium. Now that other agents are available, developing a systematic database for choosing among the augmenting strategies becomes crucial. Lamentably, such controlled data in the long-term treatment of bipolar patients do not appear to be rapidly forthcoming. Thus, like so many other areas of controversy in this field based on inadequate reference data, it remains for the clinician to judiciously evaluate the risk:benefit ratio of adjunctive treatment with the unimodal agents in comparision with the bimodal agents (such as carbamazepine and valproate) in each individual patient. Although not systematically assessed, some of the controversies regarding the liabilities of cycle induction by antidepressants may be partially resolved by the identification of rapid cycling; groups that see cycle induction as a special problem (Wehr, Kukopulos, Akiskal, Himmelhoch and

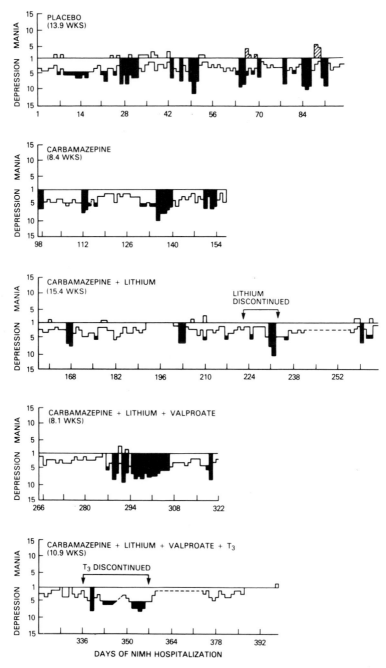

Figure 9. Pharmacological response to combination therapy in an ultra-rapid cycling manic-depressive patient.

ourselves) see a high percentage of rapid cyclers. Parenthetically, this might be an excellent area for private practice clinicians and others in non-traditional research settings to engage in clinical trials where treatment options are at least randomly assigned and patients are followed and evaluated in a systematic fashion, even if a double-blind design is not employed. Such an approach is likely to yield highly valuable data.

Carbamazepine in the prophylaxis of bipolar illness

Considerable evidence is now available suggesting that carbamazepine possesses acute antimanic efficacy. Some 19 double-blind studies reviewed elsewhere (Post, 1990a, 1990b; Post *et al.*, 1987a, 1989, 1990a) are convergent with the notion that carbamazepine exerts antimanic effects that are parallel to those of the neuroleptics. It is of significance that the antimanic efficacy of carbamazepine has now been well documented and suggests parallels with lithium in the acute and prophylactic treatment of bipolar illness.

Data from nine controlled and partially controlled studies of carbamazepine in long-term prophylaxis are illustrated in Table II. These have included patients who were studied either in a blind fashion or where a systematic cross-over design was utilized. In contrast to a much larger group of uncontrolled studies reviewed elsewhere (Post and Uhde, 1986) where the response rate was 64%, these studies indicate an approximately 72% marked or excellent response rate to carbamazepine. Thus, overall, some 344 of 526 patients (65%) have been reported responsive to carbamazepine either alone or in combination with lithium carbonate.

Our initial report of acute and long-term effects of carbamazepine prophylaxis was published in *Communications in Pschopharmacology* in 1978 and extended in 1983 when we found that 6 of 7 patients were substantially improved with the use of carbamazepine alone (3 patients) or in conjunction with lithium (3) and neuroleptics (1). Four of these patients were studied in a double-blind fashion (Ballenger and Post, 1978; Post *et al.*, 1983b). We observed, and continue to observe, in an extension of this study, a good response to the adjunctive use of carbamazepine in previously lithium-refractory patients, particularly those with rapid-cycling disorder (Post *et al.*, 1990b). Several of the patients and their initial responses are illustrated in Figure 10. Note a decrease in both frequency and severity of manic and depressive episodes with the institution of carbamazepine prophylaxis (right-hand side of figure).

A controlled study of carbamazepine compared to placebo in a double-blind fashion was reported by Okuma and colleagues (1981). In their study, 6 of 10 patients impoved on carbamazepine, while only 2 of 9 improved on placebo ($p < 0.10$). Placidi *et al.* (1986) utilized a design of carbamazepine compared with placebo in a randomized fashion. They observed 21 of 29 patients with

Table II. Controlled and quasi-controlled[a] studies of carbamazepine prophylaxis in manic-depressive illness

Study	n	Diagnosis	Design	Dose of carbamazepine (mg per day)	Other drugs	Duration	Results
Ballenger and Post (1978); Post et al. (1983b)	7	6 M–D 1 conf. psychosis	4 blind 3 open	800–2000 mg (11.3 µg ml) (7.5–15.5 µg/ml)	None for 3 patients Li in 3 Neurolep. in 1	6–51 mos	6/7 improved; esp. Li non-responsive cyclers
Okuma et al. (1981)	12 CBZ:10 placebo	M–D	CBZ v. placebo Blind randomized	400–600 mg (5.6 = 2.0 µg/ml)	Acute treatments added during episode breakthroughs	12 mos either Rx	6/10 improved on CBZ; 2/9 improved on placebo (p < 0.10 diff.)
Placidi et al (1986)	CBZ: 20 9 Li 19 8	M–D SA M–D SA	CBZ v. Li Blind randomized	400–1600 mg (7–12 µg/ml)	Acute treatments added during episode breakthroughs	36 mos	21/29 marked to moderate improvement on CBZ; 20/27 on Li improved by relapse criteria
Kishimoto and Okuma (1985)	18	PB I & II	Open crossover (A–B or B–A) v. Li (400–800 mg)	200–600 mg		>1 yr each X = 52.4 mos CBZ; X = 42.2 mos lithium	Significantly fewer hospitalizations on CBZ; CBZ effective in Li non-responders

Study	Sample	Design	Dose		Duration	Results
Watkins et al. (1987)	19 CBZ Li	7 UP 12 BP	CBZ v. Li D-blind randomized	(5–12 µg/ml)	Antidepressants as needed	16/19 improved on CBZ 15/18 improved on Li $p < 0.001$ increases in mos of remission both drugs Li > CBZ
Bellaire et al. (1988)	50 CBZ	18 UP 24 UP 8 SA	CBZ v. Li Open randomized	600–800 mg (0.2–12.5 µg/ml)	24 mos	Global efficacy and tolerance NS favour CBZ
Lusznat et al. (1988)	20 CBZ; 20 Li	M–D	CBZ v. Li Blind randomized	(6–12 µg/ml)	Neuroleptics: antidepressants as needed	12 mos	9/16 satisfactory on CBZ; 5/17 satisfactory on Li; CBZ non-significantly better than Li on readmission, depression, side effects
Cabrera et al. (1986)[a]	4 CBZ 6 Li	3 BP 1 SA 5 BP 1 SA	CBZ v. Li Randomized	1050–1350 mg/d (5.3–11.2 µg/ml)	Neuroleptic in 1 CBZ Neuroleptic in 2 Li	6–16 mos	2/4 improvement on CBZ 3/6 improvement on Li
[a] Oxcarbazepine	4 CBZ 4 BP		Open	900–1200 mg/d (6.25–15.8 µg/ml)	Li in 1	16 mos	2/4 improved on CBZ

Note: controlled studies = 60/85 (71%) response to carbamazepine. Uncontrolled studies = 288/449 (64%) response to carbamazepine. Total = 348/534 (65%) response.

[a] Blinded: cross-over or randomized.

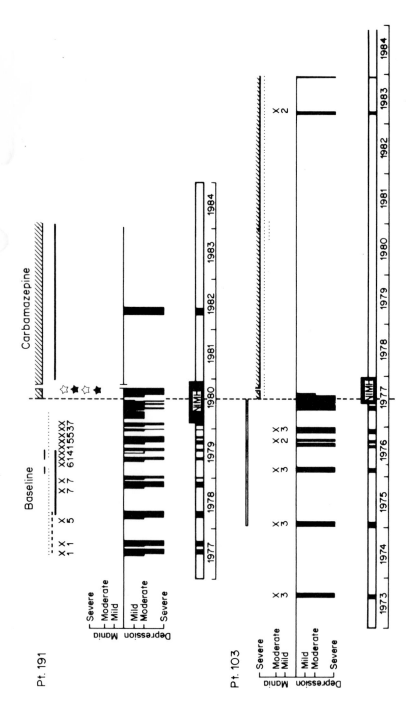

Figure 10.   Prophylactic efficacy of carbamazepine in depression (X = number of ECT).

a moderate to marked improvement with carbamazepine and an approximately similar 20 of 27 patients improving on lithium in patients who were followed for 2–36 months. Prien and Gelenberg (1989) commented on the high rate of drop-outs in this study and the lack of separation of bipolar, schizoaffective and schizophreniform patients in the efficacy analysis. Kishimoto and Okuma (1985) reported 18 patients who were studied in an open, cross-over fashion on lithium or carbamazepine. They reported significantly fewer hospitalizations on carbamazepine compared with lithium. Watkins *et al.* (1987) reported a blind randomization of carbamazepine versus lithium. The 19 patients studied on carbamazepine included 12 bipolar and 7 unipolar patients. Sixteen of 19 patients improved on carbamazepine while 15 of 18 improved on lithium. There was a highly significant ($p < 0.001$) increase in months of remission on both drugs, although lithium appeared to be superior to carbamazepine on a measure of 'additional time' in remission (9.3 ± 2.0 months lithium versus 3.3 ± 0.8 months CBZ; $p < 0.001$).

Bellaire and colleagues (1988) reported an open series of patients who were randomized to either lithium or carbamazepine for one year. In this study, global efficacy and tolerance were non-significantly different on a variety of measures but tended to favour carbamazepine. Lusznat *et al.* (1988) studied 20 patients randomized to either lithium or carbamazepine and reported a 12-month response rate of 9 of 16 patients who showed satisfactory response on carbamazepine and 5 of 17 who showed a similar response on lithium. In this instance, carbamazepine was non-significantly better than lithium on criteria such as numbers of readmissions, severity of depression and side effects.

As reviewed by Prien and Gelenberg (1989), the existing partially controlled studies have, in many instances, methodological flaws. Nonetheless, the data currently available from these studies considerably augment the uncontrolled observations that support a role for carbamazepine in the prevention of both manic and depressive episodes. Prien and Gelenberg (1989) have also noted that the strongest evidence for the prophylactic efficacy of carbamazepine was based on designs employing mirror image trials (see Figure 10), placebo discontinuation (Post *et al.*, 1984a, 1984b), and open trials in refractory patients (see Figure 5b). Nevertheless, a variety of issues remain to be further clarified. One of the most important is the delineation of clinical and biological markers of which patients may respond to this anticonvulsant compared with lithium carbonate.

Data in the literature (reviewed in Table IV) suggest that while rapid-cycling illness is a relative indicator of lithium non-response, many of these patients appear to respond to carbamazepine, either alone or in combination. The data of Okuma *et al.* (1973), reanalysed from their graphic depiction of response in their open clinical trial, actually suggest that rapid-cycling patients (those with an estimated greater than four episodes per year) have a better response to carbamazepine than those patients without such a rapid cycling pattern. When

166

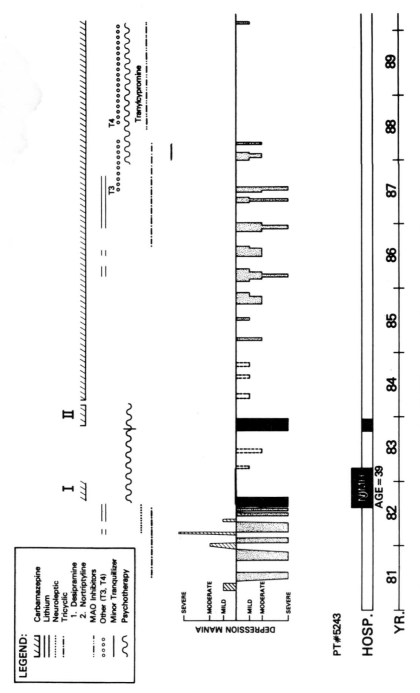

Figure 11. Good acute response to carbamazepine (I, II) but progressive emergence of episodes.

the same analysis is applied to the visual depiction of clinical response in the study of Kishimoto *et al.* (1983), however, there appears to be no preference of response of rapid cyclers compared with non-rapid cyclers. Moreover, in the study of Joyce (1988), where rapid cyclers were specifically selected for treatment, a relatively low response rate (33%) was noted for carbamazepine or the carbamazepine–lithium combination.

Thus, while it appears appropriate to conclude that many lithium-refractory rapid-cycling patients may respond to carbamazepine either alone or adjunctively, it remains to be delineated whether rapid cycling is actually a positive predictor for carbamazepine response. In addition, Frankenburg *et al.* (1988) reported that of 21 patients initially showing good acute response to carbamazepine and continued on the drug, only some 7 patients remained on carbamazepine in addition to other agents at the end of the period of approximately three to four years of follow-up. The reasons for carbamazepine discontinuation included an unusually high incidence of side effects (not observed or paralleled by results of many other clinical investigators) and, in ten instances, the development of inefficacy. Among the 7 patients who remained on carbamazepine, only 2 were noted to continue to show an excellent response. Joyce (1988) reported that of 18 rapid-cycling patients, only 12 received carbamazepine for six months or greater and 4 of these showed complete remission (2 on carbamazepine alone and 2 in combination with lithium). Three showed a mild response and 5 did not respond at all. Thus, the long-term response to carbamazepine does not appear to be as robust in some studies as in others.

In an attempt to assess further the reasons for these discrepancies, we have followed a group of patients who showed initially good response to carbamazepine in an open-label fashion in the community in a manner not entirely dissimilar to that of Frankenburg *et al.* (1988), although follow-up reports were more systematically gleaned from the patient and/or treating physician on a monthly basis by our social worker, Gabriele Leverich. We observed that carbamazepine, usually given as an addition to lithium, made a substantial impact on the course of illness in 24 patients (Post *et al.*, 1990b). On the average, patients exhibited 6.5 ± 6.3 episodes per year in the year prior to the carbamazepine trial. Following carbamazepine administration, mean episodes dropped to two to three per year in the first several years of treatment, and persisted at this level. An illness index was constructed by multiplying the duration of illness by severity. Patients showed an illness index of 22 (equivalent to 22 weeks of complete incapacitation or 44 weeks of severe impairment per year); on carbamazepine this decreased to a range of six to eight (a 72% decrease from baseline in the first year and a 66% decrease in the second year of carbamazepine treatment).

Embedded in this overall pattern of good response to carbamazepine was a subgroup of patients who showed an initial excellent response, but then demonstrated a pattern of some deterioration back toward baseline. As illustrated in Figure 11 some patients began to show the re-emergence of manic or depressive episodes. We classified patients who showed a consistent and prolonged response to carbamazepine as stable responders, while those who showed an initial response with some loss of efficacy as those who showed a pattern of escape. In patients who were followed for more than two years, 11 patients showed a stable pattern of response to carbamazepine, while 11 showed the pattern of some loss of efficacy over time. Again, all these patients were not under our direct treatment control. It was our impression that loss of efficacy in many instances occurred despite maintenance of adequate therapeutic levels of carbamazepine and, in some instances, in spite of attempts to recapture therapeutic response by raising carbamazepine dose and/or blood levels. Perhaps these data are not too different from those of Maj *et al.* (1989a), who recently reported, in patients showing an initial complete response to lithium for two years, a high percentage eventually experiencing breakthrough of manic and depressive episodes. While Page *et al.* (1987) suggest there was no loss of efficacy during lithium treatment, 22 of 10 patients were lost to follow-up and 20 had died, 6 by suicide.

A variety of explanations remain to be systematically pursued for the phenomenon of carbamazepine-induced escape (such as pharmacokinetics, illness progression, and loss of drug efficacy). We have explored an interesting preclinical model that may be relevant in the clinical sphere. We have found that rats initially showed an excellent response to the acute anticonvulsant effects of carbamazepine on amygdala-kindled seizures eventually show the development of loss of efficacy or tolerance (Weiss and Post, 1991a) upon daily repetition of drug and kindled stimulation. We have labelled this phenomenon 'contingent tolerance', as animals that receive the drug after seizures have occurred do not become tolerant. Moreover, once tolerance has been induced by repeated pretreatment, it can be reversed by a period of giving the drug after the seizure has occurred. Likewise, animals that are given kindled seizures, but do not receive any drug (for five or seven days) show renewed efficacy to carbamazepine. In contrast, animals that are merely exposed to carbamazepine without the kindled stimulation or have a period of time off without either kindling or drug (for three weeks or longer) do not show spontaneous reversal of the tolerance process. Taken together, these data suggest that the experience of seizures in the absence of drug is the requisite condition for renewal of carbamazepine's anticonvulsant efficacy or, specifically, a temporal unpairing of drug and seizure induction.

If a parallel phenomenon was occurring in the clinical sphere, the preclinical data suggest the possibility that a period of time off carbamazepine might lead to at least a transient renewal of its clinical efficacy once it is resumed. To our knowledge, such a strategy has not been pursued prospectively in the initially responsive patient who develops refractoriness. Thus, it might deserve exploration on a careful individual trial basis (Pazzaglia and Post, in press, 1992). These observations on carbamazepine-induced tolerance and its potential reversal by a medication-free period appear to parallel those in unipolar depressives whose responsiveness to MAOIs is lost, but regained after a period of drug discontinuation (J. Fawcett, personal communication, 1988).

In our preclinical studies, we did not observe cross-tolerance between carbamazepine and the anticonvulsant diazepam (Weiss and Post, 1991b). This suggests that different drugs with different mechanisms of action may not share the development of cross-contingent tolerance and raises the question of whether shifting to another anticonvulsant or alternative treatment agent might not be a more effective strategy than drug discontinuation in the face of the emergence or gradual inefficacy. By so doing, one might avoid the occurrence of an untreated episode associated with the carbamazepine discontinuation phase prior to reinitiating the drug. Obviously these therapeutic suggestions are only tenuously based on preclinical evidence at this time, but the theoretical context of contingent tolerance appears to merit discussion, and it may help provide a conceptual organization for a variety of factors that could lead to loss of efficacy over time. Such loss of efficacy does not appear to be confined to carbamazepine alone; it can occur with lithium (Maj *et al.*, 1989a) or valproate. Moreover, Baldessarini and Tohen (1988) and Fawcett have suggested that tolerance may occur to the long-term efficacy of tricyclics and MAOIs in patients with recurrent unipolar affective disorders as well. In our analysis, compared with those who showed a stable long-term carbamazepine prophylaxis, those who showed the pattern of escape (i.e., possible tolerance) had experienced a rapidly deteriorating and escalating frequency of episodes in the baseline years prior to initiation of carbamazepine treatment. Thus, it is possible that these patients had experienced a more malignant course of illness, and loss of efficacy was destined to occur regardless of which effective agent was used for initial treatment. Preliminary evidence suggests that loss of efficacy can occur with valproate as well (see Figure 12). Clearly, much information remains to be garnered on the long-term course of response in rapid cyclers, not only to carbamazepine and related novel anticonvulsant mood stabilizers, but also to lithium and more traditional agents, where a considerable degree of morbidity in spite of initial good response is increasingly being recognized (Table I and Figure 6).

Lithium–carbamazepine combination and its augmentation

Kishimoto and Okuma (1985) describe a series of patients who appear to respond to the combination of lithium and carbamazepine much better than to either drug alone. It is unclear which patients require combination versus single treatment. In light of this ambiguity, it may be useful clinically to add

170

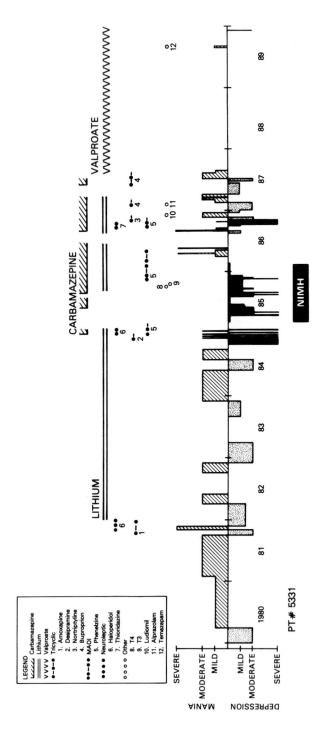

Figure 12. Prophylactic response to valproate in a non-responder to lithium/carbamazepine.

carbamazepine to existing treatment with lithium, particularly in bipolar patients who show some evidence of initial, at least partial, response to lithium. If a dramatic clinical response is observed, a decision can always be made later (although with the caveats discussed above) to discontinue lithium and see whether carbamazepine alone is capable of producing this degree of efficacy. In this fashion, considerable time might be saved in the assessment of the non-responsive patient (who would have avoided a trial of carbamazepine alone) and alternative options could then be explored. While monotherapy is currently fashionable in the treatment of seizure disorders, this academic principle does not appear to be paralleled by clinical practice. Similarly, in many series even in the best-managed lithium clinics, patients with recurrent affective disorders appear to require considerable adjunctive medication in order to maintain stability. Considerable work remains to define which affectively ill patients require combination therapy with agents with different mechanisms of action.

Obviously, recognition of the need for combination therapy in some individuals has to be tempered by the concerns of additive side effects, particularly in the use of lithium and carbamazepine, where each agent alone can have considerable and differential potential for a variety of side effects. Table III reviews, in a highly encapsulated form, the differential side-effect profiles of these two agents and some of the effects when the two drugs are used in combination. The clinical use and side effects of carbamazepine are discussed in detail elsewhere (Post *et al.*, 1984a, 1987b; Post, 1988; Jefferson *et al.*, 1987; Jefferson and Greist, 1987). Nonetheless, several systems should be briefly reviewed in relationship to long-term prophylaxis. It is our experience and that of the Japanese investigators (Okuma, 1983) and many other groups throughout the world that, in general, the combination of lithium and carbamazepine is very well tolerated (Brewerton *et al.*, 1988; Post, 1989; Kramlinger and Post, 1989a, 1989b, 1990). This contrasts with the isolated reports of neurotoxicity when the two agents are used in combination.

It should be remembered that when carbamazepine is initiated (even as a single-treatment agent) in high doses (600–800 mg/kg per day), there is an increased risk of side effects such as dizziness, ataxia and diplopia. Thus, it is important, particularly if initiating treatment during a relatively euthymic or depressive phase, to begin treatment with carbamazepine at low dose with a slow rate of dose increase. Some patients will not tolerate more than 200 mg or even 100 mg of carbamazepine at night, with increases proceeding at 200 mg every three days or more slowly.

Accordingly, as patients show an extremely wide variability in the dose and blood level at which they will demonstrate side effects, it is of considerable importance to individualize dose administration, titrating against side effects rather than proceeding with an arbitrary regimen (Tomson, 1984). In most studies, the doses for prophylaxis appear to be in the range of those used for acute treatment of manic and depressive episodes and, in these latter instances,

Table III.   Comparative clinical and side-effect profiles of lithium, carbamazepine and valproate

	Li	CBZ	Li and CBZ combination	Valproate
Clinical profile				
Mania	++	++	+++	++
Dysphoric	(+)	+	++	++
Rapid cycling	+	++	+++	++
Continuous cycling	(+)	+	++	+
Family history negative	+	++	+++	?
Depression	+	(+)	++	(+)
Prophylaxis of mania and depression	++	++	+++	++
Epilepsy	0	++	?	++
Pain syndromes	0	++	?	?
Side effects				
White blood count	↑	↓	(↑), Li*	—
Diabetes insipidus	↑	↓	↑, Li*	—
Thyroid hormones, T_3, T_4	↓	↓	↓↓	?↓
TSH	↑	—	↑, Li*	?
Serum calcium	↑	↓		?
Weight gain	↑	(−)		↑
Tremor	↑	—		↑
Memory disturbances	(↑)	(↑)		(↑)
Diarrhoea	(↑)	—		(↑)
Psoriasis	(↑)	—		—
Teratogenesis	(↑)	(↑)		(↑)
Pruritic rash (allergy)	—	↑		—
Agranulocytosis	—	(↑)		—
Thrombocytopenia	—	(↑)		(↑)
Hepatitis	—	(↑)		↑
Hyponatraemia, water intoxiation	—	↑		—
Dizziness, ataxia, diplopia	—	↑		—
Hypercortisolism, escape from dexamethasone suppression	—	↑		?

Note: *Clinical efficacy*   *Side effects*
    0,   none   ↑,   increase
    +,   effective   ↓,   decrease
    ++,   very effective   ( ), inconsistent or rare
    +++, possible synergism   —,   absent
    ( ),   equivocal   ↓↓, potentiation
                                       Li* effect of lithium predominates

there seems to be little evidence of a relationship of either dose or blood level to the degree of clinical response across patients (Post *et al.*, 1983a; Post, 1990a, 1990c). Therefore, it would appear most opportune to titrate individual patients to their side effects threshold rather than attempt to target a specific dose or blood level. In this fashion, side effects will be avoided in the majority of patients and dose can be gradually increased, particularly after three or four weeks of treatment, when hepatic enzymes are induced and patients will tolerate doses of carbamazepine not previously tolerated because of increased drug metabolism.

Patients should be warned about possible pharmacokinetic interactions with commonly used drugs that might produce marked increases in carbamazepine levels and associated toxicity. These include erythromycin and its congeners, the calcium channel blockers, verapamil, diltiazem (but not nifedipine), the MAOI iproniazid (but not, apparently, phenelzine or tranylcypromine), and propoxyphene (Davron). It is also important to note that carbamazepine will induce the metabolism of birth control pills, making them less effective, and higher-dosage forms of these medications may be necessary in order to ensure adequate birth control. Other potential interactions are summarized in Table IV.

Table IV. Life events in affective illness: relationship to number of episodes

Greater likelihood of precipitants with first episode	Equal or less likelihood of precipitants with first episode compared with subsequent episodes
1. Astrup *et al.* (1959)	1. Kennedy *et al.* (1983)
2. Ambelas (1979)	
3. Ayuso Gutierrez *et al.* (1981)	
4. Bidzinska (1984)	
5. Perris (1984)	
6. Dolan *et al.* (1985)	
7. Ezquiaga *et al.* (1987)	
8. Ambelas (1987)	
9. Ghaziuddin *et al.* (1990)	
10. Swann *et al.* (1990)	
11. Cassano *et al.* (1990, personal communication)	
12. Mendlewicz *et al.* (1990, personal communication)	

With regard to haematological problems, patients should also be given adequate informed consent and told that if any evidence of infection or bleeding disorder becomes evident (such as fever, rash, sore throat, petechiae, etc.) they should immediately contact their physician for advice regarding drug discontinuation and the necessity of obtaining a complete blood count.

Recurrent breakthrough of severe depression in bipolar patients treated with lithium, carbamazepine or other agents appears to be the most troublesome treatment issue. The use of lithium potentiation for a variety of acute antidepressant treatments, including carbamazepine, has recently been reviewed (Kramlinger and Post, 1989a) and is widely accepted. The efficacy of adding carbamazepine to lithium for the patient experiencing acute depressive breakthroughs has not been systematically explored. However, rather than automatically moving to a unimodal antidepressant such as a heterocyclic or an MAOI (with their attendant liabilities for cycle induction), and given the emerging data for substantial efficacy of carbamazepine in prophylaxis of depression (Table II and Figure 10), one might consider the addition of this bimodal mood-stablizing agent for the bipolar patient experiencing depressions on lithium. Stuppaeck *et al.* (1990) have recently reported that carbamazepine was effective in the prophylaxis in 11 of 17 unipolar depressives as well.

Even in the face of the dual mood-stabilizing agents of lithium and carbamazepine, some bipolar individuals may still be liable to manic switches induced by HCAs and MAOIs. Such a patient is illustrated in Figure 12. This 35-year-old female demonstrated lithium refractoriness, including tricyclic-induced acceleration of rapid cycling in 1984. Upon admission to NIMH, treatment with carbamazepine (initially alone and later with adjunctive lithium, also administered on a double-blind basis) was associated with a cessation of rapid cycling but persistence of a low-level depression. When attempts were made to potentiate treatment with an MAOI, a mildly hypomanic state was induced at the end of her NIMH hospitalization and this was eventually followed by a switch into severe mania that required rehospitalization in another institution. Numerous attempts were made to restabilize the patient using lithium and carbamazepine with several adjunctive antidepressant modalities, but all were unsuccessful. The patient was eventually switched to valproate and became euthymic for the first time in many years and remained stable for several years. However, by 1989–1990, the patient was showing evidence of affective breakthroughs, again suggesting that tolerance may occur to a wide variety of treatment agents, particularly in rapid cyclers.

Consequently, it appears that in some vulnerable individuals, even two mood stabilizers (lithium and carbamazepine) may be insufficient to block HCA- or MAOI-induced switches and/or rapid cycling. On the other hand, we have observed other patients in whom the introduction of MAOIs did not produce mania or rapid cycling and in whom therapeutic response in depression was achieved (see Figure 11). These individual case reports highlight the need for systematic clinical trials to document the relative utility of these agents and to uncover the possible clinical or biological markers to predict response. The patient in Figure 12 also highlights the proposition that response to one anticonvulsant may not predict response to another, and that some rapid cyclers may benefit from a shift or rotation of drugs in their regimens if there is either inefficacy or eventual loss of efficacy.

The use of bupropion (Wellbutrin) in combination with carbamazepine and lithium deserves careful systematic evaluation, particularly in light of the major concern about the induction of seizures with high doses of this agent. Theoretically, combined use of bupropion and carbamazepine would obviate this risk and, at the same time, allow systematic assessment of the efficacy of high-dose bupropion in the bipolar patient. In contrast to this hopeful perspective with bupropion, it appears that the selective serotonin (5-hydroxytryptamine, 5-HT) reuptake inhibitor fluoxetine may share some of the liabilities of the other unimodal antidepressants in terms of case reports of the occurrence of mania.

Valproate prophylaxis in affective illness

As illustrated in Figure 12 and in Table III, there is emerging case material and open clinical observations in a series of studies indicating that valproate may play a valuable role in the treatment of lithium refractoriness in bipolar patients. While none of the prophylactic studies with valproate has been blind or randomized, this drug was often successfully employed in patients refractory to lithium and/or carbamazepine. Recent data of Calabrese and Delucchi (1989) also support the efficacy of valproate in patients with ultra-rapid mood fluctuations, some of whom were unresponsive to lithium and carbamazepine. These data parallel the earlier observations of McElroy and associates (1987), who reported good responses to valproate in patients refractory to the other two treatments, but partially contrast with the poorer quality of response noted by Puzynski and Klosiewicz (1984). These later investigators observed statistically significant but at times not clinically robust prophylactic responses to valproate. In addition, there appeared to be a less good response in prevention of the depressive episodes, with some patients showing 'fragmentation' of longer episodes to more short and discrete ones. Some of the patients of Emrich and associates (1980, 1984, 1985) have been followed for a number of years on valproate therapy with continued positive responses, and systematic long-term controlled trials with this agent are eagerly awaited, as are studies aimed at elucidating possible predictors of differential response to carbamazepine versus valproate. Response to a combination of carbamazepine plus valproate has been reported in epilepsy and deserves systematic study in recurrent affective illness (see Figure 9 and Keffer and Post, 1992).

The therapeutic range of valproate is thought to reside between 50 and 120 $\mu g/ml$ in epilepsy, and preliminary data suggest that this is the same range for clinical effectiveness in manic-depressive illness. Doses to achieve these blood levels are usually on the order of 1500 mg per day (range 750–2500 mg per day). Side effects differ with valproate administration compared with lithium or carbamazepine (Table III). These have tended to be gastrointestinal disturbances (less common with the enteric-coated capsule Depakote), dose-related tremor, increased appetite and weight gain, and alopecia (which may be prevented with zinc (50 mg per day) (Pippenger, personal communication, October 1990).

According to the psychiatric series of valproate studies reported to date, there has been a relative absence of hepatic side effects. This is particularly noteworthy as there is a well-documented occurrence of severe hepatitis and some fatalities with the use of valproate for epilepsy. Children under 2 years of age appear to be particularly prone to severe hepatic reactions (Dreifuss and Langer, 1987), although cases have been reported in older individuals as well (Scheffner *et al.*, 1988). There is also some evidence that this side effect may occur more commonly during anticonvulsant combination treatment than when valproate is used alone.

As mild increases in liver enzymes are common on valproate and many of the other anticonvulsants, it is usually recommended that treatment proceed cautiously in the face of these mild elevations and the drug not be discontinued until enzymes are several times normal or clearly increasing and not tapering off. Thus, periodic checks of hepatic function are indicated during treatment with valproate. In addition, symptoms of malaise, apathy, aversion to valproate, nausea, vomiting, fever, right upper quadrant pain, dark urine, jaundice, oedema, or a bleeding tendency should all provoke an immediate call to the patient's physician and immediate drug discontinuation if these are associated with evidence of hepatic dysfunction.

Thyroid augmentation: replacement and suppressive doses

Gjessing (1975) originally suggested the use of thyroid hormone in the treatment of periodic catatonia. Stancer and Persad (1982), Wehr and colleagues (1985), and Bauer and Whybrow (1988) have studied the use of suppressant doses of thyroid hormone in the treatment of refractory bipolar patients. Wehr *et al.* (1988) reported that this treatment, which was associated with medical toxicities in a number of patients, showed eventual loss of efficacy even in patients who initially showed a good response. Stancer and Persad (1982) and now Bauer and Whybrow (1988, 1990) have recommended using high doses of thyroid hormone in the treatmnet of refractory and rapid-cycling bipolar patients, largely as an adjunctive treatment. Thyroxine (T_4) is increased until the free T_4 index is above the normal range and thyroid-stimulating hormone (TSH) falls to below normal. This is typically achieved with a dose of Synthroid 0.3–0.4 mg per day (Bauer and Whybrow, 1988, 1990). When used in this fashion, Bauer and Whybrow report an improvement in the severity of both manic and depressive symptoms in these rapid-cycling patients. The long-term effects of such treatment on the course of illness remain to be documented.

The ambiguities of evaluating the response and contribution of each of the separate drugs in a patient treated with multiple pharmacotherapies is illustrated in Figure 9. This 58-year-old single female had a greater than 20-year history of ultra-rapid cycling, as documented prospectively during evaluation of the patient on placebo (row 1). The patient was blindly assessed by nurses twice daily and global daily mania and depression ratings are plotted above and below the abscissa, respectively. Blind institution of carbamazepine treatment resulted in inhibition of hypomania, but produced little change in the rapid fluctuations of depressions (row 2). The blind addition of lithium did not substantially alter this pattern (row 3), but may have slightly attenuated episode duration or severity with the associated increase in relative euthymia (unshaded). The further addition of valproate resulted in an apparent slowing of cycling with prolongation of a depression (row 4).

When triiodothyronine (T_3) (50 µg) was added to the combination of three bimodal agents, a euthymic state was observed (row 5), and the patient was able to be discharged. She remained relatively stable, except for one moderate depression responsive to MAOIs, for approximately nine months, in contrast to her previous state of continuous illness for more than two decades. Rapid cycling of depressions then resumed which was only partially responsive to MAOIs. It is noteworthy that the carbamazepine and valproate combination that is used with some success in the treatment of refractory epileptics (Walker and Koon, 1988; Dean and Penry, 1988; Callaghan and Goggin, 1988) produced severe asterixis associated with an elevated ammonia level. It is also noteworthy that this patient was treated with T_3 and not T_4, as the literature records is generally employed for maintenance or replacement (because of the longer half-life of T_4), that the dose (50 µg) was not suppressive, and that baseline thyroid function was normal. An important role of thyroid augmentation in this patient is suggested by the on–off–on nature of her response (row 5), but not unequivocally demonstrated; i.e., it is possible that the other bimodal agents merely required a longer period of time to attenuate cycling. These ambiguities remain even with prospective double-blind evaluation of treatment. Nonetheless, we would encourage the use of daily self-ratings on a 100-mm line (0 = worst ever; 50 = normal; 100 = highest ever) in rapid-cycling out-patients, so that mood can be evaluated graphically and prospectively.

Adjunctive use of high-potency benzodiazepines for breakthrough episodes

While Chouinard (1987) reported that clonazepam and lithium were equally effective in acute mania, adjunctive use of neuroleptics was allowed in both patient populations and thus obscures the interpretation of the results. Nonetheless, it appears that clonazepam is a highly sedating benzodiazepine that may be particularly effective for night-time use in patients who show insomnia as an early sign of hypomania or depression. Wehr (1989) argues convincingly that sleep deprivation or prolonged periods of decreased sleep may, in a positive feedback fashion, exacerbate mania. Therefore, targeting the early evidence of sleep disturbance and treating it with high-potency sedating benzodiazepines such as clonazepam may be a particularly effective treatment strategy to be employed in lieu of automatic first use of neuroleptics. However, Aronson *et al.* (1989) have reported a series of five patients where clonazepam was unable to substitute for neuroleptics. The antidepressant efficacy of clonazepam also requires further investigation, with some promising studies reported (Kishimoto *et al.*, 1988, 1990).

The long-term efficacy of the benzodiazepines, either as single agents or as adjuncts in the treatment of bipolar illness, has not been very systematically explored. However, preliminary data from Kishimoto and Okuma (personal communication, August 1988) suggest that tolerance occurs in a substantial proportion of patients, and this would be the likely expectation based on the high incidence of tolerance development to the benzodiazepines in the treatment of seizure disorders. Thus, one might confine the benzodiazepines to acute, intermittent and adjunctive use rather than attempting to rely on this series of compounds as a long-term treatment strategy.

Alprazolam appears to have a more positive acute antidepressant profile than clonazepam, at least in milder out-patient depressives, but appears to share the risk of the unimodal antidepressants for manic induction.

While adjunctive use of the high-potency benzodiazepines may at times be helpful, one should give strong consideration to intervening with adjunctive use of carbamazepine or valproic acid (as discussed above) for rapid cyclers with breakthrough manic or depressive episodes; moreover, information about responsivity in an acute episode may be very helpful in assisting in the choice of agents for a long prophylaxis. Parenthetically, acute trials of carbamazepine and valproate in depression may not be as good an indicator of subsequent prophylactic antidepressant response as is the case for mania, since the percentage of response in prophylaxis of depression (as with lithium) may be higher than in acute treatment of depression.

Calcium channel blockers in the treatment of affective illness

While a series of reports indicate the efficacy of verapamil and related calcium channel blockers in the treatment of acute mania (Dubovsky *et al.*, 1986; Dose *et al.*, 1986; Brotman *et al.*, 1986), data are sparse regarding long-term efficacy of these agents in prophylactic treatment (Dubovsky *et al.*, 1985; Barton and Gitlin, 1987; Gitlin and Weiss, 1984). Moreover, the data of Hoschl and Kozeny (1989) indicated that while verapamil was as effective in the treatment of mania as lithium, or lithium in combination with neuroleptics, it was without effect in the treatment of acute depression. The time course of improvement was equal to that of placebo in depression and clearly of lesser efficacy compared with amitriptyline or other active antidepressant agents chosen by the treating physician.

Thus, the utility of verapamil in lithium-refractory patients remains to be documented, as does its potential efficacy in the prophylaxis of recurrent depressive episodes. Nonetheless, this series of agents remains promising in light of their acute antimanic efficacy and occasional case reports of longer-term efficacy. They are also of considerable interest in relationship to data implicating abnormalities in calcium metabolism in affective disorders (Dubovsky and Franks, 1983; Carman and Wyatt, 1979) and the subtleties of synaptic neurotransmission, as well as the mechanism of action of lithium (Meltzer *et al.*, 1988) and carbamazepine (Post, 1987).

Other anticonvulsants

Inoue *et al.* (1984) reported that acetazolamide (Diamox) was ineffective in some patients with atypical psychosis not responsive to lithium or carbamazepine. Possible correlates of response include puerperal and premenstrual psychosis and episodes presenting with dreamy confusional states. Efficacy in more typical bipolar patients remains to be studied.

While highly touted for a variety of neuropsychiatric illnesses (Dreyfus, 1981), phenytoin remains to be systematically tested in longer-term prophylaxis of unipolar or bipolar illness. A case report of repeated response to phenytoin and relapse on discontinuation in a patient with severe schizoaffective illness (Freyhan, 1945) suggests that some patients may respond to this agent. An isolated positive case report is also provided by Stephen G. Hayes, MD (personal communication, 6th May 1989).

In several instances, γ-aminobutyric acid (GABA) agonists have been reported to be effective in acute trials in affectively ill patients, but have not been systematically explored for long-term prophylaxis (Lloyd *et al.*, 1989). A clinical trial of γ-vinyl GABA was associated with a substantial incidence of depression, but whether this was a direct effect of this reuptake inhibitor remains to be explored.

Electroconvulsive therapy (ECT)

This somatic treatment (which is itself a potent anticonvulsant modality (Post *et al.*, 1986a) remains under-utilized in many institutions for treatment-refractory depression. Nonetheless, data are virtually non-existent for its long-term efficacy in the bipolar or rapid-cycling patient. In the patient illustrated in Figure 8, we observed an initial excellent acute response to ECT during one depressive episode, but the patient failed ECT prophylaxis and failed to respond to a new series of ECT treatments in the next depression in another hospital. Nevertheless, ECT may be life saving in treatment of acute episodes and its use may be associated with renewed efficacy to more traditional modalities (although

Sackeim *et al.* (1990) suggests this is unlikely), either on the basis of altering the neurotransmitter milieu or in providing a period of time off psychotropic medications that may be associated with reversal of contingent tolerance (see above). Maintenance ECT treatment in rapid cyclers clearly deserves systematic study.

Other approaches

Adjunctive treatment with folate (300–400 µg per day) (Coppen *et al.*, 1986) or ascorbate (3 g) (Naylor and Smith, 1981; Kay *et al.*, 1984) has been recommended in some studies but not amply demonstrated for overall clinical utility. Nonetheless, given the general lack of serious side effects of this strategy, it might be considered for the patient showing inadequate response to existing treatment regimens.

Naylor *et al.* (1986) has also hypothesized that drugs acting on vanadium (such as ascorbate, ethylenediaminetetraacetic acid (EDTA) or carbamazepine) may be effective in bipolar illness. He also found that high-dose methylene blue (300 mg/kg) as an adjunct to lithium maintenance was effective in reducing depressive but not manic symptoms. Turner (1985) did not observe positive effects, however.

Tryptophan potentiation is controversial and remains on hold because of the Food and Drug Administration (FDA) ban on sales due to the development of malignant eosinophilia; use of 5-hydroxytryptophan (5-HTP) remains a potential option (van Praag *et al.*, 1987) requiring further study, although it too has been associated with the eosinophilia–myalgia syndrome.

Sleep deprivation may provide an acute augmentation to existing and adjunctive treatments for the patient with a depressive breakthrough but inconsistency of response is problematic. We have observed either tolerance or, in contrast, a relative refractory period to positive sleep deprivation effects in some rapid-cycling bipolar patients at the onset of individual depressive episodes, but greater responsivity as the episode progresses (Roy-Byrne *et al.*, 1984; Ketter *et al.*, unpublished observations, 1990). Moreover, in one rapid cycler, an attempt at prophylactic sleep deprivation during a euthymic period precipitated a depressive episode.

High-intensity light is reported to be of prophylactic value in seasonal affective disorder (Rosenthal *et al.*, 1984) and remains to be studied in more traditional bipolar patients.

S-Adenosyl-methionine appears remarkable for its acute antidepressant properties in unipolar patients, but appears relatively contraindicated in bipolar illness because of the unusually high incidence of switches to mania (Carney *et al.*, 1988). Maintenance treatment in unipolars has not been explored, to our knowledge.

Psychosurgery remains unevaluated in systematic controlled studies and positive results are sometimes confounded with differences in adjunctive medications, including psychotropic anticonvulsants (Lovett and Shaw, 1987).

Illness evolution over time: implications for pharmacotherapy and the role of pscyhosocial stressors

Elsewhere, we have discussed in more detail how the model of kindling may be useful in conceptualizing various aspects of the long-term course of manic-depressive illness (Post *et al.*, 1984c, 1986b, 1988b; Post, 1990b). A brief synopsis is presented as it pertains to several issues of import in prophylaxis in rapid cycling depression. Kindling is the development of increasing behavioural and motor responses culminating in full-blown production of a seizure to a previously subthreshold stimulation. Thus, it is clear that kindling is not a good model for manic-depressive illness as the behaviours observed during kindling do not resemble those in manic-depressive illness. Moreover, patients with manic-depressive illness do not demonstrate an increased proclivity for seizures and, even with sophisticated electrophysiological and metabolic mapping, there is little evidence of a covert seizure disorder.

Nonetheless, kindling provides an interesting model for the progressive evolution and unfolding of a neuropsychiatric syndrome in response to the same inducing stimulus. Some of the principles of illness evolution and treatment response might be relevant to parallel processes in affective illness. Kindling may be divided into three general stages: (early) development; (mid) completed; and (late) spontaneous. During kindling development, animals proceed through a phase when electrical stimulation (i.e., once a day for one session) is subthreshold for production of even an afterdischarge (AD). With repeated stimulation, AD threshold decreases, and with sufficient repetitions the AD begins to grow in duration and complexity as well as spread through the various brain structures until a full-blown motor convulsion occurs. In the completed stage of kindling, full-blown seizures are reliably induced. Following a sufficient number of repetitions of kindled seizures, the animal enters a phase of spontaneity where exogenous electrophysiological stimulation is no longer required and the animals appear to show what might be considered spontaneous epilepsy.

It is of considerable interest that pharmacological interventions in kindling vary according to stage of evolution. For example, while carbamazepine is one of the most effective agents in inhibiting the completed amygdala-kindled seizure, it is without effect on the early development of kindled seizures, at least in the rat (Weiss and Post, 1987; Schmutz and Klebs, 1989). Carbamazepine shows the opposite profile on cocaine-kindled seizures, where it is highly effective in preventing development of these seizures, but once they are fully manifest the drug is ineffective (Weiss *et al.*,1989). An even more remarkable dissociation is evident from the data of Pinel (1983), where he has documented that diazepam, which is effective in the development and completed stages of kindling, is ineffective on the spontaneous seizures. Conversely, phenytoin, which is poorly effective in the first two stages, is highly effective in preventing spontaneous seizures. These data and others appear to amply document the principle that different phases of the evolution of what appears to be a unitary syndrome, such as kindled seizures, are, in fact, differentially responsive. Thus, in this and other preclinical models, effective pharmacological intervention may differ as a function of the stage of evolution of the syndrome.

We are now in a position to ask whether a similar principle may not be operating in the phases of evolution of manic-depresive illness. The data summarized in Table I suggest that lithium is less effective in rapid-cycling patients and that many of these patients may respond to either carbamazepine or valproate. While patients may ultimately be separated into responsive subgroups, it is also possible that the same patient is differentially responsive as a function of his stage of illness. There may be an evolution of pharmaco-responsivity in which patients early in their course are amenable to treatment interventions with lithium, but, with the occurrence of more rapid cycling which often occurs late in the illness, relative refractoriness occurs and adjunctive treatments are required.

The schema illustrated in Figure 13 is highly provisional but is presented in order to suggest that this organizing principle needs to be further systematically tested, and that clinicians may use it in order to consider different treatment options, particularly in patients who have shifted to more malignant phases of their illness. Again, we are not suggesting a literal extrapolation of one-to-one drug efficacy of the different stages of kindling to the different stages of manic-depressive illness, but only that the principle of differential pharmaco-responsivity as a function of stage may be worthy of consideration in both syndromes.

The kindling model may also provide a means for unitary conceptualization of how affective illness may progress from episodes that are precipitated by psychosocial stressors to ones that are occurring autonomously and independently. Following the early observations of this transition by Kraepelin (1921), there is considerable systematic evidence (as reviewed in Table IV) that such a transition reliably occurs; there are greater numbers of psychosocial precipitants in the first episode of affective illness than in subsequent episodes.

These observations might also predict the differential efficacy of psychotherapeutic interventions as a function of course of illness. Early episodes that are associated with specific psychosocial stressors and precipitants may be responsive to psychodynamic therapies and other therapies aimed at understanding and/or reducing the apparent stress involved. However, when the shift to automaticity occurs, typically associated with rapid cycling, more congitive and behavioural strategies may be of greater importance in an attempt to specifically desensitize or decondition the episodes triggered more easily by lesser and lesser degrees of psychosocial stress. In the late phases of the illness, a

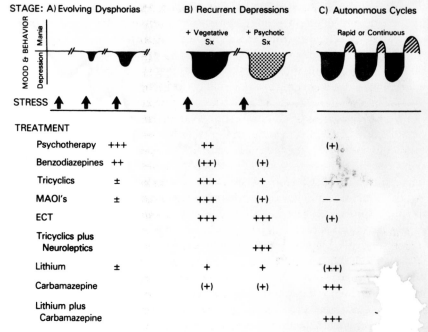

Figure 13. Psychopharmacology of affective illness as a function of stage of development (hypothetical scheme for further study).

great deal of psychosocial support may be needed in order to help the patient tolerate the recurrent dysphoric affective states while systematic clinical trials are conducted in order to assess which of a now extensive series of drugs may be effective for a given patient. Figure 5(b) also illustrates the possible role of stress sensitization in the breakthrough of previously effective pharmacotherapy (Leverich *et al.*, 1990).

The role of multi-model approaches and psychotherapy should not be underestimated for the unipolar and bipolar rapidly-cycling patient, particularly in light of recent systematic data regarding the efficacy of psychotherapeutic treatments alone in mild depression (Silver and Runkle, 1989; Elkin *et al.*, 1989) and in conjunction with phramacotherapy in a variety of treatment paradigms (Klerman and Weisman, 1987). Frank *et al.* (1991) document a weak effect of psychotherapy in delaying relapse in recurrent unipolar depression.

Conclusions

While the goal of maintaining complete prophylaxis (absence of episodes) may not be attainable for each individual patient, with the variety of available modalities even the most refractory bipolar patient has an excellent chance of a marked degree of improvement. This optimistic view needs to be balanced against the potential for malignant progression to rapid cycling and beyond (e.g., ultra-rapid cycling) and the need for close monitoring of the patient's pharmacotherapy and side effects by the patient himself and the family in a joint effort aimed at recognizing the potentially devastating long-term consequences of this illness.

Given the vagaries of clinical response and the dangers inherent in the discontinuation of an effective medication (Figures 6 and 7), it would appear that the acquisition of a regimen associated with successful prophylaxis should engender the most conservative approach to therapeutics; i.e., continued maintenance treatment. Conversely, the lack of adequate clinical efficacy should engender active and aggressive treatment responses in an attempt to arrive at the most appropriate psychopharmacological and psychotherapeutic regimens. In the face of loss of efficacy to previously effective regimes in rapid-cycling patients, novel approaches may be necessary, such as rotation among agents or temporary discontinuation of a drug. (It is noteworthy that the hypothetical effects of drug discontinuation are opposite, depending on whether the treatment is effective or loss of efficacy has occurred.)

Affective disorder, particularly of the more malignant, rapidly cycling variety, is both a potentially fatal medical illness and an eminently treatable one. Tremendous strides have been made in the development of new treatment options in the past three decades. Given the explosive accumulation of new knowledge in the neurosciences and the greatly advanced biochemical and physiological techniques and instrumentation to better understand the illness and the mechanisms of action of existing agents, it is hoped that, in the near future, not only will treatment be better targeted to individual patients, but that a new series of more effective treatments will emerge to prevent this recurrent and potentially incapacitating disorder. Much clinical and basic work remains to be performed to define and maximize the treatment options of this most difficult subgroup of the recurrent affective illnesses.

References

Abou-Saleh MT, Coppen A (1986) Who responds to prophylactic lithium. *J Affective Disord* **10**, 115–125.

Ahlfors UG, Baastrup PC, Dencker SJ (1981) Flupenthixol decanoate in recurrent manic depressive illness: a comparison with lithium. *Acta Psychiatr Scand* **64**, 226–237.

Ambelas A (1979) Psychologically stressful events in the precipitation of manic episodes. *Br J Psychiatry* **135**, 15–21.

Ambelas A (1987) Life events and mania: a special relationship. *Br J Psychiatry* **150**, 235–240.

Angst J (1986) The course of affective disorders. *Psychopathology* **19**, 47–52.

Angst J, Weiss P (1967) Periodicity of depressive psychoses. In Brill H, Cole JO, Deniker P (eds) *Proceedings of the Fifth International Medical Foundation, International Congress Series*, pp. 702–710. Amsterdam: Excerpta Medica.

Angst J, Merikangas K, Scheidegger P, Wicki W (1990) Recurrent brief depression: a new subtype of affective disorder. *J Affective Disord* **19**, 87–98.

Aronson TA, Shukla S, Hirschowitz J (1989) Clonazepam treatment of five lithium-refractory patients with bipolar disorder. *Am J Psychiatry* **146**, 77–80.

Astrup C, Fossum A, Holmboe R (1959) A follow-up study of 270 patients with acute affective psychoses. *Acta Psychiatr Scand* **34**, 7–62.

Ayuso Gutierrez JL, Fuentenebro de Diego F, Mendez Barroso R, Marteo Martin I (1981) Analysis of precipitating factors in a sample of patients hospitalized for endogenous depression. *Ann Med-Psychol (Paris)* **139**, 759–769.

Baastrup PC, Schou M (1967) Lithium as a prophylactic agent: its effect against recurrent depressions and manic-depresive psychosis. *Arch Gen Psychiatry* **16**, 162–172.

Baldessarini RJ, Tohen M (1988) Is there a long-term protective effect of mood-altering agents in unipolar depressive disorder? *Psychopharmacology Series (Berlin)* **5**, 130–139.

Ballenger JC, Post RM (1978) Therapeutic effects of carbamazepine in affective illness: a preliminary report. *Commun Psychopharmacol* **2**, 159–175.

Barton BM, Gitlin MJ (1987) Verapamil in treatment-resistant mania: an open trial. *J Clin Psychopharmacol* **7**, 101–103.

Bauer MS, Whybrow PC (1988) Thyroid hormones and the central nervous system in affective illness: interactions that may have clinical significance. *Integrative Psychiatry* **6**, 75–85.

Bauer MS, Whybrow PC (1990) Rapid cycling bipolar affective disorder. II. Treatment of refractory rapid cycling with high-dose levothyroxine: a preliminary study. *Arch Gen Psychiatry* **47**, 435–440.

Bellaire W, Demish K, Stoll K-D (1988) Carbamazepine versus lithium in prophylaxis of recurrent affective disorders (abstract). *Psychopharmacology* (suppl.) **96**, 287.

Bertollini R, Kallen B, Mastroiacovo P (1987) Anticonvulsant drugs in monotherapy: effect on the fetus. *Eur J Epidemiol* **3**, 164–171.

Bidzinska EJ (1984) Stress factors in affective diseases. *Br J Psychiatry* **144**, 161–166.

Bouman TK, Niemantsverdriet-Van Kampen JG, Ormel J, Slooff CJ (1986) The effectiveness of lithium prophylaxis in bipolar and unipolar depressions and schizo-affective disorders. *J Affective Disord* **11**, 275–280.

Bratfos O, Haug JO (1968) The course of manic-depressive psychosis: follow-up investigation of 215 patients. *Acta Psychiatr Scand* **44**, 89–112.

Brennan MJW, Sandyk R, Borseek D (1984) Use of sodium-valproate in the management of affective disorders: basic and clinical aspects. In Emrich HM, Okuma T, Muller AA (eds) *Anticonvulsants in Affective Disorders*, pp. 56–65. Amsterdam: Excerpta Medica.

Brewerton TD (1986) Lithium counteracts carbamazepine-induced leukopenia while increasing its therapeutic effect. *Biol Psychiatry* **21**, 677–685.

Brewerton T, Kramlinger KG, Post RM (1988) Combination therapy with lithium and carbamazepine. In Birch NJ (ed.) *Lithium: Inorganic Pharmacology and Psychiatric Use*, pp. 57–60. Oxford: IRL Press.

Brotman AW, Farhadi AM, Gelenberg AJ (1986) Verapamil treatment of acute mania. *J Clin Psychiatry* **47**, 136–138.

Brown R (1989) US experience with valproate in manic depressive illness: a multicentre trial. *J Clin Psychiatry* **50**, 13–16.

Cabrera JF, Muhlbauer HD, Schley J *et al.* (1986) Long-term randomized clinical trial on oxcarbazepine vs. lithium in bipolar and schizoaffective disorders: preliminary results. *Pharmacopsychiatry* **19**, 282–283.

Calabrese JR, Delucchi GA (1989) Phenomenology of rapid cycling manic depression and its treatment with valproate. *J. Clin Psychiatry* **50**, 30–34.

Callaghan N, Goggin T (1988) Adjunctive therapy in resistant epilepsy. *Epilepsia* **29**, S29–S35.

Carman JS, Wyatt RJ (1979) Use of calcitonin in psychotic agitation or mania. *Arch Gen Psychiatry* **36**, 72–75.

Carney MWP, Chary TKN, Bottigliere T, Reynolds EH (1988) Switch and *S*-adenosylmethionine. *Alabama J Med Sci* **25**, 316–319.

Chouinard G (1987) Clonazepam in acute and maintenance treatment of bipolar affective disorder. *J Clin Psychiatry* **48**, 29–37.

Coppen A, Abou-Saleh MT (1988) Lithium therapy: from clinical trials to practical management. *Acta Psychiatr Scand* **78**, 754–762.

Coppen A, Chaudhry S, Swade C (1986) Folic acid enhances lithium prophylaxis. *J Affective Disord* **10**, 9–13.

Cutler NR, Post RM (1982) Life course of illness in untreated manic-depressive patients. *Comprehen Psychiatry* **23**, 101–115.

Dean JC, Penry JK (1988) Carbamazepine/valproate therapy in 100 patients with partial seizures failing carbamazepine monotherapy: long term follow-up. *Epilepsia* **29**, 687.

Dolan RJ, Calloway SP, Fonagy P *et al.* (1985) Life events, depression and hypothalamic–pituitary–adrenal axis function. *Br J Psychiatry* **147**, 429–433.

Dose M, Emrich HM, Cording-Tommel C, Von Zerssen D (1986) Use of calcium antagonists in mania. *Psychoneuroendocrinology* **11**, 241–243.

Dostal T (1977) Double-blind study of the therapeutic and prophylactic effect of lithium salts in psychiatry. Prague: Research Institute of Psychiatry—candidate dissertation.

Dreifuss FE, Langer DH (1987) Hepatic considerations in the use of antiepileptic drugs. *Epilepsia* **28**, S23–S29.

Dreyfus J (1981) *A Remarkable Medicine Has Been Overlooked.* New York: Simon & Schuster.

Dubovsky SL, Franks RD (1983) Intracellular calcium in affective disorders: a review and an hypothesis. *Biol Psychiatry* **18**, 781–797.

Dubovsky S, Franks R, Schrier D (1985) Phenelzine-induced hypomania: effect of verapamil. *Biol Psychiatry* **20**, 1009–1014.

Dubovsky SL, Franks RD, Allen S (1986) Calcium antagonists in mania: a double-blind study of verapamil. *Psychiatry Res* **18**, 309–320.

Dunner DL, Fieve RR (1974) Clinical factors in lithium prophylactic failure. *Arch Gen Psychiatry* **30**, 229–233.

Dunner DL, Fleiss JL, Fieve RR (1976) Lithium carbonate prophylaxis failure. *Br J Psychiatry* **129**, 40–44.

Elkin I, Shea MT, Watkins JT *et al.* (1989) National Institute of Mental Health Treatment of Depression Collaborative Research Program. General effectiveness of treatments. *Arch Gen Psychiatry* **46**, 971–982.

Elphick M (1985) An open clinical trial of carbamazepine in treatment-resistant bipolar and schizoaffective psychotics. *Br J Psychiatry* **147**, 198–200.

Emrich HM, Von Zerssen D, Kissling W *et al.* (1980) Effect of sodium valproate in mania: the GABA hypothesis of affective disorders. *Arch Psychiatr Nervenkr* **229**, 1–16.

Emrich HM, Dose M, Von Zerssen D (1984) Action of sodium-valproate and of oxcarbazepine in patients with affective disorders. In Emrich HM, Okuma T, Muller AA (eds) *Anticonvulsants in Affective Disorders*, pp. 45–55. Amsterdam: Excerpta Medica.

Emrich HM, Dose M, Von Zerssen D (1985) The use of sodiuim valproate, carbamazepine and oxcarbazepine in patients with affective disorders. *J Affective Disord* **8**, 243–250.

Esparon J, Kolloori J, Naylor GJ *et al.* (1986) Comparison of the prophylactic action of flupenthixol with placebo in lithium treated manic-depressive patients. *Br J Psychiatry* **148**, 723–725.

Ezquiaga E, Gutierrez JLA, Lopez AG (1987) Psychosocial factors and episode number in depression. *J Affective Disord* **12**, 135–138.

Frank E, Kupfer DJ, Wagner MS *et al.* (1991) Efficacy of interpersonal psychotherapy as a maintenance treatment of recurrent depression: contributing factors. *Arch Gen Psychiatry* **48**, 1053–1059.

Frankenburg FR, Tohen M, Cohen BM, Lipinski JF Jr (1988) Long term response to carbamazepine: a retrospective study. *J Clin Psychopharmacol* **8**, 130–132.

Freyhan FA (1945) Effectiveness of dipheylhydantoin in management of non-epileptic psychomotor excitement stage. *Arch Neurol Psychiatry* **53**, 370–374.

Gaily E, Granstrom ML (1989) A transient retardation of early postnatal growth in drug-exposed children of epileptic mothers. *Epilepsy Res* **4**, 147–155.

Gallicchio VS, Hulette BC (1989) *In vitro* effect of lithium on carbamazepine-induced inhibition of murine and human bone marrow-derived granulocyte–macrophage, erythroid, and megakaryocyte progenitor stem cells. *Proc Soc Exp Biol Med* **190**, 109–116.

Gelenberg AJ, Kane JM, Keller MB *et al.* (1989) Comparison of standard and low serum levels of lithium for maintenance treatment of bipolar disorder. *N Engl J Med* **321**, 1489–1493.

Georgotas A, Cancro R (1988) *Depression and Mania.* New York: Elsevier.

Ghaziuddin M, Ghaziuddin N, Stein GS (1990) Life events and the recurrence of depression. *Can J Psychiatry* **35**, 239–242.

Gitlin MJ, Weiss J (1984) Verapamil as maintenance treatment in bipolar illness: a case report. *J Clin Psychopharmacol* **4**, 341–343.

Gitlin MJ, Cochran SD, Jamison KR (1989) Maintenance lithium treatment: side effects and compliance. *J Clin Psychiatry* **50**, 127–131.

Gjessing LR (1975) Academic address: a review of periodic catatonia. *Biol Psychiatry* **8**, 23–45.

Glenthoj B, Hemmingsen R, Bolwig TG (1988) Kindling: a model for the development of tardive dyskinesia. *Behav Neurol* **1**, 29–41.

Gold PW, Robertson GL, Ballenger JC *et al.* (1983) Carbamazepine diminishes sensitivity of the plasma arginine vasopressin response to osmotic stimulation. *J Clin Endocrinol Metab* **57**, 952–957.

Goldney RD, Spence ND (1986) Safety of the combination of lithium and neuroleptic drugs. *Am J Psychiatry* **143**, 882–884.

Goodnick PJ, Fieve RR, Schlegel A, Baxter N (1987) Predictors of interepisode symptoms and relapse in affective disorder patients treated with lithium carbonate. *Am J Psychiatry* **144**, 367–369.

Goodwin RK, Ebert MH (1973) Lithium in mania: clinical trials and controlled studies. In Gershon S, Shopsin (eds) *Lithium: Its Role in Psychiatric Research and Treatment*, pp. 237–252. New York: Plenum Press.

Goodwin FK, Jamison KR (1990) *Manic-depressive Illness.* New York: Oxford University Press.

Greil W, Schmidt ST (1988) Terminating lithium long-term treatment. In Bird NJ (ed.) *Lithium: Inorganic Pharmacology and Psychiatric Use*, pp. 149–153. Oxford: IRL Press.

Grof P, Angst J, Haines T (1974) The clinical course of depression: practical issues. In Schattauer FK (ed.) *Symposia Medica Hoechst: Classification and Prediction of Outcome of Depression*, Vol. 8. New York: Schattauer.

Grof P, Hux M, Grof E, Arato M (1983) Prediction of response to stabilizing lithium treatment. *Pharmakopsychiatria* **16**, 195.

Grof E, Haag M, Grof P, Haag H (1987) Lithium response and the sequence of episode polarities: preliminary report on a Hamilton sample. *Prog Neuropsychopharmacol Biol Psychiatry* **11**, 199–203.

Haag H, Heidorn A, Haag M, Greil W (1987) Sequence of affective polarity and lithium response: preliminary report on Munich sample. *Prog Neuropsychopharmacol Biol Psychiatry* **11**, 205–208.

Hales RE, Frances AJ (eds) (1987) *American Psychiatric Association Annual Review*, Vol. 6. Washington, DC: APA Press.

Hanus H, Zapletalek M (1984) The prophylactic lithium treatment in affective disorders and the possibilities of the outcome prediction. *Sbornik Vedeckych Praci Lekarske Fakulty Karlovy Univerzity V Hradci Kralove (Praha)* **27**, 5–75.

Hardy MC, Lecrubier Y, Widlocher D (1986) Efficacy of clonidine in 24 patients with acute mania. *Am J Psychiatry* **143**, 1450–1453.

Hayes SG (1989) Long-term use of valproate in primary psychiatric disorders. *J Clin Psychiatry* (suppl.), 35–39.

Haykal RF, Akiskal HS (1990) Bupropion as a promising approach to rapid-cycling bipolar II patients. *J Clin Psychiatry* **51**, 450–455.

Hays P (1976) Etiological factors in manic-depressive psychoses. *Arch Gen Psychiatry* **33**, 1187–1188.

Herridge PL, Pope HG Jr (1985) Treatment of bulimia and rapid-cycling bipolar disorder with sodium valproate: a case report. *J Clin Psychopharmacol* **5**, 229.

Himmelhoch JM, Garfinkel ME (1986) Sources of lithium resistance in mixed mania. *Psychopharmacol Bull* **22**, 613–620.

Himmelhoch JM, Thase ME, Mallinger AG, Fuchs CZ (1986) Tranylcypromine versus imipramine in manic depression. In *New Research Abstracts of the American Psychiatric Association 139th Annual Meeting*, NR 122, p. 78. Washington, DC: APA Press.

Hoschl C, Kozeny J (1989) Verapamil in affective disorders: a controlled, double-blind study. *Biol Psychiatry* **25**, 128–140.

Inoue H, Hazama H, Hamazoe K (1984) Antipsychotic and prophylactic effects of acetazolamide (Diamox) on atypical psychosis. *Folia Psychiatr Neurol Jpn* **35**, 425–436.

Itoh K, Ishigane M (1973) On the clinical effectiveness of lithium carbonate for manic-depressive reactions: therapeutic and prophylactic effects. *Shinyaku-to-Rinsho* **22**, 1001–1015.

Jefferson JW, Greist JH (1987) Lithium carbonate and carbamazepine side effects. In Hales RE, Frances AJ (eds) *American Psychiatric Association Annual Review*, Vol. 6, pp. 746–780.

Jefferson JW, Greist JH, Ackerman DL, Carroll JA (1987) *Lithium Encyclopedia for Clinical Practice*, 2nd edn. Washington, DC: American Psychiatric Press.

Jeste DV, Wyatt RJ (1982a) *Understanding and Treating Tardive Dyskinesia*. New York: Guilford Press.

Jeste DV, Wyatt RJ (1982b) Therapeutic strategies against tardive dyskinesia. *Arch Gen Psychiatry* **39**, 803–816.

Joffe RT, (1991) Carbamazepine, lithium and life course of bipolar affective disorder: a clinical evaluation. *Am J Psychiatry* **148**, 1270–1271.

Joffe RT, Post RM, Roy-Byrne PP, Uhde TW (1985) Hematological effects of carbamazepine in patients with affective illness. *Am J Psychiatry* **142**, 1196–1199.

Joffe RT, Post RM, Uhde TW (1986) Effects of carbamazepine on serum electrolytes in affectively ill patients. *Psychol Med* **16**, 331–335.

Johnson FN (1987) *Depression and Mania: Modern Lithium Therapy.* Oxford: IRL Press.

Jones KL, Lacro RV, Johnson KA, Adams J (1989) Pattern of malformations in the children of women treated with carbamazepine during pregnancy. *N Engl J Med* **320**, 661–1666.

Joyce PR (1988) Carbamazepine in rapid cycling bipolar affective disorder. *Int Clin Psychopharmacol* **3**, 123–129.

Kay DS, Naylor GJ, Smith AH, Greenwood C (1984) The therapeutic effect of ascorbic acid and EDTA in manic-depressive psychosis: double-blind comparisons with standard treatments. *Psychol Med* **14**, 533–539.

Keller MB (1990) Diagnostic and course-of-illness variables pertinent to refractory depression. In Tasman A, Goldfinger SM, Kaufmann CA (eds) *Review of Psychiatry,* Vol. 9, pp. 10–32. Washington DC: American Psychiatric Press.

Kelly TE (1984) Teratogenicity of anticonvulsant drugs. I. Review of the literature. *Am J Med Genet* **19**, 413–434.

Kennedy S, Thompson R, Stancer HC *et al.* (1983) Life events precipitating mania. *Br J Psychiatry* **142**, 398–403.

Kishimoto A, Okuma T (1985) Antimanic and prophylactic effects of carbamazepine in affective disorders. *Abstracts of the 4th World Congress in Biological Psychiatry,* 8–13 September, 363 pp, abstract no. 506.4.

Kishimoto A, Ogura C, Hazama H, Inoue K (1983) Long-term prophylactic effects of carbamazepine in affective disorder. *Br J Psychiatry* **143**, 327–331.

Kishimoto A, Omura F, Inoue K *et al.* (1986) A comparative study of carbamazepine and lithium for prophylaxis of bipolar affective disorder. *Yonago Acta Med* **20**, 76–90.

Kishimoto A, Kamata K, Sugihara T *et al.* (1988) Treatment of depression with clonazepam. *Acta Psychiatr Scand* **77**, 81–86.

Kishimoto A, Komada A, Harada Y *et al.* (1990) Prophylaxis of affective episodes with anti-epileptic drug 'clonazepam'. *Abstracts CINP* **1**, pp. 59

Klerman GL, Weissmann MM (1987) Interpersonal psychotherapy (IPT) and drugs in the treatment of depression. *Pharmacopsychiatry* **20**, 3–7.

Koufen H, Consbruch U (1989) Long-term catamnesis on the topic of uses and side effects of lithium prevention of phasic psychoses. *Fortschr Neurol Psychiatr* **57**, 374–382.

Kraepelin E (1921) In Robertson GM (ed.) *Manic-depressive Insanity and Paranoia.* Edinburgh: Livingstone ES (trans. RM Barclay).

Kramlinger KG, Post RM (1988) Ultra-rapid cycling bipolar affective disorder. Presented at the Annual Meeting of the Psychiatric Research Society, Park City, Utah, March 10–12.

Kramlinger KG, Post RM (1989a) The addition of lithium carbonate to carbamazepine: antidepressant efficacy in treatment-resistant depression. *Arch Gen Psychiatry* **46**, 794–800.

Kramlinger KG, Post RM (1989b) Adding lithium carbonate to carbamazepine: antimanic efficacy in treatment-resistant mania. *Acta Psychiatr Scand* **79**, 378–385.

Kramlinger KG, Post RM (1990) Addition of lithium carbonate to carbamazepine: hematologic and thyroid effects. *Am J Psychiatry* **147**, 615–620.

Kukopulos A, Reginaldi D, Laddomada P et al. (1980) Course of the manic-depressive cycle and changes caused by treatment. Pharmakopsychiatria **13**, 156–167.

Kukopulos A, Caliari B, Tundo A et al. (1983) Rapid cyclers, temperament, and antidepressants. Compr Psychiatry **24**, 249–258.

Kupfer DJ, Carpenter LL, Frank E (1988) Possible role of antidepressants in precipitating mania and hypomania in recurrent depression. Am J Psychiatry **145**, 804–808.

Kupfer DJ, Frank E, Perel JM (1989) The advantage of early treatment intervention in recurrent depression. Arch Gen Psychiatry **46**, 771–775.

Lambert PA (1984) Acute and prophylactic therapies of patients with affective disorders using valpromide (diprophylacetamide). In Emrich HM, Okuma T, Muller AA (eds) Anticonvulsants in Affective Disorders, pp. 34–44. Amsterdam: Excerpta Medica.

Lambert PA, Carraz G, Borselli S (1975) Le diprophylacetamide dans le traitement de la psychose maniaco-depressive. Encephale **1**, 25–31.

Linz G, Lovrek A, Thau K et al. (1988) Lithium-withdrawal study in schizoaffective patients. In Birch NJ (ed.) Lithium: Inorganic Pharmacology and Psychiatric Use, pp. 161–162. Oxford: IRL Press.

Lerer B, Gershon S (1989) New Directions in Affective Disorders. New York: Springer.

Leverich GS, Post RM, Rosoff AS (1990) Factors associated with relapse during maintenance treatment of affective disorders: case studies. Int Clin Psychopharmacol **5**, 135–136.

Lewis JL, Winokur G (1982) The induction of mania: a natural history study with controls. Arch Gen Psychiatry **39**, 303–306.

Lewis J, Winokur G (1989) Induction of mania by antidepressants (letter). Am J Psychiatry **146**, 126–128.

Lloyd KG, Zivkovic B, Scatton B et al. (1989) The GABAergic hypothesis of depression. Prog Neuropsychopharmacol Biol Psychiatry **13**, 341–351.

Lovett LM, Shaw DM (1987) Outcome in bipolar affective disorder after stereotactic tractotomy. Br J Psychiatry **151**, 113–116.

Lowe MR, Batchelor DH (1986) Depot neuroleptics and manic depressive psychosis. Int Clin Psychopharmacol (Suppl. 1) 53–62.

Lundqvist G (1945) Prognosis and course in manic-depressive psychoses. Acta Psychiatr Neurol **35**, 1–96.

Lusznat RM, Murphy DP, Nunn CM (1988) Carbamazepine vs lithium in the treatment and prophylaxis of mania. Br J Psychiatry **153**, 198–204.

Maguire J, Singh AN (1987) Clonidine: an effective anti-manic agent. Br J Psychiatry **150**, 863–864.

Maj M, Del Vecchio M, Starace F et al. (1984) Prediction of affective psychoses response to lithium prophylaxis. Acta Psychiatr Scand **69**, 37–44.

Maj M, Arena F, Lovero M et al. (1985) Factors associated with response to lithium prophylaxis in DSM III major depression and bipolar disorder. Pharmacopsychiatry **18**, 309–313.

Maj M, Pirozzi R, Kemali D (1989a) Long-term outcome of lithium prophylaxis in patients initially classified as complete responders. Psychopharmacology (Berlin) **98**, 535–538.

Maj M, Pirozzi R, Starace F (1989b) Previous pattern of course of the illness as a predictor of response to lithium prophylaxis in bipolar patients. J Affective Disord **17**, 237–241.

Mander AJ (1986a) Is there a lithium withdrawal syndrome? Br J Psychiatry **149**, 498–501.

Mander AJ (1986b) Clinical prediction of outcome and lithium response in bipolar affective disorder. J Affective Disord **11**, 35–41.

Mander AJ (1988) Use of lithium and early relapse in manic-depressive illness. Acta Psychiatr Scand **78**, 198–200.

Mander AJ (1989) Prediction of rapid relapse following lithium discontinuation. *Irish J Psychol Med* **6**, 23–25.

Mander AJ, Loudon JB (1988) Rapid recurrence of mania following abrupt discontinuation of lithium. *Lancet* **ii**, 15–17.

McElroy SL, Keck PE Jr, Pope HG Jr (1987) Sodium valproate: its use in primary psychiatric disorders. *J Clin Psychopharmacol* **7**, 16–24.

McElroy SL, Keck PE Jr, Pope HG Jr, Hudson JI (1988a) Valproate in the treatment of rapid-cycling bipolar disorder. *J Clin Psychopharmacol* **8**, 275–279.

McElroy SL, Pope HG Jr, Keck PE Jr (1988b) Treatment of psychiatric disorders with valproate: a series of 73 cases. *Psychiatr Psychobiol* **3**, 81–85.

Meitzer HL, Kassir S, Goodnick PJ et al. (1988) Activated calcium ATPase in bipolar illness. *Neuropsychobiology* **20**, 169–173.

Misra PC, Burns BH (1977) 'Lithium non-responders' in a lithium clinic. *Acta Psychiatr Scand* **55**, 32–40.

Montgomery SA (1989) New antidepressants and 5-HT uptake inhibitors. *Acta Psychiatr Scand* (suppl.) **350**, 107–116.

Nakane Y, Okuma T, Takahashi R (1980) Multi-institutional study on the teratogenicity and fetal toxicity of antiepileptic drugs: a report of a collaborative study group in Japan. *Epilepsia* **21**, 663–680.

Naylor GJ, Smith AH (1981) Vanadium: a possible aetiological factor in manic depressive illness. *Psychol Med* **11**, 249–256.

Naylor GJ, Martin B, Hopwood SE, Watson Y (1986) A two-year double-blind crossover trial of the prophylactic effect of methylene blue in manic-depressive psychosis. *Biol Psychiatry* **21**, 915–920.

Nolen WA (1983) Carbamazepine, a possible adjunct to or alternative for lithium in bipolar disorder. *Acta Psychiatr Scand* **67**, 218–225.

Okuma T (1983) Therapeutic and prophylactic effects of carbamazepine in bipolar disorders. *Psychiatr Clin North Am* **6**, 157–174.

Okuma T, Kishimoto A, Inoue K et al. (1973) Anti-manic and prophylactic effects of carbamazepine on manic-depressive psychosis. *Folia Psychiatr Neurol Jpn* **27**, 283–297.

Okuma T, Inanaga K, Otsuki S et al. (1981) A preliminary double-blind study of the efficacy of carbamazepine in prophylaxis of manic-depressive illness. *Psychopharmacology* **73**, 95–96.

Page C, Benaim S, Lappin F (1987) A long-term retrospective follow-up study of patients treated with prophylactic lithium carbonate. *Br J Psychiatry* **150**, 175–179.

Paskind HA (1930) Manic-depressive psychosis in a private practice. *Arch Neurol Psychiatry* **23**, 699–794.

Pellock JM (1987) Carbamazepine side effects in children and adults. *Epilepsia* **28**, S64–S70.

Perris H (1984) Life events and depression. Part 2. Results in diagnostic subgroups, and in relation to the recurrence of depression. *J Affective Disord* **7**, 25–36.

Pickar D, Murphy DL, Cohen RM et al. (1982) Selective and nonselective monoamine oxidase inhibitors: behavioral disturbances during their administration to depressed patients. *Arch Gen Psychiatry* **39**, 535–540.

Pinel JP (1983) Effects of diazepam and diphenylhydantoin on elicited and spontaneous seizures in kindled rats: a double dissociation. *Pharmacol Biochem Behav* **18**, 61–63.

Pisciotta AV (1982) Carbamazepine: hematological toxicity. In Woodbury DM, Penry JK (eds) *Antiepileptic Drugs*, pp. 533–541. New York: Raven Press.

Placidi GF, Lenzi A, Lazzerini F et al. (1986) The comparative efficacy and safety of carbamazepine versus lithium: a randomized, double-blind 3-year trial in 83 patients. J Clin Psychiatry **47**, 490–494.

Post RM (1987) Mechanisms of action of carbamazepine and related anticonvulsants in affective illness. In Meltzer H, Bunney WE Jr (eds) Psychopharmacology: A Generation of Progress, pp. 567–576. New York: Raven Press.

Post RM (1988) Effectiveness of carbamazepine in the treatment of bipolar affective disorder. In McElroy S, Pope HG (eds) Use of Anticonvulsants in Psychiatry: Recent Advances, pp. 1–23. Clifton, NJ: Oxford Health Care.

Post RM (1989) Introduction: emerging perspectives on valproate in affective disorders. J Clin Psychiatry **50**, 3–9.

Post RM (1990a) Alternatives to lithium for bipolar affective illness. In Tassman A, Kaufman C, Goldfinger S (eds) APA Annual Review, Vol. 9, pp. 170–200. Washington, DC: APA Press.

Post RM (1990b) Sensitization and kindling perspectives for the course of affective illness: toward a new treatment with the anticonvulsant carbamazepine. Pharmacopsychiatry, **23**, 3–17.

Post RM (1990c) Anticonvulsants for the lithium-resistant bipolar patient. In Amsterdam J (ed.) Pharmacology of Depression: Application for the Outpatient Practitioner, pp. 129–158. New York: Marcel Dekker.

Post RM, Cutler NR (1979) The pharmacology of acute mania. In Klawans HL (ed.) Clinical Neuropharmacology, Vol. 4, pp. 39–81. New York: Raven Press.

Post RM, Uhde TW (1986) Anticonvulsives in non-epileptic psychosis. In Trimble M, Bolwig TG (eds) Aspects of Epilepsy and Psychiatry, pp. 177–212. Chichester: Wiley.

Post RM, Ballenger JC, Reus VI et al. (1978) Effects of carbamazepine in mania and depression: therapeutic effects of carbamazepine in affective illness: a preliminary report. Communications in Psychopharmacology **2**, 159–175.

Post RM, Uhde TW, Ballenger JC et al. (1983a) CSF carbamazepine and its –10,11-epoxide metabolite in manic-depressive patients: relationship to clinical response. Arch Gen Psychiatry **40**, 673–676.

Post RM, Uhde TW, Ballenger JC, Squillace KM (1983b) Prophylactic efficacy of carbamazepine in manic-depressive illness. Am J Psychiatry **140**, 1602–1604.

Post RM, Ballenger JC, Uhde TW, Bunney WE Jr (1984a) Efficacy of carbamazepine in manic-depressive illness: implications for underlying mechanisms. In Post RM, Ballenger JC (eds) Neurobiology of Mood Disorders, pp. 777–816. Baltimore: Williams & Wilkins.

Post RM, Berrettini WH, Uhde TW, Kellner CH (1984b) Selective response to the anticonvulsant carbamazepine in manic-depressive illness: a case study. J Clin Psychopharmacol **4**, 178–185.

Post RM, Rubinow DR, Ballenger JC (1984c) Conditioning, sensitization, and kindling: implications for the course of affective illness. In Post RM, Ballenger JC (eds) Neurobiology of Mood Disorders, pp. 432–466. Baltimore: Williams & Wilkins.

Post RM, Putnam F, Uhde TW, Weiss SRB (1986a) ECT as an anticonvulsant: implications for its mechanism of action in affective illness. In Malitz S, Sackeim HA (eds) Electroconvulsive Therapy: Clinical and Basic Research Issues. Annals of the New York Academy of Sciences, Vol. 462, pp. 376–388. New York Academy of Sciences.

Post RM, Rubinow DR, Ballenger JC (1986b) Conditioning and sensitization in the longitudinal course of affective illness. Br J Psychiatry **149**, 191–201.

Post, RM, Uhde TW, Roy-Byrne PP, Joffe RT (1986c) Antidepressant effects of carbamazepine. Am J Psychiatry **143**, 29–34.

Post RM, Uhde TW, Roy-Byrne PP, Joffe RT (1987a) Correlates of antimanic response to carbamazepine. *Psychiatry Res* **21**, 71–83.

Post RM, Uhde TW, Rubinow DR, Weiss SRB (1987b) Antimanic effects of carbamazepine: mechanisms of action and the implications for the biochemistry of manic-depressive illness. In Swann A (ed.) *Mania: New Research and Treatment*, pp. 96–176. Washington, DC: APA Press.

Post RM, Roy-Byrne PP, Uhde TW (1988a) Graphic representation of the life course of illness in patients with affective disorder. *Am J Psychiatry* **145**, 844–848.

Post RM, Weiss SRB, Rubinow DR (1988b) Recurrent affective disorders: lessons from limbic kindling. In Ganten d, Fuxe S (eds) *Current Topics in Neuroendocrinology* pp. 91–115. New York: Springer.

Post RM, Altshuler LL, Ketter T *et al.* (1989) Anticonvulsants in affective illness: clinical and theoretical implications. In Smith DB, Treiman DM, Trimble M (eds) *Advances in Neurology* Vol. 55, *Neurobehavioral Problems in Epilepsy* pp. 239–277. New York: Raven Press.

Post RM, Kramlinger KG, Altshuler LL *et al.* (1990a) Treatment of rapid cycling bipolar illness. *Psychopharmacol Bull* (in press).

Post RM, Leverich G, Rosoff AS, Altshuler LL (1990b) Carbamazepine prophylaxis in refractory affective disorders: a focus on long-term followup. *J Clin Psychiatry* (in press).

Potter WZ, Murphy DL, Wehr TA *et al.* (1982) Clorgyline: a new treatment for patients with refractory rapid-cycling disorder. *Arch Gen Psychiatry* **39**, 505–510.

Prasad AJ (1984) The role of sodium valproate as an anti-manic agent. *Pharmatherapeutica* **4**, 6–8.

Prien RF, Gelenberg AJ (1989) Alternatives to lithium for preventive treatment of bipolar disorder. *Am J Psychiatry* **146**, 840–848.

Prien RF, Klett CJ, Caffey EM Jr (1973) Lithium carbonate and imipramine in prevention of affective episodes: a comparison in recurrent affective illness. *Arch Gen Psychiatry* **29**, 420–425.

Prien RF, Himmelhoch JM, Kupfer DJ (1988) Treatment of mixed mania. *J Affective Disord* **15**, 9–15.

Prien RF, Kupfer DJ, Mansky PA *et al.* (1984) Drug therapy in the prevention of the recurrences in unipolar and bipolar affective disorders. *Arch Gen Psychiatry* **41**, 1096–1104.

Puzynski S, Klosiewicz L (1984) Valproic acid amide as a prophylactic agent in affective and schizoaffective disorders. In Emrich HM, Okuma T, Muller AA (eds) *Anticonvulsants in Affective Disorders*, pp. 68–75. Amsterdam: Excerpta Medica.

Rosenthal NE, Sack DA, Gillin JC *et al.* (1984) Seasonal affective disorder: a description of the syndrome and preliminary findings with light therapy. *Arch Gen Psychiatry* **41**, 72–80.

Rouillon F, Phillips R, Serrurier D *et al.* (1989) Recurrence of unipolar depression efficacy of maprotiline. *Encephale* **15**, 527–534.

Roy-Byrne PP, Joffe RT, Uhde TW (1984a) Effects of carbamazepine on thyroid function in affectively ill patients: clinical and theoretical implications. *Arch Gen Psychiatry* **41**, 1150–1153.

Roy-Byrne PP, Uhde TW, Post RM, Joffe RT (1984b) Relationship of response to sleep deprivation and carbamazepine in depressed patients. *Acta Psychiatr Scand* **69**, 379–382.

Roy-Byrne PP, Post RM, Uhde TW *et al.* (1985) The longitudinal course of recurrent affective illness: life chart data from research patients at NIMH. *Acta Psychiatr Scand* (suppl.), **71**, 5–34.

Roy-Byrne PP, Post RM, Hambrick DD *et al.* (1988) Suicide and course of illness in major affective disorder. *J Affective Disord* **15**, 1–8.

Sackeim HA, Prudic J, Devanand DP (1990) Treatment of medication resistant depression with electroconvulsive therapy. In *Annual Review of Psychiatry* Vol. 9, pp 91–115. Washington, DC: APA Press.

Sandyk R (1985) Antimanic effects of clonidine and the endogenous opioid system (letter). *Am J Psychiatry* **142**, 992–993.

Scheffner D, Konig S, Rauterberg-Ruland I *et al.* (1988) Fatal liver failure in 16 children with valproate therapy. *Epilepsia* **29**, 530–542.

Schmutz M, Klebs K (1989) Kindling and antiepileptic drugs. In Bolwig TG, Trimble MR (eds) *The Clinical Relevance of Kindling*, pp. 55–68. Chichester: Wiley.

Schou M (1973) Prophylactic lithium maintenance treatment in recurrent endogenous affective disorders. In Gershon S, Shopsin B (eds) *Lithium: Its Role in Psychiatric Research and Treatment*, pp. 269–295. New York: Plenum.

Schou M (1982) Advances in lithium therapy. In Jamison KR (ed.) *Lithium: Clinical Considerations*, pp. 41–63. New York: Excerpta Medica.

Secunda SK, Swann A, Katz MM *et al.* (1987) Diagnosis and treatment of mixed mania. *Am J Psychiatry* **144**, 96–98.

Semadeni GW (1976) Etude clinique de l'effet normothymique du diprophylacetamide. *Acta Psychiatr Belg* **76**, 458–466.

Shopsin B (1983) Bupropion's prophylactic efficacy in bipolar affective illness. *J Clin Psychiatry* **44**, 163–169.

Silver FW, Ruckle JL (1989) Depression: management techniques in primary care. *Postgrad Med* **85**, 359–366.

Sovner R (1989) The use of valproate in the treatment of mentally retarded persons with typical and atypical bipolar disorders. *J Clin Psychiatry* **50**, 40–43.

Squillace K, Post RM, Savard R, Eewin M (1984) Life charting of the longitudinal course of recurrent affective illness. In Post RM, Ballenger JC (eds) *Neurobiology of Mood Disorders*, pp. 38–59. Baltimore: Williams & Wilkins.

Stancer HC, Persad E (1982) Treatment of intractable rapid-cycling manic-depressive disorder with levothyroxine. *Arch Gen Psychiatry* **39**, 311–312.

Stromgren LS, Boller S (1985) Carbamazepine in treatment and prophylaxis of manic-depressive disorder. *Psychiatr Dev* **3**, 349–367.

Stuppaeck D, Barnas C, Miller C *et al.* (1990) Carbamazepine in the prophylaxis of mood disorders. *J Clin Psychopharmacol* **10**, 39–42.

Svestka J, Nahunek K (1975) Proceedings: the result of lithium therapy in acute phases of affective psychoses and some other prognostical factors of lithium prophylaxis. *Acta Nervosa Superior (Praha)* **17**, 270–271.

Swann AC, Secunda SK, Stokes PE *et al.* (1990) Stress, depression, and mania: relationship between perceived role of stressful events and clinical and biochemical characteristics. *Acta Psychiatr Scand* **81**, 389–397.

Swift JM (1907) The prognosis of recurrent insanity in the manic-depressive type. *Am J Insanity* **64**, 311–326.

Tadokoro S, Kuribara H (1986) Reverse tolerance to the ambulation-increasing effect of methamphetamine in mice as an animal model of amphetamine psychosis. *Psychopharmacol Bull* **22**, 757–762.

Taschev T (1974) The course and prognosis of depression on the basis of 652 patients decreased. In Schattauer FK (ed.) *Symposia Medica Hoest: Clasification and Prediction of Outcome of Depression*, pp. 156–172. New York: Schattauer.

Tomson T (1984) Interdosage fluctuations in plasma carbamazepine concentration determine intermittent side effects. *Arch Neurol* **41**, 830–834.

Tondo L, Floris GF, Burrai C, Pani PP (1988) Lithium withdrawal: An outcome. In Birch NJ (ed.) *Lithium: Inorganic Pharmacology and Psychiatric Use*, pp.155–156. Oxford: IRL Press.

Turner WJ (1985) Methylene blue for MDI (letter). *Biol Psychiatry* **20**, 815.

Uhde TW, Post RM (1983) Effects of carbamazepine on serum electrolytes: clinical and theroetical implications. *J Clin Psychopharmacol* **3**, 103–106.

Van Praag HM, Kahn R, Asnis GM *et al.* (1987) Therapeutic indications for serotonin-potentiating compounds: a hypothesis. *Biol Psychiatry* **22**, 205–212.

Vencovsky E, Soucek K, Kabes J (1984) Prophylactic effect of dipropylacetamide in patients with bipolar affective disorder (short communication). In Emrich HM, Okuma T, Muller AA (eds) *Anticonvulsants in Affective Disorders*, pp. 66–67. Amsterdam: Excerpta Medica.

Vestergaard P, Poulstrup I (1988) Prospective studies on a lithium cohort. 3. Tremor, weight gain, diarrhea, psychological complaints. *Acta Psychiatr Scand* **78**, 434–441.

Vieweg V, Glick JL, Herring S *et al.* (1987) Absence of carbamazepine-induced hyponatremia among patients also given lithium. *Am J Psychiatry* **144**, 943–947.

Waddington JL, Brown K, O'Neill J *et al.* (1989) Cognitive impairment, clinical course and treatment history in out-patients with bipolar affective disorder: relationship to tardive dyskinesia. *Psychol Med* **19**, 897–902.

Walker JE, Koon R (1988) Carbamazepine versus valproate versus combined therapy for refractory partial complex seizures with secondary generalization. *Epilepsia* **29**, 693.

Watkins SE, Callender K, Thomas DR *et al.* (1987) The effect of carbamazepine and lithium on remission from affective illness. *Br J Psychiatry* **150**, 180–182.

Wehr TA (1989) Sleep loss: a preventable cause of mania and other excited states. *J Clin Psychiatry* **50**, 8–16.

Wehr TA, Goodwin FK (1987) Do antidepressants cause mania? *Psychopharmacol Bull* **23**, 61–65.

Wehr TA, Sack DA, Cowdry RW, Rosenthal NE (1985) Thyroid axis abnormalities in bipolar depression. In *Abstracts, IVth World Congress of Biological Psychiatry*, 8–13 September, abstract no. 414.6, p. 326, Philadelphia.

Wehr TA, Sack DA, Rosenthal NE, Cowdry RW (1988) Rapid cycling affective disorder: Contributing factors and treatment responses in 51 patients. *Am J Psychiatry* **145**, 179–184.

Weiss SRB, Post RM (1987) Carbamazepine and carbamazepine-10,11-epoxide inhibit amygdala kindled seizures in the rat but do not block their development. *Clin Neuropharmacol* **10**, 272–279.

Weiss SRB, Post RM (1991a) Development and reversal of conditioned inefficacy and tolerance to the anticonvulsant effects of carbamazepine. *Epilepsia* **32**, 140–145.

Weiss SRB, Post RM (1991b) Contingent tolerance to the anticonsulvant effects of carbamazepine. In *Carbamazepine: A Bridge Between Epilepsy and Psychiatry*, Proceedings of 10 June 1989 Conference in Milan, Italy (in press).

Weiss SRB, Post RM, Szele F *et al.* (1989). Chronic carbamazepine inhibits the development of local anesthetic seizures kindled by cocaine and lidocaine. *Brain Res* **497**, 72–79.

Wyatt RJ, Alexander RC, Egan MS, Kirsh DG (1988) Schizophrenia: just the facts. What do we know, how well do we know it? *Schizophrenia Res* **1**, 3–18.

Zis AP, Goodwin FK (1979) Major affective disorder as a recurrent illness. *Arch Gen Psychiatry* **36**, 835–839.

Zis AP, Grof P, Webster M (1980) Prediction of relapse in recurrent affective disorder. *Psychopharmacol Bull* **16**, 47–49.

8

Psychological treatments in prevention of relapse

Ellen Frank, Sheri Johnson and David J. Kupfer

Introduction

As better operational criteria for diagnosing depression have been developed and seeking of treatment for depression has become more socially acceptable, increasing attention has been focused on treatment efficacy. The need for controlled trials of both psychopharmacological and psychotherapeutic interventions for the treatment of the acute episode is apparent. The need to examine whether the chosen treatment is effective is perhaps obvious, not only in bringing about immediate symptomatic relief but also for a sustained period of clinical remission. In this volume, other chapters are devoted to the assessment of psychopharmacological interventions. The overall goal of this chapter is to assess the effectiveness of psychotherapeutic interventions in preventing relapse and recurrence of unipolar affective disorder.

We review the research on psychotherapy with a focus on its longer-term impact. This emphasis on relapse and recurrence is relatively recent and the number of studies which address this question is relatively limited. However, this area represents a field with significant applied and theoretical implications. Given the high rates of relapse, the clinical importance of long-term outcome research is clear. Furthermore, research in this area has great potential to elucidate mechanisms of change as well as factors which moderate onset,

---

Long-term Treatment of Depression. Edited by S.A. Montgomery and F. Rouillon
© 1992 John Wiley & Sons Ltd

maintenance, and exacerbation of episodes. It is hoped that a review of research in this area will spur increased attention to such issues.

The following review will emphasize the three forms of individual psychotherapy which have been compared empirically with antidepressant medication: behavioural, cognitive-behavioural, and interpersonal psychotherapy. To
facilitate interpretation of results, methodological issues will be discussed first.
After reporting specific outcome studies, we briefly address factors which may
moderate treatment efficacy. We conclude with directions for future research.

Conceptual issues in defining relapse

While criteria for defining the onset of single episodes of depression have long
been established, it has been much more difficult to establish criteria for
changes across time in clinical conditions. The need to capture these temporal
patterns was first recognized by Kraepelin in the latter half of the nineteenth
century (Jackson, 1986). Despite this long history of scientific concern, attempts
to define critical change points in clinical course have lagged far behind efforts
to establish operational criteria for the acute depressive episode.

As any clinician will attest, depressive symptoms often fluctuate markedly
during the course of treatment, with some fairly asymptomatic weeks interspersed with other periods of full or nearly full symptomatology. Even after
several weeks or months relatively free of depressive symptoms, exacerbations
may occur. Furthermore, especially for those patients who have already experienced a second episode, the likelihood of a subsequent episode remains increased throughout much of the subject's life (Keller et al., 1982a). In short,
there can be several change points during therapy and throughout the post-
treatment period, with patients sometimes appearing fully symptomatic, sometimes partially symptomatic, and sometimes completely asymptomatic. The
duration and sequence of these varied symptom levels also differs dramatically
across patients; some patients maintain a level of chronic mild symptomatology,
others quickly attain lasting symptomatic recovery, and still others will show full
recovery only to develop another episode months, or even years, later. These
changes, despite their complexity, are the fundamental unit which must be
evaluated in systematically comparing psychotherapeutic outcomes.

Remission, recovery, relapse and recurrence are terms that are already in
widespread use, but different investigators clearly use them with very different
definitions (Prien et al., 1991). To promote clarity, this review will rely on the
definitions suggested by the MacArthur task force (Frank et al., 1991a; described
more fully in Chapter 3).

Accordingly, *remission* refers to a brief period of time during which the
individual evidences either partial or full improvement in symptoms of sufficient magnitude so as no longer to meet diagnostic criteria for a depressive

episode. A remission which continues for a sufficient period of time will qualify as a *recovery*. A recovery suggests that the current episode is successfully terminated and that efforts may shift to prevention of further episodes.

Relapse is defined as a change from either partial or full remission to full syndrome criteria for the disorder before the person has met criteria for recovery. Hence, a person may achieve periods of complete symptomatic remission followed by full symptomatology, yet the symptomatic exacerbations may be considered part of the initial episode, depending on the duration of the symptom-free period. In contrast, *recurrence* is defined as a return of symptoms following recovery, with symptoms of sufficient magnitude to qualify for a depressive episode.

While these definitions establish theoretical guidelines, the length of time required to establish recovery remains uncertain. Naturalistic studies of course suggest that the median duration from onset of an episode to recovery is approximately one year, although 'recovery time' following treatment entry is slightly over 12 weeks (Keller *et al.*, 1982b). Data from pharmacological treatment outcome studies suggest that subjects remain vulnerable to relapse if their medication is withdrawn before they achieve 16–20 weeks of full remission (Prien and Kupfer, 1986). Recent reanalyses of the NIMH–PRB protocol by Greenhouse *et al.* (1991) suggest that abrupt discontinuation of medication substantially increases the chances of rapid return of symptoms. To date, no one has examined withdrawal of psychotherapy in a systematic fashion.

In short, studies of treatment outcome need to examine periods of four months to a year to assess relapse rates effectively, and periods of greater than a year in order to begin to address issues of recurrence. Accordingly, studies which have followed subjects for only four months or less following treatment termination will not be addressed within this review. Most studies of psychotherapeutic interventions have followed subjects for periods of one year or less after treatment termination, though there are a small number of longer-term studies (Blackburn *et al.*, 1986; Evans *et al.* (submitted); Frank *et al.*, 1990; Weissman *et al.*, 1979).

Description of psychological interventions in relapse prevention

There has been considerable research concerning the immediate impact of psychotherapy on depressive episodes, encompassing a range of modalities and approaches. A number of different forms of psychotherapy appear to facilitate recovery from depression, including group (Covi *et al.*, 1974; Gordon *et al.*, 1988; Steinmetz *et al.*, 1983; Steuer *et al.*, 1984), psychoeducational (Brown, 1980), marital (Jacobson *et al.*, 1987; O'Leary and Beach, 1990), and family (Glick *et al.*, 1985) approaches. Although there has been some attention to long-term outcome following group (Brown and Lewinsohn, 1984) and marital therapy (O'Leary and Beach, 1990), this review will focus on individual therapy and its impact.

Within the field of individual therapy, only three forms of psychotherapy have been systematically compared to antidepressant medication in regard to relapse and recurrence: behaviour therapy, cognitive-behavioural therapy, and interpersonal psychotherapy. Although each technique was developed within a specific theoretical context, the validity of the underlying aetiological premises is a separate issue from the efficacy of the intervention and will not be addressed here.

These forms of therapy share several common elements. Most important, each one was developed specifically for use with depressive disorders and has demonstrated efficacy which is comparable to tricyclic antidepressants (TCAs) in short-term outcome studies. Each form was also designed as a structured, short-term approach with a focus on experiences in the patient's current life. While acknowledging that maladaptive patterns may have developed from previous experiences, behaviour therapies, cognitive behaviour therapy and interpersonal psychotherapy all tend to assume that long-standing patterns will be expressed in the patient's current struggles and should be addressed through a focus on ameliorating current problems.

Behaviour therapists have long emphasized the need to establish empirical data concerning efficacy, and a variety of behavioural interventions have been investigated in regard to depression. With respect to long-term outcome, Lewinsohn and his colleagues (Brown and Lewinsohn, 1984) have contrasted a group versus individual psychoeducational approach which targets pleasant activities, negative thinking, relaxation skills, and social skills. However, research on outcome with individual psychotherapy for depression has been focused more specifically on enhancing social skills (Hersen *et al.*, 1984; Miller *et al.*, 1989). Social skills training is designed to address interpersonal deficits which are specifically problematic for the individual. After identification of problem areas, therapy focuses on providing instruction, feedback, and practice of appropriate responses. Additionally, patients are encouraged to monitor and reinforce their own progress (Bellack *et al.*, 1981).

Cognitive behaviour therapy (CBT; Beck *et al.*, 1979) is based on the premise that a person's unrealistically negative cognitions concerning the self, the world, and the future contribute to the onset of depression. Cognitive therapy attempts to produce symptomatic remission through challenging patients' maladaptive assumptions. First, however, patients are encouraged to increase the number of 'mastery' or 'pleasure' experiences in which they engage on a daily basis and to increase the regularity of their daily routine. This typically brings about sufficient relief of depressive symptoms so that the patient can be engaged in the cognitive-restructuring aspects of the therapy. Then, using a series of specific techniques, patients are taught to evaluate systematically the accuracy of their negative beliefs and to alter their unrealistically negative cognitions in a more positive and realistic direction. Cognitive therapy has been shown to be an effective treatment technique in a variety of short-term studies (see Bergin and Lambert, 1978) and has become a major technique for studies of psychotherapy and depression.

In contrast, *interpersonal* psychotherapy (Klerman *et al.*, 1984) aims toward symptomatic relief through addressing conflicts or deficits in the patient's social realm. Developed as a supportive intervention, interpersonal psychotherapy (IPT) emerged out of the large body of literature on interpersonal deficits associated with depression (Weissman and Paykel, 1974). In this psychotherapy, patients explore the interpersonal context surrounding the onset of their episode as well as exacerbations of interpersonal difficulties which may have emerged as a consequence of their symptomatology. Generally, the content of therapy focuses on one of four problem areas common to depression: grief, interpersonal disputes, role transitions, or interpersonal deficits. The patient is encouraged to examine the ways in which this difficulty may have contributed to their episode, and an attempt is made to resolve this prominent interpersonal difficulty. For example, if a role transition were defined as the most prominent problem area, the patient would be encouraged to evaluate the lost role, express related affect, develop social skills relevant to the new role, and establish interpersonal relationships which will be supportive of the new role. In achieving these goals, an interpersonal psychotherapist would be less likely to suggest homework than a behavioural or cognitive therapist, and would tend to adopt a less directive stance.

In addition to differences in the types of psychotherapy which have been administered, studies have varied in the timing of the interventions and whether they include a combination psychotherapy and pharmacotherapy condition. For the most part, research on the preventative capacity of psychotherapy has focused on whether short-term acute psychological interventions, typically of 12–16 sessions, decrease the probability of relapse/recurrence. However, a few researchers have also examined whether continuing psychotherapy beyond the apparent end of the episode has a prophylactic effect. While cognitive and behavioural research has focused on the impact of a limited number of booster sessions (Blackburn *et al.*, 1986; Hersen *et al.*, 1984; Jarrett *et al.*, 1990), interpersonal psychotherapy was originally designed as a treatment to be offered following initial symptom remission (Klerman *et al.*, 1974). This study focused on relapse prevention through continuing initial treatment for several months. Recently, however, a maintenance form of interpersonal pscyhotherapy (IPT-M) has been developed (Frank, 1991). IPT-M aims to delay or prevent recurrence through monthly sessions over a several-year period. IPT-M shares many features with acute interpersonal psychotherapy, yet differs in monitoring for signs of emergent episodes, development of interpersonal strategies aimed at prevention of future episodes, and allowance for a broader range of interpersonal problem areas. The effectiveness of maintenance interpersonal psychotherapy within a three-year outcome study (see below) indicates the importance of further explorations of the appropriate timing of interventions. Finally, while the vast majority of research has focused on contrasting psychotherapy with pharmacotherapy, a few studies have examined the efficacy of combining medication and psychotherapy. In order to evaluate the implications of these various studies, we will first discuss methodological issues which are of primary concern in psychotherapy outcome research.

Methodological concerns in psychotherapy outcome research

The methodological issues involved in treatment outcome research are complex and numerous. Since other researchers have provided excellent reviews of these issues (Bergin and Lambert, 1978), we will briefly summarize some of the most important dimensions for cross-study comparisons, including the adequacy of psychotherapy definitions, efficacy of comparison treatments, appropriateness of analytic strategies, and representativeness in follow-up sample definition.

Perhaps the most critical issue within this research is the degree to which psychotherapeutic techniques are well defined and executed. Fortunately, the approaches which have been used predominantly in the treatment of depression have well-developed treatment manuals (Beck *et al.*, 1979; Bellack *et al.*, 1981; Klerman *et al.*, 1984). Unfortunately, data on the degree to which therapists conform to these manuals is often less available. Although scales for assessing both the competence of the therapist and the specificity of therapy are available for both cognitive therapy (Vallis *et al.*, 1986) and interpersonal psychotherapy (DeRubeis *et al.*, 1982), analyses of data from these scales has been reported only rarely (O'Malley *et al.*, 1988). A related issue with respect to treatment quality is the extent of therapist training prior to the study and the amount of ongoing supervision during the trial. These 'pragmatic' issues can profoundly influence the adequacy of the clinical trial, the robustness of the findings and the likelihood that findings can be replicated.

In addition to conformity to the goals and techniques of the stated psychological intervention, several questions can be raised about the adequacy of control groups. Antidepressant medications have become well-established treatments and, as such, have become a standard against which other treatment approaches are evaluated. However, since a wide variety of factors influence the efficacy of psychotropic medication, studies which fail to implement standardized procedures could underestimate the impact of medication, providing a poor control for the efficacy of psychotherapy.

As suggested by Meterissian and Bradwejn (1989), several criteria must be met for an 'adequate' medication trial. Specifically, medications must be administered at an effective minimum dose, maintained at the maximum dosage for at least four to six weeks, and provided by an experienced pharmacotherapist with experience in psychiatric settings. Despite standardized administration, patients may vary greatly in their overall compliance and individual metabolism of medications, necessitating the use of plasma levels to determine whether patients are actually ingesting a sufficient dosage (Meterissian and Bradwejn, 1989). After achieving and maintaining symptom remission, medications should be withdrawn on a gradual basis to avoid increased risk of relapse (Greenhouse *et al.*, 1991). Finally, the prevailing 'ethos' of the unit or clinic in which a trial is conducted may influence the quality of either the control or experimental treatment in ways which are, as yet, poorly understood. Finally, to establish the overall efficacy of medications, a pill–placebo condition should be included (Meterissian and Bradwejn, 1989).

Given appropriate attention to providing standardized and efficacious psychotherapy and comparison treatments, the statistical analysis of data in treatment outcome studies is quite complex and a potential source of much bias. These issues have been eloquently discussed in a review by Lavori *et al.* (1984). Lavori and his colleagues point out that, traditionally, researchers have relied on two major approaches to data analysis.

Perhaps the most pervasive approach has been to analyse the mean levels of symptom severity at specific points in time, typically using ANOVAs to contrast groups. Unfortunately, such statistics do not provide critical information regarding the percentage of subjects who can be considered treatment responders or failures. A second common strategy, which does attempt to capture the distribution of responses, involves analysing the number of responders versus non-responders at different follow-up times, typically using χ^2 statistics. Unfortunately, both ANOVA and χ^2 techniques assess symptom patterns at one point in time, and consequently fail to capture critical differences between medication and psychotherapy in the timing of treatment response and relapse. For example, a subject who is symptom free at six months may have achieved a stable recovery several months before assessment or, conversely, may be fluctuating dramatically in symptom levels. A variation of this approach has been to report the number of relapses within a certain time period. With such an approach, relapse rates may be artificially elevated by subjects who cycle rapidly between health and illness. Similarly, some researchers report the average length of time to relapse. However, this measure is greatly affected by the skew caused by subjects who maintain wellness for indefinite periods of time. Across each of these measures, additional interpretive problems emerge because relapse rates are highly dependent on the length of follow-up. Because of this phenomenon, cross-study comparisons are prohibited by vastly different periods of follow-up, varying from several months to three years. Finally, none of these approaches provides a comprehensive strategy for dealing with subjects who do not complete therapy or follow-up; researchers have typically analysed drop-outs separately or have excluded these subjects entirely. In studies with significant drop-out rates, this can lead to a large decrement in the power to detect differences between groups.

Recently, survival analysis, or life table analysis, has gained increased acceptance, because of its ability to address many of the above constraints. This technique tests differences between groups in the cumulative probability of relapse across time. Individuals who drop out of treatment are included in calculations up until the time they drop out and then are considered 'censored'. Inclusion of these individuals increases the ability to detect differences between groups. Additionally, by following the clinical status of patients across time, this technique is more sensitive to differences between groups in the timing of relapses. Although this technique has been receiving more attention, it has only been used for more recent studies. Even among researchers who have employed survival analysis of relapse/recurrence status, tremendous variability still exists in definitions of relapse and recurrence. That is, dramatic cross-study differences exist in the magnitude of change required for a remission, the duration of time required for a recovery, the intensity of symptom exacerbation required for relapse or recurrence, and the blindness of the individual(s) making the determination that a relapse or recurrence has taken place.

Finally, one additional methodological issue deserves note. Studies to date have varied greatly in defining the follow-up sample. During the initial treatment period, subjects may refuse their assigned treatment, or accept their initial assignment and terminate therapy prematurely. Studies have varied as to whether they excluded refusers and drop-outs from analyses or included these patients as treatment failures. Such decisions have significant implications for conclusions. In this review, we note if treatment groups varied significantly in the percentage of treatment refusals, drop-outs, or premature terminations. Additionally, authors have varied in including all subjects for follow-up analyses versus only those subjects who responded to initial treatment. While including all subjects provides a more comprehensive understanding of overall treatment effects, only subjects who have achieved a full remission are relevant for questions of relapse/recurrence for that specific treatment. Hence, the review will emphasize results based on those subjects who responded to initial treatment; however, a few studies will be reported which included non-responders in their analyses and this discrepancy will be noted.

In summary, a full understanding of the overall efficacy of psychotherapeutic interventions in major depression is hampered by a series of methodologic problems. These include: (1) inconsistent attention to or failure to report analyses of therapist competence and treatment specificity; (2) variable adequacy of control conditions; (3) differential levels of sophistication of data analytic techniques; and (4) inconsistent criteria for inclusion of subjects in the follow-up sample.

Comparative efficacy of psychological interventions

We will now review studies which address the question of whether treatment of the acute episode with a psychological intervention has an impact on the likelihood of relapse/recurrence. First, we will discuss the few studies which have compared different individual psychotherapy approaches without a medication control group. Second, research addressing the long-term efficacy of behavioural, cognitive-behavioural, and interpersonal psychotherapy will be discussed. Finally, the value of combining psychotherapy and antidepressant medication will be briefly addressed.

There have been three studies contrasting the long-term impact of a depression-specific psychotherapy with a control psychotherapy condition. Each study documented the efficacy of cognitive and behavioural psychotherapy in preventing relapse. These studies indicate that structured short-term therapies, such as cognitive and behavioural therapy, appear to fare better than brief psychodynamic therapy (Gallagher and Thompson, 1982; Gallagher-Thompson *et al.*, 1990) or an absence of therapy (Wilson *et al.*, 1983) in terms of relapse rates for depression. However, these studies have suffered from a number of methodological problems, particularly the study by Wilson and his colleagues, which did not use diagnostic criteria in sample selection, failed to report the percentage of subjects responding to therapy, did not distinguish between responders and non-responders, included only a small number of subjects ($N = 25$), and only provided eight weeks of treatment. Finally, none of the above studies have included survival analyses.

Behavioural therapy

Although there have been multiple studies of the immediate outcome of behavioural therapy, only one study has addressed the longer-term outcome of individual behaviour therapy. Hersen *et al.* (1984) contrasted the effect of four treatments: social skills plus placebo, social skills plus amitriptyline, amitriptyline, and brief psychodynamic psychotherapy plus placebo. One hundred and twenty female patients were seen for 12 weeks of initial treatment, followed by six months of continuation treatment. During the continuation phase of treatment, psychotherapy was limited to six to eight visits, and amitriptyline levels were lowered, although the average dosage remained at 182.4 mg per day. During the initial treatment phase, significantly more of the subjects in the amitriptyline-alone condition were terminated due to a failure to respond or a deterioration in clinical status. Other than this finding, treatment groups did not appear to be significantly different at the termination of initial treatment. A non-significant trend for the social skills plus placebo group to respond more positively to initial treatment was noted. At the termination of treatment, no significant differences were found between groups for the mean level of

Table I. Treatment characteristics in long-term psychotherapy outcome studies.

Reference	Initial treatment			Follow-up after initial treatment		
	Conditions	Plasma monitoring	No. weeks	Treatment	Outcome measures	Assessment timing
Hersen et al. (1984)	SS + PBO SS + AMI AMI Dynamic	No	12	6–8 visits over 6 mos; reduced-dosage pharmacotherapy	HRSD; BDI	6 mos after initial treatment
Kovacs et al. (1981)	CBT IMI	No	CT 12 IMI 10–12	Naturalistic	HRSD; HRSA; Raskin; BDI	Monthly for 1 yr after initial treatment
Simons et al. (1986)	CBT CBT + PBO CBT + NT NT	Yes	12	NT tapered over one mo; naturalistic after 1 mo.	BDI; HRSD	1, 6, and 12 mos after initial treatment
Evans et al. (submitted)	CBT IMI CBT + IMI	No	12	50% of IMI group treated for 1 yr; naturalistic	BDI; HRSD; Raskin; MMPI-D	6, 12, 18 and 24 mos after initial treatment; BDI monthly
Shea et al. (1990)	IPT CBT IMI + CM PBO + CM	Yes	16	IMI tapered over 2 mos; naturalistic	HRSD; SCI–90; BDI; LIFE-II	6, 12 and 18 mos after initial treatment
Blackburn et al. (1986)	CBT Antidepressant of choice CBT + antidepressant	No	12–15	CBT every 5 wks for 6 mos; reduced dosage pharmacotherapy	HRSD; BDI; HS Chart review	HRSD, BDI and HS at 6 mos; chart review at 24 mos after initial treatment

Study	Treatment	Randomized	Duration	Treatment description	Measures	Follow-up
Jarrett et al. (1990)	CBT	Not applicable	16	10 sessions CBT; naturalistic	RDC	Monthly for 8 mos after initial treatment
Thase (1991)	CBT	Not applicable	4 sessions	10–20 sessions CBT; naturalistic	DSM-III RDC; HRSD	1, 3, 6, 9 and 12 mos after initial treatment
Thase et al (in press)	CBT	Not applicable	16 sessions	20 sessions CBT; naturalistic	DSM-III RDC; HRSD	1, 3, 6, 9 and 12 mos after initial treatment
Weissman et al. (1981)	IPT AMI IPT + AMI Therapy-on-demand	No	12–16	Naturalistic	Raskin; HRSD; SCL-90; SAS	1 yr after initial treatment
Weissman et al. (1976)	AMI	Yes	12–16	8 mos of AMI + IPT PBO + IPT CM + IPT AMI + monthly contact PBO + monthly contact CM + monthly contact	Raskin; CID; HRSD; SAS	6 and 12 mos after continuation treatment
Frank et al. (1990)	IPT + IMI	Yes	Until HRSD ≤ 7 and Raskin ≤ 5 for 20 weeks	3 yrs of IPT IPT + PBO IPT + IMI CM + PBO CM + IMI	RDC; HRSD; Raskin	monthly for 3 y

Table II.   Sample characteristics in long-term psychotherapy outcome.

Reference	N	Criteria[a]
Hersen et al. (1984)	120	Feighner criteria for primary unipolar non-psychotic depression Raskin ≥ 7 No history of hypomanic episodes No family history of bipolar disorder
Kovacs et al. (1981)	44	Out-patients of the Mood Clinic at the University of Pennysylvania Feighner criteria for non-psychotic non-bipolar major depression HRSD ≥ 14 BDI ≥ 20 Age 18–65 No history of non-response to TCAs
Simons et al. (1986)	87	DIS criteria for primary affective disorder, unipolar, depressed type BDI ≥ 20 HRSD ≥ 14 Age 18–60
Evans et al. (submitted)	107	RDC for major depressive disorder, unipolar type Several exclusionary diagnoses, including anxiety-related disorders
Shea et al. (1990)	239	RDC for major depressive disorder Symptom duration ≥ 2 wks Several exclusionary diagnoses HRSD ≥ 14
Blackburn et al. (1986)	64	RDC and PSE criteria for primary major depressive disorder, unipolar non-psychotic subtype BDI ≥ 14 40 psychiatric out-patients 24 general practice patients
Jarrett et al. (1990)	32	RDC for major depressive disorder
Thase et al. (1991)	16	In-patients RDC and DSM-III criteria for non-bipolar, primary major depressive disorder, probable or definite endogenous subtype HRSD ≥ 15
Thase et al. (in press)	48	Outpatients RDC and DSM-III criteria for non-bipolar, primary major depressive disorder, probable or definite endogenous subtype HRSD ≥ 15

Table II.   (cont.)

Reference	N	Criteria[a]
Weissman *et al.* (1981)	81	RDC for primary major depressive disorder, non-bipolar non-psychotic type Raskin ≥ 7 Age 18–65 No trial of amitriptyline in the past three months No history of non-response to psychotherapy
Weissman *et al.* (1976)	278	DSM-II criteria for depression Raskin ≥ 7 Women only
Frank *et al.* (1990)	230	RDC for primary major depression, non-bipolar type Third episode Remission ≥ 10 wks before current episode HRSD ≥ 15 Raskin ≥ 7 Age 21–65
Wilson (1982)	64	BDI ≥ 20 Self-report symptom duration ≥ 2 mos Absence of other major disorders Age 20–55
Miller *et al.* (1989)	45	Depressed in-patients at private psychiatric hospital DIS criteria for major depression Absence of other major disorders BDI ≥ 18 HRSD ≥ 18 Age 18–65
Beck *et al.* (1985)	33	Out-patients at the Center for Cognitive Therapy Feighner criteria for definite depressive syndrome No psychotic symptoms Absence of other major disorders BDI ≥ 20 HRSD ≥ 14

[a] Feighner criteria (Feighner *et al.*, 1972).
DIS (Diagnostic Interview Schedule; Robins *et al.*, 1981).
RDC (Research Diagnostic Criteria; Spitzer *et al.*, 1978).
PSE (Present State Exam; Wing *et al.*, 1974).
DSM-III (Diagnostic and Statistical Manual of Mental Disorders, 3rd edn; American Psychiatric Association, 1980).

symptomatology or the percentage of subjects who scored 10 or less on both the Beck Depression Inventory (BDI; Beck, 1961) and the Hamilton Rating Scale for Depression (HRSD; Hamilton, 1960). Overall, 40/92 subjects were free of significant symptoms at the end of continuation therapy. Unfortunately, this report does not document the number of people who maintained a stable remission, and fails to include statistics such as survival analysis which consider the temporal course of symptoms.

Cognitive therapy
The impact of cognitive therapy during the acute episode on relapse or recurrence   In the past few years, four studies have emerged which contrast the response and relapse rates following cognitive therapy versus antidepressant medications (see Table III). In general, these studies have found equivocal (Kovacs *et al.*, 1981; Shea *et al.*, 1990) or positive results (Evans *et al.*, submitted; Simons *et al.*, 1986) for cognitive therapy in terms of long-term outcome.

In one of the first long-term treatment outcome studies, Kovacs *et al.* (1981) found that, one year following treatment, subjects treated with cognitive therapy displayed significantly lower BDI scores than subjects treated with TCAs and subsequently discontinued. Unfortunately, many of the recently established methodological standards, such as plasma monitoring of anti-depressant levels, were not used. Furthermore, the authors did not provide specific data on relapse rates, pooled subjects who had and had not responded to treatment, and conducted their analyses of symptomatology levels at only six and 12 months, rather than examining temporal patterns of relapse. Furthermore, insufficient attention was given to the abrupt discontinuation of medication and how this may have affected outcome in the drug-treated group.

Despite these limitations, their results provide some relevant information. Although none of the categorical analyses were significant, a number of trends consistently indicated an advantage for the cognitive therapy group. Among these, a series of risk ratios indicated that subjects who had received antidepressant medication were twice as likely to relapse, whether this was defined as achieving a BDI score above 16 or returning to mental health treatment. Additionally, while only 35% of the medication treatment group remained well throughout the year, 56% of the cognitive group remained well. In summary, the pattern of these findings suggests that 'prophylaxis' following cognitive therapy was better than following TCA treatment. However, the small number of subjects ($N = 35$) and the lack of survival analyses may have limited the power to detect meaningful differences in this sample.

Simons and her colleagues documented some advantages for cognitive behaviour treatment in longer-term outcome. However, results at treatment termination did not differentiate subjects who had received 12 weeks of cognitive therapy treatment alone, cognitive therapy with placebo, cognitive therapy with nortriptyline or nortriptyline alone (Simons *et al.*, 1986). Additionally, survival

Table III. Relapse rates in long-term psychotherapy outcome studies

Reference	Relapse definition	Separated responders	Proportion of treatment completers who relapsed				
			SS	CBT	IPT	Medication	Combination
Hersen et al. (1984)	BDI or HRSD > 10	No	7/21[a]			5/12	6/16[a]
Kovacs et al. (1981)	BDI ≥ 16 Received MH treatment Met either definition	No		7/18 9/18 10/18		11/17 13/17 14/17	
Simons et al. (1986)	BDI ≥ 16 within 6 months Received MH treatment Met either definition	Yes		0/10 2.10 2/10		1/9 5/9 6/9	2/14 4/14 6/14
Evans et al. (submitted)	BDI ≥ 16 for 1 wk	Yes		4/23		5/10	3/11[a] 2/13
Shea et al. (1990)	RDC for definite major depressive disorder for 2 weeks	Yes		8/22	7/21	9/18	
	Received MH treatment Met either definition			3/22 9/22	9/21 12/21	8/18 11/18	
Blackburn et al. (1986)	BDI ≥ 9 and HRSD ≥ 8	Yes		3/10[a]		7/9[a]	3/14[a]
Jarrett et al (1990)	RDC for major depression	Yes		13/20 2/12[a]			
Thase et al. (1991)	DSM-III for major depression and HRSD ≥ 14	Yes		3/4 1/10[a]			
Thase (in press)	DSM-III for major depression and HRSD ≥ 14	Yes		16/48			
Weissman et al. (1981)	Received MH treatment	No			7/13	11/15	12/18
Frank et al. (1990)	RDC for major depression HRSD ≥ 15 Raskin ≥ 7	Yes			16/26[a]	6/28[a]	6/25[a]
Miller et al. (1989)	HRSD > 17; BDI > 16; SSI[b] > 7; or Rehospitalization	Yes				3/6[a]	4/20[a]

[a] Continuation treatment received.
[b] SSI (Scale for Suicidal Ideation; Miller et al. 1986).
Note: Weissman et al. (1976) and Wilson (1982) did.

analysis of the one-year follow-up period did not support any differences among the four groups. After collapsing their groups into subjects who received cognitive therapy (with or without TCAs) or did not (medication treatment) significant findings did emerge. Relapse, defined as a BDI score greater than 15 or a return for mental health treatment, occurred in 28% of the cognitive therapy group (with or without placebo) versus 66% of the TCA group.

The work of Evans and his collaborators (submitted) replicates these findings and extends them in two significant ways. First, this study involved follow-up for two years following treatment termination. Second, two comparison medication conditions were included. In addition to a group which received a standard three-month imipramine treatment, a second group received imipramine on a continuation basis for one year following acute treatment. As discussed elsewhere in this volume, an increasingly common pharmacological strategy in the prevention of relapse has been to increase the duration of antidepressant treatment. In short, a 'continued imipramine' group provides a much more stringent test of whether acute cognitive therapy provided protection against relapse. In this investigation, medication was tapered over a two-week period.

Results were comparable to the findings of Simons *et al.* (1986). At the conclusion of acute treatment, groups did not differ in mean levels of symptomatology nor did groups differ in the proportion of subjects who responded to treatment with a BDI score of less than 16 (Evans *et al.*, submitted). Across the two years of follow-up, however, survival analyses indicated that the cognitive therapy patients experienced significantly fewer relapses than subjects who had been treated with medication-without-continuation. This result was supported across several definitions of relapse, based on both BDI scores and treatment-seeking. Interestingly, the medication-continuation group displayed relapse rates which were not significantly different from either of the other two conditions, being intermediate between the cognitive therapy group and the medication-without-continuation group.

Finally, recent findings from the NIMH Treatment of Depression Collaborative Research Program (Shea *et al.*, 1990) have addressed questions of long-term efficacy through an 18-month follow-up of interpersonal psychotherapy, cognitive therapy, imipramine plus clinical management, or placebo plus clinical management (Elkin *et al.*, 1989). Results of this study have been particularly important, since many of the previous therapy studies have been criticized because they were conducted at centres which were involved in the original development of the treatment approaches. In contrast, the NIMH-TDCRP study was a multi-site investigation, with none of the sites having a prior identification with any of the specific techniques employed. Additionally, all therapists received training until they reached specific criteria. Ongoing supervision was less frequent following this training, although conformity to the goals and techniques of the specific approaches was monitored throughout the course of treatment.

At the termination of treatment, when the whole sample is considered, cognitive therapy was not significantly different from imipramine or interpersonal psychotherapy in terms of the level of symptoms or percentage of subjects evidencing recovery; however, it was also not significantly different from the effects of placebo plus clinic management. During follow-up, few significant differences emerged among responders to the various treatments. Survival analyses did not indicate significant differences between any of the groups in relapse rates. Although non-significant, there was a tendency for the cognitive behaviour group therapy to be less vulnerable to relapse, particularly when examining relapse in terms of seeking additional treatment.

In summary, although there have only been a few comprehensive research programmes examining the prophylactic efficacy of CBT, the studies appear to be fairly methodologically sound and the results relatively consistent. It should be noted that the issues of attrition and bias introduced when only responders to acute treatment are followed are not addressed in these reports. Methodological questions have been raised about pharmacotherapy validity in one study (Kovacs *et al.*, 1981), but a similar pattern of findings has held across studies. On the other hand, the major evidence against the efficacy of CBT derives from the failure to document an advantage beyond clinical management plus placebo in the NIMH–TDCRP study. However, in this study, IPT and imipramine treatment also failed to achieve results which were discriminable from clinical management with placebo among those patients with mild to moderate severity of illness at baseline. For those patients who scored ≥20 on the HRSD (Hamilton, 1960), however, imipramine proved superior to the three treatments. Although cognitive therapy results have not been consistently statistically significant, small sample sizes and choices in analytic techniques may have limited the ability to detect differences.

Several questions remain to be addressed. First, the limited length of follow-up has constrained most of these studies to addressing questions of relapse and leaving recurrence issues unexamined. Second, each of the above studies has had a naturalistic follow-up period, in which ongoing treatment is not provided and patients are allowed to seek treatment as they see fit. A large proportion of subjects do seek further treatment, despite efforts within some studies to discourage patients unless a full relapse is documented. Ethically, patients must be able to pursue further treatment, yet methodologically, the impact of these uncontrolled interventions is difficult to determine. One design which does allow for the investigation of therapeutic effects without other interventions involves the provision of ongoing psychotherapy following the acute episode. More important, several researchers have postulated that continuation treatment may provide considerable benefit in reducing the risk of relapse.

The impact of ongoing cognitive therapy on relapse/recurrence Several studies have examined the prophylactic impact of ongoing cognitive therapy; these studies have assessed a range of treatment provisions, from a few 'booster' sessions to continuation treatment, which provides ongoing treatment at a reduced frequency. Blackburn *et al.* (1986) compared cognitive therapy, antidepressant medication, and combination psychotherapy and pharmacotherapy in both a hospital and a general practitioner sample. Subjects who had responded to initial treatment were assigned to ongoing therapy for six months; pharmacotherapy was continued, although sometimes at a reduced level, and psychotherapy was continued as booster sessions offered every six weeks. At the conclusion of the initial 12–15-week treatment, only one of the seven subjects in the general practitioner pharmacotherapy condition had recovered. All other treatments were successful in achieving remission. Despite these differences, primary analyses were conducted pooling the hospital and general practice patients. At the termination of the continuation phase, analysis of the HRSD and the BDI revealed no significant differences between cognitive therapy and pharmacotherapy in either mean symptom levels or the percentage of symptom-free patients. Eighteen months after the termination of continuation treatment, relapse/recurrence using a definition based solely on the presence of physician's notes indicating a need for a return to treatment was more prevalent in the pharmacotherapy group. While 78% of this group had a relapse/recurrence using this definition, only 23% of the cognitive-therapy-alone group and 21% of the combination group suffered a relapse or a recurrence. Unfortunately, more comprehensive data regarding symptomatology were not available at the 18-month follow-up, so these rates may represent substantial underestimates. A second concern centres around the validity of the medication control in the general practice condition, in light of the low rates of initial recovery and limited experience of the prescribing general practitioners (Hollon *et al.*, 1991). However, within the hospital sample, adequate pharmacotherapy appears to have been administered, yet recipients were still more vulnerable to relapse than the cognitive therapy recipients. Finally, the authors did not include a comparison group without booster sessions, so it is difficult to draw conclusions regarding the advantages of continuing treatment from this study. Using their definitions, Blackburn and colleagues found an exceptionally low rate of relapse/recurrence across the first six months (6% of the cognitive therapy group, 0% of the combination group, and 30% of the medication group), pointing to the need to examine the impact of booster sessions more systematically.

In a recent pilot study, Jarrett and colleagues have examined the impact of continuation cognitive therapy. Twelve patients who responded to an initial 20 sessions of cognitive therapy were assigned to additional therapy, which involved ten sessions over eight months (Jarrett *et al.*, 1990). Sessions were conducted every other week for two months, then monthly. In comparison with 20 responders who had received only the initial treatment, substantially fewer subjects met Research Diagnostic Criteria for major depression during the eight months following initial treatment. While 51% of the control sample had relapsed, 20% of the continuation sample had relapsed. In another pilot investigation involving in-patients, Thase (1991) found that subjects who received cognitive therapy after hospital discharge were strikingly less likely to relapse than patients who did not receive out-patient psychotherapy. While 75% of subjects who did not receive continuation therapy relapsed, only 10% of the subjects who received continuation therapy relapsed.

In general, preliminary results indicate that continuing cognitive therapy following symptomatic remission is helpful. To date, only one study has suggested otherwise. Baker and Wilson (1985) found no advantage to adding four group therapy booster sessions across a three-month period. However, the limited duration of their treatment, the changing composition of their groups during follow-up, and the reliance on graduate student therapists may have limited efficacy within this trial.

Overall then, while continuation therapy appears promising, several questions remain unaddressed, and methodological difficulties coupled with the limited number of studies prohibit strong conclusions. These CBT results, however, certainly merit further research, with one critical focus being the impact of such interventions over a longer period of time, in order to address questions of recurrence.

Interpersonal psychotherapy

The impact of interpersonal psychotherapy (IPT) during the acute episode on subsequent recovery and relapse   Despite the widespread interest in using IPT for the acute treatment of depression, only two primary studies have addressed this specific issue. Weissman and colleagues (1979) conducted a study in which 81 patients received 16 weeks of IPT, pharmacotherapy, combination IPT and pharmacotherapy, or non-scheduled supportive therapy-on-demand. During the initial treatment period, a significant proportion of the patients assigned to IPT refused treatment (32%). Only subjects who completed at least one week of treatment were included in analyses. 'Symptomatic failure' was the primary outcome variable used in survival analyses, and was defined as a Raskin depression score of 9 or more after eight weeks of treatment. This criterion merged patients who had never achieved remission with those who had relapsed following remission. During the initial treatment period, all three active treatments performed comparably and significantly better than the non-scheduled treatment in preventing symptomatic failure, even accounting for the significant proportion of the pharmacotherapy group (66%) that dropped out of treatment prematurely. There was a non-significant trend for the combination treatment to be more successful (Weissman *et al.*, 1979).

At one year follow-up, no group differences emerged on the mean levels of symptomatology, nor the percentage of subjects reporting recovery, remission, or intermittent symptoms. Nor were differences observed with respect to treatment-seeking. However, the interpersonal psychotherapy patients were significantly more functional in the social realm, particularly as parents, extended family members, and in leisure activities (Weissman *et al.*, 1981). These social adjustment effects were particularly interesting in light of the failure to demonstrate differences in social adjustment at the termination of treatment (Weissman *et al.*, 1979).

Finally, it should be noted that the authors of this study included treatment refusers and non-completers in most of their analyses. This controls for the higher percentage of IPT subjects who refused treatment and is thus a more stringent test of the efficacy of the treatment. Further exploration of the groups of subjects who completed the treatment would be of interest, as these are the only subjects who would be assumed to have derived the full benefit. In addition, use of survival analysis might have enhanced the power to detect meaningful differences in this follow-up sample.

The second source of data concerning the impact of acute IPT is the NIMH Treatment of Depression Collaborative Research Program discussed above (Elkin *et al.*, 1989). At the conclusion of initial treatment, the overall outcome of interpersonal psychotherapy appeared comparable to imipramine or cognitive therapy in terms of symptom levels, but was not significantly different from clinical management plus placebo. Nevertheless some evidence emerged that a higher percentage of IPT patients demonstrated full symptom remission than clinical management plus placebo patients, especially if baseline severity was taken into account. Follow-up assessments were conducted at six, 12, and 18 months following therapy termination, and survival analyses demonstrated no significant differences in relapse rates for groups receiving IPT, cognitive therapy, imipramine and clinical management, or placebo and clinical management (24% of CBT patients, 23% of IPT patients, 16% of IMI + CM patients, 16% of PBO + CM achieved recovery and remained well through 18 months; mean weeks of survival before relapse: 65.8 CT, 54.1 IPT, 47.2 IMI, 62.5 PBO) (Shea *et al.*, 1990). Given the small range of studies and the methodological limitations, conclusions would be premature. Preliminary evidence from these two studies suggests that beneficial social effects may emerge following therapy, yet the implications of these effects for relapse/recurrence remain unclear.

Does continuation or maintenance IPT protect against relapse and recurrence? IPT differs from most forms of psychotherapy in that it was originally developed for the provision of ongoing care *following* a response to pharmacotherapy. In the original study of this treatment approach, Klerman and colleagues (1974) assessed the impact of IPT in 150 depressed out-patients who had responded to four to six weeks of amitriptyline therapy.

Following acute treatment, they were assigned to eight months of continuation treatment within a 2 × 3 factorial design. Half of the subjects were assigned to weekly psychotherapy, while half of the subjects were assigned to a low-contact condition. Additionally, subjects were assigned to receive amitriptyline, a placebo, or no pill. Following treatment, subjects were followed for another 12 months.

As noted by the authors, several factors may limit the effectiveness of this design for studying psychotherapy. First, the initial administration of medication alone for treatment of the acute episode may have established lower expectations about the efficacy of psychotherapy. Second, patients began psychotherapy following two months of treatment, soon after achieving remission. The fragility of this new-found relief from symptoms may have changed the manner in which therapists and patients would address problems, possibly limiting the intensity of therapeutic work.

At the conclusion of continuation treatment, life table analyses indicated that subjects receiving medication had a significantly lower chance of relapse than subjects receiving a placebo or no pill. There was a non-significant trend for subjects receiving IPT to have lower relapse rates than subjects in the low-contact condition (Klerman *et al.*, 1974). Patients receiving no treatment demonstrated a relapse rate of 36%, compared with a relapse rate of 12% in the amitriptyline group, 16.7% in the IPT-alone group, and 12.5% in the combination psychotherapy and medication group. The comparable rates of relapse in the amitriptyline and the interpersonal psychotherapy groups raise questions of whether this study included a sufficiently large number of treatment responders to capture clinically significant effects. Patients receiving IPT demonstrated a significantly more positive social adustment than patients receiving medication alone (Weissman and Paykel, 1974).

During the first year of follow-up, few between-group differences emerged (Weissman *et al.*, 1976). Within the first six months after termination, subjects who had received amitriptyline were more likely to seek medications, while subjects who had received IPT were more likely to seek therapy. The authors did not conduct survival analyses, nor did they analyse the proportion of subjects who remained well, relapsed, or continued to experience chronic symptoms. However, ANOVAs revealed no group differences in symptom levels or social adjustment at either six or 12 months.

While the above data provide some estimate of the efficacy of IPT in relapse prevention, recent findings by Frank and her colleagues (1990) address issues of recurrence in maintenance therapy. These investigators conducted the first three-year outcome study in relation to IPT alone and in combination with medication. In this trial, initial treatment consisted of combined imipramine (150–300 mg) and IPT given in weekly sessions for 12 weeks followed by bi-weekly sessions for eight weeks, followed by monthly sessions until the patients stabilized. This study is also unique in providing psychotherapy until the patients had demonstrated evidence of recovery. Following stabilization, patients were treated on a monthly basis until their HRSD and Raskin scores had remained within the remission range for a total of 20 weeks. Following this combined continuation treatment period, the 128 subjects who had achieved recovery were randomly assigned to one of five treatments: IPT alone, IPT with a placebo, IPT with imipramine, medication clinic with placebo, or medication clinic visits with imipramine. In the two active imipramine groups, medication was maintained at the dose which was used in treating the acute episode. As discussed earlier, the maintenance form of IPT was developed for this study, and consists of monthly visits focused on interpersonal problems in the subject's life. Entrance criteria for this study were particularly stringent, requiring subjects to be in their third or greater episode of major depression. Survival analyses revealed significant effects for medication ($p < 0.0001$) and for psychotherapy ($p < 0.05$), but no interaction between medication and psychotherapy. Of particular interest, the mean survival time in weeks was 45 for the medication clinic/placebo group, 74 for the IPT-M and placebo group, 82 for the IPT-M-alone group, 124 for the medication clinic/imipramine group, and 131 for the IPT-M and active imipramine group.

Summary of IPT findings   Overall, IPT, like cognitive therapy, has fared reasonably well in studies of relapse and recurrence. Acute trials of IPT have found an outcome comparable to antidepressant medication, yet have also had difficulty demonstrating significant advantages in symptom relief above medication clinic or placebo treatment. There is some evidence to suggest that IPT exerts a more specific influence on social adjustment. In regard to effects of continuing therapy, the recent three-year outcome findings suggest that psychotherapy, even when limited to monthly contacts, may play a significant role in extending the well interval even for patients with highly recurrent forms of the disorder. These results, coupled with the low relapse rates in cognitive therapy continuation treatment studies, emphasize the need to examine issues of 'dosage' and 'duration' in continuation and maintenance psychotherapy much more closely and systematically.

Combination treatment
The investigation of combination treatment has centred around two questions. First, is there an advantage to providing medication in addition to psychotherapy? Second, is there an advantage to providing psychotherapy in addition to medication?

Only two studies have examined the long-term impact of behavioural therapy with and without antidepressant medication. Briefly, Wilson (1982) did not find any decrement in symptom levels at six-month follow-up when adding amitriptyline treatment to a behavioural therapy which included relaxation therapy and pleasant activities. Similarly, Hersen et al. (1984) found a non-significant trend for combination treatment to produce lower relapse rates during the maintenance phase of therapy than social skills training alone.

In regard to the prophylactic effects of providing acute medication in addition to a cognitive therapy treatment, current research has not documented any significant differences between groups in rates of relapse/recurrence or treatment-seeking (Evans *et al.*, submitted; Simons *et al.*, 1986; Beck *et al.*, 1985; Blackburn *et al.*, 1986). While Simons *et al.* (1986) found a non-significant trend toward poorer outcome within the combination treatment group, Beck and his colleagues (1985) found trends toward better outcome in the combination treatment group. Several methodological issues preclude firm statements on the basis of this research. First, preliminary evidence suggests that subjects receiving combination therapy may be more likely to achieve remission and may do so at a more rapid pace. Given these findings, decisions about whether to include treatment non-responders in follow-up analyses become particularly important. Studies which include only initial treatment responders in their analyses (Evans *et al.*, submitted; Simons *et al.*, 1986) may correctly document comparable rates of relapse following recovery. However, such findings may disguise a greater overall percentage of subjects who are able to recover and then remain well given combination therapy. It is particularly important within samples which have responded differentially to initial treatment to analyse both the responders and the non-responders. Other problems include: (1) a reliance solely on statistics which tabulate the percentage of subjects with symptomatology at a given point in time (Beck *et al.*, 1985; Blackburn *et al.*, 1986); (2) an inordinately large proportion of subjects seeking additional treatment during the follow-up period (91% of the combination group and 71% of the cognitive therapy group in the groups studied by Beck and colleagues; (3) minimal dosage levels of medication treatment (amitriptyline 100–150 mg per day) (Beck *et al.*, 1985; Wilson, 1982); (4) failures to assess plasma levels for compliance (Beck *et al.*, 1985; Blackburn *et al.*, 1986; Wilson, 1982); (5) abrupt discontinuation of medication which may produce withdrawal effects which mimic relapse (Wilson, 1982); and (6) small sample sizes (Wilson, 1982).

Despite the difficulty in reaching conclusions regarding combination behavioural or cognitive therapy, the results of IPT studies have been quite comparable, with no statistically significant advantage for combination therapy in initial (Weissman *et al.*, 1981), continuation (Klerman *et al.*, 1974), or maintenance therapy (Frank *et al.*, 1990).

In regard to combination therapy versus pharmacotherapy alone, results have been fewer and more discrepant. A series of findings have indicated that medication is not more prophylactic with the addition of acute CBT (Simons *et al.*, 1986), acute IPT (Weissman *et al.*, 1981), continuation IPT (Weissman *et al.*, 1976), or maintenance IPT (Frank *et al.*, 1990). However, Evans, in the above-mentioned two-year follow-up study, found that the provision of short-term cognitive therapy in addition to a three-month course of antidepressant medication significantly decreased relapse rates, and seemed to exert the same level of prevention as continuing medications for an additional year.

Finally, a recent study (Miller *et al.*, 1989) examined the long-term impact of providing cognitive therapy and behavioural therapy to a standard in-patient treatment consisting of milieu therapy, antidepressant medication, and other psychotropic medication as indicated. Psychotherapy was administered throughout the in-patient stay and for 20 weeks after discharge. While results at termination significantly favoured the combination treatment in terms of treatment completion and symptom levels, differences in relapse rates at 12-month follow-up were not found. However, power was severely limited in conducting follow-up analyses, as only six subjects completed and responded to the standard treatment. Secondary analyses were conducted which included non-responders to initial treatment; these indicated a significant advantage for the combination treatment at 12-month follow-up (Miller *et al.*, 1989). Further analyses on a larger sample revealed an interaction between the level of cognitive dysfunction at treatment entry and the response to different forms of treatment (Miller *et al.*, 1990). Subjects who had low scores on the Dysfunctional Attitudes Scale and the Cognitive Bias Questionnaire responded equally well to pharmacotherapy alone or in combination with cognitive therapy. However, subjects who had high levels of cognitive dysfunction responded significantly better when cognitive therapy was provided in addition to antidepressant medications. These results held for the mean levels of symptomatology as well as the percentage of responders. Survival analyses were not conducted.

In summary, differences in samples, treatment provision, and analytic strategies preclude conclusions concerning the advantages of combination therapy for relapse prevention. Preliminary data indicate that combination therapy is roughly comparable to the provision of psychotherapy alone, and may have advantages when compared to acute medication treatment alone, but not when compared to continuation or maintenance pharmacotherapy. Regardless of the impact of combination therapy for long-term outcome, the indication that this treatment provides greater hope during the initial episode may be sufficient justification for further investigation of this common clinical strategy.

Finally, questions remain concerning the impact of combining cognitive therapy with other interventions. It appears that marital therapy provided in addition to cognitive therapy (Jacobson *et al.*, 1987; O'Leary and Beach, 1990) or IPT (Foley *et al.*, 1987), particularly for samples selected on the basis of marital dissatisfaction, is comparable in terms of initial symptom reduction, yet holds the additional benefit of increasing marital satisfaction levels. Certainly, given the interwoven and complex relationship between depression and disturbances in social functioning, particularly marital distress (Rounsaville *et al.*, 1979), one might expect that addressing marital problems could enhance the length of recovery. Findings to date have suggested that the addition of marital therapy may not produce differential symptom reduction at one-year outcome, but that couples who received marital therapy continue to report higher levels of marital satisfaction at follow-up than couples who received cognitive therapy alone (O'Leary and Beach, 1990). Although the reports currently in the literature do not include results in terms of long-term outcomes of responders or the temporal pattern of relapse, both Jacobson and colleagues and Foley and colleagues are currently collecting information on the long-term benefits of combining marital and individual therapy in the treatment of depression.

Summary: prophylactic efficacy of psychotherapy

Although there have been a limited number of studies with a range of methodological rigour, several findings emerge. First, although there has been a paucity of long-term research on behavioural therapy, preliminary results suggest that this may be an efficacious treatment in the prevention of relapse. Second, cognitive therapy during the acute episode appears to be equivocal or better than acute pharmacotherapy in relapse prevention. Ongoing 'booster' sessions or continuation treatments appear to hold promise for increasing these preventative effects. Third, while results of interpersonal psychotherapy during the episode have not demonstrated any long-term advantages in symptom reduction as compared with TCAs, IPT may have long-term effects on social adjustment. Fourth, recent evidence indicates that the provision of IPT maintenance sessions on a monthly basis has a significant impact on recurrence rates. Finally, combination treatment does not seem more helpful than psychotherapy or pharmacotherapy alone in preventing relapse or recurrence.

At present, the factors which may moderate the long-term efficacy of psychotherapy have not been systematically investigated. However, a number of factors seem to influence naturalistic course and response to pharmacotherapy. As comprehensively reviewed by Belsher and Costello (1988), four domains have been particularly consistent in their predictive ability, including a history of depressive episodes, major life events, social support deficits, or neuroendocrine dysregulation after recovery. Demographic variables have not been particularly consistent, although factors such as age and gender have been predictive within a large community sample (Lewinsohn *et al.*, 1989). Recent research also suggests that the persistence of sleep abnormalities may be a particularly useful indicator of relapse and recurrence (Giles *et al.*, 1987). Finally, a number of variables which have been found to be intimately linked to depression are poorly understood in relation to relapse and recurrence. These include the quality of ongoing interpersonal relationships and the impact personality traits, domains which may interact with the provision and efficacy of psychotherapy and/or pharmacotherapy. In short, it is important for psychological treatment outcome studies to address a broad range of variables in addressing which subjects are most vulnerable to relapse.

Although treatment outcome studies have typically investigated a small subset of variables in relation to relapse and recurrence, Gonzales *et al.* (1985) comprehensively assessed predictors of three-year outcome following psychotherapy. They assessed a range of demographic, symptom, and life circumstance variables in a sample of CBT recipients who had major depression, intermittent depression, or double depression. The enormous difficulty involved in conducting this form of research is highlighted by the fact that less than 25% of the original 113 patients completed the study. Results of this study indicated that previous episodes of depression, positive family history, medical problems, life dissatisfaction, depression level at entry to the study, and younger age accounted for 38% of the variance in time to relapse, as assessed using life tables.

Preliminary research investigating demographic, symptomatic, and social predictors of long-term treatment outcome has documented few consistent effects. Several studies, however, sugest that clinical status at treatment termination is predictive of relapse. Simons *et al.* (1986) found that the combination of BDI and DAS scores at termination of acute treatment predicted relapse and recurrence with 73% accuracy. BDI scores of less than 4 at treatment termination seemed particularly predictive of sustained recovery. Evans and colleagues also found that post-treatment BDI scores were highly predictive of relapse; while patients with BDI scores of less than 5 demonstrated a 22% relapse rate, patients with BDI scores greater than 9 demonstrated a 40% relapse rate.

Although other variables have been investigated, it is difficult to separate the impact of symptom levels from other factors. For example, Weissman *et al.* (1978) examined predictors of depression up to 48 months after treatment entry. They found that neuroticism scores on the Maudsley Personality Inventory, administered after one month of acute treatment, were predictive of ongoing, chronic symptoms, particularly for subjects who did not receive further treatment. Similarly, Thompson *et al.* (1988) found that within a sample of elderly depressed patients, the presence of an Axis II disorder during depression was associated with a decreased likelihood of achieving recovery by six months. However, symptom levels, which overlap highly with personality symptoms, were not controlled for in either of these analyses. In fact, assessments of personality before and after recovery from depression have documented the artificial elevation of personality diagnoses during episodes (Hirschfeld *et al.*, 1983). Because of this high degree of overlap, it is unclear whether these findings are best attributed to personality features or would be more appropriately related to residual levels of symptomatology. Taken together, these findings indicate the extreme importance of monitoring any signs of clinical disturbance before the termination of therapy. Subjects who retain even residual levels of symptomatology may be particularly vulnerable to relapse after psychotherapy (see Prien and Kupfer, 1986). If additional research replicates this finding, it may be important to re-examine data on the acute response to psychotherapy, with an emphasis on the percentages of subjects who achieve full remission.

In addition to further research efforts on predictors or relapse and recurrence, there is a strong need to develop a better understanding of the processes which are involved in recovery. Investigators in this direction may be hindered by a tendency to focus solely on symptom levels as outcome variables. For example, IPT appears to exert major influence through changing the person's social adjustment. Future research could expand on this interesting result by tracking whether patients who achieve substantial social improvements are less vulnerable to relapse. Similarly, in the cognitive literature, researchers have begun to address the question of whether lingering negative cognitive attributions or styles impact on the probability of relapse (Fennell and Teasdale, 1987; Hollon *et al.*, in press; Simons *et al.*, 1986). While these results are certainly quite interesting, further replication is required. At present, the degree to which these findings reflect underlying levels of residual symptomatology is often unclear. Regardless, these findings hold potential for matching individuals with the most appropriate therapy. There may be certain individuals with high levels of cognitive distortion (Miller *et al.*, 1990) who would benefit more fully from CBT; similarly, subjects with more prominent interpersonal difficulties may receive more ample benefits from IPT.

In short, there may be separate pathways to recovery, just as there are multiple factors which can contribute to the onset of illness. It is unclear how much different therapies rely on the same or different mechanisms of change. These factors which suggest treatment-specific processes of change have just begun to be explored. The multi-dimensionality of the recovery process is supported by the findings of DiMascio and colleagues (1979), who discovered that medication and psychotherapy, while comparable in efficacy, were affecting different symptom clusters. Medication appears to act primarily on vegatative symptoms; psychotherapy appeared more efficacious for symptoms of mood and apathy; and combination therapy seemed to address both clusters. In addition to affecting different symptoms, these treatments show different timing of response, with pharmacotherapy acting more rapidly (DiMascio *et al.*, 1979; Elkin *et al.*, 1989).

The validity of attending to more specific aspects of the psychotherapy is illustrated by a recent finding of particular importance in the prediction of relapse and recurrence following psychotherapy (Frank *et al.*, 1991b). Recently, treatment quality, defined as the conformity to specific IPT techniques and goals, was found to be highly predictive of long-term treatment outcome. While patients who received less specific IPT demonstrated a median survival time of 18.1 weeks, patients who received more specific IPT demonstrated a median survival time of 101.7 weeks.

Conclusions

Overall, then, the field of psychotherapy research in depressive disorders has witnessed enormous advances in methodological sophistication and increasing attention to long-term outcome. Results of these efforts have been promising across several different forms of psychotherapy. Despite significant advances, conclusions have been limited by the small number of studies and a series of methodological problems. The most pervasive methodological difficulties have included a failure to report treatment specificity, inadequate provision of medication, most frequently in the form of abrupt withdrawal, analyses of discrete points in time rather than cumulative probability of relapse, and small sample sizes.

Despite these problems, one conclusion emerges across a range of studies. As is the case with pharmacotherapy, continuing psychotherapy after initial recovery is a powerful technique in the prevention of relapse and recurrence. The importance of ongoing therapy is supported by findings that patients who display even low levels of residual symptomatology are vulnerable to relapse. Hence, even when patients appear substantially improved, continuation treatment may be essential for stable recovery.

The impact of longer-term therapy is a critical area for future research. In particular, research addressing the minimum 'dosage' and length of continuation therapy is greatly needed. Finally, although there have been very few studies which adequately addressed recurrence, this appears to be an area which may be quite sensitive to psychological interventions, and would be a particularly important area for further research.

Acknowledgements

This work was supported in part by National Institute of Mental Health grants MH29618 and MH30915 and by The John D. and Catherine T. MacArthur Foundation Network on the Psychobiology of Depression and Related Affective Disorders.

References

American Psychiatric Association (1980) Diagnostic and Statistical Manual of Mental Disorders, 3rd edn. Washington, DC: APA.

Baker AL, Wilson PH (1985) Cognitive-behavior therapy for depression: the effects of booster sessions on relapse. *Behav Ther* **16**, 335–344.

Beck AT, Beamsderfer A (1974) Assessment of depression: the depression inventory. In Pichot P, Olivier-Martin R (eds) *Psychological Measurements in Psychopharmacology: Modern Problems in Pharmacopsychiatry*, Basel: S. Karger.

Beck AT, Ward CH, Mendelsohn M *et al* (1961) An inventory for measuring depression. *Arch Gen Psychiatry* **4**, 561–571.

Beck AT, Weissman A, Lester D, Trexler L (1974) The measurement of pessimism: The Hopelessness Scale. *J Consult Clin Psychol* **42**, 861–865.

Beck AT, Rush AJ, Shaw BF, Emery G (1979) *Cognitive Therapy of Depression: A Treatment Manual.* New York: Guilford.

Beck AT, Hollon SD, Young JE *et al.* (1985) Treatment of depression with cognitive therapy and amitriptyline. *Arch Gen Psychiatry* **42**, 142–148.

Bellack AS, Hersen AM, Himmelhoch J (1981) Social skills training for depression: a treatment manual. *J Abstract Service Catalog Selected Documents* **11**, 36.

Belsher G, Costello CG (1988) Relapse after recovery from unipolar depression: a critical review. *Psychol Bull* **104**, 84–96.

Bergin AE, Lambert MJ (1978) The evaluation of therapeutic outcomes. In Bergin G, Bergin AE (eds) *Handbook of Psychotherapy and Behavior Change: An Empirical Analysis*, 2nd edn, pp. 139–190. New York: Wiley.

Blackburn IM, Eunson KM, Bishop S (1986) A two-year naturalistic follow-up of depressed patients treated with cognitive therapy, pharmacotherapy and a combination of both. *J Affective Disord* **10**, 67–75.

Brown RA, Lewinsohn PM (1984) A psychoeducational approach to the treatment of depression: comparison of group, individual, and minimal contact procedures. *J Consult Clin Psychol* **52**, 774–783.

Brown SD (1980) Coping skills training: an evaluation of a psychoeducational program in a community mental health setting. *J Counseling Psychol* **27**, 340–345.

Covi L, Lipman RS, Derogatis LR *et al.* (1974) Drugs and group psychotherapy in neurotic depression. *Am J Psychiatry* **131**, 191–198.

Derogatis LR, Lipman RS, Rickels K *et al.* (1974) The Hopkins Symptom Checklist (HSCL): a self-report symptom inventory. *Behav Sci* **19**, 1–15.

DeRubeis RJ, Hollon SD, Evans MD, Bemis KM (1982) Can psychotherapies for depression be discriminated? A systematic investigation of cognitive therapy and interpersonal therapy. *J Consult Clin Psychol* **50**, 744–756.

DiMascio A, Weissman MM, Prusoff BA *et al.* (1979) Differential symptom reduction by drugs and psychotherapy in acute depression. *Arch Gen Psychiatry* **36**, 1450–1456.

Elkin I, Shea T, Watkins JT *et al.* (1989) National Institute of Mental Health treatment of depression collaborative research program: general effectiveness of treatments. *Arch Gen Psychiatry* **46**, 971–982.

Evans MD, Hollon SD, DeRubeis RJ *et al.* (submitted) Differential relapse following cognitive therapy, pharmacotherapy, and combined cognitive-pharmacotherapy for depression.

Feighner JP, Robins E, Guze SB *et al.* (1972) Diagnostic criteria for use in psychiatric research. *Arch Gen Psychiatry* **26**, 57–63.

Fennell MJV, Teasdale JD (1987) Cognitive therapy for depression: individual differences and the process of change. *Cognitive Ther Res* **11**, 253–271.

Foley SH, Rounsaville BJ, Weissman MM *et al* (1987, May) Individual vs. conjoint interpersonal pschotherapy for depressed patients with marital disputes. Paper presented at the annual meeting of the American Psychiatric Association, Chicago.

Frank E (1991) Interpersonal psychotherapy as a maintenance treatment for patients with recurrent depression. *Psychotherapy* **28**, 259–266.

Frank E, Kupfer DJ, Perel JM *et al.* (1990) Three year outcomes for maintenance therapies in recurrent depression. *Arch Gen Psychiatry* **47**, 1093–1099.

Frank E, Prien R, Jarrett RB *et al.* (1991a) Conceptualization and rationale for consensus definitions of terms in major depressive disorder: Remission, recovery, relapse, and recurrence. *Arch Gen Psychiatry* **48**, 851–855.

Frank E, Kupfer DJ, Wagner EF *et al.* (1991b) Efficacy of interpersonal psychotherapy as a maintenance treatment for recurrent depression: contributing factors. *Arch Gen Psychiatry* **48**, 1053–1059.

Gallagher DE, Thompson LW (1982) Treatment of major depressive disorder in older adult outpatients with brief psychotherapies. *Psychother Theory Res Pract* **19**, 482–489.

Gallagher-Thompson D, Hanley-Petersen P, Thompson LW (1990) Maintenance of gains versus relapse following brief psychotherapy for depression. *J Consult Clin Psychol* **58**, 371–374.

Giles DE, Jarrett RB, Roffwarg HP, Rush AJ (1987) Reduced REM latency: a predictor of recurrence in depression. *Neuropsychopharmacology* **1**, 33–39.

Glick ID, Clarkin JF, Spencer JH *et al.* (1985) A controlled evaluation of inpatient family intervention. *Arch Gen Psychiatry* **42**, 882–886.

Gonzales LR, Lewinsohn PM, Clarke GN (1985) Longitudinal follow-up of unipolar depressives: an investigation of predictors of relapse. *J Consult Clin Psychol* **53**, 461–469.

Gordon VC, Matwychuk AK, Sachs EG, Canedy BH (1988) A three-year follow-up of a cognitive-behavioral intervention. *Arch Psychiatr Nursing* **2**, 218–226.

Greenhouse JB, Stangl D, Kupfer DJ, Prien RF (1991) Methodological issues in maintenance therapy clinical trials. *Arch Gen Psychiatry* **48**, 313–318.

Hamilton M (1959) The assessment of anxiety states by rating. *Br J Med Psychol* **32**, 50–55.

Hamilton M (1960) A rating scale of depression. *J Neurol Neurosurg Psychiatry* **23**, 56–62.

Hamilton M (1967) Development of a rating scale for primary depressive illness. *Br J Soc Clin Psychol* **6**, 278–296.

Hathaway SR, McKinley JC (1951) *The Minnesota Multiphasic Personality Inventory Manual*. New York: Psychological Corporation.

Hersen M, Bellack AS, Himmelhoch JM, Thase ME (1984) Effects of social skill training, amitriptyline, and psychotherapy in unipolar depressed women. *Behav Ther* **15**, 21–40.

Hirschfeld RMA, Klerman GL, Clayton PJ *et al.* (1983) Assessing personality: effects of the depression state on trait measurement. *Am J Psychiatry* **140**, 695–699.

Hollon SD, Evans MD, DeRubeis RJ (in press). Cognitive mediation of relapse prevention following treatment for depression: implications of differential risk. In Ingram RE (ed.) *Psychological Aspects of Depression*. New York: Plenum Press.

Hollon SD, Shelton RC, Loosen PT (1991). Cognitive therapy and pharmacotherapy for depression. *J Consult Clin Psychol* **59**, 88–99.

Jackson SW (1986) *Melancholia and Depression from Hippocratic Times to Modern Times*. New Haven: Yale University Press.

Jacobson NS, Schmaling KB, Salusky S *et al.* (1987, November) Marital therapy as an adjunct treatment for depression. Paper presented at the annual meeting of the Association of the Advancement of Behavior Therapy, Boston.

Jarrett RB, Gullion CM, Basco MR, Rush AJ (1990) Are the effects of short-term cognitive therapy short lived? *Biol Psychiatry*. 158A.

Keller MB, Shapiro RW, Lavori PW, Wolfe N (1982a) Relapse in major depressive disorder: analysis with the life table and regression models. *Arch Gen Psychiatry* **39**, 911–915.

Keller MB, Shapiro RW, Lavori PW, Wolfe N (1982b) Recovery in major depressive disorder: analysis with the life table. *Arch Gen Psychiatry* **39**, 905–910.

Keller MB, Lavori PW, Friedman BL *et al.* (1987) The LIFE: a comprehensive method for assessing outcome in prospective longitudinal studies. *Arch Gen Psychiatry* **44**, 540–549.

Klerman GL, DiMascio A, Weissman M *et al.* (1974) Treatment of depression by drugs and psychotherapy. *Am J Psychiatry* **131**, 186–191.

Klerman GL, Weissman MM, Rounsaville BJ, Chevron ES (1984) *Interpersonal Psychotherapy of Depression.* New York: Basic Books.

Kovacs M, Rush J, Beck AT, Hollon SD (1981) Depressed out-patients treated with cognitive therapy or pharmacotherapy: a one-year follow-up. *Arch Gen Psychiatry* **38**, 33–39.

Lavori PW, Keller MB, Klerman GL (1984) Relapse in affective disorders: a reanalysis of the literature using life table methods. *J Psychiatry Res* **18**, 13–25.

Lewinsohn PM, Zeiss AM, Duncan EM (1989) Probability of relapse after recovery from an episode of depression. *J Abnormal Psychol* **98**, 107–116.

Lovibund SH (1981) The differentiation and measurement of depression, anxiety and tension. Paper presented at Rutgers University.

Meterissian GB, Bradwejn J (1989) Comparative studies on the efficacy of psychotherapy, pharmacotherapy, and their combination in depression: was adequate pharmacotherapy provided? *J Clin Psychopharmacol* **9**, 334–339.

Miller IW, Norman WH, Bishop WH, Dow MG (1986) The modified scale for Suicidal Ideation: reliability and validity. *J Consult Clin Psychol* **54**, 724–725.

Miller IW, Norman WH, Keitner GI (1989) Cognitive-behavioral treatment of depressed inpatients: six- and twelve-month follow-up. *Am J Psychiatry* **146**, 1274–1279.

Miller IW, Norman WH, Keitner GI (1990) Treatment response of high cognitive dysfunction depressed inpatients. *Compr Psychiatry* **30**, 62–71.

O'Leary KD, Beach SRH (1990) Marital therapy: available treatment for depression and marital discord. *Am J Psychiatry* **147**, 183–186.

O'Malley SS, Foley SH, Rounsaville BJ *et al.* (1988) Therapist competence and patient outcome in interpersonal psychotherapy of depression. *J Consult Clin Psychol* **56**, 496–501.

Paykel ES, Klerman GL, Prusoff BA (1970) Treatment setting and clinical depression. *Arch Gen Psychiatry* **22**, 11–21.

Prien RF, Kupfer DJ (1986) Continuation drug therapy for major depressive episodes: how long should it be maintained? *Am J Psychiatry* **143**, 18–23.

Prien RF, Carpenter LL, Kupfer DJ (1991) The definition and operational criteria for treatment outcome of major depressive disorder: a review of the current research literature. *Arch Gen Psychiatry* **48**, 796–800.

Raskin A, Schulterbrandt JG, Reatig N *et al.* (1970) Differential response to chlorpromazine, imipramine, and placebo: a study of subgroups of hospitalized depressed patients. *Arch Gen Psychiatry* **23**, 164–173.

Robins LN, Helzer JE, Croughan J, Ratcliff KS (1981) National Institute of Mental Health Diagnostic Interview Schedule: its history, characteristics and validity. *Arch Gen Psychiatry* **38**, 381–389.

Rounsaville BJ, Weissman MM, Prusoff BA, Herceg-Baron RL (1979) Marital disputes and treatment outcome in depressed women. *Compr Psychiatry* **20**, 483–490.

Shea MT, Elkin I, Imber S (1990) Course of depressive symptoms over follow-up: findings from the NIMH treatment of depression collaborative research program. Paper presented at the meeting of the Society for Psychotherapy Research, June, 1990.

Simons AD, Murphy GE, Levine JL, Wetzel RD (1986) Cognitive therapy and pharmacotherapy for depression: sustained improvement over one year. *Arch Gen Psychiatry* **43**, 43–48.

Spitzer RL, Endicott J, Robins E (1978) Research Diagnostic Criteria: rationale and reliability. *Arch Gen Psychiatry* **35**, 773–782.

Steinmetz JL, Lewinsohn PM, Antonuccio DO (1983) Prediction of individual outcome in a group intervention for depression. *J Consult Clin Psychol* **51**, 331–337.

Steuer JL, Mintz J, Hammen CL *et al.* (1984) Cognitive-behavioral and psychodynamic group pscyhotherapy in treatment of geriatric depression. *J Consult Clin Psychol* **52**, 180–189.

Thase ME, Bowler, K, Harden T (1991) Cognitive behavior therapy of endogenous depression: Part 2. Preliminary findings in 16 unmedicated inpatients. *Behav Ther* **22**, 469–477.

Thase ME, Simons AD, McGeary J *et al.* (in press) Relapse following cognitive behavior therapy of depression: potential implications for longer courses of treatment. *Am J Psychiatry.*

Thompson LW, Gallagher D, Czirr R (1988) Personality disorder and outcome in the treatment of late-life depression. *J Geriatr Psychiatry* **21**, 133–153.

Vallis TM, Shaw BF, Dobson KS (1986) The cognitive therapy scale: psychometric properties. *J Consult Clin Psychol* **54**, 381–385.

Weissman MM, Paykel ES (1974) *The Depressed Woman: A Study of Social Relationships.* Chicago: University of Chicago Press.

Weissman MM, Kasl SV, Klerman GL (1976) Follow-up of depressed women after maintenance treatment. *Am J Psychiatry* **133**, 757–760.

Weissman MM, Prusoff BA, Klerman GL (1978) Personality and the prediction of long-term outcome of depression. *Am J Psychiatry* **135**, 797–800.

Weissman MM, Prusoff BA, DiMascio A *et al.* (1979) The efficacy of drugs and psychotherapy in the treatment of acute depressive episodes. *Am J Psychiatry* **136**, 555–558.

Weissman MM, Klerman GL, Prusoff BA *et al.* (1981) Depressed outpatients: results one year after treatment with drugs and/or interpersonal psychotherapy. *Arch Gen Psychiatry* **38**, 51–55.

Wilson PH (1982) Combined pharmacological and behavioral treatment of depression. *Behav Res Ther* **20**, 173–184.

Wilson PH, Goldin JC, Charbonneau-Powis M (1983) Comparative efficacy of behavioral and cognitive treatments of depression. *Cognitive Ther Res* **7**, 111–124.

Wing JK, Cooper JE, Sartorius N (1974) *The Description and Classification of Psychiatric Symptoms: An Instruction Manual for the Present State Examination and CATEGO Programme.* Cambridge University Press: London.

9

Comorbidity of mood disorders and anxiety states: implications for long-term treatment

Giovanni B. Cassano, Mario Savino and Giulio Perugi

Overlap between diagnostic categories in mood disorders and anxiety states

Advances in the pharmacological treatment of anxiety states have favoured the adoption of operative diagnostic criteria within the wide area of neurotic disorders, and have led to the supersession of the 'hierarchical diagnostic approach', so enabling both researchers and clinicians to direct new attention to comorbidity among various psychopathological conditions. The recent 'nosographic revolution' has permitted the assessment of the co-occurrent diagnostic categories—a phenomenon that is recognized to have considerable pathophysiological and therapeutic implications for individual patients.

Anxiety states concomitant with depression have often been considered 'secondary' conditions, as symptoms or features associated with the latter disorder. Such interpretations were also due to the fuzzy diagnostic boundaries falling within the neurotic spectrum, where the term 'anxiety' was, until recently, used to refer to an aspecific condition of acute or chronic apprehension, tension and agitation, with neurovegetative phenomena. The loss of information resulting from such loose terminology has been largely responsible for diagnostic and

Long-term Treatment of Depression. Edited by S.A. Montgomery and F. Rouillon
© 1992 John Wiley & Sons Ltd

therapeutic shortcomings in the management of patients presenting concomitant syndromes or symptoms of anxiety and depression.

Increasing interest has been stimulated by the comorbidity of anxiety and mood disorders, whose relationships have been a long-standing focus of investigation (Freud, 1894; Lewis, 1934; Roth, 1959). Comorbidity of mood and anxiety disorders is a frequent phenomenon. Estimates of intra-episodic and lifetime comorbidity between anxiety and major depression range widely from 19% (Fawcett and Kravitz, 1983) to 91% (Bowen and Kohout, 1979), depending on the length of follow-up and on the diagnostic criteria adopted.

Comorbidity between mood disorders and anxiety states has been found to be associated with greater severity of the psychopathology (Angst and Dobler-Mikola, 1985), higher rates of chronicity (Stavrakaki and Vargo, 1986), lower response to treatment (Van Valkenburg et al., 1984), and poorer prognosis (Wittchen and Essau, 1989; Hecht et al., 1989). Thus, comorbidity appears to be frequent in the patient's lifespan, but it also affects the family area. Anxiety and mood disorders are common among the first-degree relatives of both anxious and depressive probands (Leckman et al., 1983). Family studies in young probands (Weissman, 1990) reported the following conclusions: (a) there is a high risk of comorbidity phenomena in children with anxious or depressed parents; (b) relatives of children with anxiety or mood disorders are frequently affected by anxiety or depression; (c) children show a high degree of comorbidity between anxiety and mood disorders.

Clinical research on intra-episodic and lifetime comorbidity has been focused mainly on the relationship between anxiety disorders and major depression. This latter condition has been considered either as a consequence of prolonged anxiety states, or as an independent illness. In contrast, the co-occurrence of anxiety disorders with the full range of mood disorders, such as bipolar I and II disorders, dysthymia, cyclothymia, and even mild affective temperamental dysregulations, has not been systematically explored. In a recent inquiry, we investigated the comorbidity phenomenon in 103 outpatients with panic disorder (Cassano et al., 1991). Major depression was found in 29% of this sample, within which the recorded frequency of bipolar II disorder was 12%, while the frequency of cyclothymic and hyperthymic temperamental dysregulation was 34%. Thus the bipolar spectrum disorders appear to be quite common in patients suffering from an anxiety state such as panic disorder.

We will concentrate on the short and long-term treatment implications of those common conditions in which panic disorder and generalized anxiety disorder (GAD) co-occur with the entire spectrum of mood disorders.

Implications of comorbidity for the long-term pharmacological treatment of anxiety states

Comorbidity between anxiety and mood disorders such as bipolar disorder, recurrent unipolar depression, dysthymia and cyclothymia should be considered when contemplating treatment in a short or long-term perspective; the adoption of pharmacological combinations may be required and the co-occurrence of different disorders may affect a patient's drug compliance, as well as response to medication. Syndromic complexity may be made apparent by the contrasting effects of treatments, which often improve one disorder while worsening another; it is mainly on phenomena such as these that treatment-resistant conditions are grounded. In confronting such 'mosaic' syndromes, clinicians may find it difficult to sharply delineate features to be treated specifically and to draw up a set of outcome measures; moreover, the contrasting effects of medication on each of the concomitant disorders may complicate the clinical picture. When mood and anxiety disorders are concomitant, the condition is often labelled as borderline personality disorder, and psychotherapy becomes the most commonly used treatment; in other cases, the diagnosis of 'atypical depression', 'hysteria', or 'neurotic-hypochondriacal-phobic depression' is applied; in others the diagnosis of 'anxious depression' is formulated to account for the concomitant anxious disorder. The loss of information brought about by such diagnostic labels has a negative impact on treatment selection, on pharmacotherapeutic conduct and on the management of cases in which one disorder may predispose to another and/or interfere with its course and evolution.

Panic disorder

The primary role of imipramine in the treatment of panic disorder was shown by Klein (1964) and subsequently confirmed in several controlled studies (for revue see Cassano *et al.*, (1988a). Clinical experience and a large number of reported observations suggest that other tricyclic and tetracyclic drugs, such as clomipramine (Gloger *et al.* 1981; Cassano *et al.*, 1988b), maprotiline (Sheehan, 1982), desipramine (Rifkin *et al.*, 1981), nortriptyline (Muskin and Fyer, 1981) and trimipramine (in our clinical experience) can have similar antipanic effects.

Various studies have proved the efficacy of monoamine oxidase inhibitors (MAOIs) in panic anxiety and avoidance behaviour (Sargant and Dally, 1962; Tyrer *et al.*, 1973; Mountjoy *et al.*, 1977; Sheehan *et al.*, 1984). Phenelzine can be more potent and more rapidly effective than imipramine in patients with a wide range of avoidance behaviour and less frequent panic attacks.

There is a wide consensus of the efficacy of benzodiazepines on anticipatory anxiety and their lack of efficacy in blocking panic attacks (Noyes *et al.*, 1984);

Chouinard *et al.* (1982), and Sheehan *et al.* (1984) reported the specific efficacy of alprazolam, a new triazol-derived benzodiazepine. The two phases of the Worldwide Multicenter Upjohn Study (Ballenger *et al.*, 1988) confirmed that the optimal panic-blocking dose of alprazolam varied from 6 mg to 8 mg per day, a dosage that is equivalent to about 60–100 mg per day of diazepam. Controlled studies with other benzodiazepines at such doses still need to be performed before concluding that alprazolam is unique among these compounds in its antipanic properties. More recently, claims have been made about the antipanic effect of clonazepam (Spier *et al.*, 1986), a high-potency benzodiazepine, and about the serotonin (5-hydroxytryptamine, 5-HT) uptake inhibitor fluoxetine (Gorman *et al.*, 1987).

Studies of panic-agoraphobic patients on long-term treatment with tricyclic antidepressants (TCA) (Zitrin *et al.*, 1980) revealed that their condition continued to improve during several months of medication, especially as regards the delayed and slow remission of phobic avoidance and the progressive recovery of social adjustment. On this basis, it does not seem to be advisable to reduce or interrupt treatment until the remission of symptoms has become stable and secondary maladaptive phenomena have been overcome (Ballenger, 1986). It is considered advisable to attempt the discontinuation of treatment after a six to eight-month period free from major or minor panic attacks, anticipatory anxiety, phobic avoidance and residual phenomena. Whatever the drug given, TCA, MAOI or alprazolam, discontinuation should be gradual, taking place over a period of one to three months.

Data on the rate of relapses after the interruption of drug treatment are scarce. Zitrin *et al.* (1980) reported that about 15–30% of agoraphobics relapsed within two years of discontinuing 26 weeks of imipramine treatment. Cohen *et al.* (1984) obtained a similar relapse rate in another two-year follow-up study. There are no published data concerning the frequency of relapses following MAOI discontinuation. Generally, when relapse does occur, patients respond positively to resumption with the same compound, and a new attempt to withdraw the drug can be tried three to six months after treatment has been resumed. By adopting this strategy it is possible to discontinue the drug treatment of most patients during the second year (Ballenger, 1986). Some patients must continue with pharmacological therapy much longer, even if at lower dosages.

Panic disorder with agoraphobia can be subdivided into two subcategories on the basis of medium and long-term response to TCA: in one, avoidance phenomena disappear immediately after panic attacks have been blocked, and patients start to move and interact very easily; in another, anticipatory anxiety and avoidance behaviour persist longer after the disappearance of panic attacks, or decrease very slowly, so calling for a cognitive and behavioural therapeutic approach. Nevertheless, a progressive increase in TCA may be needed to achieve therapeutic effects on avoidance behaviour, which may improve several months after doses have been increased. The length of this initial stage and the dosage regimens vary in each case according to the sensitivity of individual patients to long-term side effects with TCAs, such as gastrointestinal symptoms and weight gain, tremor, decreased libido, and impaired intellectual performance.

In the cases of comorbidity of depression and panic disorder, a relatively high proportion of patients start with a depressive episode before panic disorder; this proportion may vary according to whether the observation was made in depressive or anxious patients. More frequently, depression starts after the onset of panic disorder and may occur during the acute phase of the illness or later in the course of panic disorder. When panic disorder appears in a patient with a past history of bipolar I or II disorder or with an early-onset depressive episode, it is necessary to allow for the possibility that antidepressants could favour the onset of continuous or rapid cyclicity. The co-occurrence of bipolar I or II disorder and panic disorder should induce the clinician to have recourse to high dosages of TCA for short periods only and with caution, so as to avoid the risk of mixed-manic or hypomanic switches. Benzodiazepines should be given for short periods or not at all and, once the diagnosis of bipolar disorder is formulated, TCAs should be combined with mood-stabilizing drugs such as lithium salts or carbamazepine (CBZ). For these cases the use of low doses (50–150 mg per day) of trimipramine, a sedative antidepressant which has an antipanic action at doses which seem to have a negligible mood-elevating effect, has in our experience proved highly effective; the main problem in the long-term administration of trimipramine is weight gain.

The concomitance of recurrent unipolar episodes and panic disorder should not influence the treatment choice of TCAs or MAOIs for the anxiety disorder. The long-term follow-up of these patients does, however, show that the maintenance treatment that is effective in preventing panic-agoraphobic symptoms often fails to prevent the recurrence of depression. Some patients show a full-blown depressive episode after the TCA-induced recovery from panic symptomatology even when maintained on the drug. In these cases either an increase in the dosages of the same compound, or additional antidepressant treatments to overcome the co-occurring mood syndrome are needed. The fact that the doses of TCAs which were effective in preventing panic attacks do not prevent the recurrence of depressive episodes indicates a significant degree of independence between the two concomitant disorders.

The treatment of panic disorder with concomitant major affective disorders should exclude the long-term use of benzodiazepines. The prolonged administration of benzodiazepines may, in fact, affect the course and symptomatology of depression; in addition, the subsequent withdrawal of these drugs may easily trigger a severe major episode, with a higher risk of suicidal behaviour.

When the combined feature is that of an 'atypical depression' in which panic attacks and phobic symptoms are associated with rejection sensitivity, mood reactivity, hypersomnia, and hyperphagia, treatment with MAOIs would be advisable (Quitkin *et al.*, 1988). It should, however, be borne in mind that the long-term administration of these drugs in atypical depression with panic disorder may produce temperamental changes in the direction of mania which in some cases are associated with paranoid thinking. Long-term treatment with MAOIs may induce dependency, with tolerance for the therapeutic effects. After two to three years of MAOI treatment, some of our patients had frequent depressive recurrences, with chronic mood instability and generalized anxiety.

If the depressive episode starts during an acute phase of panic disorder or develops in the post-critical phase of panic attacks it tends to last for short periods and to respond to the same treatment employed for the panic disorder (Cassano *et al.*, 1989a). When recurrent or bipolar depression occurs later, months or years after complete recovery from panic disorder, short and long-term treatment can be mainly targeted on the mood disorder, with the awareness of the risk of a recurrence of full-blown panic symptomatology. Even so, most patients with depressive symptomatology who have a history of panic disorder do reveal at least 'soft' signs of the panic–agoraphobic spectrum, such as isolated and/or atypical minor attacks, claustrophobia and mild separation anxiety; in these patients it is advisable to treat the depressive episodes with antidepressants such as imipramine or clomipramine—compounds which also have an effect on panic-related phenomena.

Panic disorder may also appear in subjects with dysthymia, cyclothymia and subclinical mood dysregulations such as dysthymic, hyperthymic and cyclothymic temperament. In the post- and inter-critical phases of panic disorder a dysthymic disorder may become the most significant clinical phenomenon; dysthymia is often complicated by inappropriate long-term treatments with different combinations of benzodiazepines. Such a dysthymic condition is often co-occurent with other residual panic or avoidance phenomena, and generally responds to treatment with phenelzine or fluoxetine. In some patients concomitant panic disorder and dysthymia simultaneously disappear with the same treatment. When the chronic depressive state continues after the complete remission of the panic disorder symptomatology, trials with other antidepressants, as well as electroconvulsive therapy (ECT), should be taken into consideration.

TCA long-term high-dosage regimens in patients with sub-bipolar temperamental dysregulations can induce significant mood changes; in particular, assertiveness, extrovertness, and hyperactivity with intrusiveness and reduced insight to the point of unreserved expansiveness. Even if only rarely, the remission of phobic-anxiety symptoms may be followed by a return to temperamental characteristics which preceded the onset of panic disorder; at other times, a slight tinge of expansive mood is perceived by the patient and his family as being quite different from his or her previous temperament. These changes usually remain at a subclinical level and a reduction in TCA dosage is sufficient to avoid more serious episodes.

Mild mixed chronic states, characterized by depression, anxiety, mood instability, agitation, irritability and impulsivity, and panic disorder with phobic avoidance may co-occur and the cross-sectional feature can attain the characteristics of a 'pan-anxiety' syndrome with neurotic-histrionic aspects. The cognitive profile of these subjects and the characteristics of their syndrome are such that it may be hard to convince them of the usefulness of combined long-term treatment with both antipanic and mood-stabilizing drugs.

When panic disorder co-occurs with bipolar spectrum disorders a concomitant obsessive-compulsive disorder (OCD) or an obsessive-compulsive personality disorder (OCPD) is quite often encountered (Cassano *et al.*, 1991). In our studies on patients suffering from OCD (Lensi *et al.*, unpublished data) as the index episode the comorbidity with panic disorder was 11.7%. In the investigation on panic disorder mentioned above, comorbidity with OCD and OCPD was 3.1% and 26.8%, respectively. In these cases the best results are those obtained by administering clomipramine, on the basis of its proven efficacy in both disorders (OCD and panic disorder). When the obsessive symptoms have lasted longer than the panic-agoraphobic ones, high doses are often needed for long periods. In some rare cases reversible psychotic features may be triggered; in others irritability, impulsiveness and aggressiveness. These latter phenomena, though rare, must be taken into consideration, as well as the risk of bipolar switches mentioned above; it follows that if soft bipolar predictors are detectable in the family and lifetime history, a preventive combination with CBZ should be adopted. In these cases CBZ or valproic acid should be preferred to lithium as it also enhances the epileptogenic threshold in these patients, who are treated with high doses of TCA compounds. Weissman *et al.* (in press) have, in fact, drawn attention to comorbidity between panic disorder and epilepsy. The risk of epileptic attacks should be anticipated when treating panic disorder with high doses of TCA, as well as when these patients are being withdrawn from benzodiazepines while being maintained on a medium–high treatment regimen with antidepressants.

Another frequently associated condition in patients with panic disorder and mood spectrum disorders is derealization–depersonalization (DD). DD was present during panic attacks in 34.7% of our patient sample (Cassano *et al.*, 1989b). In a number of cases DD, whether or not associated with other symptoms or signs of temporal lobe involvement, may precede or follow the attack. In others it may simply be a post- or inter-critical phenomenon lasting for weeks or months and accompanied by extremely high levels of emotional involvement and anxiety. Quite commonly, patients with panic derealization show a combination of phobic and obsessional symptoms, so displaying the classic 'pan-anxiety, pan-neurosis syndrome'. These feature are such that, even if the initial treatment may utilize relatively high dosages of benzodiazepine sedatives, the medium and long-term treatment calls for a combination of TCAs together with CBZ.

The co-occurrence of social-phobic phenomena, which is not rare in panic disorder patients, enhances the risk of concomitant dysthymia or that of full-blown depressive episodes. In our samples (Perugi *et al.*, 1990) a social phobia secondary to panic disorder was present in 17.1%. 'Secondary' social phobia responds to TCAs, while primary social phobia responds selectively to treatment with the MAOI phenelzine.

Generalized anxiety disorder (GAD)
Pharmacotherapy for GAD is usually considered to be a short-term—sometimes intermittent—complement to non-pharmacological approaches, when anxiety symptoms show episodic aggravation (Greenblatt and Shader, 1974); but when such symptoms display a persistent pattern and a prolonged course, different pharmacological strategies are required. Benzodiazepines are considered the preferential short-term treatment for non-psychotic anxiety. Only a limited number of clinical trials conducted on patients selected according to DSM-III criteria for GAD have been published (Rickels *et al.*, 1983). All these studies reported that benzodiazepines produced greater improvement than placebo after the first week of treatment. The rapid onset of their therapeutic action and the limited number and severity of unwanted effects tend to raise the level of patients' compliance. On the other hand, the development of dependence on benzodiazepines has been identified as one of the risks of chronic treatment with these compounds. Dependence has been produced by chronic treatment with high doses of benzodiazepines (Hollister, 1973) and, more recently, it has become clear that this may occur even when benzodiazepines are prescribed for long periods at low dosages (Marks, 1978; Rickels *et al.*, 1990; Schweizer *et al.*, 1990). Predictably, these features have led to a search for safer and more selective antianxiety agents that do not have sedative effects and do not pose any abuse/dependence risk.

Buspirone is a new anxiolytic that is structurally unrelated to other anti-anxiety agents (Goldberg *et al.*, 1983). This drug has no effect on *in vitro* or *in vivo* binding to the benzodiazepine receptor system (Schoemaker *et al.*, 1981) and it does not interact with uptake sites for monoaminergic systems (Riblet *et al.*, 1982). Buspirone has a certain affinity for serotonergic type 1 receptors located in the hippocampus, and some studies have indicated various interactions of the drug with the dopaminergic receptor system (Riblet *et al.*, 1982).

A series of clinical studies have shown that the efficacy of buspirone in the treatment of GAD is similar to that of various benzodiazepines, and that it has relatively few side effects (Goldberg and Finnerty, 1982; Cohn and Wilcox, 1986). Unlike benzodiazepines, buspirone produces its anxiolytic effects without sedation or psychomotor impairment. Experimental data from animals and clinical studies seem to indicate a low potential for buspirone abuse (Hendry *et al.*, 1983). Abrupt discontinuation of the drug does not seem to produce rebound anxiety or withdrawal symptoms after 6–12 weeks (Tyrer *et al.*, 1985) or even six months (Rickels *et al.*, 1985) of continuous administration. Despite the lack of evidence of physical dependence and tolerance, patients should be closely monitored when buspirone is given for longer than six months because of the lack of long-term experience with this drug.

Previous research has focused on the efficacy of TCAs in the treament of GAD (Kahn *et al.*, 1986). Controlled studies on more restrictively diagnosed GAD populations are needed to confirm or reject any specific anxiolytic role for TCAs when prescribed for non-depressed GAD patients. Antidepressants might also be of some use when there has been an inadequate therapeutic response to benzodiazepines, or, possibly, when patients need long-term treatment (Rickels and Schweitzer, 1987). GAD has often been found to be associated with panic disorder and depressive symptoms. In most cases the treatment of panic disorder or depression with TCAs produces a resolution of all these conditions. Even so, some patients maintain their tendency to excessive chronic worries with a concomitant state of tension and hyperarousal, and a pessimistic attitude towards life. In our experience fluvoxamine seems to produce a substantial long-term anxiolytic effect in patients with GAD as well as with panic disorder. Controlled clinical trials with this compound in large clinical samples are needed to confirm these personal observations.

Problems with benzodiazepines in long-term treatment of anxiety states

The capacity of benzodiazepines to produce dependence, abuse and a withdrawal syndrome means that, in treating anxiety, they should not be used for longer than four weeks (Committee on Safety of Medicines, 1988). Nevertheless, a high proportion of patients with anxious disorders are benzodiazepine dependent, some because of prescriptions issued by GPs or psychiatrists, and others because of self-prescriptions. The pharmacokinetics of benzodiazepines may influence the choice of treatment, since the risks of dependence and side effects induced by these substances are related to the rates of body distribution and excretion. It seems to be less likely that long-acting benzodiazepines will induce dependence. These compounds have a more gradual tapering effect when discontinued. And the elimination time of this form of the drug and its active metabolites is long enough to make withdrawal symptoms milder. On the other hand, long-acting benzodiazepines accumulate in the body; after the primary compound has been eliminated, its metabolite is left in the body and builds up with successive administrations. Elderly and liver-impaired subjects have a low capacity for benzodiazepine elimination, with consequent drug accumulation and toxicity. Several benzodiazepine-related side effects, such as drowsiness, sedation, lethargy, and impaired motor and cognitive functioning, are related to drug accumulation.

Conversely, short-acting benzodiazepines do not show such a 'built-in' tapering-off action, and abrupt discontinuation of these drugs (e.g. triazolam, lorazepam) seems to induce more severe withdrawal reactions than those associated with long-acting benzodiazepines. Benzodiazepines with short half-lives may show rapid fluctuations in drug blood levels and pose an increased risk of minor withdrawal symptoms during treatment. Moreover, the return of symptoms may induce patients to take benzodiazepines more frequently or at higher doses.

The benzodiazepine withdrawal syndrome, when doses are at therapeutic levels, is characterized by minor symptoms such as tension, irritable mood, depression, derealization, sweating, insomnia, and loss of appetite. Seizures and delirium are rare features of the low-dose benzodiazepine withdrawal syndrome. This symptomatology mostly appears one to ten days after the last dose of benzodiazepines and may last from a few days up to six months (Ashton, 1984). The minimum length of treatment capable of producing withdrawal symptoms ranges from four weeks (Fontaine *et al.*, 1984) to eight months (Rickels *et al.*, 1983). According to Rickels *et al.* (1983), a history of past administration of treatment with benzodiazepines—and other sedatives—may predispose a patient to develop withdrawal symptoms after the discontinuation of a new benzodiazepine medication. In anxious and/or depressed patients it is often difficult to distinguish between mild withdrawal symptoms and the reappearance of original symptoms. Conditions specific to withdrawal seem to include irritable mood, impulse dyscontrol, and neurovegetative symptoms such as nausea, headache, dizziness, weight loss, misperceptions, and supersensitivity to environmental stimuli; the quick improvement of this symptomatology that follows the resumption of benzodiazepine administration is very helpful to differential diagnosis.

Dependence on benzodiazepines affects a high percentage of patients suffering from anxiety and mood disorders; these are common conditions which require prolonged treatments. The withdrawal syndrome in panic disorder patients is accompanied by the recurrence of panic attacks now showing a severer symptomatology (Fyer *et al.*, 1987); the ultimate effect is that of reinforcing dependence. As far as GAD is concerned, long-standing anxious symptomatology increases the chances of a prolonged administration of benzodiazepines. This explains why increasing number of patients suffering from GAD turn to the clinician for help because of drug dependence problems rather than a GAD-related symptomatology.

The comorbidity of anxiety states and mood disorders favours the development of dependence on anxiolytic drugs, and prolonged benzodiazepine administration is associated with a chronic course of depressive symptomatology. Long-lasting mild manifestations such as anxiety, irritable mood, and memory impairment are also commonly observed. The relationship between the chronic administration of benzodiazepines and bipolar disorders needs to be confirmed. Sudden manic or hypomanic switches have been observed when benzodiazepines were withdrawn; but mixed states, with agitation, depressed mood, irritability, impulse dyscontrol and anger have also been found; in patients with mixed states and melancholic syndromes the withdrawal of benzodiazepines may aggravate impulse dyscontrol and trigger suicidal behaviour (Himmeloch, 1987).

Symptoms of withdrawal from therapeutic doses of benzodiazepines are seldom a major problem. In most cases a slow tapering with long half-life compounds under careful monitoring is sufficient to minimize withdrawal effects. Major difficulties arise from the chronic misuse of benzodiazepines in patients with anxiety states and mood disorders. These subjects start to take these compounds occasionally and continue for many years, developing tolerance to their therapeutic effects after a few months. When they try to discontinue, the withdrawal syndrome is generally interpreted as a reappearance of severe anxiety symptoms; this forces the patient to continue the drug in the conviction that it will prevent relapses. The chronic use of benzodiazepines produces an unstable condition and favours the chronicization of anxiety and depressive features. These patients often show other symptoms such as cognitive impairment—for instance loss of memory and difficulties in concentrating—as well as some personality changes including irritability, hostility and mood reactivity. Even when benzodiazepines are being taken daily, frequent subclinical withdrawal phenomena due to fluctations in drug blood levels can themselves produce anxiety and worsen mood instability to the point of inducing depressive or mild mixed states.

The extensive experience derived from the Worldwide Upjohn Study (Pecknold *et al.*, 1989) has demonstrated that alprazolam can be tapered off without substantial withdrawal problems after a two-month treatment at effective dosages. Withdrawal phenomena have been reported in only 35% of cases, and only 10% showed from moderate to severe withdrawal symptoms. It is, however, widely accepted nowadays that abrupt drug withdrawal should, as far as possible, be avoided. When abstinence symptoms occur, patients should be put back on a benzodiazepine, preferably one with a long half-life, after which medication should be slowly tapered off. The presence of suicidal thinking points to a probable need for hospitalization.

Concluding remarks

The contributions made by Roth and Harper (1962), Marks (1969) and Klein (1964) on anxiety and phobic derealization syndromes, simple and complex phobias, and panic disorder/agoraphobia have significantly sharpened the diagnostic and therapeutic approaches to anxious neurotic disorders, and therapeutic results have been optimized over the short and long term. The overlapping areas between different anxious categories are now undergoing a process of precise delimitation in which special attention is being devoted to the entire spectrum of manifestations of each single disorder by considering their most atypical and mild sub-syndromic features. Such definitions are pertinent to clinical and scientific aims. The criteria that are widely adopted nowadays in defining the spectrum of mood and pesonality disorders have also made for greater accuracy in detecting the modalities and frequency of the co-occurrence of phenomenologically independent anxiety and mood disorders that often appear as a mild stable temperament trait. At least as far as onset and course are concerned, the lifespan and intra-episodic comorbitity of mood and anxiety disorders have shown the clinical autonomy of these conditions, which may, however, share common genetics or pathophysiology. In most cases under our observation, mood and anxiety disorders had an independent and different age at onset, course, and treatment response, so that each often required a selected, specifically targeted drug therapy both for the initial and subsequent phases of the treatment.

At present, long-term placebo-controlled studies on comorbid conditions are not available and, as a result, any conclusions regarding treatment choice and management are very limited. The logical application of what empirical evidence is available with regard to the efficacy of different treatments for each single disorder, even when occurring in comorbid conditions, is largely arbitrary, since, as yet, these are recognized independent pathophysiological causative processes. On the other hand, the adoption of a comorbidity model would appear to be a useful tool in defining outcome measures and in considering future clinical trials. Pharmacological studies, as well as family, genetic, developmental and biological research, can then be used to test the validity of this model.

There is substantial evidence of a less favourable outcome occurring amongst subjects with both anxiety and mood disorders which would seem to underline the potential usefulness of the comorbidity concept. As a rule, the physician is requested to formulate one single diagnosis in order to simplify communication and treatment choice; although this procedure is adequate in most cases, with a large number of patients it may represent an excessive restriction of information. In approaching patients with chronic and/or resistant affective disorders, the clinician should perhaps take into account an accurate assessment of comorbid syndromes, in order to optimize therapeutic approach and management.

Acknowledgements

This study was in part supported by a grant from the Italian Ministero della Pubblica Istruzione and Consiglio Nazionale delle Ricerche (CNR).

References

Angst J, Dobler-Mikola A (1985) The Zurich study, VI: a continuum from depression to anxiety disorders? *Eur Arch Psychiatry Neurol Sci* **235**, 179–186.

Ashton H (1984) Benzodiazepine withdrawal: unfinished story. *Br Med J* **288**, 1135–1140.

Ballenger JC (1986) Pharmacotherapy of the panic disorders. *J Clin Psychiatry* **47**, 27–32.

Ballenger JC, Burrows GD, DuPont RL *et al.* (1988) Alprazolam in panic disorder and agoraphobia: results from a multicenter trial. I. Efficacy in short-term treatment. *Arch Gen Psychiatry* **45**, 413–422.

Bowen RC, Kohout J (1979) The relationship between agoraphobia and primary affective disorders. *Can J Psychiatry* **24**, 317–322.

Cassano GB, Perugi G, McNair D (1988a) Panic disorder: review of the empirical and rational basis of the pharmacological treatment. *Pharmacopschiatry* **21**, 157–165.

Cassano GB, Petracca A, Perugi *et al.* (1988b) Clomipramine for panic disorder: I. The first 10 weeks of a long term comparison with imipramine. *J Affective Disord* **14**, 123–127.

Cassano GB, Perugi G, Musetti L, Akiskal HS (1989a) The nature of depression presenting concomitantly with panic disorder. *Compr Psychiatry* **21**, 157–165.

Cassano GB, Petracca A, Perugi G *et al.* (1989b) Derealization and panic attacks: a clinical evaluation on 150 patients with panic disorder/agoraphobia. *Compr Psychiatry* **30**, 5–12.

Cassano GB, Savino M, Musetti L, Perugi G (1991). Comorbidity of mood and anxiety disorders. In Cassano GB, Akiskal HS (eds) *Serotonin-Related Psychiatric Syndromes*, Vol. 165, pp 73–82. London, New York: Royal Society of Medicine Services.

Chouinard G, Annable L, Fontaine R (1982) Alprazolam in the treatment of generalized anxiety and panic disorders: a double blind placebo-controlled study. *Psychopharmacology* **77**, 229–223.

Cohen S, Montiero W, Marks IM (1984) Two-years follow-up of agoraphobia after exposure and imipramine. *Br J Psychiatry* **144**, 276–281.

Cohn JB, Wilcox CS (1986) Low sedation potential of buspirone compared with alprazolam and lorazepam in the treatment of anxious patients: a double blind study. *J Clin Psychiatry* **47**, 409–412.

Committee on Safety of Medicines (1988) Systematic review of the benzodiazepines. *Br Med J* **i**, 910.

Fawcett J, Kravitz HM (1983) Anxiety syndromes and their relationships to depressive illness. *J Clin Psychiatry* **44**, 8–11.

Fontaine R, Chominard G, Annable L (1984) Rebound anxiety in anxious patients after abrupt withdrawal of benzodiazepines treatment. *Am J Psychiatry* **141**, 848–852.

Freud S (1894/1959) The justification for detaching from neurasthenia a particular syndrome: the anxiety-neurosis. In *Collected papers*, Vol. 1. New York: E. Jones.

Fyer AJ, Liebowitz MR, Gorman JM (1987) Discontinuation of alprazolam treatment in panic patients. *Am J Psychiatry* **144**, 303–308.

Gloger S, Grunhaus L, Birmacher B, Troudart T (1981) Treatment of spontaneous panic attacks with clomipramine. *Am J Psychiatry* **138**, 1215–1217.

Goldberg HL, Finnerty RS (1982) Comparison of buspirone in two separate studies. *J Clin Psychiatry* **43**, 92–94.

Goldberg ME, Salama AI, Patel JB, Malick JB (1983) Novel non-benzodiazepines anxiolitics. *Neuropharmacology* **22**, 1499–1504.

Gorman JM, Liebowitz MR, Fryer AJ (1987) An open trial of fluoxetine in the treatment of panic attacks. *J Clin Psychopharmacol* **7**, 329–332.

Greenblatt DJ, Shader RI (1974) *Benzodiazepines in Medical Practice.* New York: Raven Press.

Hecht H, Von Zerssen D, Krieg C *et al.* (1989) Anxiety and depression: comorbidity, psychopathology, and social functioning. *Compr Psychiatry* **30**, 420–433.

Hendry JS, Balster RL, Rosencrans JA (1983) Discriminative stimulus properties of buspirone compared to central nervous system depressant in rats. *Pharmacol Biochem Behav* **19**, 97–101.

Himmeloch JM (1987) Lest treatment abet suicide. *J Clin Psychiatry* **48**, 44–54.

Hollister LE (1973) *Clinical Use of Psychotherapeutic Drugs.* Springfield IL: Charles Thomas.

Kahn RJ, McNair DM, Lipman RS *et al.* (1986) Imipramine and chlordiazepoxide in depressive and anxiety disorders. II. Efficacy in anxious outpatients. *Arch Gen Psychiatry* **43**, 79–85.

Klein DF (1964) Delineation of two drug responsive anxiety syndromes. *Psychopharmacologia* **5**, 397–408.

Leckman JR, Weissman MM, Merikangas KR *et al.* (1983) Panic disorder and major depression. *Arch Gen Psychiatry* **40**, 1055–1060.

Lewis AJ (1934) Melancholia: a clinical survey of depressive states. *J Ment Sci* **80**, 277–278.

Marks IM (1969) *Fears and Phobias.* London: Heinemann.

Marks J (1978) *The Benzodiazepines: Use, Overuse, Misuse, Abuse.* Lancaster: MTP Press.

Mountjoy CQ, Roth M, Garside RF, Leitch IM (1977) A clinical trial of phenelzine in anxiety depressive and phobic neuroses. *Br J Psychiatry* **131**, 486–492.

Muskin PR, Fyer AJ (1981) Treatment of panic disorder. *J Clin Psychopharmacol* **1**, 81–90.

Noyes R, Anderson D, Clancy J (1984) Diazepam and propranolol in panic disorder and agoraphobia. *Arch Gen Psychiatry* **41**, 287–292.

Pecknold JC, Swinson RP, Kuch K, Lewis C (1989) Alprazolam in panic disorder and agoraphobia: results from a multicenter trial discontinuation effects. *Arch Gen Psychiatry.*

Perugi G, Simonini E, Savino M *et al.* (1990) Primary and secondary social phobia: psychopathologic and familial differentiations. *Compr Psychiatry* **31**, 245–252.

Quitkin FM, Stewart JW, McGrath PJ *et al.* (1988) Phenelzine vs imipramine in probable atypical depression: defining syndrome boundaries of selective MAOI responders. *Am J Psychiatry* **145**, 306–312.

Riblet LA, Taylor DP, Eison MS *et al.* (1982) Pharmacology and neurochemistry of buspirone. *J Clin Psychiatry* **43**, 11–16.

Rickels K, Schweizer EE (1987) Current pharmacotherapy of anxiety and panic. In Meltzer HY (ed.) *Psychopharmacology: The Third Generation of Progress.* New York: Raven Press.

Rickels K, Weisman K, Norstad N. *et al.* (1982) Buspirone and diazepam in anxiety: a controlled study. *J Clin Psychiatry* **43**, 81–86.

Rickels K, Case G, Downing RW (1983) Long term diazepam therapy and clinical outcome. *JAMA* **250**, 767–770.

Rickels K, Csanalosi I, Chung H, Case WG (1985) Buspirone, clorazepate and withdrawal. *138th Annual Meeting of the American Psychiatric Association.* Dallas.

Rickels K, Schweizer E, Case WG, Greenblatt DJ (1990) Long-term therapeutic use of benzodiazepines. I. Effects of abrupt discontinuation. *Arch Gen Psychiatry* **47**, 899–907.

Rifkin A, Klein DF, Dillon D (1981) Blockade by imipramine or desipramine of panic induced by sodium lactate. *Am J Psychiatry* **138**, 676–677.

Roth M (1959) The phobic anxiety-depersonalization syndrome. *Proc R Soc Med* **52**, 587–595.

Roth M, Harper M (1962) Temporal lobe epilepsy and the phobic-anxiety-depersonalization syndrome. Part II: Practical and theoretical considerations. *Compr Psychiatry* **3**, 215–226.

Sargant W, Dally P (1962) Treatment of anxiety states by antidepressant drugs. *Br Med J* **i**, 6–9.

Schoemaker H, Bliss M, van Yamamura HI (1981) Specific high-affinity saturable binding of 3H-RO5-4864 to benzodiazepine binding sites in the rat cerebral cortex. *Eur J Pharmacol* **71**, 173–174.

Schweizer E, Rickels K, Case WG, Greenblatt DJ (1990) Long-term therapeutic use of benzodiazepines. II. Effects of gradual taper. *Arch Gen Psychiatry* **47**, 908–916.

Sheehan DV (1982) Current views on the treatment of panic and phobic disorders. *Drug Ther* **12**, 74–93.

Sheehan DV, Claycomb JB, Surman OS (1984) The relative efficacy of alprazolam, phenelzine, and imipramine in treating panic attacks and phobias. In *Abstracts of the Scientific proceedings of the 137th Annual Meeting of the American Psychiatric Association*, Los Angeles.

Spier SA, Tesar GE, Rosenbaum JF (1986) Treatment of panic disorder and agoraphobia with clonazepam. *J Clin Psychiatry* **47**, 238–242.

Stavrakaki C, Vargo B (1986) The relationships of anxiety and depression: a review of literature. *Br J Psychiatry* **149**, 7–16.

Tyrer P, Candy J, Kelly D (1973) A study of the clinical effects of phenelzine and placebo in the treatment of phobic anxiety. *Psychopharmacologia* **32**, 237–254.

Tyrer P, Murphy S, Owen R (1985) The risk of pharmacological dependence with buspirone. *Br J Clin Pract* **39**, 91–93.

Van Valkenburg C, Akiskal HS, Puzantian V, Rosenthal T (1984) Anxious depression: clinical, family history and naturalistic outcome: comparisons with panic and major depressive disorders. *J Affective Disord* **6**, 67–82.

Weissman MM (1990) Evidence for comorbidity of anxiety and depression: family and genetic studies of children. In Maser JD, Cloninger CR (eds) *Co-morbidity of Mood and Anxiety Disorders*, pp. 13–37. Washington, DC: American Psychiatric Press.

Wittchen HU, Essau L (1989) Natural course and spontaneous remissions of untreated anxiety disorders. In Hand I, Wittchen HU (eds) *Panic and Phobias*. Berlin: Springer.

Zitrin CM, Klein DF, Woerner M (1980) Treatment of agoraphobia with group exposure in vivo and imipramine. *Arch Gen Psychiatry* **37**, 63–72.

10

Psychopharmacological and psychotherapeutic strategies in intermittent and chronic affective conditions

Hagop S. Akiskal

Introduction

Systematic longitudinal clinical observations, family studies and sleep neuro-physiological findings have led to the suggestion that many patients with inter-mittent or chronic affective symptomatology—conventionally subsumed under such rubrics as 'characterologic depressives' and 'dependent' or 'borderline' characters—represent common variants of mood disorder (Akiskal, 1981, 1983, 1984, 1991a). Furthermore, old (Kraines, 1967) and new research (Cassano *et al.*, 1983) has shown that pernicious personality changes—constituting the 'post-affective personality'—often complicate the course of recurrent mood disorders. This chapter will consider the long-term treatment implications of these American developments for the practice of psychiatry.

DSM-III-R (American Psychiatric Association, 1987) now officially recognizes two such chronic depressive patterns: residual depression, representing inade-quate recovery from depressive episodes; and dysthymia, a disorder which pursues a low-grade fluctuating course and which can serve as the substrate for recurrent depressive episodes. The latter pattern of low-grade depression pre-ceding major depressions is more prevalent than depression followed by

Long-term Treatment of Depression. Edited by S.A. Montgomery and F. Rouillon
© 1992 John Wiley & Sons Ltd

low-grade chronic depression (Lewinsohn *et al.*, 1991). Furthermore, major depression superimposed on cyclothymia also often pursues a subacute and protracted course (Akiskal *et al.*, 1979). Finally, the deletion in DSM-III-R of hierarchical principles in the diagnosis of major depressive and panic disorders has led to the recognition of protracted depressions with fatigue and reverse vegetative signs against a background of panic-phobic symptomatology. Many patients with the latter condition feel literally exhausted after many years of self-induced exposure to a variety of social and life situations to which they are constitutionally oversensitive (Akiskal and Lemmi, 1987); often labelled as 'atypical' depressives, the extreme fatigue of these patients is presently as common a cause for medical consultation as a hundred years ago when Beard (1972 reprint) aptly described them under the rubric of 'neurasthenia'.

After being unfashionable until the mid-1970s, psychopharmacological applications in out-patient psychiatry in North America have benefited from a neo-Kraepelinian renaissance (Akiskal, 1989; Klerman, 1990). These applications represent innovative clinical uses of thymoleptic and related substances most of which, like the Kraepelinian philosophy endorsing their uses, were largely imported from Europe. Such biologically oriented practice (Klein *et al.*, 1980) is being increasingly supported by an expanding double-blind literature on the utility of a variety of thymoleptic agents in most of the foregoing chronic affective subtypes (reviewed in Shader *et al.*, 1985; Howland, 1991). This may come as a surprise to those clinicians who have not followed these clinical research developments. Reconceptualizing certain character pathologics as affective disorder has actually brought new hope and substantial alleviation of suffering to many patients previously deemed 'refractory' to chemotherapy, typically administered in suboptimal doses (Akiskal, 1985; Scott, 1988; Kennedy and Joffe, 1989; Nierenberg and Amsterdam, 1990; Guscott and Grof, 1991). In some communities, undertreatment—one of the contributory causes of chronicity in depressive illness—has actually dropped from 90% in the decade of the 1970s to under 40% in the 1980s (Akiskal *et al.*, 1989).

In another chapter (Akiskal, 1991c) in Volume 2 in this series, I have outlined a classificatory schema of chronic-resistant depressions developed at the University of Tennessee, and described clinical presentations and aetiological aspects; in that chapter 'psychopharmacological dissection' strategies were discussed to the extent they supported the proposed clinical subtyping. Although the present chapter has a broader treatment focus, omitted from discussion are considerations of dysphoric manic and rapid-cycling disorders arising from a more classical manic-depressive substrate. Following a brief discussion of psychopathological considerations pertaining to trait–state issues in intermittent and chronic affective conditions, this chapter reviews the existing systematic literature on their psychopharmacotherapy, and concludes with practical psychotherapeutic principles in their long-term management. The review of the literature is primarily targeted to emerging empirically tested strategies in the long-term management of these protracted low-grade affective conditions.

Dysthymic and related low-grade depressions

The gradual shift of psychiatric care to the out-patient setting over the past two to three decades has confronted psychiatrists with a prevalent group of low-grade affective conditions which pursue a subacute or chronic course. Epidemiological estimates indicate that 3.3% of the US population suffers from such conditions subsumed under the broad rubric of 'dysthymia' (Regier *et al.*, 1988).

Patients with these conditions typically complain of long-standing depressive suffering—often with insidious indeterminate onset—thereby creating difficulty in distinguishing their symptoms from their habitual selves (Akiskal *et al.*, 1980). Lacking the well-defined episodic course of the endogenous depressives, these patients are often relegated to the realm of neurosis. Yet upon closer look, subtle 'endogenous' features can be discerned in a special subgroup meeting the description of the classical melancholic (depressive) temperament with habitual gloominess, brooding, anhedonia, lethargy—all of which are pronounced in the morning—and increased need for sleep rather than insomnia. University of Tennessee research (Akiskal, 1983, 1990) has put this temperament in operational terms based on Kurt Schneider's empirical work (Table I). Dysthymics meeting these criteria often test positive on such markers of mood disorders as shortened REM latency and loaded family history for these disorders. The foregoing considerations in turn support the thesis that in many dysthymic patients the low-grade symptomatology represents a 'subaffective' expression of primary affective illness where temperament and affective symptomatology merge imperceptibly.

Traditionally subsumed under neurotic depressions, the affinities of intermittent and chronic affective conditions to major mood disorders were unsuspected. Their more recent reclassification under the DSM-III (1980) mood

Table I.   Depressive temperamental attributes

1. Gloomy, humourless or incapable of fun
2. Given to worry, brooding or pessamistic cognitions
3. Introverted, passive or lethargic
4. Habitually long sleeper (>9 hours of sleep) or suffering intermittent insomnia
5. Preoccupied with inadequacy, failure and negative events
6. Sceptical, overcritical or complaining
7. Self-critical, self-reproachful and guilt prone
8. Dependable, devoted and self-sacrificing

Modified from Akiskal (1983, 1990).

disorder subtype of 'dysthymia' is upheld by prospective research on neurotic depressives (Akiskal *et al.*, 1978; Bronisch *et al.*, 1985) which has shown such unexpected outcomes as endogenous episodes, bipolar switches, completed suicide and, generally, as unfavourable a course as that of their psychotic counterparts.

Such data have further supported the view that major mood disorders often originate in relatively 'minor' depressions with neurotic or characterologic guises. The concept of 'double depression' (Keller *et al.*, 1983) underscores this frequent superimposition of major episodes on low-grade chronic depressive symptomatology. Recent epidemiological data from Zurich (Angst *et al.*, 1990) further suggest that brief depressions which pursue a recurrent course are more prevalent than full-blown major depressions with which they often co-exist. We have elsewhere (Akiskal and Weiss, 1992) summarized the evidence for a spectrum concept of depressive illness whereby depressive temperament, recurrent brief depression, dysthymia and major depressive episodes form a continuum.

Not all low-grade chronic depressions represent the precursor of major depressions. Thus, DSM-III-R distinguishes dysthymia proper—reserved for low-grade depressive conditions of early insidious onset and protracted course for many years or decades before superimposed episodes, if any—from the chronic depressive residuals representing inadequate recovery following single or multiple episodes of major depression. Such residuals are more likely to arise from the substrate of single unipolar episodes in later life than from that of bipolar disorder and related recurrent depressions (Cassano *et al.*, 1989).

Although the DSM-III and DSM-III-R conceptualizations of dysthymia are still controversial in Europe (Burton and Akiskal, 1990), they have drawn clinical and research attention to the existence of a hitherto unsuspected, overlooked or misdiagnosed universe of low-grade intermittent and chronic depressions (Weissman and Klerman, 1977; Akiskal *et al.*, 1981). By legitimizing their affective status, these manuals accelerated the widespread clinical use of innovative psychopharmacological interventions for these chronic sufferers of depression.

Cyclothymia, bipolar II and borderline epiphenomena

This is not to say that such progress occurred without opposition or controversy in North America. The very fact that borderline conditions defined largely in affective language (Table II)—overlapping with dysthymic and cyclothymic disorders (Akiskal, 1981)—are, nonetheless, listed as prominent instances of 'erratic' personality disorder on Axis II, is indicative of ambivalence in DSM-III on whether to classify low-grade affective symptomatology as mood or personality disorders. Such ambivalence, in turn, reflects a schism in North American psychiatry on how best to characterize non-classical affective conditions.

Table II.   DSM-III-R (1987) criteria of borderline personality rearranged to highlight affective dysregulation

---

- Object hunger—intolerance of abandonment
- Splitting—unstable intense relationships
- Mercurial moods—affective instability
                     —angry outbursts
- Behavioural dyscontrol—physical self-damage
                               —impulsive or unpredictable
- Unstable sense of self—identity disturbances
- Chronic emptiness—boredom

Updated from Akiskal (1981) and Gardner and Cowdry (1985).

Despite claims to the contrary summarized by Gunderson and Phillips (1991), the affinity of borderline conditions to mood disorders is supported by shortened REM latency (Akiskal, 1981; Bell *et al.*, 1983; McNamara *et al.*, 1984; Reynolds *et al.*, 1985; Akiskal *et al.*, 1985), thyroid-stimulating hormone (TSH) blunting upon thryrotropin-releasing hormone (TRH) challenge (Garbutt *et al.*, 1983), as well as familial loading for mood—including bipolar—disorders (Stone, 1980; Akiskal *et al.*, 1985). However, unlike dysthymia with depressive temperamental traits, the list of flagrant borderline psychopathology shown in Table I is rarely antecedent to major depression (Friedman *et al.*, 1982); instead, it appears to reflect a more complex interaction between pre-existing impulsive tendencies which, for unknown reasons, manifest in affective storms during depressive episodes and their aftermath. The dysphoria in borderline personality is so intense—and the behaviour of patients so erratic—that one should think of it more as an intermittent mixed state with bipolar II background rather than dysthymia *per se* (Akiskal, 1987). Here, the periodic intrusion of an underlying cyclothymic vulnerability into the phenomenology of depressive episodes probably accounts for the 'characterologic' instability and the chain of improvident activities and tempestuous life course of borderline conditions which brings so much pain to the patients and their loved ones.

The sensitive-avoidant temperament and atypical depressions

Another DSM-III personality construct—the avoidant type characterized by sensitive-anxious traits—overlaps considerably with social phobic and related depressive conditions (Turner *et al.*, 1986), again testifying to the fluid boundary between traits (Axis II) and psychopathological states (Axis I). The biological underpinnings of these shy-inhibited conditions—manifested in an autonomic nervous system overreactive to novel social interactions—have been underscored in recent research by Kagan *et al.* (1988). This hyperarousal can be seen in the sleep EEG of adult depressives with past history of somatic anxiety and phobic tendencies; unlike dysthymic and borderline conditions, they exhibit delay in the first appearance of REM due to multiple arousals especially prominent in the first half of the night (Akiskal *et al.*, 1984).

Intermittent and chronic affective conditions as subaffective disorders

To recapitulate the psychopathological considerations reviewed thus far, intermittent chronic affective conditions may represent symptomatic extensions of a depressive temperament, the residuum of incompletely remitted major depression, they could arise in the setting of an anxious-sensitive-avoidant temperament, or reflect the dysphoric phases of an impulse-ridden cyclothymic temperament. Thus, the boundary between trait and state is hard to define in these conditions.

Although it is customary to designate these trait conditions as 'character' or 'personality' disorders—with the implication that they are 'learned' attributes of developmental origin—systematic long-term clinical studies conducted at the University of Tennessee (Akiskal *et al.*, 1979; Yerevanian and Akiskal, 1979; Akiskal, 1981) have led to the conceptualization of many of them as subaffective disorders, representing temperamental dysregulations of constitutional origin. This biological viewpoint is further supported by past and current genetic research on personality and its disorders (Eysenck,1967; Cloninger, 1987; Bouchard *et al.*, 1990). Such a conceptualization provides the philosophical rationale for relatively specific psychopharmacotherapy geared to their hypothesized underlying biological dysregulations.

The notion that chemistry is relevant to long-term traits exhibited by the four temperaments goes back to Hippocratic medicine (Klibansky *et al.*, 1979). Thus, an excess of black bile was related to the melancholic, yellow bile to the choleric, phlegm to the phlegmatic, and blood to the sanguine temperaments. For those exhibiting an imbalance of the four humours, ancient treatments consisted of such procedures as special diets, herbs or blood-letting to restore chemical balance with an optimum mixture of temperament necessary for adaptation in life. Balance tilted towards the sanguine type—with its zest for life and fun—was considered the most desirable.

Strategies for two types of atypical depressions

More specific chemical interventions had to await the modern era of psychopharmacology. One of the first dramatic successes along these lines were reported in the late 1950s by West and Dally (1959) and Sargent (1962), who used the monoamine oxidase inhibitor (MAOI) iproniazid in chronically anxious, neurasthenic and hypochondriacal individuals with secondary or atypical depressions characterized by initial insomnia, yet with a tendency to oversleep, irritability, fatigue, overeating and evening worsening of mood.

Given a past history of somatic anxiety and phobic tendencies, these patients with protracted fatigue states typically exhibited sensitive-avoidant personality attributes (Akiskal, 1988). Not only have these patients been shown to respond to currently marketed MAOIs such as phenelzine in double-blind studies (Davidson and Pelton, 1986; Liebowitz *et al.*, 1988), but these personality attributes appear to be the most robust predictors of response in the atypical depressive syndromes, especially in women. Indeed, the avoidant 'personality' itself and associated interpersonal difficulties appear responsive to MAOIs (Stewart *et al.*, 1988) and, possibly, to specific serotonin (5-hydroxytryptamine, 5-HT) reuptake inhibitors such as fluoxetine (Deltito *et al.*, 1991). Whereas comparatively the response to classical tricyclic antidepressants (TCAs) has generally been found inferior to MAOIs in atypical depressions, clinicians should remain alert to the possibility that some atypical depressives will respond to TCAs (Paykel *et al.*, 1983). Behavioural regimens that emphasize proper sleep hygiene will often enhance the therapeutic gains made through medication; in particular, patients must understand the mechanisms of their disorder and the need to avoid caffeine, alcohol and sedative-hypnotics in general. However, alprazolam or clonazepam given before bedtime might benefit those whose sleep is disturbed by sleep-onset panic attacks (Akiskal and Lemmi, 1987).

There exists another low-grade fluctuating affective condition with fatigue, weight gain, and hypersomnia (Davidson *et al.*, 1982)—which clinically overlaps with the atypical depressions in the British sense—but where the temperament is more extraverted, consisting of what is often referred to as 'hysteroid' or 'borderline' characterologic pathology, but which should more accurately be considered cyclothymic. That is, the intermittent depressions of these patients commonly coalesce into major depression which, in turn, are punctuated by brief hypomanic periods leading to the bipolar II pattern (Akiskal, 1981). In a new study (Himmelhoch *et al.*, 1991), the MAOI tranylcypromine has been shown to be clearly superior in a double-blind comparison against the TCA imipramine; indeed, TCAs often induced highly dysphoric mixed-manic type symptomatology. An earlier systematic but open study at the University of Tennessee (Akiskal *et al.*, 1979) had shown TCA-induced aggravation in the course of 44% of cyclothymics, and lithium stabilization over a 6–12-month period in 60%, with significant reduction in such traits and characteristic behaviours as impulsivity, explosive anger outbursts, promiscuous behaviour and ill-advised romantic liaisons, uneven employment history and substance abuse; unpredictability in mood, which had been a major source of distress to these patients—undermining their sense of self because they did not know how they were going to feel from one moment to the next—also responded to lithium, thereby attenuating such a core borderline feature as identity disturbances. Two double-blind studies subsequently verified the beneficial effects of lithium in reducing depressive recurrences in cyclothymic (Peselow *et al.*, 1982) and anger outbursts in borderline (Links *et al.*, 1990) probands. These positive responses echo findings by Rifkin *et al.* (1972), who used a double-blind placebo cross-over study in what they termed 'emotionally unstable character disorder', possibly a more flagrant or 'antisocial' variant of cyclothymia. More recently, bupropion—buttressed with lithium and/or thyroid augmentation—has shown promise over a two-year period of maintenance in cyclothymic–bipolar II patients refractory to other interventions (Haykal and Akiskal, 1990).

It is beyond the scope of this chapter to discuss the treatment of all patients in the heterogeneous realm of borderline conditions. Suffice it to mention that their psychopharmacological response profile—now documented in several controlled investigations (Soloff *et al.*, 1986; Cowdry and Gardner, 1988)—overlaps considerably with that of bipolar II disorder (Akiskal, 1985): aggravation with TCAs, alleviation of depression with MAOIs, symptomatic control with low-dose neuroleptics, and stabilization with such antikindling drugs as carbamazepine. Given recent reports of electro-encephalographic abnormalities in borderlines (Snyder and Pitts, 1984; Cowdry *et al.*, 1985), a subgroup might have affinities to patients manifesting subictal or interictal disturbances of complex partial seizures (Bear and Fedio, 1977; Himmelhoch, 1987; Blumer *et al.*, 1988). As for low-dose neuroleptics, their efficacy transcends their potential utility in those with schizotypal features (Goldberg *et al.*, 1986) observed in about one in five patients meeting the criteria for borderline personality (Akiskal *et al.*, 1985); they seem to offer stabilization for intensely dysphoric unstable moods as well as reducing impulsive suicide attempts (Montgomery, 1987). Finally, adult attention-hyperactivity disorder with intermittent depressions, meeting borderline criteria, might benefit from stimulant medication (e.g., methylphenidate given in maintenance doses of 5–10 mg b.i.d. (Wood *et al.*, 1976).

Strategies for dysthymia and residual depressions

Patients in both of the foregoing groups—whether sensitive-anxious-avoidant or impulsive-hysteroid-borderline—will technically meet the DSM-III-R criteria for dysthymia (Trull *et al.*, 1990). I have elsewhere (Akiskal, 1983, 1990) argued that such broad usage of the term is to be discouraged, because then dysthymia will deteriorate into a synonym for all low-grade depressive conditions. Research conducted at the University of Tennessee (Akiskal *et al.*, 1980; Rosenthal *et al.*, 1981) focused on a core group of early-onset primary dysthymia which is not secondary to another psychiatric disorder. Many of these patients meet the criteria for the classic melancholic temperament. Their chronic anhedonia is particularly striking, typically manifested in deficits in leisure functions and inability to find joy in anything. Their lifelong suffering does not appear to originate in any obvious environmental adversity and lends some credence to their complaints that they were 'born depressed' or that they have been 'depressed since conception'. Indeed, all studies (Rosenthal *et al.*, 1981; Kocsis *et al.*, 1988; Klein *et al.*, 1988) that have examined their familial background reported loaded history for mood—including bipolar—disorders. Primary dysthymia pursues a fluctuating course and most patients eventually, albeit briefly, meet criteria for syndromal depressions that typically resolve with a return to the dysthymic baseline (Keller *et al.*, 1983). The sombre introverted personality of these patients is one of the core characteristics of dysthymia (Yerevanian and Akiskal, 1979), and contrasts with the more extroverted baseline observed in the atypical depressive subtypes (Liebowitz and Klein, 1979).

Encouraged by sleep EEG findings of short REM latency in some dysthymic patients (Akiskal *et al.*, 1980)—and the presence of family history for both unipolar and bipolar illness (Rosenthal *et al.*, 1981)—our mood clinic coupled vigorous and sequential trials of at least two TCAs (desipramine and nortriptyline) with behavioural strategies such as social skills training. These patients had previously failed on multiple courses of monotherapy with either medications or individual psychotherapy. Our rationale for combined treatment was that psychotherapy alone would prove ineffective in reversing the temperamentally based inertia so characteristic of these patients; pharmacotherapy alone, on the other hand, was unlikely to improve significantly the social deficits of these patients. With our strategy of combined treatment, not only did we observe gradual attenuation of the low-grade depressive suffering in one-third of the entire patients, but also brief hypomanic responses in some of the TCA-responsive subgroup. Hypomanic features have also been observed in the prospective follow-up of both dysthymic children (Kovacs and Gastsonis, 1989) and adults (Klein *et al.*, 1988; Rihmer, 1990). Such data provide an explanation for the potential usefulness of lithium carbonate with or without secondary amine TCAs in some dysthymic patients (Akiskal *et al.*, 1980). MAOIs may still benefit others (Vallejo *et al.*, 1987). Ritanserin, an experimental S_2-antagonist, has also shown promise in a double-blind placebo-controlled study (Lapierre 1991). In another Memphis study (Haykal and Akiskal, in preparation), we found TCAs and fluoxetine to be effective in roughly two-thirds of dysthymics, but fluoxetine having a significant edge in terms of social functioning; this open trial was continued over a 34-month period, testifying to the stability of thymoleptic response in dysthymia. Whether serotonergic antidepressants work on the core depressive features, or comorbid eating, sleep and substance abuse problems, is uncertain (Akiskal, 1991b). It is nevertheless impressive that many patients whose existence had been immersed in perpetual gloom, lack of confidence, anhedonia, fatigue and hypersomnia had a reversal to essentially normal functioning which they had never known before.

To date, the largest double-blind placebo controlled trial of dysthymia is the

Kocsis *et al.* study (1988) which has shown imipramine to be highly efficacious in two-thirds of dysthymics. Finally, some dysthymics respond to sleep deprivation (Rihmer, 1990). This is of both theoretical and practical interest in that it contrasts with worsening of anxious-depressive manifestations in panic disorder (Roy-Byrne *et al.*, 1986), which forms the substrate of the neurasthenia observed in many atypical depressives. The practical implication here is that the sensitive-avoidant temperament should avoid sleep deprivation, whereas those with the depressive temperament may derive transient benefit from it.

The last group of chronic depressions to be considered is represented by major depressions with incomplete recovery. After ruling out inadequate treatment (Table III; Akiskal, 1985), the main aetiological correlates of chronicity in these patients include familial affective loading, concurrent disabling medical disease, use of depressant antihypertensive agents, multiple bereavement, disabled spouses (with medical or psychiatric disease), and secondary sedativism. The sleep EEG of these patients with residual depressive symptomatology is indistinguishable from that of acute depressive episodes, suggesting that these depressive residuals represent an unresolved affective process and hence the necessity for a vigorous chemotherapeutic approach (Akiskal, 1981). There are no published studies of antidepressant trials on residual depressive symptomatology *per se*, but earlier studies (e.g., Ayd, 1984), documenting the utility of maintenance antidepressant treatment in chronic depressives, and emerging data (Frank *et al.*, 1990) on the desirability of maintaining the acute antidepressant dose in optimizing relapse prevention, should serve as useful guidelines. Such dose considerations also appear relevant to early-onset dysthymics with superimposed major depressive episodes (Kocsis *et al.*, 1988).

Table III.   Factors in the undertreatment of depressive illness

Pharmacological factors:
    Inadequate dosage or duration of antidepressant trials
    Polypharmacy
    Disabling side effects
    Low TCA blood level despite adequate dose

Patient factors:
    Rejection of pharmacological 'crutch'
    Fear of 'addiction' to medication
    Hypochondriasis about side effects
    Feeling unworthy of being helped

Physician factors:
    Failure to educate patient or family
    Reluctance to use MAOIs
    A more generalized ambivalence about prescribing medication
    Undue emphasis on characterologic aspects

Modified from Akiskal (1985).

In treating residual depressions, the physician should first eliminate contributory drug factors (e.g., depressant antihypertensives, benzodiazepines, or alcohol), before embarking upon a vigorous chemotherapeutic regimen (Akiskal, 1985). This can be accomplished with nortriptyline, which can be conveniently given in effective doses, because its pharmacokinetics are well established. It can be coupled, if needed, with a low-dose neuroleptic such as thiothixene in patients with delusional features. For those with severe insomnia, trimipramine often improves sleep without adverse effects on REM parameters. Despite the Nolen *et al.* study (1988) reporting no advantage of going from a noradrenergic to a serotonergic antidepressant, we do recommend one of the new serotonergic re-uptake inhibitors based on clinical experience and experimental data implicating the 5-HT system in treatment resistance (reviewed in Akiskal, 1991b). In view of the common association of chronicity of depression with medical illness, patients with residual depressions are not easily managed with the classic MAOIs; however, the recent availability of reversible MAOIs free of adverse interaction with medication in current medical use, represents yet another promising approach to resistant depressives. Residual symptoms would further respond to a course of electroconvulsive therapy (ECT) in most of the remaining unresponsive patients (Akiskal *et al.*, 1989). Those few who remain 'ultra-refractory' often prove to have endocrine abnormalities, occult malignancies or neurological disease (Akiskal, 1985; Akiskal *et al.*, 1989).

Strategies for protracted mixed states

In the 1970s, inadequate antidepressant treatment was a major contributor to the genesis of residual depression. Recent clinical observations, however, suggest that overzealous TCA treatment of a special subgroup of depressives in young and middle-aged depressives may lead not only to rapid cycling (Koukopoulos *et al.*, 1980; Wehr and Goodwin, 1987), but also to chronicization (Akiskal and Mallya, 1987), especially in those with premorbid hyperthymic tendencies (Tondo *et al.*, 1981). These highly dysphoric residual states are characterized by psychomotor inertia co-existing with intense emotional arousal, insomnia, anxiety, panic, agitation, suicidal preoccupations, racing thoughts and other evidence for subtle hypomanic intrusions into depression (e.g., intense sexual appetite and extraverted behaviour against a background of genuine expressions of depressive suffering). Thus, the residual symptomatology in some recurrent depressions in reality represents a protracted mixed state. In our experience, lithium augmentation championed by De Montigny *et al.* (1981)—now buttressed by other investigators (reviewed by Price *et al.*, 1986, and by Schopf, 1989)—is particularly relevant to such pseudo-unipolar depressions (it is doubtful if lithium augmentation is ever useful in strictly unipolar patients). Furthermore, once lithium augmentation converts a

TCA non-responder to a responder, in our experience in many cases the TCA can be discontinued within a few weeks, and the patient maintained on lithium monotherapy. Although MAOIs are not entirely benign from the standpoint of rapid cycling or chronicization, but when combined with lithium, they are a better alternative to TCAs (Himmelhoch *et al.*, 1991). Some patients can be maintained on lithium alone; others require low-dose neuroleptics for brief periods—certainly no more than two to three weeks—superimposed on a lithium maintenance regimen. Thyroid augmentation of lithium (Extein and Gold, 1986) and carbamazepine or valproate augmentation of lithium (Post *et al.*, 1986; Emrich *et al.*, 1985) represent additional empirically tested strategies of potential benefits relevant to this recalcitrant group of protracted dysphoric suffering.

The search for the three humours

Except for the sanguine temperament—which today we might call hyperthymia—the remaining three temperaments described in Greco-Roman medicine seem to embody the biochemical underpinnings of the low-grade affective conditions considered in this chapter. Cloninger's portrayal of personality pathology (1987) as a function of hypothesized disturbances along serotonergic, noradrenergic and dopaminergic axes represents a modern version of this ancient theory.

The data reviewed on the pharmacotherapy of low-grade affective conditions are not easily superposable on the biogenic amines favoured by Cloninger. There generally seems to be more evidence for the involvement of the 5-HT than the other systems in these subaffective dysregulations (reviewed in Akiskal, 1991b), especially as it pertains to patients with prominent disturbances along the introversion-extraversion dimension. Disturbances in the noradrenergic system—when superimposed on those of the serotonergic system—might account for anxious (neurotic) symptomatology (Akiskal, 1990); finally, the dopaminergic system might be especially relevant to depressive and schizotypal features, which when combined mimic the negative symptom complex of schizophrenia with anhedonia, avolition and social withdrawal (Lecrubier, 1989).

Such speculative correlations might one day explain why a large class of thymoleptic medications have been found useful in protracted low-grade depressive conditions. Unfortunately, despite nearly four decades of intense search for the three humours, black or yellow bile and phlegm are still as 'valid' as any others that have been proposed in recent times and, therefore, clinicians are admonished to treat chronic affective disturbances on the basis of empirical psychopharmacological considerations. The literature summarized in this chapter—which with few exceptions is based on *acute* studies in chronic patients—should serve as a general guideline and philosophical justification for more sophisticated and long-term studies.

Psychological principles in treating chronic depressions

The long-term psychopharmacological management of this very complex group of chronic patients is still very much of an art that each clinican must develop by informed 'trial and error' on a large number of patients examined over long periods of personal follow-up. Such experience will teach the physician that psycho-educational and psychotherapeutic approaches can considerably enhance the gains made through chemotherapy.

However, long-term psychotherapy deriving from psychodynamic theory—commonly used with the ambition to modify the character pathology in depressives (Arieti and Bemporad, 1980)—is of unproven value for this purpose. To put it bluntly, personality disturbances observed in chronic affective conditions represent either constitutional givens which are mininally responsive to insight-oriented therapies, or are epiphenomenal to the affective pathology and are unlikely to recede without significant improvement in this pathology. What is needed are more focused practical supportive and interpersonal interventions (Weissman and Akiskal, 1984) and psycho-educational approaches for both patient and spouse, to combat the demoralization of a chronic illness with devastating effects on scholastic, vocational and personal life (Akiskal, 1985), and to enhance rapport, hope and compliance with medication regimens (Table IV). Most importantly, the physician himself should maintain an attitude of optimism and cite to the patient the increasing availability of more specific thymoleptic agents. Maintaining empathy is not always easy, as many chronic depressives tend to irritate and alienate their physicians. In the case of these more impulsive, dysphoric patients, it is necessary to set clear limits right from the outset of treatment: repeated angry outbursts directed at the physician are

Table IV. Psychological principles in treating chronic affective conditions

---

- Provide a believable dose of optimism
- Set limits on the destructive expression of anger
- Support patient's significant others
- Enlist supportive relationships for patient
- Treat patient in a 'group practice' setting in order to dilute countertransference reactions
- Periodically consult mood disorder specialists
- Explore vocational—and object—choices best suited for patient's temperament

---

counter-therapeutic and will not be tolerated. This is also to signal to the patient the destructive effect of anger on interpersonal relationships outside therapy.

Price (1978) has pointed out how mediocre responses to half-hearted attempts to treat chronic depression might lead the clinician to change the patient's diagnosis to character disorder. Affective reconceptualization of 'character' disorders within a biological framework not only brings the potential benefit of innovative psychopharmacological strategies to this 'difficult' group of patients, but could reduce physicians' countertransference to the patient (Gardner and Cowdry, 1985), and thereby lead to more efficient treatment.

The long-term clinical management of patients with chronic affective dysregulation requires versatility in biological and psychosocial interventions—and medical competence to address comorbid physical conditions—as well as the stamina to endure their hopeless despair which is often 'contagious', especially when treatment is not progressing optimally. The physician himself may need periodic support; indeed, such patients are best treated in the setting of group practice.

The reward of pulling out of despair patients 'written off' as incurable by themselves, family or previous therapists is one of the most gratifying professional experiences in the field of medicine. Despite opinion to the contrary, depressives with personality disorders do respond to antidepressants (Joffe and Regan, 1989). Even malignant characterologic distortions brought about by protracted depression can often be attenuated (Akiskal *et al.*, 1988) with the sophisticated psychopharmacological care available today for chronic affective conditions.

Vocational guidance which attempts to match the patient's temperament to a specific type of work (Akiskal, 1991a) or object choice in which he/she will be in optimum harmony ultimately represents a more realistic goal than modifying the personality structure (Akiskal and Akiskal, 1992). For instance those patients who are unable to get up at the 'societal' hours of 7–8 a.m. to go to work should be encouraged to seek jobs with more flexible hours to accommodate the peculiarities of their sleep requirements. Cyclothymic individuals might consider acting or other domains of art where their tempestuous moods might be 'useful', if not better tolerated. The overdedication of dysthymic individuals to jobs which require 'suffering' for others or institutions is well known since Schneider's classic description (1958), now verified in empirical research (Cassano *et al.*, 1990). Such harmony between temperament and the work environment could, ideally, obviate the need for chemotherapy—or at least reduce the dosage needed for optimum affective equilibrium.

The foregoing vocational considerations represent future challenges for psychosocial interventions in those with chronic affective dysregulations. At present, competent psychopharmacotherapy—buttressed with supportive and psycho-educational approaches—represents state-of-the-art treatment for most low-grade affective conditions which are woven into the personality structure of the patient.

References

Akiskal HS (1981) Subaffective disorders: dysthymic, cyclothymic and bipolar II disorders in the 'borderline' realm. *Psychiatr Clin North Am* **4**, 25–46.

Akiskal HS (1983) Dysthymic disorder: psychopathology of proposed chronic depressive subtypes. *Am J Psychiatry* **140**, 11–20.

Akiskal HS (1984) Characterologic manifestations of affective disorders: toward a new conceptualization. *Integrative Psychiatry* May–June, 83–96.

Akiskal HS (1985) A proposed clinical approach to chronic and 'resistant' depressions: evaluation and treatment. *J Clin Psychiatry* **46**, 32–37.

Akiskal HS (1987) The milder spectrum of bipolar disorders: diagnostic, characterologic, and pharmacologic aspects. *Psychiatr Ann* **17**, 32–37.

Akiskal HS (1988) Personality in anxiety disorders. *Psychiatrie Psychobiol* **3**, 161s–166s.

Akiskal HS (1989) Classification of mental disorders. In Kaplan HI, Sadock BJ (eds) *Comprehensive Textbook of Psychiatry*, pp. 583–598. Baltimore: Williams & Wilkins.

Akiskal HS (1990) Toward a definition of dysthymia: boundaries with personality and mood disorders. In Burton SW, Akiskal HS (eds) *Dysthymic Disorder*, pp. 1–12. London: Gaskell.

Akiskal HS (1991a) Chronic depression. *Bull Menninger Clin* **55**, 156–171.

Akiskal HS (1991b) Chronic-resistant depressions: are serotonergic mechanisms relevant? In Cassano GB, Akiskal HS (eds) *Serotonin-Related Psychiatric Syndromes: Clinical and Therapeutic Links*, pp. 171–174. London: Royal Society of Medicine Services.

Akiskal HS (1991c) Clinical subtypes of chronic-resistant depression. In Feighner J (ed.) *Diagnosis of Depression*, pp 149–162. Chichester: Wiley.

Akiskal HS, Akiskal K (1992, in press) Cyclothymic, hyperthymic and depressive temperaments as subaffective variants of mood disorders. In Tasman A (ed.) *American Psychiatric Association Review*, pp 43–62. Washington DC: American Psychiatric Press.

Akiskal HS, Lemmi H (1987) Sleep EEG findings bearing on the relationship of anxiety and depressive disorders. In Racagani G, Smeraldi E (eds) *Anxious Depression: Assessment and Treatment*, pp. 153–159. New York: Raven Press.

Akiskal HS, Mallya G (1987) Criteria for the 'soft' bipolar spectrum: treatment implications. *Psychopharmacology Bull* **23**, 68–73.

Akiskal HS, Weise R (1992) The clinical spectrum of so-called 'minor' depressions. *Am J Psychother* **46**, 1–14.

Akiskal HS, Bitar AH, Puzantian VR *et al.* (1978) The nosological status of neurotic depression: a prospective three- to four-year follow-up examination in light of the primary–secondary and unipolar–bipolar dichotomies. *Arch Gen Psychiatry* **35**, 756–766.

Akiskal HS, Khani MK, Scott-Strauss A (1979) Cyclothymic temperamental disorders. *Psychiatr Clin North Am* **2**, 527–554.

Akiskal HS, Rosenthal TL, Haykal RF *et al.* (1980) Characterological depressions: clinical and sleep EEG findings separating 'subaffective dysthymias' from 'character spectrum disorders'. *Arch Gen Psychiatry* **37**, 777–783.

Akiskal HS, King D, Rosenthal TL *et al.* (1981) Chronic depressions: Part 1. Clinical and familial characteristics in 137 probands. *J Affective Disord* **3**, 297–315.

Akiskal HS, Lemmi H, Dickson H *et al.* (1984) Chronic depressions: Part 2. Sleep EEG differentiation of primary dysthymic disorders from anxious depressions. *J Affective Disord* **6**, 287–295.

Akiskal HS, Chen SE, Davis GC *et al.* (1985) Borderline: an adjective in search of a noun. *J Clin Psychiatry* **46**, 41–48.

Akiskal HS, Cassano GB, Musetti L *et al.* (1989) Psychopathology, temperament, and past course in primary major depressions. 1. Review of evidence for a bipolar spectrum. *Psychopathology* **22**, 268–277.

American Psychiatric Association (1980, revised, 1987). *Diagnostic and Statistical Manual of Mental Disorders*, 3rd edn. Washington, DC: American Psychiatric Association.

Angst J, Merikangas K, Scheidegger P, Wicki W (1990) Recurrent brief depression: a new subtype of affective disorder. *J Affective Disord* **19**, 87–98.

Arieti S, Bemporad JR (1980) The psychological organization of depression. *Am J Psychiatry* **137**, 1360–1365.

Ayd FJ Jr (1984) Long-term treatment of chronic depression: 15-year experience with doxepin HCl. *J Clin Psychiatry* **45**, 39–46.

Bear DM, Fedio P (1977) Quantitative analysis of interictal behaviour in temporal lobe epilepsy. *Arch Neurol* **34**, 454–467.

Beard GM (1972 reprint) *American Nervousness, Its Cause and Consequences: A Supplement to Nervous Exhaustion (Neurasthenia)*. New York: Arno Press.

Bell J, Lycaki H, Jones D *et al.* (1983) Effect of preexisting borderline personality disorder on clinical and EEG sleep correlates of depression. *Psychiatry Res* **9**, 115–123.

Blumer D, Heilbronn M, Himmelhoch J (1988) Indications for carbamazepine in mental illness: atypical psychiatric disorder or temporal lobe syndrome. *Compr Psychiatry* **29**, 108–122.

Bouchard TJ, Jr, Lykken DT, McGue M *et al.* (1990) Sources of human psychological differences: the Minnesota Study of Twins Reared Apart. *Science* **250**, 223–228.

Bronisch T, Wittchen HU, Krieg C *et al.* (1985) Depressive neurosis: a long-term prospective and retrospective follow-up study of former inpatients. *Acta Psychiatr Scand* **71**, 237–248.

Burton SW, Akiskal HS (eds) (1990) *Dysthymic Disorder*. London: Gaskell.

Cassano GB, Maggini C, Akiskal HS (1983) Short-term, subchronic, and chronic sequelae of affective disorders. *Psychiatr Clin N Am* **6**, 55–67.

Cassano GB, Akiskal HS, Musetti L *et al.* (1989) Psychopathology, temperament, and past course in primary major depressions. 2. Toward a redefinition of bipolarity with a new semistructured interview for depression. *Psychopathology* **22**, 278–288.

Cassano GB, Perugi G, Maremmani I, Akiskal HS (1990) Social adjustment in dysthymia. In Burton SW, Akiskal HS (eds) *Dysthymic Disorder*, pp. 78–85. London: Gaskell/Royal College of Psychiatrists.

Cloninger CR (1987) A systematic method for clinical description and classification of personality variants: a proposal. *Arch Gen Psychiatry* **44**, 573–588.

Cowdry RW, Pickar D, Davies R (1985) Symptoms and EEG findings in the borderline syndrome. *Int J Psychiatry Med* **15**, 201–211.

Cowdry RW, Gardner DL (1988) Pharmacotherapy of borderline personality disorder: alprazolam, carbamazepine, trifluoperazine, and tranylcypromine. *Arch Gen Psychiatry* **45**, 111–119.

Davidson J, Pelton S (1986) Forms of atypical depression and their response to antidepressant drugs. *Psychiatry Res* **17**, 87–95.

Davidson JR, Miller RD, Turnbull CD, Sullivan JL (1982) Atypical depression. *Arch Gen Psychiatry* **39**, 527–534.

Deltito JA, Poeschla BD, Stam M, Martin Y (1991) Monoamine oxidase inhibitors or fluoxetine in the treatment of avoidant personality disorder. In Cassano GB, Akiskal HS (eds) *Serotonin-Related Psychiatric Syndrome: Clinical and Therapeutic Links*, pp. 107–114. London: Royal Society of Medicine Services.

De Montigny C, Grunberg F, Mayer A, Deschenes J-P (1981) Lithium induces rapid relief of depression in tricyclic antidepressant drug non-responders. *Br J Psychiatry* **138**, 252–256.

Emrich HM, Dose M, von Zerssen D (1985) The use of sodium valproate, carbamazepine and oxcarbazepine in patients with affective disorders. *J Affective Disord* **8**, 243–250.

Extein I, Gold MS (1986) Psychiatric applications of thyroid tests. *J Clin Psychiatry* **47** (Suppl. 1), 13–16.

Eysenck HJ (1967) *The Biological Basis of Personality.* Springfield, IL: Thomas.

Frank F, Kupfer DJ, Perel JM *et al.* (1990) Three-year outcomes for maintenance therapies in recurrent depression. *Arch Gen Psychiatry* **47**, 1093–1099.

Friedman RC, Clarkin JF, Corn R *et al.* (1982) DSM-III and affective pathology in hospitalized adolescents. *J Nerv Ment Dis* **170**, 511–521.

Garbutt JC, Loosen PT, Tipermas A, Prange AJ Jr (1983) The TRH test in patients with borderline personality disorder. *Psychiatry Res* **9**, 107–113.

Gardner DL, Cowdry RW (1985) Suicidal and parasuicidal behavior in borderline personality disorder. *Psychiatr Clin North Am* **8**, 389–403.

Goldberg SC, Schulz SC, Schulz PM *et al.* (1986) Borderline and schizotypal personality disorders treated with low-dose thiothixene vs placebo. *Arch Gen Psychiatry* **43**, 680–686.

Gunderson JG, Phillips KA (1991) A current view of the interface between borderline personality disorder and depression. *Am J Psychiatry* **148**, 967–975.

Guscott R, Grof P (1991) The clinical meaning of refractory depression: a review for the clinician. *Am J Psychiatry* **148**, 695–704.

Haykal RF, Akiskal HS (1990) Bupropion as a promising approach to rapid cycling bipolar II patients. *J Clin Psychiatry* **51**, 450–455.

Himmelhoch JM (1987) Cerebral dysrhythmia, substance abuse, and the nature of secondary affective illness. *Psychiatr Ann* **17**, 710–727.

Himmelhoch JM, Thase ME, Mallinger AG, Houck P (1991) Tranylcypromine versus imipramine in anergic bipolar depression. *Am J Psychiatry* **148**, 910–916.

Howland RH (1991) Pharmacotherapy of dysthymia: a review. *J Clin Psychopharmacol* **11**, 83–92.

Joffe RT, Regan JJ (1989) Personality and resopnse to tricyclic antidepressants in depressed patients. *J Nerv Ment Disord* **177**, 745–749.

Kagan J, Reznick JS, Snidman N (1988) Biological bases of childhood shyness. *Science* **240**, 167–171.

Keller MB, Lavori PW, Endicott J *et al.* (1983) Double depression: two-year follow-up. *Am J Psychiatry* **140**, 689–694.

Kennedy SH, Joffe RT (1989) Pharmacological management of refractory depression. *Can J Psychiatry* **34**, 451–456.

Klein DF, Gittelman R, Quitkin F, Rifkin A (1980) *Diagnosis and Drug Treatment of Psychiatric Disorders: Adults and Children,* 2nd edn. Baltimore: Williams & Wilkins.

Klein DN, Taylor EB, Harding K, Dickstein S (1988) Double depression and episodic major depression: demographic, clinical, familial, personality, and socioenvironmental characteristics and short-term outcome. *Am J Psychiatry* **145**, 1226–1231.

Klerman GL (1990) The contemporary American scene: diagnosis and classification of mental disorders, alcoholism and drug abuse. In Sartorius N, Jablensky A, Regier DA *et al.* (eds) *Sources and Traditions of Classification in Psychiatry,* pp. 93–137. New York: WHO/Hans Huber.

Klibansky R, Panofsky E, Saxl F (1979) *Saturn and Melancholy.* Liechtenstein: Nendeln (Kraus reprint).

Kocsis JH, Frances AJ, Voss C *et al.* (1988) Imipramine treatment for chronic depression. *Arch Gen Psychiatry* **45**, 253–257.

Kovacs M, Gastsonis C (1989) Stability and change in childhood—onset of depressive disorder: longitudinal course as a diagnostic validator. In Robins LN, Barrett JE (eds) *The Validity of Psychiatric Diagnosis*, pp. 57–73. New York: Raven Press.

Kraines SH (1967) Therapy of the chronic depressions. *Dis Nerv System* **28**, 577–584.

Koukopoulos A, Reginaldi D, Laddomada P *et al.* (1980) Course of the manic-depressive cycle and changes caused by treatment. *Pharmakopsychiatria* **13**, 156–167.

Lapierre Y (1991) Evaluation of treatment of dysthymic disorder with antidepressants. *Paper presented at World Congres of Biological Psychiatry, Florence, Italy, 9–14 June*.

Lecrubier Y (1989) Thymasthenia: clinical and pharmacological aspects. *Psychiatry in the 80's* **7**, 5–6.

Lewinsohn PM, Rohde P, Seeley JR, Hops H (1991) Comorbidity of unipolar depression: I. Major depression with dysthymia. *J Abnormal Psychol* **100**, 205–213.

Liebowitz MR, Klein DF (1979) Hysteroid dysphoria. *Psychiatr Clin North Am* **2**, 555–575.

Liebowitz MR, Quitkin FM, Stewart JW *et al.* (1988) Antidepressant specificity in atypical depression. *Arch Gen Psychiatry* **45**, 129–137.

Links PS, Steiner M, Boiago I, Irwin D (1990) Lithium therapy for borderline patients: preliminary findings. *J Pers Disord* **4**, 173–181.

NcNamara E, Reynolds CF III, Soloff PH *et al.* (1984) EEG sleep evaluation of depression in borderline patients. *Am J Psychiatry* **141**, 182–186.

Montgomery SA (1987) The psychopharmacology of borderline personality disorders. *Acta Psychiatr Belg* **87**, 260–266.

Nierenberg AA, Amsterdam JD (1990) Treatment-resistant depression: definition and treatment approaches. *J Clin Psychiatry* **51**, 39–47.

Nolen WA, van de Puttee JJ, Dijken WA *et al.* (1988) Treatment strategy in depression. I. Non-tyricyclic and selective reuptake inhibitors in resistant depression: a double-blind partial crossover study on the effects of oxaprotiline and fluvoxamine. *Acta Psychiatr Scand* **78**, 668–675.

Paykel ES, Parker RR, Rowan PR *et al.* (1983) Nosology of atypical depression. *Psychol Med* **13**, 131–139.

Peselow ED, Dunner DL, Fieve RR, Lautin A (1982) Lithium prophylaxis of depression in unipolar, bipolar II, and cyclothymic patients. *Am J Psychiatry* **139**, 747–752.

Post RM, Uhde TW, Roy-Byrne PP, Joffe RT (1986) Antidepressant effects of carbamazepine. *Am J Psychiatry* **143**, 29–34.

Price JS (1978) Chronic depressive illness. *Br Med J* i, 1200–1201.

Price LH, Charney DS, Heninger GR (1986) Variability of response to lithium augmentation in refractory depression. *Am J Psychiatry* **143**, 1387–1392.

Regier DA, Boyd JH, Burke JD Jr *et al.* (1988) One-month prevalence of mental disorders in the United States based on five Epidemiologic Catchment Area sites. *Arch Gen Psychiatry* **45**, 977–986.

Reynolds CF III, Soloff PH, Kupfer DJ *et al.* (1985) Depression in borderline patients: a prospective EEG sleep study. *Psychiatry Res*, **14**, 1–15.

Rifkin A, Quitkin F, Carrillo C *et al.* (1972) Lithium carbonate in emotionally unstable character disorder. *Arch Gen Psychiatry* **27**, 519–523.

Rihmer Z (1990) Dysthymia: a clinician's perspective. In Burton SW, Akiskal HS (eds) *Dysthymic Disorder*, pp. 112–125. London: Gaskell/Royal College of Psychiatrists.

Rosenthal TL, Akiskal HS, Scott-Strauss A *et al.* (1981) Familial and developmental factors in characterological depressions. *J Affective Disord* **3**, 183–192.

Roy-Byrne PP, Uhde TW, Post RM (1986) Effects of one night's sleep deprivation on mood and behavior in panic disorder: patients with panic disorder compared with depressed patients and normal controls. *Arch Gen Psychiatry* **43**, 895–899.

Sargent W (1962) The treatment of anxiety states and atypical depressions by the monoamine oxidase inhibitor drugs. *J Neuropsychiatry* **3**, 96–103.

Schneider K (trans. MW Hamilton) (1985) *Psychopathic Personalities*. Springfield, IL: Thomas.

Schopf J (1989) Treatment of depressions resistant to tricyclic antidepressants, related drugs or MAO-inhibitors by lithium addition: review of the literature. *Pharmacopsychiatry* **22**, 174–182.

Scott J (1988) Chronic depression. *Br J Psychiatry* **153**, 287–297.

Shader RI, Scharfman EL, Dreyfuss DA (1985) Toward a psychobiologic view of selected personality disorders. In Michels R, Cooper AM, Guze SB *et al.* (eds) *Psychiatry*, pp. 1–11. Philadelphia: Lippincott.

Snyder S, Pitts WM Jr (1984) Electroencephalography of DSM-III borderline personality disorder. *Acta Psychiatr Scand* **69**, 129–134.

Soloff PH, George A, Nathan RS *et al.* (1986) Progress in pharmacotherapy of borderline disorders: a double-blind study of amitriptyline, haloperidol, and placebo. *Arch Gen Psychiatry* **43**, 691–697.

Stewart JW, Quitkin FM, McGrath PJ *et al.* (1988) Social functioning in chronic depression: effect of 6 weeks of antidepressant treatment. *Psychiatry Res* **25**, 213–222.

Stone MH (1980) *The Borderline Syndrome*. New York: McGraw-Hill.

Tondo L, Laddomada P, Serra G *et al.* (1981) Rapid cyclers and antidepressants. *Int Pharmacopsychiatry* **16**, 119–123.

Trull TJ, Widiger TA, Guthrie P (1990) Categorical versus dimensional status of borderline personality disorder. *J Abnormal Psychol* **99**, 40–48.

Turner SM, Beidel DC, Dancu CV, Keys DJ (1986) Psychopathology of social phobia and comparison to avoidant personality disorder. *J Abnormal Psychol* **95**, 389–394.

Vallejo J, Gasto C, Catalan R, Salamero M (1987) Double-blind study of imipramine versus phenelzine in melancholias and dysthymic disorders. *Br J Psychiatry* **151**, 639–642.

Wehr TA, Goodwin FK (1987) Can antidepressants cause mania and worsen the course of affective illness? *Am J Psychiatry* **144**, 1403–1411.

Weissman MM, Akiskal HS (1984) The role of psychotherapy in chronic depressions: a proposal. *Compr Psychiatry* **25**, 23–31.

Weissman MM, Klerman GL (1977) The chronic depressive in the community: unrecognized and poorly treated. *Compr Psychiatry* **18**, 523–532.

West ED, Dally PJ (1959) Effects of iproniazid in depressive syndromes. *Br Med J* **1**, 1491–1494.

Wood DR, Reimherr FW, Wender PH, Johnson GE (1976) Diagnosis and treatment of minimal brain dysfunction in adults: a preliminary report. *Arch Gen Psychiatry* **33**, 1453–1460.

Yerevanian BI, Akiskal HS (1979) Neurotic, characterological, and dysthymic depressions. *Psychiatr Clin North Am* **2**, 595–617.

Index

Index compiled by June Morrison